RELIGIOUS REFUGEES IN THE EARLY MODERN WORLD

The religious refugee first emerged as a mass phenomenon in the late fifteenth century. Over the following two and a half centuries, millions of Jews, Muslims, and Christians were forced from their homes and into temporary or permanent exile. Their migrations across Europe and around the globe shaped the early modern world and profoundly affected literature, art, and culture. Economic and political factors drove many expulsions, but religion was the factor most commonly used to justify them. This was also the period of religious revival known as the Reformation. This book explores how reformers' ambitions to purify individuals and society fuelled movements to purge ideas, objects, and people considered religiously alien or spiritually contagious. As an alternative history of the Reformation, it:

* Aims to explain religious ideas and movements of the Reformation in non-technical and comparative language.
* Moves Jews and Muslims from the margins of the traditional Reformation narrative and considers how the exile experience shaped early modern culture, art, politics, and cities.
* Traces the historical patterns that still account for the growing numbers of modern religious refugees.

Nicholas Terpstra is Professor and Chair of History at the University of Toronto. He has been a visiting professor at Sydney, Tel Aviv, and Warwick Universities and at the Harvard Center for Italian Renaissance Studies. His books have shown how Renaissance cities handled orphans, abandoned children, criminals, and the poor in the fifteenth and sixteenth centuries. His most recent book, *Cultures of Charity: Women, Politics, and the Reform of Poor Relief in Renaissance Italy* (2014), won prizes from the Renaissance Society of America and the American Historical Association.

RELIGIOUS REFUGEES IN THE EARLY MODERN WORLD

An Alternative History of the Reformation

NICHOLAS TERPSTRA

University of Toronto

CAMBRIDGE UNIVERSITY PRESS

CAMBRIDGE
UNIVERSITY PRESS

One Liberty Plaza, 20th Floor, New York, NY 10006, USA

Cambridge University Press is part of the University of Cambridge.

It furthers the University's mission by disseminating knowledge in the pursuit of education, learning, and research at the highest international levels of excellence.

www.cambridge.org
Information on this title: www.cambridge.org/9781107652415

© Nicholas Terpstra 2015

This publication is in copyright. Subject to statutory exception and to the provisions of relevant collective licensing agreements, no reproduction of any part may take place without the written permission of Cambridge University Press.

First published 2015
Reprinted 2017

Printed in the United States of America

A catalog record for this publication is available from the British Library.

Library of Congress Cataloging in Publication Data
Terpstra, Nicholas.
Religious refugees in the early modern world : an alternative history of the Reformation / Nicholas Terpstra, University of Toronto.
  pages cm
Includes bibliographical references and index.
ISBN 978-1-107-02456-4 (alk. paper)
1. Reformation. 2. Religious refugees – History. 3. Europe – History – 1492–1648.
 I. Title.
BR305.3.T47 2016
270.6086′91–dc23   2015005133

ISBN 978-1-107-02456-4 Hardback
ISBN 978-1-107-65241-5 Paperback

Cambridge University Press has no responsibility for the persistence or accuracy of URLs for external or third-party Internet Web sites referred to in this publication and does not guarantee that any content on such Web sites is, or will remain, accurate or appropriate.

To the memory of Anne & Klaas and Jean & John, whose own migrations, shaped deeply by religion, closed some horizons but opened many others

CONTENTS

	Introduction	*page* 1
	On the Move	1
	Reformation Histories	7
	Persecution Paradigms	11
	Toleration and Co-Existence	15
	Body Politics	17
1	**The Body of Christ: Defined and Threatened**	21
	Purity and Community in the Body	22
	Threats to the *Corpus Christianum*	38
2	**Purifying the Body**	74
	Separation	77
	Containment	84
	Prosecution	94
	Purgation	105
3	**Dividing the Body: People and Places**	133
	People	134
	Places	157
4	**Mind and Body**	184
	Ways of Thinking: Purity of Thought	186
	Ways of Living: Purity of Action	218
5	**Re-Forming the Body: The World the Refugees Made**	241
	Tools	242
	Personnel	257
	Spaces	269
	Imagination	289
	Confession and Culture	305
6	**Re-Imagining the Body**	309
	Select Bibliography	331
	Index	337

INTRODUCTION

ONE OF THE HARSHEST REALITIES OF THE MODERN WORLD IS the plight of refugees. War, brutal dictators, and inter-communal tensions regularly send tens of thousands fleeing for their lives over the nearest border. Race, ethnicity, and religious identity often provide the overt reasons for exile and expulsion. Some refugees settle in camps, hoping to return, while others keep moving from country to country in search of a new life. Families are torn apart, and those who choose not to flee risk being killed by armies, guerillas, or neighbours. The twentieth century saw millions killed, millions flee as refugees, and millions more forced to migrate when war destroyed their homelands. In 2014 the United Nations High Commission on Refugees estimated that the current global total of displaced peoples had risen beyond 50 million. Has it always been this way? When did refugees first become a common phenomenon, and why?

On the Move

European states began using exile and expulsion as deliberate tools of policy about six hundred years ago, in the period known as the late Middle Ages or Renaissance. This was when the religious refugee in particular became a mass phenomenon. Medieval traditions regarding purity, contagion, and purgation took a sharper definition in the fifteenth century. Political and economic realities deeply shaped the many cultural forces and historical events that then spurred institutional religious reformation in the sixteenth and seventeenth centuries. Towns, cities, and states had long been concerned with asserting their religious character and spiritual purity. As power began flowing towards monarchs and central governments, French king Henry IV's goal of "one faith, one law, one King" took hold across the continent. Those who fell outside this unity were not just alien, but also impure and possibly contagious. Any society that took its responsibilities to God seriously might have to purge itself in order to purify its population and so maintain its own health.

The sharp language of purification and purgation came out of medicine, but was adopted by religious reform movements. The drive to purge and purify reshaped Europe and the globe throughout the early modern period. This book will argue that because purgation was so central a part of religious reform, we should include the expulsion of the Jews from Spain in 1492 as one of the critical events marking the start of 'the Reformation' – no less significant than Martin Luther's posting of the Ninety-Five Theses in 1517 or English king Henry VIII's divorce controversy of the 1520s and '30s. Iberian Jews were given the choice to be baptised as Christians or to leave the land that they had lived in for over a thousand years. Iberian Muslims, who had lived in Spain for seven hundred years, were given the same ultimatum in 1502. These were not the first or last threats – Jews had faced similar demands in 1391, and Muslims would face them again in 1609–14. Yet the 1492 decree of King Ferdinand and Queen Isabella was the most ambitious in its national scope, numerical scale, and religious focus. To its proponents, it was an exercise in community building and a pious act. It was also the wave of the future. It set membership in the national community on the foundations of religious truth and individual will, rather than on accidents of birth. Within decades, Dutch Anabaptists, Italian Calvinists, English Catholics, and Bohemian Hussites would all be offered the same choice: join or leave.

Mass expulsions did not come overnight. Throughout the course of the fifteenth century, an accelerating wave of expulsions across Europe forced hundreds of thousands of people out of their homes for reasons of religion: 20,000 Jews were expelled from towns across Germany and France throughout the century, before Spain's unlucky 80,000 were given three weeks to leave in 1492. A decade later, the 200,000 who remained of Granada's half-million Muslim population were given the choice of baptism or exile. Anabaptists began fleeing from west and central to Eastern Europe in the 1520s and 1530s; *spirituali* fled Italy from the 1540s; Protestant Marian exiles abandoned England in the 1550s and Catholics left under Elizabeth I. Larger and larger groups were on the move: 10,000 Catholics fled the Netherlands when Calvinists seized power in the 1570s and early 1580s, and then 150,000 Protestants fled from Flanders when Spanish troops retook the region later in that decade. In the 1570s and 1580s, 80,000 *moriscos* were moved from Granada and Valencia into Castile.

The scale of expulsions only increased through the seventeenth century as nations gained a firmer shape and identity, and as governments gained greater policing power: 300,000 Muslims fled from Iberia in 1609–14, 150,000 Huguenots from France after 1685, and 20,000 Protestants from the bishopric of Salzburg in 1731–32 in the last large religiously motivated expulsion in premodern Europe. Outside Europe, the British forcibly relocated more than 11,000 French Catholic settlers from Acadie from 1755. They hoped it would be the final solution for a determined guerrilla movement that was resisting absorption into the British Empire. It would be the last time a European colonial power forcibly resettled European settlers for reasons of religion or nationality. Of course, all colonial powers would continue exploiting and indeed inventing religious, tribal, and racial distinctions in their efforts to divide and conquer the various peoples and territories in their American, African, and Asian empires.

Not all exiles were driven out by formal proclamations, and not all migrants fled for their lives. The early modern period also saw 'voluntary' migrations of religious groups with effects that would resonate through later centuries. Some were engineered by governments to secure political control of contested areas, as when English governments moved Protestants into northern Ireland in what were known as the 'Ulster plantations'. In other cases, whole communities relocated overseas, either to have a chance to exercise their own restrictive notions of religious purity or at least to escape interference and persecution from neighbours and officials. The same European governments that persecuted them at home sometimes supported their move to overseas colonies. French Protestants initially moved freely to Brazil and New France with the eager support of Parisian officials who were finding it difficult to persuade other Frenchmen to occupy the newly claimed lands. Yet these same officials soon began to fear that these settlers might become a fifth column of resistance to the crown and so prohibited Protestants from moving to these colonies or publicly worshipping there. Portuguese Jews settled Recife in Brazil and then, when uprooted by the Inquisition, established plantations in Suriname. So many Spanish Jews who had formally converted to Catholicism moved to Mexico in the sixteenth century – more than half of all Spanish settlers by some estimates – that the Inquisition felt compelled to follow them by 1571.

Of course, not all migrants wore their religious convictions so prominently on their sleeves, or even much in their hearts. Many moved to pursue trade or avoid prison, to follow or flee family, or simply to find opportunities not available at home. They could still get caught up in the rhetoric of exile and expulsion. Perhaps the most self-conscious *religious* exiles were the English Puritans, who seized on the name of 'pilgrims' and on the biblical model of the Israelites fleeing Egypt when they left England from the

1620s-40s in search of a Promised Land in America. Their exile experience led them to see themselves as a Chosen People who were to be a Light on a Hill. That same conviction, without the Puritan creed, informed many of the English Catholics who later followed them to Maryland and Rhode Island. The strong sense of being an exceptional nation with a divine destiny, first framed by religious exiles in the seventeenth century, has since become a fundamental part of American identity, embraced by Jews, Muslims, Hindus, and Christians as a secularized civic religion.

In light of these dynamics, the Reformation stands out as the first period in European and possibly global history when the religious refugee became a mass phenomenon. Europe was certainly no stranger to exile, crusade, and heresy hunting. The origins of what has been called its 'persecuting society' lay further back in time. Yet never before had so many people of so many different faiths — hundreds of thousands certainly and perhaps millions — been forcibly relocated by the demands of religious purity. Some, like Iberia's Jews or France's Huguenots, were being pushed out of a nation that was self-consciously purifying itself. Others, like Munster's apocalyptic Anabaptists and Massachusetts Bay's Puritans were being pulled to a Promised Land where they could form their own pure communities. In most cases, push and pull were just two sides of the coin in the new currency of religious community. For many refugee communities, exile was internalized to the point where it became a key element in how its members defined themselves. They embraced it, and even continued doing to themselves what others had done to them. Being exiled sometimes made refugees less rather than more tolerant of others. Persecution and martyrdom pushed some Radical Anabaptists to isolated agricultural communities in central and eastern Europe where they disciplined their own erring or dissident members with the choice of compliance or exile. Refugee status sharpened Calvinists' conviction that they were the Chosen People of God living like latter-day children of Israel exiled from slavery in Egypt. In a series of promised lands from Geneva and Emden to New England and South Africa, the pain of exile became for Calvinists a badge of courage, a mark of election, and a form of discipline. Across the globe, returned refugees or transplanted exiles became some of the most hard-line advocates of religious intolerance and purification.

Exile did not always mean relocation over the nearest border. It could also mean forced removal to some secure or enclosed place within the city or territory. An accelerating cascade of expulsions across Europe through the fifteenth century propelled increasing numbers of Jews into Italy, where by mid-century some preachers began sounding alarm bells about a rising

'Jewish contagion'. Civic governments, trying to calm these fears without risking the loss of Jewish capital, built walls and gates around Jewish neighbourhoods and thus created the enclosed ghetto as a solution to protect the Christian community from this new 'contagion'. But who did those hastily-erected walls and gates protect? Ironically, the ghettos consolidated Jewish community and reinforced the authority of rabbis and religious councils in the world that the Jews made within the walls. This certainly frustrated those Christian authorities that had built "conversion houses" just outside the ghetto gates in order to draw out Jews into Christendom. Despite these frustrations, enclosure in a walled and gated building or neighbourhood became a common cultural form that was almost like a kind of internal exile. And throughout the early modern period, Christian authorities trusted in enclosures to separate, protect, punish, or convert a wide range of groups. They built many kinds of enclosures for nuns, orphans, the poor, and other marginal people, although it was not always clear whether these marginal groups were being protected from their surrounding communities, or whether those communities were being protected from them.

Even as a mass phenomenon, religious exile had an individual face. It was the common experience of many of the key thinkers of the period, and many worked their experience as religious refugees into their thinking and writing: Isaac Abravanel, Juan Luis Vives, Martin Luther, John Calvin, Menno Simons, Reginald Pole, Lelio Socinio, Fernando Cardoso, Johan Comenius, Mary Ward, and many others. Some, like Michael Servetus and Giordano Bruno, moved back and forth across Europe and finished their migrations only when they were burned at the stake as heretics. Others like Elizabeth Dirks, Janneken Muntsdorp, and Margaret Polley went to the stake before they could hit the road, becoming a cautionary lesson for those who might be slow to flee.

Forced expulsion reshaped Europe's social geography through the early modern period by creating diasporic communities across and beyond the continent. At a time when few Europeans wanted to move to remote overseas colonies, refugees and religiously-driven migrants figured disproportionately as the source of settlers. In some colonies like Portuguese Goa or Angola, they would impose regimes as restrictive as the ones they had fled. In others like Brazil and parts of New England they would develop more open forms of co-existence and hybridity. Some European communities, like Emden and Geneva, became temporary shelters for thousands of transient refugees. Others like Amsterdam and Salonika developed into international entrepots whose open social atmosphere attracted migrants of all kinds and revolutionized economic life. Many of these refugee communities lasted for

6   INTRODUCTION

Map 1. Cities of Early Modern Europe & the Mediterranean. Produced by Colin Rose.

centuries, like those of the Mennonites in the Ukraine, the Al-Andalus Moriscos in Istanbul and Algiers, and the Jews in Salonika and Eastern Europe. Diasporic communities established by Jews around Europe and the Mediterranean remained intact until new waves of expulsion, ethnic cleansing, and Holocaust crashed over the twentieth century and swept them into Auschwitz and Bergen Belsen. The twentieth century's religion was a racialized nationalism, but its drive to purge various impure groups and purge the community remained as strong as ever.

Religious exile and forced migration were not limited to Christendom. Greek Orthodox believers fled the steady expansion of Ottoman Turks into the Byzantine Empire. The Ottoman policy of *sürgün*, or resettling, forced criminals, colonists, and immigrants around the Empire according to local need, and was sometimes applied collectively to distinct religious and ethnic groups like the Jews. Jews fleeing Spain or the Holy Roman Empire were steered towards a few specific centers like Istanbul, Salonika, Safed, Edirne, and Izmir. Those same cities received Jews who had been caught up in the Ottoman military advance into central Europe in the 1520s, when thousands fled from Buda and Belgrade. The Ottomans moved fewer peoples around the Mamluk empire after conquering it in 1517, but their chief Islamic opponents in the Persian Safavid Empire also created religious refugees. As Persian Shi'ite clergy gained power from the late sixteenth century, they steadily increased pressure on Jewish communities and pushed for forced conversion campaigns which led many Jews to flee to Baghdad by the mid-seventeenth century.

Reformation Histories

What is 'Reformation'? Historians used to describe the period in terms of the search for a purer faith and simpler community in reaction to supposed abuses and corruption in the institutional Catholic Church. Histories of the Reformation were deeply shaped by the religious and national divisions the period created: Catholics and Protestants wrote very different accounts, but so too did French, English, or German historians. For centuries, most historians focused on the lives of particular religious reformers and the development of particular national church institutions. They lionized national heroes and demonized national enemies. From the nineteenth century, many asserted that the period's disputes triggered a series of developments that created the modern age. They found in the Reformation the birth of modern sensibilities about conscience, nation, and political liberty that were grouped together and described as 'modernity' – a cultural and intellectual development that many liberals praised and many conservatives condemned. Martin Luther's intellectual conflicts and refusal to bend to the pope were portrayed as assertions of individual freedom of conscience. Henry VIII's decision to break with Rome so he could break with his wife and secure his dynasty was a firm assertion of state power over the church. The Jesuit missions that accompanied Spanish and French colonists and framed a global Catholicism were confirmations of Catholicism's universality. The Calvinist framing of political responsibility confirmed representative government and the right to resist tyranny. There were few key values of modern Western society that historians could not trace back to the European Reformation, for better or worse.

If our search for origins – itself very controversial – now takes us beyond a theologian's intellectual breakthrough in a German university town and back further to a religious community's forced removal from Iberia, we are acknowledging that the Reformation was not just a movement for intellectual and religious change. It was also Europe's first grand project in social purification. Of course, these two phenomena are still intimately related. We cannot ignore how the period redefined theological doctrines, created new hybrid political-ecclesiastical institutions, or experienced economic shifts and social changes. These were both cause and consequence of the broader efforts to create purified communities of faith by means of exile and enclosure. Historians have always framed the chronology of events and movements according to the interests and values of their time. Every period, including our own, must re-evaluate the Reformation according to new priorities. Catholic and Protestant historians of the Reformation and Enlightenment periods saw sex, corruption, money, and possibly the devil at the root of each other's successes. By the nineteenth century, Friedrich Hegel and Thomas Carlyle saw it as demonstrating the catalytic force of a Great Man who could trigger historical change by uniting intellectual innovation with courageous individual will. Karl Marx and Friedrich Engels saw the Reformation as a deft manoeuvre by the capitalist mercantile class to wrench economic authority away from the landed aristocracy by undermining a church that had given nobles and kings their land, legitimacy, and power. When twentieth-century social history put the Reformation into a longer *durée*, historians who were curious about the experience of women or of the poor began rewriting the narrative. In each case, changing interpretations were driven not just by what historians discovered in archives and manuscripts but also by the social and political movements swirling outside the archive walls. Those movements helped them read familiar documents in new ways or led them to look for new documents that addressed questions no one had thought to ask before.

The resulting phases of Reformation historiography have not been sequential but concentric in their relations one to the other. New interpretations more often absorb than overturn their predecessors. They also put familiar sources under a new light that may turn up previously hidden meanings or connections. The political realism of the 1960s led historians to reread Luther's inspiring writings about the 'priesthood of all believers' as being in practice the more limited 'priesthood of all qualified burghers' – and male burghers at that. In the same way, a Reformation whose origins are redated to include the Jews' expulsion from Spain, and whose focus expands to include the refugee, the exile, the forcibly enclosed cannot ignore famous texts like the *Twelve Articles of the Peasantry*, *The Institutes of the Christian Religion*, or the *Edicts of the Council of Trent*. It rereads them. In the process, it highlights how profoundly the language of purity and purgation frame them, and how naturally exile and enclosure flow from them. As societies composed clearer definitions of what was good and normal and holy, they had to decide what to do with those who were now defined as bad and deviant and unholy. This is one reason why the Reformation saw the emergence of more efficient state-church institutions that were expected to police new boundaries. The realities of exile and of enclosure put these developments into a different framework and should lead us to question some of the optimism behind earlier interpretations.

Through much of the nineteenth and twentieth centuries the Reformation was seen as a critically important period in the history of western progress and civilization – it was a key initial stage in the story of modernity. Yet faith in modernity collapsed through the last decades of the twentieth century. Gandhi quipped that 'Western Civilization' sounded like a good idea that perhaps ought to be tried, and in that one joke put his finger on the absurdity and hypocrisy of modernity's deeply Eurocentric approach to global history. Historians now are sceptical about the possibility of tracing causality so far back through time. They are also more alert to and critical of the special interests that might be driving the effort. In post-modern historiography, treatments of the Reformation are often more local, individual, and cultural. Our sensitivity to the complicated dynamics of the particular in the past make us wary of finding the birth of anything in the period, let alone our own 'modern age'.

More to the point, we now find more continuities that cross what used to be the sharp boundary of the sixteenth century with its border posts in famous events like Luther's appearance at the Diet of Worms in 1521, Calvin's publication of one edition of *Institutes* after the other from 1536, and the gathering of Catholic churchmen at the Council of Trent from 1547 to 1563. Words like 'corruption' are used less often to describe the period that lies on the medieval side of that boundary, and 'reform' is now not always seen as positive for all those it affected. Current Reformation histories put theology and politics more securely into the contexts of anthropology and sociology to better assess how the period's dynamics interact with gender, class, marginality, ritual, art, violence, and popular culture. The Reformation is like a house with many windows, and each gives a different view on to the life and relationships of those inside.

Approaching the Reformation by looking into the window of religious expulsion and exile puts the themes of purity, contagion, and purgation into the foreground and gives us an angle of vision that allows us to explore the movement for religious reform cross-culturally, across many faiths, and as a global phenomenon. Focusing on exiles and refugees re-arranges our sense of how ideas and institutions relate. We may rethink what influenced what. We may be surprised by the appearance of people and relationships we had not noticed before. Looking at Luther as a refugee may draw out new dimensions of his work, as it has done in recent years for Calvin. None of this negates the view we have long had by looking through other more familiar windows. Yet it may lead us to think differently about the house itself.

And that different thinking will happen regardless. Reformation studies continue taking their shape from the lives, concerns, and questions of those who are writing them. Fewer students or scholars are fascinated by the fine shadings of Protestant and Catholic theology and Church Order than they would have been forty years ago. Fewer identify closely with the churches that split apart into warring groups as a result of the upheavals of the sixteenth century. Many are deeply suspicious of institutions generally, and of religious institutions above all. And more now are themselves exiles, immigrants, and refugees, and these personal realities point their historical curiosity in new directions. There is far more interest in what happened at the boundaries of belief and race because there are far more people whose lives stretch across those boundaries. We study, live, and marry across lines of race, ethnicity, or religion that were once heavily policed by familial, social, and national disapproval. That policing acted at every level, delivering both the genocidal holocausts of Armenians and Jews in the twentieth century, and also the mundane regulations that tried to prevent Catholics from applying for jobs in Protestant shops, or Jews from buying property in 'Christian' suburbs. Our recent wars have been described by some as a 'clash of civilizations' between Christianity and Islam, but they have seen equally violent clashes between Shia, Sunni, and Alawite. Such frequent examples of bloody hatred and banal prejudice make us more curious about past times when religious communities either lived together more peaceably or when they decided that co-existence was no longer possible. Our experiences of tension, collaboration, and cross-cultural relations make us more curious about how past cultures fought, co-existed, and mixed.

To acknowledge that the Reformation period was *deeply* about exile, expulsion, and refugees is not to say that it was *only* about them. Nor is it to say that its theologies and religious institutions were universally or necessarily oppressive. Religion was not the only factor behind expulsions, but it often provided the critical justification and language. The forced mass migration of religious minorities became a normal, familiar, and expected feature of a public policy that was oriented towards building a stronger society. If we ask why, we often hear distinctly religious language of purity, contagion, and purgation. These are recurring motifs that we can find in everything from sermons and tracts to plays and songs. They are found in royal decrees, popular ballads, and children's proverbs, sometimes on the surface but more often as a recurring subtext. We need to ask: why do these themes seem to accelerate in the fifteenth century? Why they are so enduring? Above all, how did they shape cultures through the past four or five hundred years?

Persecution Paradigms

The persecution of minorities was not itself a new thing. The medievalist R. I. Moore first traced how social fears, political ambitions, and emerging states came together in the eleventh century and led to what he described as a 'persecuting society'. Heretics, lepers, and Jews were singled out by authorities in church and state as Others whose very existence threatened the cohesion and survival of society. Their difference was a sin, a pollution, or a disease; and only a stiff purging would restore health to the social body. Some medieval authorities stirred up mob violence against these three target groups, and used arrest and trial, prison, and expulsion to push them to the margins of society, into exile, and even to death. Moore claims that a mentality of segregation, suppression, and purgation eventually took hold, but he argued that even when angry crowds were involved, this mentality was not the work of a blind and violent mob as the famous French sociologist Emile Durkheim thought. Rather, as Durkheim's equally famous German contemporary Max Weber argued, the instigators and beneficiaries of this purgative violence were to be found further up the social ladder among political and religious authorities and literary elites who were more cynical and strategic. Scapegoating and prosecuting a common social enemy paid benefits to those religious authorities who could name the threats and to those political authorities who could prosecute them. This was authorized violence that built the apparatus of the state.

Moore controversially drew a connection between the medieval hounding of Jews, heretics, and lepers, and twentieth century pogroms and genocides. Once the persecuting society emerged, it never lacked for fresh targets. Following Michel Foucault, Moore found that governments' drives for obedience and power were a powerful force behind each new generation of state persecution. Foucault thought that the persecuting drive characterized the seventeenth and eighteenth centuries above all, while the Italian historian Carlo Ginzburg thought that it emerged in the early fourteenth century. The American historian David Nirenburg has argued that local contexts and immediate material motives usually offer better ways to explain violence than abstract structures and stereotypes traced over long periods. Nirenburg found that violence could sometimes be ritualized and staged, like the violence against Jews during Holy Week. On those occasions it certainly reinforced social boundaries and benefited those in authority; communities united when they could direct their violence against common enemies. On the whole, however, Nirenburg rejects generalizations that describe violence as a state plot, a mass phenomenon, or an expanding cultural animus against a single target group like the Jews. He sees many persecutions but no persecuting society.

Whether universal or local, violence is only half the story. Communities needed ideas to unite around and people to galvanize them. Benedict Anderson's typology of the 'imagined community' aimed to explain how nationalism took shape and took hold in the nineteenth and twentieth centuries. We cannot simply project his analysis back to the Reformation period, yet the complex of five factors that he identifies as shaping the modern imagined communities of nationalism will be eerily familiar to an early modernist: the territorialization of religious faiths, the idea of sacred kingship, the development of print capitalism, the emergence of vernacular national languages, and changing conceptions of time. Anderson argued that their coming together in the nineteenth century facilitated the emergence of modern nationalism, particularly in Europe's overseas colonies. We might see that their conjunction at the dawn of the early modern age would turn the exodus of Spain's Jews from a single action into the first of a series of state acts bent on creating exclusive religious 'imagined communities' across Europe. These imagined communities of faith would also shape how Europeans defined insiders and outsiders in the world they were coming to explore.

More recently, the Renaissance historian Guido Ruggiero has used the term 'consensus realities' to describe how the leaders within a class or culture can agree on what a phenomenon looks like or means. Ruggiero describes Italian civic humanism as one such Renaissance 'consensus reality': many elite men who had read Aristotle and Cicero agreed with its ideal of civic politics even if they often undermined it in their actual political machinations. In this book, we will use the medieval idea of the *Corpus Christianum* or social Body of Christ as one example of a consensus reality, and the early modern witch hunt as another. Both the *Corpus Christianum* and witchcraft were intellectual constructs or metaphors that were believed in so widely and strongly that contemporaries considered them to be self-evident and 'real'. Influential authors, preachers, and magistrates could draw on them when aiming to explain either what made a community strong or what threatened to overturn it. Their words, whether preached from pulpits, published in pamphlets, or set out in laws provided what we can describe as a 'legitimizing discourse' that obligated authorities to act, or that justified the actions that they took. There was in fifteenth-century Spain – as in mid-twentieth-century Germany – a powerful consensus reality about the threat that Jews posed to society. And there was a powerful legitimizing discourse that could turn that reality into action.

This book will not argue that there was a single cause of violence against religious minorities or single line forward from the expulsions of the Reformation to the pogroms and Holocausts of the twentieth century. Nor will it argue that episodes of violence were purely episodic: locally generated, materially driven, and never the expression of some broader impulse that transcended time and space. The developments sketched here did have medieval precedents in the persecution of the Jews, heretics, and others who were seen as contagious. These medieval precedents demonstrate how important the language of purity, contagion, and purgation can be, particularly when it is rooted in religion and spoken by church and state officials. It was an ancient and timeless language. We can hear it spoken by ancient Israelites, Greeks, and Romans. Renaissance and Reformation authors, who were transfixed by the idea of returning *ad fontes*, or 'to the sources', would sometimes imitate the very words of these classical authors. Yet the language was not peculiarly European or Western. The same words and images, and often the same metaphor of society as a sick and endangered body in need of strong purgative medicine, could be found in China, Persia, Africa, and pre-Columbian America. It constitutes a recurring vocabulary of responses to perceived threats. But this seeming universality raises the question: can a language of purity, contagion, and purgation that is so common help us understand any particular situation?

Local conditions determined the discourse of contagion and purification in any particular time or place. There was a wide variety of voices in early modern society, but every now and then a charismatic individual or group seized the public stage and articulated a single compelling doctrine. It might have been for a short period, and it might have been for personal benefit, and reactions inevitably set in. But regardless of that, crisis, challenge, or opportunity could allow a Cardinal Ximenes, or Martin Luther, or Jan of Leiden to emerge and dominate in a locality or polity for a few years, drawing on a familiar stock of concepts, terms, and consensus realities to justify radical action against particular targets. These radical activists framed the legitimating discourse that preceded and incited violence, or that might even be used to justify or explain violence which had just happened. The discourse might be voiced by perpetrators or observers with very different agendas. Jesuits in New France wrote of the elimination of the Huron Wendat by the Iroquois Confederacy (allies of the British) in 1649, even though small Huron convert communities continued to exist right outside Jesuit settlements in Quebec. In this case, the invented account of how Iroquois-British forces had completely purged Huron lands allowed the Jesuits to claim that the lands were now vacant and open to French occupation. They also argued that French soldiers could and should support Jesuit missionary efforts. The semifictional Jesuit accounts did more than just serve church and state purposes. They reinforced the sharp rhetorical drive we see in all legitimating ideologies, as friends are described as purely good and enemies as purely evil. This kind of black and white contrast was the staple of popular religious rhetoric in the period, and did much to shape popular attitudes to religious others.

Similarly, events in one place might spur talk of purity, contagion, and purgation in another in a gathering snowball effect. The metaphors of the time provide an apt parallel. Plagues did not spontaneously combust across Europe, but travelled with merchants, preachers, soldiers, and migrants along vectors of infection. In the mid-fourteenth century it took two years for the bubonic plague to travel from the ports of Italy to the highlands of Scotland. Syphilis travelled the same route a century and a half later in about the same time. Travellers and highways carried songs, letters, sermons, pamphlets, and gossip telling of the Jews' desecration of eucharistic hosts, of Radicals' destruction of religious images, or of witches' search for unbaptized infants. In some places, the news got a skeptical response. In others it resonated more deeply and broadly, reinforcing existing fears, explaining local problems, intensifying local rivalries, and legitimizing local purges. This in part explains how a series of cities across Europe could one after the other expel their communities of Jews throughout the fifteenth century. Urban burghers picked up the fears of their neighbors and learned from their responses.

Legitimizing discourses braided together strands of tradition, legal custom, and religious metaphor. The most powerful of these were also the most elastic: scripture and religious history. As we will see, models and metaphors drawn from both sources refracted and gave meaning to local experiences by setting them into a divine history and plan. Millenarian radicals found their marching orders when merging the story of Israel's conquest of the Promised Land with the apocalyptic promise of the Last Judgment and the end of time. More pacifist Anabaptists looked instead to the model of the early church in the book of Acts in the Christian Bible, with its egalitarian order and communitarian sharing of goods. Calvinists and Puritans found their experience reflected in the account of God's Chosen People persecuted in Egypt and liberated in the Exodus to make their way to a Holy Land. Jews took hope from the narrative of Esther, who saved her people from elimination and secured a cathartic and liberating settling of accounts against those who had sought to destroy them. Muslims looked to collections of hadiths for the stories of Mohammed's persecution and exile.

Jews, Muslims, Catholics, and Protestants all absorbed the lessons of martyrs who had been constant and hopeful in the face of persecution. Printing allowed these narratives to become almost as ubiquitous as the Torah, Bible, or Qu'ran, turning the legitimating discourses around purity, contagion, and purgation from an elite obsession into a popular movement in any and all religious traditions. In Christian Europe, printing democratized the Renaissance humanist movement's turn to classical sources, and made the Roman model of the sovereign state more accessible to those schoolboys who, as merchants, professionals, and bureaucrats, helped drive the more extensive purgations of seventeenth-century absolutist monarchies. It made possible the broadsheets that illustrated the 'crimes of the Jews', but also made cheaper those manuals which detailed how best to identify and prosecute enemies of the state. It produced both the popular martyrologies and the equally popular medical texts that explained why purgation was the key to a body's health.

Toleration and Co-Existence

Did it work? The language of purity and purgation was clearly important, but historians now are exploring how the many gaps between words and actions left room for common sense and practical toleration. The walls that separated faiths or that enclosed marginal peoples held for centuries, but cracks appeared in them quite quickly. Schism proved to be the reflex action that allowed Protestant denominations to go forth and multiply into a host of imagined communities, and this would eventually undermine the cherished idea that each one had of being God's only truly chosen church. Nuns found ways to make their convent walls more porous. Jewish merchants sailed between confessions as they moved around Mediterranean ports. Not all religious travellers were refugees. The missionaries who rode the waves of Europe's global exploration and exploitation may have aimed to convert, but were frequently drawn into conversation. Although grammarians of the imagined communities of faith aimed for rules, that conversation always moved inevitably and increasingly into local dialects. We now see these not as degenerations of a pure form, but as local expressions of new possibilities and new purities.

In a world of consensus realities, imagined communities, and legitimating discourses many languages co-existed. There were many who disagreed with, ignored, or subverted official policies mandating expulsion. As a result, there was always a broad gap between prescription and reality that might extend to the highest levels. The same magistrates in Amsterdam, Strasbourg, or Venice who passed laws curbing the activities of religious 'deviants', also protected and did business with those same deviants who went about their affairs discretely.

Yet we should remember that these were exceptions to rules that were still on the books across Europe – and that were multiplying. Despite many examples of individual acts of toleration and co-existence, the later sixteenth and seventeenth centuries also witnessed an intensification of those same concerns with purity, contagion, and purgation which we can see behind the expulsions of fifteenth-century Jews, sixteenth-century Christians, and seventeenth-century Muslims. Re-catholicization campaigns transformed Poland, Austria, and Bohemia from mixed communities into Catholic strongholds, and England's wars, expulsions, and plantations aimed to make Ireland wholly Protestant. Monarchies in France, Iberia, and England embraced the Defense of the Faith as a nationalist project because it so conveniently cast heresy as treason. Confessions and catechisms etched new doctrines more sharply, and offered standards for judging obedience and giving access to political office, social institutions, schools of all kinds, and the professions.

Governments both Protestant and Catholic may not have been entirely consistent or immediately effective in their 'confessionalization' campaigns, but these campaigns did eventually help establish official narratives and drive official policies. That the English should for so long consider themselves 'naturally' Protestant, and the Spanish just as 'naturally' Catholic was due less to the patient pastoral work of an attentive church than to the powerful alliance of church and state in creating a national Establishment that was selectively exclusive and that knew how to use propaganda effectively. The slow processes of bureaucracy would prove to be a more effective tool of confessional discipline than either inflammatory sermons or violent pamphlets. Exclusion may not have been immediate, but it was not just a metaphor: we cannot forget that the largest mass movements of religious dissenters, whether Christian, Jewish or Muslim, both 'voluntary' and forced, happened a full century or more after Martin Luther's appearance before the Holy Roman Emperor at the Diet of Worms, Ignatius Loyola's foundation of the Jesuit order, and Elizabeth I's accession to the English throne.

The early modern paradox is that confessionalist exclusivity could develop alongside practical co-existence. Confessionalism normalized and legitimated religious differences, and shaped people's expectations of themselves and others. Long after they ceased fearing the devil in the Other, communities continued *voluntarily* to separate themselves, preferring to live with their peers, associates, and co-religionists. Much of religious practice took place in the home, around the table, or in the neighbourhood, and many valued having easy access to foods and friends. At the same time, many governments allowed some degree of co-existence if the marginalized community kept its activities to these private realms and out of the public eye. Dutch Catholics and Mennonites built churches in attics and courtyards for precisely this purpose. The social geographer Bruce Masters has noted that 'religious clustering' was a form of psychological distancing that reinforced and reciprocated geographic distancing. He notes that non-Muslims never formed part of the collective 'we' in Ottoman consciousness. Co-existence under the *millet* system was purely practical, and the so-called mutual respect that kept the Ottoman Empire in a state of social harmony was more coerced than genuine. The Ottoman social system was not built on collective respect, and failed to forge cordial ties and genuine connection.

This describes the situation in England, France, Germany, Italy, Spain, and the Netherlands equally well. The Ottoman example is raised here only because Ottomans are often singled out for their exceptional toleration of minorities. As Benjamin Kaplan has argued, we do well to remember that early modern co-existence was not the same as modern toleration. It was practical and grudging, and driven more often by necessity than ideology. The number of Europeans willing to acknowledge that their religious or confessional rivals had a point, let alone a truth, was minuscule. And it would remain that way until at least the later eighteenth century.

Body Politics

When early modern people referred to their families, their social groups, and communities, they often talked about the Body. Towns were bodies, confraternities and guilds were bodies, the church was a body, and the eucharistic host used in the mass was the ultimate Body that brought all these other ones together – the Body of Christ. A healthy body was open and balanced, while a sick one might be constipated or blocked up and full of festering materials which could become contagious. To bringing a sick body back to health and prevent infecting others, you had to be willing to cut into it, bleed it, force out rotting matter, and then rebuild the proper balance of food, rest, and emotions.

What worked for the physical body, worked for the social body, and so this book takes the Body as its organizing metaphor. Chapter 1 explores how Europeans defined the Body of Christ, and what threats they feared for it. It opens by reviewing the three interconnected meanings of the Body of Christ: as the physical body of Jesus the human being, as the Host representing Christ the Lord, and as the social body or *Corpus Christianum*. After exploring how the social body was celebrated in political life and social rituals, we will consider four of the key threats to that Body that troubled early moderns: the encircling military threat posed by Ottoman Islam; the contagious inner threat posed by heretics, witches, and Jews; the threat of internal division caused by corruption in the Catholic Church; and threat of God's judgment posed by various natural disasters.

Chapter 2 then considers four ways by which Europeans aimed to Purify the Body: by separation (looking at Observance Movements in the church); by containment (the enclosure of nuns, marginals, and Jews by physical or legal means); by prosecution (the Inquisition and other forms of communal and legal discipline); and finally by Purgation (the expulsion of Jews, Muslims, and other Christians). The purges that produced exiles and refugees came in waves that intensified and became more overtly political throughout the sixteenth and into the seventeenth and eighteenth centuries.

Chapter 3 puts a human face on the process of Dividing the Body by considering a variety of exiles, refugees, and martyrs ranging from Andalusian aristocrats to Jewish *conversos* to Christian theologians. Some fled for their lives, and others for opportunities. Some spent a limited time in exile before returning home, while others were permanent migrants to a new home or perpetual refugees who never settled long in any single place. We then turn to compare eight of the places that refugees and exiles flocked to across Europe, around the Mediterranean, and in America. We see here that the ways in which cities responded to refugees could send their own economies and histories in very different directions. Some aimed to become the monocultural ideal paradise for a particular religious group, while others allowed different groups to co-exist so long as there were firm legal or physical walls separating them, and yet others allowed different religious groups to live and worship openly. There was no single model for a refugee city, but the varying degrees of open-ness or restriction profoundly shaped these cities' economic and social life through the early modern period and beyond.

Chapter 4 then turns to consider some of the religious ideas and practices driving change, or what we might call Mind and Body. The purgations and purifications of the period were as much intellectual as physical. Rather than attempt to review all of Reformation theology, this chapter singles out three common themes in religious thinking or doctrine, and how they changed in this period. 'Initiation', which could take the form of circumcision or baptism, brought an individual into the Body of the community; this was one of the earliest and most critical points dividing religious communities. 'Presence' explores how people thought about the relation between divine transcendence and physical reality – that is, how they thought that God was present among them. 'Authority' looks at how religious texts or 'scriptures' functioned in different communities, and compares who had the right or authority to interpret them and so set the standards for life in the Body. Each religious tradition combined abstract doctrines with concrete guides to action, and every woman and man regardless of creed had to put faith into practice through acts of charity. This brought Mind and Body together, and so the second half of this chapter considers conceptions of and reform to Charity. Charity was as much about setting boundaries as it was about caring for other parts of the Body. In the refugee context, it became critical to determine who got charity, and how, and why, and above all what they had to do in order to keep it. In this period, charity also became a critical agent for reforming or purifying those who were immoral, lazy, and delinquent. It was a means of keeping members of the community in line.

Chapter 5 on Re-Forming the Body continues to look at how the ideas and forms of purgation and discipline were exercised, and above all how they shaped social and cultural life. Exiles and refugees were extraordinarily active and creative wherever they landed. What kind of world did they make, and how much of what we take for granted about early modern culture is actually a direct or indirect result of the exile experience? We look first at the printing press and some of the main texts for instruction and discipline that it made possible: woodcuts, confessions, catechisms, and bibles. As printing became cheaper, these became longer, more detailed, and more available. We turn then to the personnel of the reforming churches: priests, pastors, nuns and monks, and rabbis and imams. As religious demands increased, the training of clergy evolved to keep up. Clergy became more highly educated, professional, and socially distant from their parishioners. As religious confessions became more important to national identity, and states wanted more demographic records kept more consistently, the clergy became important public officials whose role in registering births, marriages, and deaths allowed them to police religious boundaries. We turn then to look at how church buildings were reshaped under the impact of the reform movements and the schisms that divided them. Churches and religious institutions like orphanages, schools, and workhouses were like architectural catechisms. They demonstrated and taught the truth of a faith's superiority by moving far beyond words into the senses of smell, sight, and sound. Reformation could never succeed by discipline alone – it had to engage the senses and the imagination. So this chapter closes by looking at what some have described as 'the imaginary', that collection of stories, images, myths, traditions, and other forms of creative imagination that refugees and exiles used in order to pass on their convictions and preoccupations. Each religious group used stories of heroes and villains, aimed at young members in the first instance, to pass on concepts of truth, understandings of who to trust or fear, models of behaviour, attitudes, and even more abstract doctrines.

I

THE BODY OF CHRIST: DEFINED AND THREATENED

IN ORDER TO UNDERSTAND HOW EXILE AND EXPULSION COULD become mass phenomena from the late fifteenth century, we need to look at how European Christians of the centuries before this pictured their society and their relation to God. There was little unity and certainly no uniformity of views, and broad gaps between ideal and reality were the norm. When many Christians described community, they used the metaphor of a human body and in particular the Body of Christ. The metaphor of the Body had different linked dimensions: the social Body of Christians (*Corpus Christianum*) drew ultimately on the spiritual Body of Christ (*Corpus Christi*). This physical metaphor for the social community of believers distinguished Christianity from Judaism and Islam, and provided a very powerful imaginative framework for thinking about what characterized a pure social community and what threatened it.

Pictures and rituals put the idea of a *Corpus Christianum* at the centre of the Christian imaginary, and European Christians took responsibility for failing to reach the ideal community that it represented. But throughout the fourteenth century they became increasingly aware of other threats to that Body. There were threats from outside: the Ottoman Turks represented the biggest external threat, and the rising tide of Islam seemed repeatedly to be on the verge of drowning the *Corpus Christianum* entirely. And there were threats from within: heretics who rejected Catholic doctrines and structures, witches in league with the devil, and Jews who stubbornly refused to accept Christianity were all infections in one or another part of the body. Left unchecked, these infections would spread like a contagion across the whole Body of Christ. Religious leaders and institutions ought to be the spiritual doctors who could halt this contagion, but they often seemed too divided and preoccupied with their own interests to do much good. A Body thus weakened needed strong purgative medicines to restore it to health: doctors cut into the veins of sick patients to release bad and infected blood, gave emetics to trigger violent vomiting, enemas to empty the bowels, and diuretics to clear the bladder. The source of sickness had to be eliminated from the body before healing could begin. Many saw recurring plagues and famines as God's own purgations of the *Corpus Christianum*, a bracing reminder that the threats to the body were not matters of abstract debate and discussion, but of life and death, and thus of eternity.

The Body of Christ shaped both the late medieval Christian imagination and its imaginary – that complex of beliefs, assumptions, and images through which Christians understood the world. The narrative of purity, impurity, and judgment framed Christian discourse. Yet these were fundamentally metaphors. What mattered historically was who manipulated the images and discourse, and how and why. This chapter will look first at how late medieval Christians pictured and thought about society and some of the religious institutions and rituals by which they put their ideas about the social body – the *Corpus Christianum* – into practice. It will turn then to consider some of the threats that they feared most, from the Turks at their borders; to heretics, witches, and Jews in their towns and cities; to internal divisions that weakened the church's ability to defend them spiritually against these threats. The results were anything but abstract – and we will close with these Christians' powerful sense that the plagues and famines they experienced were both God's punishment and His challenge to repent and reform.

Purity and Community in the Body

People of the late medieval and Renaissance periods often thought visually, and they popularized two images over the course of the fifteenth and sixteenth centuries. One showed the Virgin Mary, the human mother of Jesus Christ and a powerful spiritual figure in the Christian message, standing with outspread arms to form a tent or canopy out of her long flowing cloak. Mary's sheltering mantle covered a different range of people in each individual image: nuns or monks, well-dressed nobles or merchants, the select members of a family, artisans of a guild, or masses of ordinary people. Male, female, young, old – the mix of those huddled under the cloak varied, although they were inevitably praying to the Virgin. She, in turn, seemed to ignore them and looked out impassively. This was the Madonna of Mercy – *misericordia* in Latin – and Europeans fashioned thousands in paintings, sculptures, woodcuts, and manuscript illustrations. She became one of the most common holy images they encountered in their daily life.

The second popular image was the bird's eye view of a city or town. Artists produced many hundreds to feed demand that began locally with prints of particular cities like Ghent, Avignon, or Geneva and then spread across Europe in published atlases containing dozens of images. From a vantage point high up in the sky, buildings, squares, and crowded neighbourhoods stood out in sharp relief within the encircling walls. Towering steeples marked the main churches, and the densely packed streets of a city's old Roman or medieval centre gave way on the outskirts to larger open blocks marked with monasteries, convents, and sometimes even fields and orchards stretching out to the city walls. No one had ever actually seen a city from this vantage point, and no one would until the Mongolfier brothers sent the first hot air balloons into the skies above Paris in 1783. This was the city as God could see it. The novelty of aerial views added to their fascination while the printing press made these woodcuts and engravings cheap and popular. One of the earliest and largest was an enormous woodcut view of Venice published by Jacopo de' Barbari in 1500. Within decades, Sebastian Munster (1488–1552), a former Franciscan friar who had converted to Protestantism and fled to Basel, published *Cosmografia* (Cosmography), a compendium of geographical knowledge that featured many city views. It was wildly popular soon after appearing in 1544, with twenty-four Latin editions appearing in the next century and many vernacular translations as well. Munster's success prompted Lodovico Guicciardini, a Florentine writer and merchant (and nephew of the famous historian and diplomat Francesco Guicciardini) who had resettled in Antwerp, to publish *The Description of the Low Countries* (*Descrittione di Tutti i Paesi Bassi* 1567) illustrated with dozens of aerial views and city profiles. Five years later Georg Braun (1541–1622) started publishing *The Cities of the World* (*Civitatis Orbis Terrarum* 1572) offering views of 546 city cities drawn by Franz Hogenburg (1535–90). It would take forty-five years to complete the six-volume project. And there were many more.

The Madonna of Mercy and the aerial city view were found everywhere but seldom as abstract images. They always showed particular people and places. The image of the Madonna of Mercy first emerged in a collection of saints' lives written in the 1230s by the Cistercian hagiographer Caesarius of Heisterbach. Marian devotion was starting to include the idea that Jesus' mother shared some of her son's powers to protect and even redeem sinners. Caesarius wrote dozens of tales about Mary protecting priests, nuns, and monks from thunderstorms and devilish temptation, and then closed the collection with a Cistercian monk's vision of the Virgin Mary surrounded by many high clerics. The monk was disturbed when he could see no Cistercians, but when she was asked why, she threw open her cloak to reveal a host of Cistercians in a privileged place under her mantle. This proved an extraordinarily compelling image, and clergy in particular competed for that favoured place under the Virgin's protective cloak. Many late medieval frescoes and paintings show Franciscan and Dominican nuns or friars under the mantle.

The Misericordia image spread rapidly through the fourteenth century, when plagues like the Black Death in 1348 drove Christians to seek shelter under Mary's cloak. By the end of the century, recurring plagues, a widening split in the church, and growing fears of the devil's work on earth made many fear that final Judgment Day was coming. A French peasant had a vision of the Virgin Mary appealing desperately with an angry Jesus, who was preparing to unleash purgative judgment on a sinful earth. As she pleaded with her son to show mercy, she spread her cloak protectively over the people whom Jesus wanted to punish. We need to remember that the plagues, famines, and sicknesses which the Virgin's protective cloak held at bay could represent either the devil's torments or God's punishments of a community. Preachers spread the French peasant's vision, and across Europe believers got to their knees to pray for Mary's protection. A devotional movement of 1399 featured vast public processions of penitents dressed in white robes, sometimes whipping themselves, and crying out for 'Misericordia', or 'Mercy'. They moved in their hundreds and thousands from city to city to quite literally transfer the devotion from one community to the next in a slow progress that climaxed in 1400 in Rome. This popular devotional movement helped spread the concept and iconic image of the Madonna of Mercy and her protective cloak across Europe: in Italy as the *Madonna della Misericordia*, through France as the *Vierge de Miséricorde*, and in Germany as the *Schutzmantelmadonna*.

The cult of the Madonna of Mercy expanded rapidly through the fifteenth century. As icons, frescoes, and statues multiplied, so too did a host of new hospitals and confraternities dedicated to the 'Misericordia' and to the idea that all those under Mary's cloak had to express charity towards each other. Some images show a broad range of needy men and women from different social classes, while others focus on narrower groups of courtiers, confraternity members, guildsmen, or clergy who provided charity to the needy. Votive images produced in the central Italian towns of San Gimigniano and Perugia after a virulent plague in 1467 showed all the townsfolk huddled together for protection [Fig 1]. Under the Virgin's cloak, many disparate groups found spiritual equality and sometimes even a degree of social equality – they were united together as a believing community protected by their patroness from evil and punishment.

1. Benedetto Bonfigli, *Madonna of Mercy* (1467). Perugia. Scala/Art Resource, New York.

While images of the Madonna of Mercy emphasized community as a bounded group of people protected by a cloak, the aerial views emphasized community as a bounded space protected by walls. Almost inevitably, that space was crowded with the houses, church towers, and market squares of a vibrant urban community, while the space outside the walls was shown as open farmland or sometimes even left completely blank. Yet this was hardly what city dwellers saw when they walked out of the gates in their city walls. Houses, shops, hostels and shrines lined the main highways for quite a distance. Communities of monks or nuns settled outside the walls out of financial necessity or devotional preference, or possibly because the city council had decided that the value of their prayers and hospitality did not outweigh their traditional immunity from property taxes. So while you could walk out of the gate in Ghent or Antwerp or La Rochelle and see houses and shops marking the roads and farms and market gardens dotting the surrounding fields, you would see none of these when you opened the atlases of Munster, Guicciardini, or Braun & Hogenburg. The artists who had followed de' Barbari depicted their cities almost as he had depicted Venice: as though these were islands in an empty sea, even if they were hundreds of miles from water and surrounded by densely populated suburbs. In most aerial views or city profiles, the city sits walled, isolated, and sharply defined in a deserted landscape [Fig 2a & 2b].

Looking at these images of walled cities and protective Madonnas helps us understand how Europeans thought about community. Community was both a built environment and a collection of people, and the popular images pictured them in ways that drew a sharp boundary between inside and outside. The area outside the city walls was as barren and unprotected as the area outside the Madonna of Mercy's cloak. To live there was to be vulnerable, foreign, possibly an outcast and certainly an outsider. By contrast, the community within the walls lived together under the Virgin's protection. The influential fifth-century theologian Augustine had distinguished between the City of God and the City of Man, and an early sixteenth century woodcut visualized two walled European cities where angels and demons challenged each other from the ramparts [Fig 3]. Citizens had the duty to work together in order to turn their city into a pure and sacred space. They rooted this conviction in the powerful metaphor of the Body of Christ. This Body took three distinct forms: physical, spiritual, and symbolic. It was Christ's human and physical body, while also being the eucharistic host in the Catholic sacrament of communion, and also the broader community of believers gathered in the church. These three dimensions depended on each other and turned the Body of Christ into one of the most powerfully resonant metaphors picturing Christian community as both sacred and secular, both transcendent and earthly. We can unpack these meanings briefly.

The first form of Christ's Body was physical – Christ as a human being. Sculptures, altarpieces, and simple images showing Christ at various ages were everywhere – to the point that no one regardless of religious belief

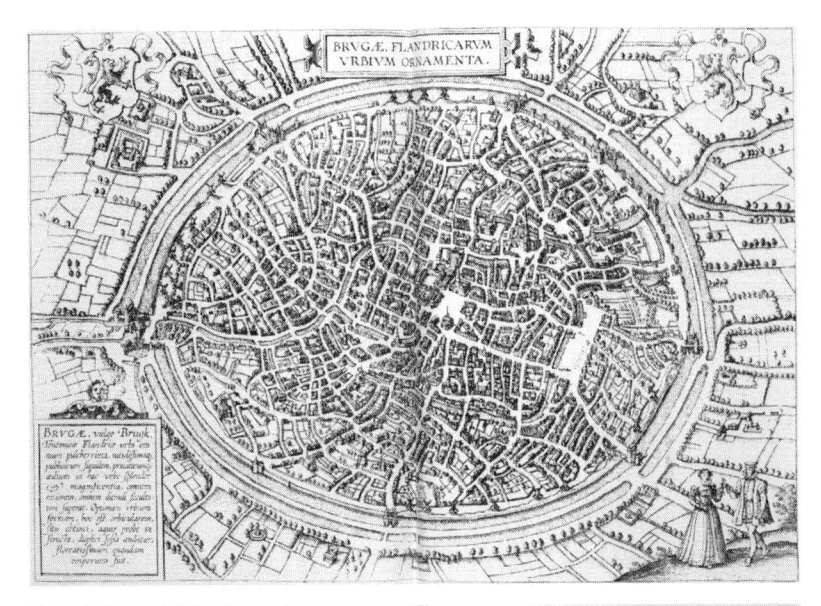

2(a). Bruges, Braun & Hogenberg, *Civitates orbis terrarum* (1572). Courtesy of the Thomas Fisher Rare Book Library, University of Toronto.

2(b). Augsburg, Braun & Hogenberg, *Civitates orbis terrarum* (1572). Courtesy of the Thomas Fisher Rare Book Library, University of Toronto.

28 THE BODY OF CHRIST: DEFINED AND THREATENED

3. Woodcut of Augustine in his Study and the Two Cities, Augustine, *De civitate dei* (1515). Courtesy of the Thomas Fisher Rare Book Library, University of Toronto.

could avoid seeing them when walking through a town. Images of Christ on Mary's lap had grown steadily more human and lifelike from the early medieval images of Mary as the Throne of Wisdom. In these, mother and son posed rigidly and impassively in rich fabrics to emphasize their nobility and divine authority. Christ might be shown as an infant, or simply as a smaller-scaled adult sitting stiffly on Mary's lap. Emotion started warming these images from the twelfth century onward, and by the fifteenth devotional images of a teenage Mary playing with a sometimes mischievous baby Christ were common. Mary might still be dressed as richly as a queen, but she might also wear the clothes of an ordinary adolescent. These very human scenes of infancy found a sobering counterpart in wretched scenes of Christ's passion and crucifixion, with northern artists in particular outdoing each other in gory depictions of Christ's suffering on the cross and Mary's anguish. Emotion had transformed Christian piety, and the deepest emotions were maternal love and adult pain and suffering. Those who wanted to follow Christ most closely had to be prepared to imitate his endurance and suffering by spending hours in prayer, days at fasting, and nights in whipping themselves.

The second form of Christ's Body was spiritual – Christ represented in the small wafer or host (known in Greek as the *eucharist* and in Latin as the *corpus christi*) that a priest consecrated in the mass before giving it individually to believers in the sacrament of communion. This central ritual of the Christian faith derived from Jesus' last meal with his disciples before his crucifixion, when he shared bread and wine with them and declared 'Take, eat, this is my body ... this is my blood' (Matthew 26:26). Only an ordained priest could perform the ritual by which a thin wafer of bread was miraculously transformed into Christ's actual physical body without ever losing the size and shape of a piece of baked dough (called 'transubstantiation'). Entire communities mobilized to celebrate the Real Presence of Christ in their church or town. This was a powerful spiritual magic with awesome results. Fear of the divine presence kept so many medieval Christians from taking communion that an important church Council in 1215 ordered all believers to receive it at least once annually in their parish church. Friars and other clergy also aimed to increase devotional exercises around the small wafer. Pope Urban IV instituted the feast of Corpus Christi in 1263 to commemorate a miracle in the small Italian town of Bolsena when a host just consecrated by a priest began bleeding. This miracle, and the many others which soon followed, made the powerful transformative magic of transubstantiation more vivid and physical. Throughout the centuries that followed, devotional exercises, frequent communion, and community-wide processions would bring Christ's Real Presence more directly into the physical realities, regular rhythms, and familiar spaces of believers' lives.

The third form of the Body of Christ was symbolic – the Body as neighbours, friends, and the whole of community of local believers gathered as the Christian Church. In a New Testament passage, the apostle Paul wrote: 'For the body is one and has many members', comparing individuals to the hands, feet, eyes, and ears which worked together for the good of the whole: 'now you are the Body of Christ and individually members of it' (I Corinthians 12: 12–13). It was known in Latin as the *Corpus Christianum*, and clergy and laity collaborated to realize this Body of Christ by offering and receiving the sacraments, marking holy days and holy spaces, and feeding and clothing the poor. They also competed to outdo each other in actions and artwork. Urban lay corporate groups like guilds and confraternities thought that their religious obligations were no less important than their social, economic, or political roles in the town or city, and no less spiritual than what monks, friars, and nuns might do. Venice's major confraternities outdid the city's religious houses in the extravagance of their shrines and processions, and in the number of people tended in their hospitals. Guilds in York and Coventry put on plays where apprentices, journeymen, and masters acted out stories from the Bible and the lives of the saints. City councils everywhere gave funds to build distinctive church towers and outfit them with flights of bells that would sound through the whole town. They outlawed swearing, shuttered markets and shops on holy days, and competed to hire public preachers in Lent or Advent who would stir up the thousands who crowded into a big church or public square.

The push and pull of laity and clergy collaborating to raise devotional awareness, pious practices, and charitable activity to an ever higher level is at the heart of what we can call 'civic religion'. Civic religion worked with all three forms of the Body of Christ: physical, spiritual, and symbolic. We often associate Catholicism primarily with the clergy: friars in monasteries, nuns in convents, and priests and bishops in parish churches and cathedrals. We define it by the theological concepts clergy developed in councils and wrote up in treatises and taught in universities, or by the vital spiritual rituals like the sacrament of communion which only they could perform. The fact that this comes first to mind reflects the reality that it was literate monks, friars, priests, and nuns who most often wrote about what it meant to be a Christian. It can come as a surprise to realize just how active male and female laity of all ages and social classes were in articulating the ritual life, charitable outreach, artistic creativity, and even physical structure of the *Corpus Christianum*. Civic religion built on the idea of the city as a holy community, protected by saints, bounded by shrines in the city walls, nourished by hospitals offering charity to citizens and pilgrims, and governed by lay people who actively promoted civic spiritual health through their communal councils, trade guilds, and confraternities. Each of these was itself a community with its own members, traditions, resources, and activities, and a Catholic town or city grew stronger as its constituent communities multiplied.

There were certainly key rituals that only ordained priests and friars could perform: hearing the confessions of individual believers, offering absolution for the sins they had confessed, consecrating hosts, casting out demons, conducting funeral rituals. This gave them a special status in the community, but it did not necessarily elevate them beyond it. Secular clergy and nuns often came from local families, while friars and monks might come from places further afield. Yet all could be deeply involved in local politics and social life, particularly those from wealthy families. Although the life and teachings of a wandering Galilean carpenter and his ragtag band of followers animated the Catholic imaginary, when it came to property and power the social and economic hierarchies of church and state usually reflected, supported, and perpetuated each other – and sometimes fought as well. In 1520s Nuremburg, the patrician Wilibald Pirckheimer fought against religious reforms being engineered by his colleagues on the city council because they would undermine a Catholic religious establishment that included the St. Clare Franciscan convent where his sister Caritas was abbess. In 1540s Florence, Duke Cosimo I cleared the Dominican house of St. Mark of a group of friars who had long opposed his family, and he barred Archbishop Antonio Altoviti from entering the city because Altoviti's father had taken up arms to resist Cosimo I's coming to power.

So we should not understand the civic religion of the *Corpus Christianum* as something that separated lay people from clergy. They did not divide their sacred from their secular lives, but saw these as being woven together just as tightly as the fabric in the robes they pulled on when entering their confraternal oratories, or in the banners that bobbed above their heads in frequent processions around the shrines, churches, hospitals, and squares of the city. Their faith brought heavenly power down to the level of the street and into the rhythms of clock and calendar. Civic religion was above all deeply *local* religion, tied to the times and spaces of the town itself.

The French market city of Lyon lay at the foot of the hill of Fourvière where the slow-moving Saone met the fast-flowing Rhone, and its merchants, artisans, and clergy threw themselves into frequent religious ceremonies. Some of their religious processions paced the walls and marked boundaries, often with Christ present in the form of a consecrated host, to protect the spaces and people within. Others connected the bridges and gates that brought food to daily markets and traders to seasonal fairs, often with an image of the Virgin Mary borne aloft by confraternity members. Both city council and church authorities might order processions to honour patron saints, mark a military victory, or observe the end of a plague. Confraternities, guilds, hospitals, and parish churches added others of their own. Italian printers, German artisans, and Flemish cloth merchants walked with native Lyonaise, because the city was a magnet for foreigners, and civic religion's devotional exercises were about all those who lived in the community and not just the much smaller number who were formally citizens. Artisans from the St. Nizier district criss-crossed the Saone with bankers from the Fourvière district, visiting churches, hospitals, and religious houses, entering the Cathedral of John the Baptist to venerate this preacher-saint's jawbone in its elaborate container (called a 'reliquary') on the high altar, or climbing up the Fourvière hill to reach the chapel where an icon of Mary and the Infant Jesus kept watch over the city. The Lyonaise wanted the Virgin Mother and Holy Child to see the city and its people face to face, and so staged richly sensory services that had bells ringing, priests and people chanting, choirs singing, candles burning, and incense smoking. They held most of their processions in the span of months from Christmas through June that were filled with holy days marking the key points of Christ's life, death, and resurrection, thereby connecting the life of the town with the life of the Saviour.

Spiritually significant spots and days marked the town and its calendar in what seemed like a purely random order. Yet the uneven spacing of place and time reflected one key belief of civic religion: it was God, working through his son Jesus and his saints and by means of miracles, who identified the key local holy places and times. A plague stopped, a blind man healed, a flood averted, or a drought ended by rains – these miracles were examples of God's work in Lyon, and the Lyonaise's work in turn was to remember and give thanks by building shrines and holding commemorative processions. But the Lyonaise were not passive; they knew that God only worked when people prayed and pleaded. So they bargained with God and the saints, using processions, shrine-building, charity, and other pious acts as currency in their efforts to purchase the divine protection that would keep the Rhone bridges from being swept away in floods or to secure the favour that would keep foreign bankers and traders coming to the four main seasonal fairs.

All civic religion was local, and all included this kind of negotiation and exchange with saintly protectors. A complicated ritual hierarchy kept some saints' images outside the city walls and others in, and valued some as moveable pieces that could be taken out into the streets in procession while others remained fixed in their shrines to draw pilgrims and penitents towards them in devotion. Florentines brought an image from an outlying town into the city during times of environmental crisis, particularly if too much rain was falling – or not enough. The Bolognese saw this and deliberately imitated it in 1433 with an image that, as in Lyon, sat atop a hill just outside of town. It worked, and over the next century Bolognese confraternities established eleven new shrines in the city walls, on bridges, and on hills outside the city. A series of processions brought the images out to visit each other on key feast days, creating a holy geography of roads and buildings. Shrines and processions marked the city as a sacred space and recruited saints as leading citizens.

The shrine-building strategies of Bologna's confraternities seem too deliberate for us to accept without question the contemporary conviction that it was God or the saints who chose the places and images of the holy in the city. With civic religion no less important than any other belief, the stories told about the faith wove hopes together with facts. The gaps between pious accounts and practical actions were sometimes widened by political agendas or unscrupulous operators. One of Bologna's shrines filled up the former city gate where a political enemy had fled. Another had its miracle-working image replaced twice as confraternity members experimented to find one that would attract more donations. We may also be puzzled when confronted with sacred rituals that seem to date from pre-Christian times and express a more animistic spirit. At Pentecost, a spring-time holy day, the young men of Lyon would put on horse costumes and dance their way from the point where the Rhone and Saone rivers met through the streets to the major Rhone bridge. In nearby Vienne, four men chosen by the local high clergy were stripped naked, blacked all over, and ran from the archbishop's palace around all the key institutions including the town hall and the leading abbey to receive, in stages, a guard, a 'king', a 'queen', and an ever-lengthening trail of hooting and yelling adolescents and young boys. In Autun, a heifer was sacrificed to the Virgin to avert plague.

If local religion incorporated these apparently animistic and even pagan elements so easily into the practice of the Catholic faith, should we really consider it Christian at all? Most historians now take the view that people who considered themselves good Catholics should be taken at their word. Since it was Catholic missionaries of the early medieval period who had first turned pagan deities into saints and had redirected devotion from holy wells and trees to new saintly shrines, we should not be surprised if lines remained blurred on these points.

As new waves of missionaries and preachers moved through and beyond Europe in the medieval centuries, the meaning of 'conversion' and the faith of converts would be questioned more and more. Were ancient legends and rituals more superstitious than spiritual? Was it enough to simply follow the public exercises of the *Corpus Christianum*: to walk in processions, give charity to beggars, make confession and receive communion annually, abstain from working on religious feast days, join a confraternity? What of spiritual exercises: the private life of faith as this might be expressed inside home and family by the prayers you prayed, the foods you ate, the clothes you wore, or the names you gave your children?

Medieval civic religious piety had been largely collective, formal, and ritualized. Through the fifteenth century new devotional movements exploded across Europe that began emphasizing individual emotions, senses, and inner states, and purity in morals and belief. The *Imitation of Christ* written by Flemish cleric Thomas à Kempis from 1418 to 1427 is usually taken as the leading example of this drive towards developing an intense and emotive inner devotional piety by directly following Christ's example. It quickly became and still remains a very popular guide for those aiming to convert from a life of spiritual indifference to a life of focused and intentional discipleship, but it was just one of many similar works. Although Thomas addressed himself primarily to fellow clergy, other authors wrote for lay believers, and 'imitative piety' transformed lay groups like confraternities. For all its deeply mystic interiority, the new piety drew believers into rituals that imitated Christ's physical actions and particularly his suffering: the hunger when he fasted, the anguish of his prayers, the torture when he was whipped, the bleeding when he was crucified. Known in northern Europe as the Modern Devotion, it emphasized helping believers to merge the physical, spiritual, and symbolic forms of the Body of Christ through pious exercises of introspection and meditative prayer, mutual correction in small groups of believers, reading and giving sermons, regular fasting and feasting, and even whipping oneself. These intense devotions were important to the collective life of a new form of confraternity that emerged through the fifteenth century: often smaller, more intense, and more determined to hold each other to higher standards of belief and action from the time they joined the brotherhood. The new groups sometimes limited their numbers to twelve in imitation of Christ's own band of disciples. They often banned women as sources of temptation, and they regularly expelled members who failed to live up to strict standards of pure morals and doctrine.

Imitative piety was as much communal as individual. Rooted in the person of Jesus, re-created regularly in the miracle of the mass, and offered through revelation in sacred texts as the model for the church, the Body of Christ in its three dimensions defined the Christian church. Individual men and women could live in, as, and with this Body in its physical, spiritual, and symbolic forms. Each springtime, the annual feast of *Corpus Domini* brought these three forms together when all members of the *Corpus Christianum* processed together with a consecrated host (the *Corpus Christi*), marking the bounds of the community and visiting its key shrines, and practicing the *Imitatio Christi* through intense prayer and fasting.

By some measures, the *Corpus Christianum* was broad and inclusive. It incorporated a wide range of believers ranging from large crowds of the spiritually indifferent to select gatherings of the pure and holy. The intense spiritual life of these latter drew in only a fraction of the people living in any one town or city. Their neighbours might be well-disposed to them, but most townspeople were likely indifferent or content simply to follow along with traditional rituals. A sizeable number might even find their aggressively pious neighbours to be tedious, interfering, or dangerous. Many Florentines initially followed the charismatic Dominican friar Savonarola in the 1490s, but they quickly cooled and then gave this reformer's more devoted followers the insulting nickname of 'the Snivellers' (*piagnoni*) to mock their weepy and emotional public behavior. Their pious wailing simply did not match the common idea of how you should conduct yourself with dignity and reserve in public.

Is there any way to measure the ranks of the truly pious? Joining a confraternity was one measure of collective spirituality. It was voluntary, although we should treat all numbers cautiously since membership brought many social privileges and benefits, and could be hedged with limits based on occupation, gender, class, and neighbourhood. Numbers of groups and of members grew rapidly in most cities and towns through the fifteenth century. Lubeck had 67 (for a population of 25,000 in 1400), Lyon had 68 (for 55,000), Florence 75 (for 60,000), and Hamburg 99 (for 18,000). The first confraternity in the Castillian town of Zamora emerged in 1230; by 1400 there were 10, and by the later sixteenth century there were 150 in a town of only 8,600. At that same point, Valladolid had 100 confraternities (for a population of 30,000) and Toledo 143 (for 60,000). Iberian territories recently reclaimed from Muslims in the Catholic Reconquista saw the most rapid growth of all through the fifteenth century. In some rural hamlets all residents were gathered into a confraternity, while in a town like Borgo San Sepolcro south of Florence about a third of all households had a male confraternity member (1,200 members in a population of less than 5,000). On average across Europe the total number of confraternity members averaged around 10 to 15 percent of the overall population.

Whether in confraternities or not, pious reformers were often disproportionately influential. They were the organizers, the true believers, and the ones who imagined themselves the most pure and holy of the community. They may have been small in number, but committed reformers are often a minority who exercise a significant influence on public policy thanks to time and circumstance. They may seize that influence by riot or impose it by force. As a result, their actions often trigger resistance, particularly when their ideas depart radically from long-standing practices. In late medieval and early modern Europe, religious radicals and impassioned reformers were often able to seize public power by fluke, but if their reforms changed familiar patterns and landscapes too radically, they could trigger a reaction that would bring them down again. Savonarola and his followers dominated Florence in 1496, but the friar was burned as a heretic only two years later, and his Snivellers were forced underground soon after. Martin Luther saw the radical reformers who took over Wittenberg in 1521 as more dangerous than Catholics, and fought hard to regain control of the city and reverse many of their changes. The Huguenots of Lyon seized power in 1562 only to lose it violently after a decade of religious reforms that rode over traditional Catholic sacred spaces and cut festive celebrations out of the calendar. When the Catholics counter-attacked in the St. Bartholomew's Day Massacre of 1572, their virulence in Lyon and elsewhere in France came out of a deep well of anger at new spiritual practices introduced by Huguenots, who were themselves often relatively new to the city.

The dynamics of power are as important as the dynamics of piety, and opposition to devotional 'reform' was common. A famous passage in the New Testament used the metaphor of many different parts making up the one Body of Christ to emphasize just how hard this was. As the apostle Paul wrote, the head often felt superior to the feet, and the eye thought it did not need the hand. The New Testament gospels likewise showed the disciples arguing frequently over who was closer to Christ's affections on earth, and so could expect to be greater in heaven. Some historians have argued that since real *communitas* and a peaceful *Corpus Christianum* were never entirely realized, they cannot have been a vital ambition for medieval urban citizens. They are reacting in part to some twentieth-century German historians who described late medieval German towns too romantically as self-fashioned 'sacred societies', and who argued that the civic reformations of the sixteenth century happened so quickly because townsmen had developed the habit of civic religious co-operation led by their town councils. This is an idealized picture that glosses over the power relations that shaped cities then as now.

More recent studies have explored the sharp and bloody divisions between quarters and social groups in medieval German towns. On Christmas Eve 1332, all the residents of one of the quarters of the small town of Hildesheim were massacred by other townsmen, and their houses and churches were burned to the ground; hardly a stirring vision of *communitas*. Journeymen in Nuremburg, one of the leading cities of the Holy Roman Empire, fought against their masters for the right to organize and be treated fairly, and similar disputes across the Upper Rhine area gathered force and exploded in a series of urban and rural revolts from 1493 to 1517 before the so-called Peasants' War of 1524–45. Rural discontent rocked England in the same period. Factionalism in Italian cities led repeatedly in the fifteenth century to pitched battles in the streets, conspiracies to assassinate rulers, and the slaughter, exile, or flight of hundreds of those on the losing side. And while Italian, German, and Flemish artisans marched in the processions of Lyon, we saw that these foreigners were also attacked when, in the 1560s and 1570s large numbers of them abandoned the local rituals of Catholic civic religion in favor of the Protestant ideas of the Huguenot movement. In London, Dutch migrants and refugees were honoured patrons of floats and ceremonial arches in the coronation processions of Elizabeth I (1559) and James I (1603), but were roundly condemned when economic conditions flagged some years later.

Cities were fractured and faction-ridden places. That poses a problem for anyone who believes in vague and romantic ideas of a peaceful medieval sacred society or civic *communitas*. Yet laypeople at the time accepted that the very concept of the *Corpus Christianum* was predicated as much on division as on union – why else would the apostle Paul have written about all the parts of the body quarrelling together? People fought hard and often over religion. Yet religious ritual was also a particularly effective way of dealing with disunity. On one hand, it had an imperative force that transcended the locality by setting local life in the context of heaven and eternity. On the other, performing ritual acts of unity helped city dwellers find a way of co-existing when their divisions were so deep. This much was unremarkable. Much of religion is shaped around the reach that exceeds the grasp, by aspirations for what can never be achieved, and with public expressions of sorrow for the failure to achieve a divine standard of perfection. Broken-ness, animosity, and violence are what religion is about, and many of its civic forms assumed these divisions and aimed to moderate, mediate, and possibly repair them. Failing that, they aimed for co-existence.

The *Corpus Christianum* was a model and goal more than it was ever a fully achieved reality. Those living in towns and cities would have been the first to acknowledge this, in part because they were aware of many threats to the Body, both from enemies outside it and divisions within it. It was these very threats that challenged their notion of the *Corpus Christianum*, and reinforced their determination to defend it – by force if necessary.

Threats to the *Corpus Christianum*

Most cultures fear particular threats to their survival: we now fear environmental degradation, overpopulation, and economic collapse. Within the past century, a whole range of threats were identified ranging from terrorist groups, to particular races, to nuclear annihilation, to so-called rogue states, to ideologies like communism, fascism, and capitalism, to religious fundamentalism. Political and cultural leaders could identify each as a threat to a particular way of life – to 'our' way of life – and the fear of them has fed extraordinary arms races, wars, and holocausts. The specific threats facing any particular family, town, or region vary with time and circumstance. Sickness, famines, floods, plagues, war, economic collapse, and political turmoil come and go. Some threats are real, and some invented; some people will feel threatened while others do not. Particular individuals or groups sometimes advertise or exaggerate a threat in order to stoke fear, gain power, or promote radical action. Fear and hatred can trigger a sharp and violent response.

European Christians of the late medieval period understood material threats as part of a larger spiritual drama. They saw themselves as players in a cosmic struggle going on between Good and Evil that had begun soon after Creation and would end only in the Last Judgment at the end of time. Scriptural texts in all traditions taught that God and the devil fought their ongoing battles in the day to day and here and now – this was the drama that preachers taught, that scripture and saints' lives narrated, and that ordinary Christians participated in directly. Human actions had eternal consequences, and disasters or threats were never random – they were either God's testing or punishing his people, or the devil's relentless assault. The Old Testament book of Job suggested that they might be both at the same time if God allowed the devil to test His followers' faith. In this cosmic drama, every disaster and threat became a test of obedience or disobedience. Your personal fate was wrapped together with the fate of your community.

No threat was too distant or metaphorical to be real. Preachers readily fit contemporary actors into an ancient Biblical script. The modern Turks threatening Vienna were like the ancient Babylonians who had conquered Jerusalem. The Jews of Augsburg, Prague, or Paris were the same enemies who had gloated over the death of Christ on Calvary. The divided church was like the many ruptured or disobedient communities of the Old and New Testaments. Plague and natural disasters were recurring elements of the cosmic drama from the time of Noah's flood. The paradox of spiritual literature was that the more distant the threat the more immediate the lesson. Throughout the fourteenth and fifteenth centuries some distant threats seemed very real challenges to the health and even survival of the Body of Christ.

We can look at four threats to the Body of Christ that people across Europe talked about, feared, and sometimes acted on: the threat of violent assault from outside posed by Islam and the Turks, the threat of an infection within the Body caused by those like heretics, witches or Jews who were secret enemies of Christ, the threat of division and corruption within the church itself, and the threat of God's judgment in the form of plagues and natural disasters. They were not the only threats, and they were not feared equally by everyone across Europe. Yet they measure the temper of the times. Some had been around for centuries and others were relatively new. Yet all of them intensified sharply in the fifteenth and early sixteenth centuries, raising new anxieties and leading some to propose radical solutions.

The Body Besieged — Islam

The external threat that most preoccupied and frightened Europeans was Islam. The faith founded on the prophecies of Mohammed (570–632) had quickly superseded Judaism as Christianity's sharpest and most immediate religious opponent. Islam's expanding presence was a continuing theme in literature, ballads, stories, and sermons throughout the later middle ages until the final siege of Vienna in 1683. It took different forms in different places, but almost always had a distinctly military character which directly threatened the *Corpus Christianum*. That threat intensified dramatically in the fifteenth and sixteenth centuries.

Islamic armies had first moved across the Middle East and North Africa in the seventh century, sweeping through those parts of the Christian Byzantine Empire where Jesus had walked and Augustine had preached. They crossed into Iberia and pushed relentlessly into France until halted in 732 by defeats at Tours and Poitiers, a few days march south of Paris. Their rapid advance left a profound impact. The earliest work of French literature is a ballad, the *Chanson de Roland* (Song of Roland), memorializing this struggle. Roland is the nephew of the great Frankish king Charlemagne, ambushed and killed when the Franks are returning from a mission to Spain to rout the Muslims and Jews. With his dying breath he sounds a horn which brings Charlemagne to wreak revenge. Dating from the mid-twelfth century and popular into at least the fourteenth, the *Song of Roland* with its ruthless Islamic soldiers, brave Christian knights, and theme of holy vengeance became the basis for a host of chivalric ballads. In 1516, the Italian poet Ludovico Ariosto wrote a new epic account, *Orlando Furioso*, which spread quickly across the continent.

Although Ariosto's epic is marked more by surreal comedy than naked fear, his choice of setting and actors shows the enduring hold that the story of Islam's conquest had on the European imagination.

Ariosto was writing a little more than a decade after Christian knights had finally expelled the Muslim armies from Iberia after a centuries-long reconquest (*Reconquista*) that culminated in the fall of the last Moorish kingdom, Granada, in 1492. The tables were turned at the other end of the Mediterranean, where Islamic armies were very much on the offensive. Christian armies had carried out a series of military assaults to retake the Holy Land from 1095 through 1270. They seized Jerusalem and established a Christian kingdom for a time. Yet the seven crusades carried out over these two centuries had very mixed results. The European armies had sometimes fought more enthusiastically against each other and against the Byzantine Empire, as when they sacked the Byzantine capital of Constantinople in 1204 and established a Latin Kingdom there. The crusade strategy died when the final Christian port-fortress of Acre fell in 1291.

Within decades, a new threat had emerged. Turkish nomads began migrating into Asia Minor in the mid-thirteenth century, and proclaimed their own Ottoman empire under Sultan Osman I in 1301. They expanded rapidly through the remnants of the Byzantine Empire in the fourteenth century, effectively isolating Constantinople by 1361, taking much of Serbia after the Battle of Kosovo in 1389, and extending north into the Balkans and modern-day Bulgaria and Romania by the 1390s. The *Corpus Christianum* in Eastern Europe was like a sand castle eroding under waves of steady Ottoman expansion. Resistance seemed futile. The wealthy and populous coastal city of Salonika, long the second-largest in the empire, was besieged and then sacked in 1430. Salonika's utter devastation triggered alarm across Europe and brought desperation in Constantinople, which had held out against repeated assaults. Emperor John Paleologus VIII (ruled 1425–48) sailed for Italy to negotiate directly for help from wealthy Italian states and the Roman Catholic Church. He had little to offer, and a weight of history to carry in the form of longstanding political, economic, and religious rivalries between East and West. Pope Eugenius IV (1431–47) used the opportunity to win submission of the Eastern Orthodox to the Roman Catholic Church in a grand Council held in Florence in 1439. On paper this achieved a grand reunion of the *Corpus Christianum*, which had been divided into Eastern Orthodox and Western Catholic churches since 1054. But there was little beyond the paper. Pope Eugenius's manoeuvrings so angered North European rulers and ecclesiastics that they expelled him and appointed a new Pope Felix V. Orthodox churchmen in Constantinople repudiated the theological

4. Ottoman archer from Nicolay, *Navigations, Peregrinations and Voyages Made into Turkey* (1577). Courtesy of the Thomas Fisher Rare Book Library, University of Toronto.

concessions and church union which their delegates had agreed to in Florence. A papal army sent to defend Bulgaria was devastated in battle in 1444. And the Turks kept coming [Fig 4].

The fall of Constantinople in 1453 was more significant psychologically than militarily. Its once impregnable walls had been built to protect a population of more than a million, but when the Turks finally broke through after a brilliant campaign led by twenty-one year old Sultan Mehmed II (1432–81), there were only 30,000 inhabitants left. In that way, Constantinople was not unlike contemporary Rome, where a population not much greater occupied the ruins of a once much larger metropolis and dreamed of reviving ancient glory. In Rome, a series of popes translated these imperial ruins and dreams into the new avenues, bridges, churches, and palaces of a universal capital – *Roma Caput Mundi* – over the next two centuries. In Constantinople, a series of sultans would do the same, proclaiming themselves Roman Caesars in the line of Augustus and Constantine. They rebuilt the old city into the capital of a new empire and religion, which they considered as fully and dominantly a part of Europe as the old Roman Empire had been. As part of the propaganda war behind their frequent battles, both the Ottoman sultans and Catholic rulers like the popes and the Hapsburg emperors claimed that they were the fulfilment of ancient Judeo-Christian prophecies of the coming of a universal empire at the end of time.

The sultan-cum-emperor Mehmed II the Conqueror pushed north immediately after seizing Constantinople. The Turks were sometimes defeated in individual battles, but came back and back again as a relentless threat, taking Serbia (1459), Bosnia (1463), Albania (1478), Herzegovina (1482), Montenegro (1498), and the entire territory around the Black Sea by 1499. More worrying for the Italians, they pushed the Genoese out of the Aegean by 1462 and launched a series of wars against the far-flung Venetian Empire the following year. Ottoman troops invaded the Italian peninsula itself in 1480, occupying the town of Otranto at the tip of the heel and massacring all its inhabitants, including the women and children who had fled to the churches for shelter.

There seemed to be no effective response. The humanist Pope Pius II (1458–64) spent his brief pontificate trying unsuccessfully to organize a crusade, and died in the Italian coastal town of Ancona as he prepared to lead it personally. Mehmed II's own death in 1481 gave brief respite, and led the Ottomans to abandon Otranto as a base for further Italian expansion. Yet within decades the Ottomans would rebound as an even greater threat.

A European observer identifying the most important world events in 1517 would not have included an obscure German monk attaching a list of theological arguments to a church door in some remote Saxon town. In that year, Sultan Selim I (1465?–1520) defeated the Mamluks in Egypt, completing the conquest of their empire begun with the seizure of Syria and Palestine the year before. Three years earlier in 1514, he had defeated the Safavid Persians of Baghdad and seized western territories of their empire as well. The world of Islam had for centuries been divided into three powerful military empires, and in the space of less than three years the Ottomans had defeated their two rivals. In 1517, Selim I sealed his victory by assuming the ceremonial title of

5. Erhard Schon, *Süleyman I 'the Magnificent'* (1532). Image courtesy Getty Open Content Program.

caliph, signalling military-religious authority over all the world of Islam. This was the immediate geopolitical backdrop for Ariosto's *Orlando Furioso*. That epic's Islamic enemy was Saracen rather than Turk, and the chivalric poem had fantastical voyages, comic characters, and doomed romances which moved it far beyond current events. Yet those Europeans who made it a best-seller after the completed version was published a few decades later may have been looking for some hope and relief from a threat that was no laughing matter.

They would not find it soon. Under Süleyman I (ruled 1520–66), the Ottomans once more turned towards Europe with a terrifyingly rapid advance through Hapsburg and Venetian territories in the 1520s: Belgrade (1521) and Rhodes (1522) fell, King Louis II of Hungary and Bohemia was defeated and killed with many of his knights at the Battle of Mohacs in 1526, and by the end of the decade the Ottoman armies had Vienna under siege [Fig 5]. The German reformer Martin Luther was only one of many in this decade who saw the Turks both as God's punishment for a corrupt Catholic Church, yet also as an immediate threat which Germans in particular had to fight against. Although 'The Terrible Turk' might be used by God to judge Christians, he was still the Antichrist in league with the devil. What else could explain his unstoppable advance? Over the course of his rule,

Süleyman II the Magnificent would capture Budapest (1541), absorb much of Hungary (1547), expand east into Iraq (1533) and west along the North African coast to Algiers (1525), Tunis (1534, 1574), and Tripoli (1551), giving the Ottomans control of much of the Mediterranean. And he was not simply on the fringe of European politics. French King Francis I, while proud of his title of 'Most Christian King', allied with Süleyman I against Holy Roman Emperor Charles V in 1536. As part of their joint operations, Francis allowed an Ottoman fleet to winter in Toulon (1543–44). He ordered all Christians out of Toulon for the season and allowed the Ottomans to purge its cathedral for use as a mosque. The alliance shocked many in Europe, including Luther, although ironically Francis' manoeuvring saved both France and Germany's protestant states from being overwhelmed by Charles V. Süleyman II 'the Magnificent' was now Ottoman sultan, caliph of Islam, and Roman emperor. Some Europeans thought so rapid and complete an advance could only signal that his was indeed the Universal Empire prophesied in the Book of Daniel for the apocalyptic end times before the Last Judgment. This was the end of history.

King Francis I's alliance may have shocked Christians, but its realpolitik cynicism also recognized that the Ottomans were now integrally part of European politics. Ambassadors and merchants were drawn to the wealth and power of Constantinople, and a growing role emerged for those who could cross the boundaries and interpret one to the other. An ambivalence settled in: some saw the Turks as a threat and a divine punishment, but others considered them wealthy, powerful, and cultured allies. Travellers praised their efficiency, the cleanliness of their cities, their apparently fair regimes, and what seemed like an administration based on merit rather than birth.

Yet for all this appreciation and budding signs of normality, the sense of threat never entirely faded. No one knew that the period of dramatic Ottoman expansion into Europe was coming to an end. The advances may have slowed but the troops and ships were still there. The Ottomans continued seizing Venetian islands, and on taking Cyprus in 1571, they flayed the commander alive, stuffed his skin with straw, and put it on display as a lesson to others. The sea battle of Lepanto that followed was a critically successful joint military action by Christian states against the Ottomans. Yet even after their decisive victory, the Venetians were not able to recover Cyprus, and all the Mediterranean maritime powers feared an angry Ottoman response. Italian, French, and Spanish ships and coastal areas remained targets for pirates operating out of Ottoman-controlled North African ports. While both sides engaged in piracy and slave-taking, as many as a million Christian captives were seized from the sixteenth through the eighteenth centuries, and held as slaves for ransom. Some returned to write profitably hair-raising stories of brutal captivity by 'The Terrible Turk', feeding a demand for some dramatically evil enemy or Other to occupy the European imagination. Conveniently ignoring their own wartime brutality, European authors emphasized tales of Ottoman atrocities, with every siege ending in the Turks beheading commanders, impaling soldiers, and massacring or enslaving hundreds or thousands of civilian Christians.

What made this evil Other even more terrifying was the fact that in some respects it was not 'other' at all. Some captured Christian slaves 'turned Turk', converting to Islam and becoming the builders, sailors, and captains of the pirate vessels which preyed on Christian ships. The most feared Ottoman troops were the janissaries, young Christian boys (ages eight to twenty) who from the 1390s were taken from conquered territories in a regular quota system (*devsirme*) and converted and trained in Constantinople to become the personal bodyguards and most dedicated soldiers of the Sultan [Fig 6]. Some European Jews and Jewish converts to Christianity (called *conversos*) moved to the Ottoman Empire and rose to prominent positions in trade, finance, administration, and the professions. For the Ottomans, this was an entirely normal part of their history and practice. As an empire of many peoples, races, and religions, they found strength in deliberately integrating different peoples and groups into a common enterprise that was vaguely Islamic but determinedly Ottoman. For European Christians more attuned to a cosmic battle of good versus evil which emphasized the importance of differences of race and religion, it was deeply unsettling: our own people – *our own children* – are the warriors against us. At a certain level, Ottoman universalism was about uniting difference under one broad tent, while Christian universalism was about reducing it to a single narrow path.

From 1480 to 1610, European presses put out twice as many books about the Turkish threat as about the American discoveries. Diplomats and traders might practice co-operation, but apocalyptic preachers, ambitious authors, and political opportunists could still raise audiences by playing to fears of the 'Terrible Turk'. Continuing Ottoman military successes made these fears far from abstract. No other earthly enemy outside its boundaries was as immediate, powerful, and threatening to Europe's *Corpus Christianum*.

The Body Infected – Heretics, Witches, and Jews

The Turkish threat was immediate and vivid. Invincible leaders like the Sultans Mehmed II the Conqueror and Süleyman I the Magnificent racked up a string of victories. Large armies in extravagant uniforms wielded exotic

6. Ottoman janissary from Nicolay, *Navigations, Peregrinations and Voyages Made into Turkey* (1577). Courtesy of the Thomas Fisher Rare Book Library, University of Toronto.

weapons like scimitars. Frightening customs like impaling, beheading, or flaying enemies alive made every battle a fight to the death. Threats arising from within the Body of Christ were no less dangerous, but much harder to identify and depict than the kinds of extravagant propaganda generated around the Turks. These inner threats were often deliberately subversive, and the first challenge lay in identifying the infectious evil posed by someone who was a neighbour, acquaintance, or friend. We can look at three such threats to the purity of the *Corpus Christianum* that increasingly preoccupied

Christians across different parts of Europe throughout the fifteenth century: heretics, witches, and Jews. Each was believed to be working for that ancient enemy of God, the devil. This made the handfuls of religious fanatics, old women, and Jewish merchants that much more fearful. As servants of God's most bitter enemy, they were a contagion in the Body. A very small number could spread far and do extraordinary harm. These threats inside the Body were often framed as threats above all to Blood: authorities believed that it was Christ's Blood above all that the devil wanted to claim, and so they projected on to the supposed enemies of Christ a similar obsession with obtaining that same Blood. Protecting Christ's Blood became the key concern for many of those who feared the infection of the *Corpus Christianum* by heretics, witches, or Jews.

Heretics

For all the emphasis on unity in the *Corpus Christianum*, the Christian church had been shaped by intense fights over points of belief and practice from the very beginning. Throughout this long series of theological debates, the winners labeled the losers as heretics, and some ancient heresies got new life in the sixteenth century – or at least the labels did. Those who doubted either that Jesus was equal to God or that God took the form of an indivisible Trinity of Father, Son, and Holy Ghost could be tagged as 'Arians' (Arius, 250–336). Those who rejected the idea of Original Sin, and who thought that humans could choose between good and evil without God's help were called 'Pelagians' (Pelagius 354–442/440). Those purists who thought that believers had to hold themselves apart from the state, pursue social justice, and accept sacraments only from priests of pure morals might be dismissed as 'Donatists' (Donatus, d. 335). The list of ancient heresies went on and on, and the sixteenth century fights were no less virulent than those in the fourth or fifth centuries.

Some theological fights of the sixteenth century were a form of professional name-calling that seemed as much about testing opponents' knowledge of church history as about challenging error. Many thought that the battle was half won if they could make the point that new and dangerous ideas were simply old and discredited heresies. In the centuries before this, the medieval church had broader concerns. It branded as heretical those movements that had a wide popular appeal and that as a result seemed to constitute a deeper and more contagious threat. Among the earliest of these were the Cathars or Albigensians, a group expanding from the twelfth century that framed the world in starkly dualistic terms – God was entirely spiritual and good while the material world was entirely material and evil.

Faith and worship should take a simple form based on acts of charity. Cathars seem to have rejected the institutions, clergy and sacraments of the church as corrupt and ineffective, and they aimed to gain heaven by a very ascetic lifestyle. If the material world was so thoroughly evil, then Christ could hardly have taken physical human form. Similarly, any sacraments involving physical materials like water, bread, and wine would be sacrilegious and hence useless. These Cathar beliefs posed a direct challenge to the Blood of Christ. By some accounts, Cathars believed in two Gods, one of light and one of darkness, and they rejected absolutely all those things which they thought belonged to the God of Darkness – including the pope and the Catholic Church.

Most of our sources for Cathar beliefs come from the Catholic Inquisitors who prosecuted them, so what we really know about Cathar beliefs is shaky. Yet we do know that they spread rapidly across parts of southern France and Italy from the twelfth century. This so alarmed church authorities that they approved the establishment of the Dominican Order in 1216 to preach to Cathars, planned a crusade to wipe them out, and developed the Inquisition to prosecute those who survived. Cathar ideas continued circulating in France and Italy until at least the early fifteenth century. A separate group known as *Alumbrados* or *Illuminati* later developed in Spain. Although they had no direct link to Cathars, they too believed that the soul could reach perfection and union with God by intense meditation and rejection of the things of the material world. Those evil things of the world included the church, the sacraments, and public worship services with candles, incense, and rituals. Some also believed that once you had reached a mystical state of perfect union with God, it was impossible to sin, no matter what bodily appetites you indulged in. The *Alumbrados* were never a large group, but they gave a lot of work to the Spanish Inquisition well into the sixteenth century and later spread into France.

Two religious orders emerged in the early thirteenth century to challenge heresy. Followers of the Spanish priest Dominic de Guzmán (1170–1221) focused on educational and legal means. The early Dominicans developed theological studies, preaching, and sustained investigation as key tools in this work, and as such were critical to the spread of universities and to the organization and staffing of the Inquisition. Followers of the Italian Francesco di Pietro di Bernadone (1181–1226) also had university-trained theologians, yet in the main Franciscans believed that lives of poverty, charity, and preaching were more effective ways of answering critics like the Cathars and others who claimed that all clergy were remote and corrupt.

In the fight against the contagion of heresy, the Dominicans generally emphasized professional expertise, while the Franciscans emphasized popular access. Both of these new religious orders established themselves within cities and towns, where they built enormous churches and large residences, and aimed to gain supporters by preaching and offering religious services including confession, communion, and burial. Both soon established lay confraternities to help gather followers and spread their message. While Dominican confraternities were often small elite groups that helped the friars with their Inquisitorial investigations, Franciscan brotherhoods gathered hundreds of members to run hospitals, stage public religious plays, and sing spiritual music together. At the same time, the Franciscans attracted many men and women from wealthy families who aimed to find ways of preserving their personal wealth, and this triggered sharp opposition from nuns and friars who saw extreme poverty as a critical part of the order's identity. The order began fracturing on this point within a few years of Francis's death. Some advocates of poverty claimed that clergy should possess nothing at all, and denounced popes, priests, and property-owning Franciscans as illegitimate. One group, the *Fraticelli* (little friars) became so openly critical of all clerical wealth that Pope Boniface VIII declared them heretical in 1296. Harsh persecution and executions, like the 1389 burning of Friar Michele Berti at the stake in Florence, curbed, but did little to eliminate, a group whose message of absolute poverty clearly resonated with many.

Many of the movements that authorities judged as heretical were sharply critical of all clergy from priests to popes, and were determined to stir up faith and action in ordinary people. This often included variations on three key points: challenging the spiritual powers and special status of the clergy, making the central sacrament of Communion more inclusive, and putting the Bible into the language and into the hands of ordinary believers. These populist ideas resonated far across Europe. In England, a diffuse group known as Lollards (likely from the Middle Dutch *lollaerd*, meaning 'mumbler' or 'mutterer') emerged around the mid-fourteenth century, taking some of their ideas from the Oxford theologian John Wycliffe (c. 1320–84). They had no central organization or doctrines, but most believed in opening the priesthood to married men, keeping clergy out of politics while making them subject to civil law, and making the eucharist a simpler ritual in which all believers shared wine and bread as reminders of Christ's sacrifice, rather than as potent magical carriers of divine power. They claimed to draw these views from scripture, and Wycliffe worked to translate the Bible into English so more could read it. While some nobles adopted Lollard ideas, church and state authorities found them subversive, and actively persecuted the Lollards

7. The Burning of John Hus from Foxe's *Actes and Monuments* (1563). Courtesy of the Thomas Fisher Rare Book Library, University of Toronto.

from the 1380s. The Lollard John Badby became the first English layman executed for heresy in 1410. Yet he was not the last, and the movement soon went underground.

Remarkably similar ideas emerged in Bohemia by the late fourteenth century around the figure of Jan Hus (c. 1369–1415), a priest who became the Rector of Charles University in Prague, and who was influenced by John Wycliffe's writings. Sharply critical of papal authority, a believer in laity taking Communion as clergy did, and an advocate of translating the scriptures into common vernacular languages for laypeople to read, Hus was excommunicated four times. He was summoned to a major church Council in Constance in 1414 to explain his views. Even though Holy Roman Emperor Sigismund I guaranteed Hus safe passage, he was arrested, tried, and burned as a heretic within a space of eight months in 1414–15 [Fig 7]. The Constance theologians wanted to do the same to John Wycliffe, who had died three decades earlier; in 1428 his remains were dug up and burned at papal command, with the ashes thrown in a river.

Bohemia exploded in reaction after Hus's execution. Nobles, clerics, and commoners banded together in a movement aimed as much at strengthening the Czech community within the Holy Roman Empire as at promoting a particular set of religious beliefs. Major anti-Hussite crusades in 1420 and 1431 were unsuccessful, and in spite of sharp and ongoing internal divisions, Bohemia developed a separate Catholic church by the 1430s, characterized by more open communion, a commitment to scriptures, and a rejection of papal authority.

Heresy clearly took many forms in the fourteenth and fifteenth centuries. Some movements were more mystical, some more political. Most were regional and some, like the Hussite movement, were distinctly national. Most were populist to some degree, challenging the special powers of the clergy and advocating a more egalitarian and lay-directed religion with full and equal access to the scriptures and sacraments. As one part of this, many rejected the idea that Christ's Body and Blood were physically present in the bread and wine of the eucharist. What may seem a minor point of doctrine was actually a critical disagreement that went to the heart of God's presence in the world, and the role of clergy in the *Corpus Christianum*. By rejecting the physical Blood of Christ in the host, the Cathars, Lollards, and Hussites were thought to be rejecting the very idea of Christian society as a Body of Christ that was mystically united in worship by the mass and led by the clergy. These challenges to traditional Catholic theology would expand through the fifteenth century. As we will see below, all sixteenth-century reformers either completely rejected or radically redefined the real, physical presence of Christ's Body and Blood in the eucharist. This was one of the key beliefs that divided them from the Catholic Church, but it is worth noting here that it was also a significant factor that kept them from uniting together. Division on the Blood made it virtually impossible to have unity in the Body.

The medieval and Renaissance Catholic Church generally harboured quite diverse forms of worship at this time, and even varieties of belief. We may then wonder why authorities in church and state became so deeply worried and so determined to crush these ideas, particularly when some of those they labelled heretics were clearly intensely sincere Christians. It was order they were worried about, and when order in church and state was directly challenged, they responded harshly. Sacred and secular authorities believed that they had a duty to preserve the *Corpus Christianum* against infections that would sicken it, or against temptations that would lead simple believers to disobedience and hell, triggering God's judgment on a whole city or society. From the fourteenth through the sixteenth centuries, many of their fears around infectious and contagious ideas went back in some direct or indirect way to blood – either the Blood of Christ or, as we will see later in relation to converts to Catholicism from Judaism and Islam, the blood of believers. As these concerns increased, so too did the tools they developed and the determination they showed in combating what they took to be heresy.

Without justifying the authorities' often violent response to what they condemned as heresy, we also need to remember that many so-called heretics were equally if not more judgmental and intolerant. Just like the Inquisitors pursuing them, they believed that their opponents were a dangerous, contagious impurity that would infect and sicken the whole *Corpus Christianum*. And they wanted these opponents removed, by violence if necessary. The threat of impurity was not simply an abstraction on the level of ideas, but an immediate challenge on the level of the Body – both the *Corpus Christi* and the *Corpus Christianum* – and so inevitably on the level of Blood. As such, threats of impurity were far sharper and more vital than disagreements in the realm of ideas which could be challenged in polite scholarly discussion. This common language of perfection, infection, and contagion, rooted in multiple understandings of the Body and Blood, became part of a shared discourse across Europe. It was a discourse that authorities and heretics across Europe would use to justify their intense efforts at prosecution and purgation.

Witches

Not all Europeans believed in witches, or even thought that they were a serious threat. Yet many did, and for them the sense of threat increased significantly over the course of the fifteenth century. Theologians and legal scholars began arguing that all witches were servants of the devil, and that witchcraft was the devil's way into the heart of the *Corpus Christianum*. Around 1140, the influential legal scholar Gratian developed what became the medieval Catholic legal consensus in his compilation of canon law (the *Corpus juris canonici*), the body of ecclesiastical pronouncements and regulations which governed the church and its personnel. Gratian classed sorcerers and magicians together with other sinners and emphasized that demons' power to harm was distinctly limited by God's superior power and care. Much of what demons seemed to be able to do, like night flight, was just an illusion, dream, or nightmare. In this environment, people believed that there could be good and bad witches, and that sorcerers or sorceresses might be able to summon and manipulate demons to positive or negative ends. Inept and easily duped comic devils filled plays and stories, making the demonic world something of a joke. Although this tradition continued, by 1434 Pope Eugenius IV was warning against 'Christian and Jewish magicians, diviners, invokers of demons, enchanters ... who use nefarious and forbidden arts, through whose efforts the Christian people, or at least a numerous and simple-minded part of them, are stained and perverted'. In 1484, Innocent VIII issued the bull *Summis desiderantes* (Desiring with supreme ardour) urging prosecution of those who gave themselves over to demons and used witchcraft to blight the Body of Christ. The devil made all the difference, and he was no longer a joke.

Fear of the devil increased markedly from the early fifteenth century. Theologians, jurists, and inquisitors began writing more frequently on the subject as they wrestled to understand threats like the Hussite and Lollard heresies. At least thirty different treatises on the devil's power appeared around the time that the Council of Basel was meeting in the 1430s. Theologians at the Council were worried about unity of the church, and feared that the devil's servants were spreading fear, division, and heresy. The Franciscan *converso* theologian Alfonso da Spina, confessor to King John II of Castile and later regent of the Faculty of Theology at the University of Salamanca, famously estimated the number of demons at 133,306,668 in his 1459 *Fortress of Faith* (Fortalitium fidei) an exposition of the many threats to the church. Spina's views about demons' powers were similar to Gratian's, but many of his contemporaries were becoming more fearful and more vocal. From mid-century an increasing number of works emphasized that demonic activity was far from illusion or dream.

Demons could work their evil in the physical world, both directly and through witches. Johannes Nider's *Formicarius* was written in 1436–37, but gained traction after being printed in 1475. The volume which is now most famous was the *Malleus Maleficarum* (*Hammer of Witches*) published in 1487 by the Dominican inquisitor Heinrich Kramer. Kramer drew on his own considerable experience to write this encyclopaedic guide on to how to identify, prosecute, and execute witches, and claimed support from Innocent VIII's *Summis desiderantes'* and the Faculty of Theology at the University of Cologne and its dean, Jacob Sprenger. Kramer claimed Sprenger as a collaborator in order to gain authority, although it is now clear that the dean actually opposed the inquisitor. The *Malleus Maleficarum* is not the most complete guide to contemporary beliefs about witches, and its influence has often been overstated. Yet it was reprinted fourteen times over the next four decades, and translated into all the main vernacular languages. Clergy and judges could easily consult the Latin text, while vernacular editions, pamphlets, and preaching helped spread its ideas to a broader audience.

Kramer summed up four key beliefs that recur in works written a century or more later, like Jean Bodin's *Demon Mania* (1580), Nicholas Remy's *Demonolatry* (1595), and Stefano Guazzo's *Compendium Maleficarum* (1610):

1) All witchcraft is devil worship. This absolute statement went beyond earlier views that implicitly recognized various degrees of witchcraft.
2) Witches renounce the Christian faith and make a deliberate pact with the devil. In return, the devil may put his mark or sign on them, and may give them a companion (a *familiar*). This emphasized that witches knew fully what they were doing, could not claim that they had been misled or duped, and so were entirely responsible before God and the law for their actions.
3) The effects of demonic power are not illusory or confined to dreams. Witches work with the devil to ruin God's world and the lives of God's followers. Their spells damage crops, hinder human and animal fertility, and cause sickness and plague. The demonic threat is real, and affects daily life.
4) 'All witchcraft is born from human lust, which in women is insatiable' (*Malleus Maleficarum*). Women are more gullible, less rational, and more lustful than men. As a result, they are more likely to be tempted by the devil, and are more likely to give in to that temptation. Poor, widowed, and marginalized women were seen as particularly vulnerable to the devil, since they had great needs and few resources, and no male relatives to guide and govern them.

An idea not found in the *Malleus*, but spread in other texts was that witches did not act individually, but gathered regularly in great feasts called *sabbats* to honour and worship the devil. Preachers imagined a cult of devil worshippers who inverted familiar elements of Christian faith in their own rituals: witches were initiated with baptisms where they received a new name, they held a form of mass at the *sabbat* with turnip slices for a host, and their version of the kiss of peace involved oral sex and carnal orgies [Fig 8].

The most troubling inversion that we find in treatises and trials again involved blood. Human blood was the carrier of life, and Christ's Blood was the guarantee of salvation. By contrast, the devil had no blood, which was one reason why intercourse with him was cold and uncomfortable. So he sought it in every form and aimed to drain it where he could in order to blight fertility, life, and salvation. Witches were accused of stealing consecrated eucharistic hosts and turning them over to the devil. Some were accused of stealing the bodies of unbaptized infants in order to use their blood in preparing potions; Kramer claimed that midwives were particularly dangerous because of their access to newborns. Infant death rates were indeed staggering at the time, although we have no evidence that midwives suffered increased surveillance or prosecution. Young couples unable to conceive, cows or goats giving little milk, a crop levelled by hail – these, too, were considered to be the witches' victims, and their infertility

8. Witch and Demon on Horseback, from the *Nuremburg Chronicle* (1493). Courtesy of the Thomas Fisher Rare Book Library, University of Toronto.

threatened families and villages. This was the devil's threat to life and blood, channelled through women's weakness, and it made witchcraft a particularly fearful and subversive danger to the *Corpus Christianum*.

We need to remember that what some have described as a 'witch craze' was always more localized and limited than the term 'craze' implies. It is hard to measure levels of fear or to identify how a fear of witches may have led people to protect themselves or shaped how they treated widows, poor women, or other marginalized characters. One imperfect index of fear is the hunts, and these were episodic. A first wave of prosecutions developed in parts of Switzerland and Savoy from the early fifteenth century, picking up and spreading from the 1480s to the 1520s before dying back. A second wave of hunts then expanded from the 1560s to about 1630, with peaks in the 1590s and 1620s. Through the decades in between, Europeans paid less attention. One simple measure of this is that no printer published the *Malleus Maleficarum* between 1521 and 1576, though it was widely translated, printed, and sold from 1486 to 1520 and from 1580 to 1650.

A resilient myth holds that millions of women died in a holocaust or 'gynecide', and that widows and particularly midwives had to be on their guard at all times during what have been called 'the Burning Times'. Disputes over numbers detract from the sobering reality that the 80–100,000 prosecutions and perhaps 50,000 executions across Europe through these centuries were driven by an effort to purge society of a very particular set of internal enemies. And the purge went further, because many more victims – most of them women – suffered suspicion, accusation, trials, violence, and expulsion. Rough justice that left little trace in legal records forced many to flee their localities and join the period's flood of refugees. Yet many local studies confirm that authorities executed more women for infanticide than for witchcraft. Some parts of Europe were hardly affected, and in others the stereotypes barely held: a Scottish witch hunt in 1620 had no reference to the devil, and in parts of Alsace more men than women were prosecuted.

What is more critical to remember for our purposes here is that the witch hunt was neither a popular 'craze' nor an exclusively religious issue. It began among lawyers, theologians, clerics, and nobles, and was spread primarily among and by them using the tools that they controlled – the law and the media above all. This demonstrates the dynamics of a 'legitimating discourse' as few other examples do: when minorities were being targeted as threats to be officially suppressed, then it took no more than a few persecutors with status, drive, and access to power to have a great impact, particularly when the victims were further marginalized by gender or race. The Holy Roman Empire's Carolina law code of 1530 made witchcraft a civil offense, as did English parliamentary statutes of 1542, 1563, and 1604. When French authors Bodin and Remy wrote their treatises in the following decades, they described witchcraft as primarily a political threat, not a religious problem.

The secularizing and criminalizing of what had been considered a largely ecclesiastical issue came about because political elites believed that churchmen were not being vigilant enough in prosecuting what they thought was a threat to political order and social health. These elites were the ones most concerned with purity, contagion, and purgation. These were also the ones who used religious discourses to promote fear, and judicial systems to prosecute other ends. As Charles Zika has shown, fears of witchcraft would continue to be stoked up into the eighteenth century through trial accounts, ballads, and stories, and even through reference to the Old Testament story of the Witch of Endor summoning up the Prophet Samuel to predict King Saul's death. To doubt the devil, his demons, and the witches who served him was to doubt God, his angels, and the priests and pastors who served him.

Jews

Jewish-Christian relations were marked by tensions from the start. Christianity was fundamentally Jewish in its origins. Jesus was a Jew, as were all the early apostles and the first Christian believers. The Christian Bible combined Jewish scriptures (the 'Old Testament') with gospel accounts of Jesus' life and letters to early Christian communities (the 'New Testament'). Yet within a few centuries, Christians came to believe that Christianity not only arose out of and continued Judaism, but that it superseded or replaced it, meaning that Christians had replaced the Jews as God's Chosen People. According to the influential theologian Augustine, the main reason to preserve Jewish communities was so that the Jews might see, at the end of time, how wrong they had been to reject Christ and carry on following the rules and rituals of the Old Testament while they waited for the promised Messiah to come and deliver them. Most Jews lived in relatively small communities across different parts of Europe, mainly in close neighbourhoods within towns. The oldest communities were around the Mediterranean in Rome and in ports like Marseilles and Barcelona, while the largest were in Iberia, where about 80,000 Jews lived in urban and rural areas. Some Italian city-states allowed Jews to be citizens, but this was an unusual carryover from laws rooted in the early medieval period.

Through the Middle Ages, Christians tolerated, persecuted, and attempted to convert Jews, depending on local political, religious, and economic dynamics. The rise of Islam from the seventh century made relations more complicated. Islamic rulers were generally less hostile to Judaism as a competing Abrahamic faith, seeing it as incomplete but not in competition with Islam. They were also more appreciative of Jews as productive merchants, artisans, and professionals. They did not try to convert or expel Jews, although they did segregate and tax Jewish populations, and some Muslim rulers acted before Christians in forcing Jews to identify themselves by wearing a yellow badge. By the end of the Middle Ages, the great majority of the world's Jews – possibly 90 percent – lived in Islamic states, where they sometimes served as intermediaries or interlocutors between Christian and Muslim populations [Fig 9a & 9b]. Yet unlike Christians and Muslims, the Jews had no state of their own in Europe or beyond. There was no Jewish nobility or monarchy in control of lands and an army, and there were in fact strict laws in both Christian and Islamic states limiting what they could own, what work they could do, and what political status they could enjoy.

To Muslim rulers, Jews were subjects; to Christians, they were a threat. Judaism was Christianity's source and closest parallel, its nearest Other. And while Muslims lived beyond Europe's eastern and western boundaries, Jews

9(a). Jewish Woman in Ottoman Empire from Nicolay, *Navigations, Peregrinations and Voyages Made into Turkey* (1577). Courtesy of the Thomas Fisher Rare Book Library, University of Toronto.

9(b). Jewish Merchant in Ottoman Empire from Nicolay, *Navigations, Peregrinations and Voyages Made into Turkey* (1577). Courtesy of the Thomas Fisher Rare Book Library, University of Toronto.

were dispersed in small groups throughout large parts of continental Europe. There was nothing in their numbers or activities that could credibly be seen as threatening to the *Corpus Christianum*, although many Christians resented Jewish economic activity and competition. With the rise of religious orders like the Dominicans and Franciscans and the emergence of the Inquisition, a Jewish threat was defined more explicitly. As with heretics and witches, theologians cast the Jews as devil-driven enemies of God, using all three as foils against which to articulate and defend a version of the Christian faith which emphasized purity, contagion, and purgation.

Blood again figured prominently. Both Judaism and Islam rejected the Christian concept of the Incarnation, in which God took human form in Christ and then suffered capital punishment in the crucifixion as a form of taking on the death penalty for sin. It was Christ's humanity – and hence the role of his physical blood in Christian thought, ritual, and metaphor – that most separated Christianity from Judaism and Islam. And it was his Blood that most animated Catholic Christianity. As we will see in Chapter 4, the Franciscans in particular began emphasizing Christ's Blood in their theology and preaching as part of their effort to make the things of faith immediately present and physically real. Out of this there grew a set of so-called blood libels against the Jews in particular – that is, charges that they were obsessed with the Blood of Christ and the blood of Christians to the point that they would stop at nothing to obtain both: stealing and desecrating eucharistic hosts and kidnapping and murdering Christian children. Like witches, Jews supposedly did this in league with the devil in order to subvert God's truth and weaken the *Corpus Christianum*. The accusation was pure fiction, but theologians and preachers used blood libels and miracle stories to chide their own followers and persuade them of the truth of Catholic doctrines centred on Blood: if even witches and Jews believe in the power of Christ's Blood, what business do you have in doubting it? Many preachers galvanized crowds with the question: how could true Christians who aimed to gather under the Virgin's cloak tolerate the presence of God's sworn enemies living within the walls that defined the *Corpus Christianum*?

Preachers used these accusations from the early thirteenth century in order to build belief in the miracle of transubstantiation, and to argue for the forced conversion or expulsion of Jews. Soon blood libels appeared in popular songs, poems, and plays. They multiplied even more with the emergence of widely sold narrative woodcuts in the fifteenth century which showed Jews buying consecrated hosts and then stabbing or burning them. The woodcuts told their story like a cartoon, with short captions or verses under each box. In one of these, produced in Passau in 1477, the host survives while the Jews are eventually caught and punished with the same mutilation and burning that they exercised against Christ. Woodcut series became critical tools for spreading the story of the case against Jews in the town of Trent in 1475 who were accused of kidnapping a two-year-old Christian boy named Simon and bleeding him to death [Fig 10]. Prints and pamphlets spread details of the notorious case that ended in the execution of eight men for the crime itself, followed by the arrest and torture of the entire Jewish community in Trent and the burning of fifteen of them at the stake. The martyred St. Simon of Trent was credited with hundreds of miracles and became the patron saint of kidnap and torture victims until he was removed from the Catholic Calendar of Saints in 1965.

A separate charge against the Jews was that of plague spreading, and here the concept of contagion was both literal and metaphorical. Jewish religious and dietary customs kept them from using wells or eating certain foods and

10. The Torture of Simon of Trent, from the *Nuremburg Chronicle* (1493). Courtesy of the Thomas Fisher Rare Book Library, University of Toronto.

encouraged a higher standard of hygiene than Christians normally practiced. In most parts of Europe they also lived together in neighbourhoods separated formally or informally from Christians. Some opponents seized on these differences in times of plague, particularly if fewer Jews were sick and dying, claiming that the Jews had poisoned the food and drink of Christians. Some argued, more indirectly, that God was punishing Christians for sheltering His enemies, and that He would not rid them of plague until they had rid themselves of Jews. The charge could come at any time, but the Black Death of 1348–50 proved particularly dangerous. The Jewish community in the French port of Toulon was the first to be sacked by gentile neighbours in April 1348, and the Aragonese port of Barcelona soon followed. Sacks and massacres killed hundreds and possibly thousands in Augsburg, Nuremburg, Erfurt, Freiburg, Basel, Strasbourg, Cologne, Mainz, and Antwerp – all of them major trading centres with large Jewish populations. More than 60 major Jewish communities and 150 smaller ones were sacked and often destroyed from 1348 to 1351.

The subtleties of eucharistic theology were not enough on their own to trigger violence on such a scale, and in many cases local economic and political resentments drove the massacres forward. Jews were usually prohibited from owning property or practicing most trades and occupations, but were permitted by local authorities to practice others, chiefly small-scale pawn broking and larger money lending which Christians were not supposed to engage in. Some civil authorities invited Jews into towns and protected them as an economic resource, but their economic role and geographic segregation left them vulnerable. The same authorities who had protected Jewish merchants and artisans might either fall silent or be powerless to defend them when conditions suddenly worsened. Pope Clement VI issued two bulls in July and September 1348 ordering clergy to protect the Jews and stating that those blaming the Jews for the advancing plague were being 'seduced by that liar, the Devil'. Yet a papal bull had no power to stop a raging crowd. In some instances, and particularly in towns of the Holy Roman Empire like Strasbourg, the Jews' protectors were distant rulers and ecclesiastics, while their opponents were neighbours bent on eliminating competition or cancelling their own debts, seizing goods, or challenging higher authorities.

As with the witch hunts, theological justifications were often secondary, but lent a spiritual justification to the persecution. Economic and political factors drove many attacks, but religion justified them; a violent pogrom was an act of piety. Jews were enemies of Christ who served the devil. They rejected Christ's Blood, they assaulted Christians through plague spreading, and they made Christian towns vulnerable to the assaults of an angry God. All these made them a contagious threat within the *Corpus Christianum*, and in the eyes of many the only way to handle this threat was to remove practicing Jews from the Christian social Body. The two linked ways of doing this were forced conversion to Christianity or forced expulsion from Christian communities. As we will see in the next chapter, both of these final solutions to the medieval and Renaissance Jewish problem became increasingly widespread through the late fourteenth and fifteenth centuries.

The Body Divided and Corrupted

Challenged with serious threats from Muslims beyond its borders, and from heretics, witches, and Jews within its heart, the Body of Christ needed to offer a unified response, and the Catholic Church would ideally frame and promote it. Yet at different points in the fourteenth and fifteenth centuries, the church was in fact deeply divided. For a few decades there were two and even three popes competing for primacy. The religious orders, which were meant to be the church's chief defense against spiritual threats, also split and fought. The great majority of lay believers may not have been much troubled by this division, because they may not have been much aware of it. Yet it was a troubling contradiction for the many professionals, merchants, clergy, and nobles who had positions of authority within the *Corpus Christianum* at both the church and state levels. Some looked for solutions by further dividing all authority and empowering the various members of the Body, while others took the opposite tack and aimed to eliminate rivals and concentrate power at the Head.

The result was an atmosphere of rivalry, criticism, and confusion and, for some, a growing sense that the church's structures themselves were the problem. Literate critics, ranging from Marsilius of Padua to Savonarola to Erasmus, wrote blistering critiques of the church and churchmen. These were so pungent that earlier generations of historians assumed that the entire fifteenth century church was corrupt at the head and practically dead in all its members. Far from it – we actually see an intense explosion of piety at the level of the laity and even among many clergy. Division can reflect healthy diversity, but in the case of the papacy and the religious orders, the splits were seen by many literate and influential laymen and clergy as a sickness that once again pointed to the work of the devil and that threatened the Body of Christ. This conviction and fear shaped their thinking, their writing, and their actions.

Division at the Top – the Papacy

Some fourteenth-century Italians believed that the papacy's weakness was most glaringly revealed in its absence from Rome, which had been the heart of the western church for well over a millennium. Pressure from French King Philip IV led the cardinals to abandon Rome for Avignon in 1309, at that time on the southeastern boundary of the kingdom of France. The papal court remained there until 1377, and on the whole it was a period of financial and bureaucratic consolidation. Yet the Italian poet Petrarch labeled it the 'Babylonian Captivity of the Church,' referring to an episode in Old Testament history when the people and rulers of Israel were forcibly taken in exile to Babylon by their Assyrian conquerors. Removal to France was not likely a major problem for Christians outside of Italy – royal courts were always on the move, and throughout the twelfth and thirteenth centuries, popes had resided in Rome only about 40 percent of the time. What was more worrying to many was that the church itself was becoming increasingly French: all eight popes elected in Avignon were French, and of the 134 cardinals they appointed 113 were also French. A church proclaiming itself universal should not be in the possession of a single nation or king.

Various pressures from Italy, including erosion of papal territories there, led Gregory XI to return to Rome in 1377. He died shortly thereafter, and the cardinals initially elected an Italian, Urban VI, in his place. Pressure from France led a group of French cardinals to return to Avignon, where they claimed to have been intimidated by Roman nobles and mobs, and promptly elected another Frenchman to become Pope Clement VI. The underlying politics of the dispute were now fully in the open, and Europe divided into two churches along the lines of national rivalries. France, the Kingdom of Naples, Scotland, Savoy, and the Iberian peninsula recognized the Avignon pope, while most of Italy, the Holy Roman Empire, England, Hungary, Poland, and Scandinavia recognized the Roman pope. Each pope declared the other to be a heretic and excommunicate, as though exclusion and purgation might solve the problem.

This schism into two Bodies was a paradox that denied the very concept of the *Corpus Christianum*, and it gave impetus to a radical solution: curb the power of the pope by sharing his authority with the lower ranks of the church hierarchy: bishops, archbishops, abbots, and cardinals. In their diversity and origins they represented a wider swathe of the different nations and peoples that comprised the Catholic Church. They could periodically gather as a council to review the state of the church and either approve or revise the actions of the executive curia and pope. Numerous councils had addressed problems in the early church, including Nicea (325), Ephesus (431), Chalcedon (451), and many in Constantinople, and there had been at least six more councils through the twelfth and thirteenth centuries. The conciliar approach had ample historical precedent, but could conciliarism solve the problem of a divided church? Both the Roman and Avignon popes refused to come to a council held at Pisa in 1408–09 to repair the division, so the Pisan conciliarists expelled both and elected a third pope in their place.

The conciliarists were more effective with a larger council held in Constance, just north of the Alps, in 1414. Thousands of delegates from across Europe attended to deal with the three main challenges facing the church: unity (*causa unionis*), heresy (*causa fidei*), and spiritual and institutional reform (*causa reformationis*). Over the next three years, they demonstrated their own legitimacy by responding decisively to each. They handled unity by deposing all three popes and electing a new one to rule from Rome. They handled heresy by burning Jan Hus and Jerome of Prague and ordering the posthumous burning of Wycliffe. They handled reform in a series of measures that empowered the cardinals and instituted regular councils, thereby

11. The Council of Constance as a gathering of high clerics under the Holy Spirit, from the *Nuremburg Chronicle* (1493). Courtesy of the Thomas Fisher Rare Book Library, University of Toronto.

curbing the authority of the popes and effectively sharing his power across the upper ranks of the church, as suggested in an image from the *Nuremburg Chronicle* [Fig 11].

Far from solving the sickness in the Body of Christ, the conciliarists' radical cure set the stage for a century and a half of fighting, manoeuvring, and denunciation that would lead to the three distinct visions of the Christian church that had emerged in different parts of Europe by the late sixteenth century: one headed by a pope with the powers of a monarch, one governed by groups of clergy working possibly but not necessarily with political authorities, and one consisting of national churches under a monarch with the powers of a pope.

Papal efforts to restore authority to the office of pontiff faced stiff resistance, above all at the Council of Basel called in 1431 following a schedule determined at the Council of Constance. When Pope Eugenius IV attempted to move the Basel Council south of the Alps to Italy, the suspicious conciliarists expelled him and in 1439 elected a Savoyard nobleman as Pope Felix V in his place. Once again there were two popes in Europe. Political assemblies north of the Alps in France, Bohemia, and the Holy Roman Empire all adopted laws or resolutions limiting the power of the pope to appoint bishops or collect taxes in their lands. Yet the conciliarists lacked the political power to evict Eugenius IV from Rome, and some prominent thinkers such as Nicholas of Cusa, Giuliano Cesarini, and Aeneas Silvius Piccolomini soon decided that unity was more important than purity. As a result, it was Felix V who stepped down within a decade.

Later popes built on this strategic victory by declaring conciliarism heretical and adopting ever more regal trappings and absolute powers as though they were the new emperors of Rome. An imperial papacy required palaces, armies, retainers, and displays of wealth and power. It became ever more deeply embedded in Italian power politics as popes packed the curia and College of Cardinals with the sons of Italian nobles, rulers, and bankers, not to mention their own relatives. The Constance conciliarists had set an upper limit of twenty-four to the College of Cardinals, and when Martin V died in 1431, there were only nineteen; by 1500 there were thirty-five, and in 1586 Sixtus V set a new limit of seventy. These became predominantly Italian, and after the death of the Dutchman Adrian VI in 1523 it would take more than 450 years before another non-Italian was elected. The French popes in Avignon had run the church with a bureaucracy (the curia) of 400–500; there were 2000 secretaries, officials, and administrators by the time that Giovanni de' Medici, son of Florence's de facto ruler Lorenzo de' Medici and appointed cardinal at age fourteen, become Pope Leo X in 1513. Conciliar concordats and legislation had cut revenues from Germany, France, and England in half, and popes bridged the yawning budget gap by raising taxes in the Papal State and creating positions in the curia which were sold to the highest bidder.

The bloated, venal, and largely Italian bureaucracy disgusted reformers of all stripes across Europe, and critics as diverse as Savonarola and Erasmus together thought that the sickness had settled in the heart of the papacy itself. By the early sixteenth century, Germans, Scandinavians, Swiss, French, and English reformers found that they could play on the growing anti-Italian sentiment by framing their critiques as an assault on 'Rome' and a defense of the local *Corpus Christianum*. Many saw a solution in conciliarism, in part because the Councils of Constance and Basel had organized themselves around different 'nations'. Yet popes resisted calls for a council to reunite the church for fear that this would let the conciliarist genie out of the bottle once again. The council which did finally open in 1545 at Trent, in the very southern reaches of the Alps, was the result of the protracted negotiations between Pope Paul III and Holy Roman Emperor Charles V. This political compromise was a pathetic shadow of past councils. Although thousands of clerics had gathered from across Europe at Constance and Basel, the few dozen who limped into Trent exemplified just how sorry a state the Catholic church had sunk to – boycotts, wars, political rivalries, and sheer inefficiency kept away all but a handful of French, German, and English clergy. That this council could subsequently emerge as more influential than most of its predecessors says a great deal about how religious politics were shifting, and how small numbers of organized and motivated elites could be more effective than large numbers of the great and the good.

A distinctly *Roman* Catholic church, more authoritative and aiming to be more unitary, would eventually emerge from this manoeuvring. Yet it was in some ways an empty victory. Those parts of the *Corpus Christianum* which had wanted more national churches under more political control simply asserted this, either within the Catholic Church or by severing themselves from it. If the church needed a head at all – and not everyone agreed that it did – then a king, or a duke, or even a city council could perform the function as well or better.

Division through the Body – in the Religious Orders

Clergy divided into two basic groups whose distinctions were expressed in two Latin words. Monks, friars, and nuns were known as 'regular clergy' because they followed a rule or *regula* which governed lives centered on poverty, chastity, and obedience and lived in closed communities. The different rules they followed set them into one of many different orders, beginning with the Benedictines in the sixth century and multiplying as reforms of the eleventh, thirteenth, and sixteenth centuries created new orders with new missions and rules. Priests who provided the sacraments to people living in a town or neighbourhood or rural area were called secular clergy, since they served in the everyday world or *saeculum*. Regular and secular clergy were the professionals who conducted the spiritual, ritual, and ecclesiastical life of the *Corpus Christianum*. Although many Christians could live for years without ever seeing a cardinal or even knowing who was pope, they would have close relations with local priests, friars, monks, and nuns.

Secular and regular clergy certainly vied with one another for the devotion and alms of laypeople, but their roles were distinct enough that they did not necessarily compete. Secular clergy tended to come from within their localities and followed local customs. Most trained through a virtual apprenticeship with existing priests, and if they could memorize the sacramental rituals around feast days and the mass, confession and communion, and birth, marriage, and death, they did not need to be literate. They might work communal plots of land and raise children with concubines. Many would be hard to distinguish from laypeople. They were appointed by and responsible to bishops, who were in turn responsible for looking to their training and discipline. We will see more about their evolving role in Chapter 5.

Regular clergy stood out through their distinctive robes; their separate communities; their higher level of education; and their social activities of preaching, organizing charity, and conducting religious services. Within the broad group of regular clergy there was far more competition and acrimony because each religious order defined a distinct mission and each house competed for financial supporters. The oldest orders established rural communities of monks following rhythms of prayer, agricultural labour, and charity set out in the Rule of St. Benedict in the sixth century. The legacies of hundreds of donors over the centuries gave some of these foundations extensive farm properties and extraordinary wealth. As towns and cities grew from the twelfth century, charismatic pious individuals established communities which developed into new orders dedicated to addressing urban needs and challenges, and supporting themselves by begging. For this reason, they were called mendicants, from the Latin *mendicare* (to beg). The Dominicans and Franciscans were the chief mendicant orders, but there were many others, including Servites, Augustinians, Vallombrosans, Carmelites, and Lateran Canons. The diversity of new orders reflected the diversity of pious founders and movements, and many also founded or co-operated with lay confraternities. Joining a confraternity allowed a layperson to follow a version of a mendicant rule adapted to a life of marriage, work, and family.

Monastic and mendicant rules were hard. Since many men and women joined orders less out of religious devotion than due to family pressures, educational and professional opportunities, or other practical benefits, it is not surprising that many regular clergy bent both the spirit and the letter of the rules. Geoffrey Chaucer's fat friars and soft-living nuns on pilgrimage to Canterbury, and Giovanni Boccaccio's sexually vigorous nuns and monks have their echoes in every European literature. To these we can add those who lived in more open religious communities without taking full or formal orders, like the *beguines* and *beghards* in Flanders, the *bizzoche* and *pinzochere* in Italy, and the *tertiaries* across Europe. Some might appear as clerical as the local parish priest or friar, although without ordination they had no sacramental powers or religious authority.

Fat friars, nuns living off of their investments, priests with concubines and children, and bishops neglecting their pastoral duties all challenged the ideal of purity in the *Corpus Christianum*. We have already seen that the Franciscan

Order divided when some friars felt that their brothers were not following St. Francis's rule of poverty. This happened almost immediately, repeatedly, and always with very sharp critiques. The Franciscans were the most sharply critical — of themselves above all — yet by the fifteenth century reform movements had emerged in almost every religious order and also in many confraternities, causing intense divisions and stirring charges of heresy. Parish priests were disciplined less often, but this only made it harder to argue why they ought to have special status and powers that separated them from the laity.

The Dominican friar Savonarola preached blistering sermons against the high clergy and other religious orders. The Dutch Augustinian canon Erasmus used satire to mock clerical pretensions and to ask rhetorically whether all Christians were not equally members of One Body of Christ. Erasmus was more moderate and certainly much funnier than Savonarola, but both described their enemies among the clergy in absolute terms as being in league with the devil — Erasmus' *Julius Excluded from Heaven* (1514), in which St. Peter refuses to let Pope Julius II into heaven because of his militarism, immorality, and pride, was no less a sharp dig for being a satire. Was it really that bad? We need to account for their rhetoric, and acknowledge that many laity and clergy were content with the situation. There were very active religious movements in the fifteenth century, and both Savonarola and Erasmus in their separate ways were part of them. Their sharp critiques received a wide hearing, and each gathered a wide following because many Europeans maintained high standards and expectations for purity among the clergy who served and led the Body of Christ. Yet we also need to recall that both were eventually repudiated. Savonarola was burned at the stake as a heretic. Erasmus was eventually seen as dangerous by some and devious by others, and he was abandoned by most of his former followers. That both these clergymen could go in a few short years from being considered the moral hope of the *Corpus Christianum* to the very sign of its deep problems shows how sharply divided opinion on the clergy had become by the early sixteenth century.

The Body Judged – Plagues and Natural Disasters

One reason why people in the fourteenth and fifteenth century clung to the idea of taking shelter under the mantle of the Virgin Mary was because the alternatives were so frightening. Death was an ever-present reality, both as tragic events in families and households and as epidemics that swept through cities. It can be difficult for us now to think of death as a form of divine

Threats to the *Corpus Christianum* 69

12. Triumph of Death. Bibliotheque Nationale, Paris. France/Bridgeman Images.

judgment when we encounter it largely in old age, in hospitals or through accidents. But in the fourteenth and fifteenth centuries, death could take an infant in hours, clear out a neighbourhood in a few days, and pluck children and youths step-by-random-step out of large families. Death stalked the *Corpus Christianum* in ways that led people to ask hard questions about their lives – or their neighbours' lives. Death certainly hit individuals, and in that form it is familiar to us as well. But death rolling unstoppably through whole communities at a time was a reality that most medieval and early modern people would encounter again and again from the time that they were young children [Fig 12]. It was an immediate reality that triggered spiritual doubts: was the devil at work, acting through his witches? Was Christ upset with local impurity or heresy, and sending plague to warn of the greater punishment that awaited everyone at the Last Judgment if they did not repent and expel the impure? Had the saints turned their backs and the Virgin Mary drawn up her cloak out of disgust at how the community sheltered the enemies of Christ and their contagion?

Much of medieval and Renaissance Christianity was structured around death. It was at the core of the story of faith. In the book of Genesis that opens the Judeo-Christian Bible, death was promised to Adam and Eve, the original human couple, as the punishment for disobeying God's explicit order not to eat the fruit of a particular tree in the Garden of Eden. Their disobedience constituted humanity's Original Sin, and the penalty for sin was death. Within the Christian narrative, Christ took human form and came to earth so that he could pay that penalty – this was why his death had to be the kind of violent execution reserved for serious criminals. The Blood of Christ had such resonant meaning only because it had been shed violently in his death. The Catholic imagination expanded in literature, paintings, stories, and sermons far more around the death than the birth of Christ. The ceremonies around Christmas paled beside those that marked his death – from the forty days of preparation through Lent through the emotional intensity of Holy Week to the Passion and violent Crucifixion (sometimes including mob violence against Jews) before the victory of Easter, which marked Christ's return to life in the resurrection.

Death also shaped personal piety. From the fifteenth century onward, Europeans bought printed tracts and guidebooks in a rapidly expanding literature on 'the art of dying well', and they were encouraged to think of every part of life as a preparation for death. Each Catholic sacrament from baptism on to extreme unction paved the way towards final judgment. Believers aimed to steer their way through the vividly forbidding imaginary landscape of purgatory and hell that waited after death by commissioning masses to be said in their name by regular clergy. One of the main emotions driving people to join confraternities was not the joy of worshipping in a community, but the fear of dying alone with no security that anyone would bury, remember, or pray for them. Salvation was collective, but so too was damnation. And death was its foretaste.

More children died by age ten than lived. Most died in their first weeks or years. Average life expectancy at birth was thirty to forty years, but statistics are skewed because so many died at a very young age. It was unusual for people to know their grandparents, and not uncommon for them to bury their parents when they were just teenagers or in their twenties. Poor sanitation bred gastro-intestinal illnesses, poor nutrition created endemic health problems like rickets, and poor living conditions left people at all ages vulnerable to tuberculosis and other respiratory illnesses. The deaths that followed were seldom peaceful – they came with wasting, pain, fever, and violence. This was simply what everyone experienced and could expect.

And then there was plague. The devil's curse and God's anger seemed frighteningly close when plague or famine hit, and from the mid-fourteenth century onwards Europeans saw no end of it. The Black Death of 1346–53 swept away a third to two thirds of Europeans as it raced from Mediterranean ports along routes inland and north, reaching Scotland and Sweden by 1350. It had emerged in the Middle East, claiming a third of the populations of Persia and the Levant and up to 40 percent of Egypt. Jan de Vries estimates that Europe's population dropped from around 100 million to about 60 million, while J. C. Russell sees a decline from 80 to 55 million. Any continental estimates mask regional variations; Italy and France were far harder hit than England and Germany. Crowded cities saw greater drops than rural areas: Florence's population of 90,000 collapsed to 36,000, half of Paris' population of 100,000 simply disappeared, and London went from 60,000 to 40,000. Most of these cities would take 150–200 years to regain their pre-plague population, in part because urban congestion ensured that various plagues returned again and again. Some plagues singled out children and youths, others adults. Some were local and regional: Venice was scourged in 1570, Milan in 1630, Barcelona in 1653, London in 1665. Some of these later plagues matched the spread of the Black Death if not quite the scale: disease swept large parts of Europe in the 1420s–30s, 1527, 1590s, and 1630. Famine often joined plague, sometimes preceding, sometimes following, or sometimes on its own. Harvests failed frequently, and familiar trading links did not reach far enough or carry enough volume to make up the difference. But famine and plague did not work alone to correct overpopulation: they triggered wars, economic depressions, and other social upheavals which led many people to put off marriage and so slow down population recovery.

How did plague and famine affect the European psyche? Since many took mass death as a form a judgment, few saw these blows to the Body as being the work of natural forces alone. The Black Death unleashed an orgy of local pogroms in which hundreds and thousands of Jews in communities across the continent were killed, often in terrible explosions of mass burnings and drownings. This was not repeated as consistently in later outbreaks of plague, although there were numerous local examples where Jews or other marginal groups were attacked. Were these non-Christians a contagious force that actively spread disease so as to kill believers? Were they an alien and infectious presence within the *Corpus Christianum*? The sheer speed of a plague's advance made the search for causes extraordinarily intense, and the language of infection, contagion, and disease transferred readily from the physical to the social body and could be used to trigger violent executions and expulsions. By contrast, although sudden hailstorms, torrential rains, or crop-killing frosts were part of the common discourse around witches, we do not find that serious witch hunts were triggered by natural disasters alone.

But seeing mass death as judgment also meant looking within the Body for the source of infection, and looking to religious ritual for acceptable forms of purgation. Devotional processions, laws against blasphemy, public flagellation, fasting and prayer, and public vows of repentance and reformation were common ways of persuading Mary to once again spread her protective cloak, and once the plague abated, these vows might produce a banner or fresco (as in Perugia and San Gimigniano in 1467 – Fig 1) or an entire church (as in Santa Maria della Salute in Venice in 1570). We need to remember that the Virgin's cloak protected communities from the spears and arrows of God's anger – the lesson was that they were morally *responsible* for the plague or famine, and that physical plague was a result of spiritual sickness. Their actions had brought it on, and their actions could send it away again. The discourse around plague emphasized that each individual, each confraternity or guild, and each city had responsibility for its health and sickness. As a result, spiritual actions existed alongside responses that we might think of as more scientific or secular: quarantines of goods and people, cleaning up noxious wastes, and sealing up, burning, or disinfecting with vinegar the homes where plague victims had died. For most Europeans the spiritual and the secular intertwined thoroughly, such that action in one did not negate action in the other. They used isolation and purgation to purify both the physical and social body.

Christian Europeans believed intensely in the *Corpus Christianum*. But what was this Body? Religious faith was collective, and the actions of every individual and all members of a group had consequences both now and in eternity. Few understood fully the doctrines of the Catholic faith, but most could follow the rituals. Few had much sense of the broader intellectual framework behind the scriptures, the sacraments, or the ecclesiology of a universal church. Most operated on a more basic animism that played good forces against bad in the visible and invisible worlds, and kept alert to rhythms of the seasons in nature and in human life. They thought about communities and boundaries, and how these were to be protected here and now, and on into eternity. Most also shaped their spiritual practice around forms of kinship. The language of brother and sister, father and mother occurs at every level of faith and church life: from Christ's words, to the saints' lives, to the whole hierarchy ranging from pope to priest and friar, to the relations between members of guilds, confraternities, and other social groups. Kinship connected your obligations to God with those to your community, and kinship ensured that it was a two-way relation in which God, the saints, and Mary also had obligations to you as well. All these kin groups were families that together constituted the *Corpus Christianum*, and what gave that Body its life was Blood.

Although Christianity, Judaism, and Islam were intimately connected to a common root as Abrahamic faiths, the idea of God taking human form in Christ put Christianity on a completely different path that was defined by the metaphors of Body, Blood, and Kinship. Every altarpiece and devotional sculpture emphasized a human expression of God's existence that Jews and Muslims found completely unacceptable. Yet a Christian could barely pass a day without encountering those human forms. They were the fundamental metaphors of a faith expressed in stories and pictures. Human forms and relationships defined Christianity and made it intensely personal and intensely moral. These included good relationships, but even more so bad ones: the devil's jealousy triggered his rebellion against God and his defeat catapulted him to Hell where his seething resentment lost no opportunity for revenge. In the Christian imaginary, the devil's hatred struck at the very Body and Blood of God. Christianity may have been distinctive in the way that it demonized its enemies and personalized threats, but this was just the flip side of its having humanized all relations between God and the world. Hatred was a human relationship, too. If the devil was so determined to contaminate the *Corpus Christianum*, the biggest question facing Christians was: What would they do about it?

2

PURIFYING THE BODY

G IVEN THE RANGE OF THREATS COMING FROM INSIDE AND outside the *Corpus Christianum*, there could be no single way of acting to purify the Body of Christ. The Turks posed an external military threat that could be answered by defensive actions, organized crusades, or diplomatic negotiation. Threats from inside the Body were usually handled in one of four ways: by separation, by containment, by prosecution, or by purgation. The strength of the response depended on the seriousness of the threat, on local social and political dynamics, and on the time period. As we have seen, Europeans became more anxious about a wide range of threats from the fifteenth century onwards, and their rhetoric and actions became steadily more harsh through the sixteenth and seventeenth centuries.

Harsh rhetoric did not always result in harsh purifying actions, particularly in the early stages. It was easier to preach or threaten purgation than to carry it out, and in fact not everyone in a community agreed on who was a threat or how they should be dealt with. Yet cultural stereotypes, hard words, and images taken from the Bible, classical authors, or medical texts merged into an evolving discourse that legitimized purity and purgation of individuals and whole societies. This legitimizing discourse spread far thanks to a range of traditional and new methods including public preaching, woodcuts, cheap pamphlets, inexpensive vernacular texts on theology and philosophy, expanding school systems, and books of manners. Purity and discipline were common themes outside the realm of religion: in humanist political texts, in medical treatises, in legal codes, and in educational treatises. The language became so common and ubiquitous that it shaped the expectations of new generations of artisans, merchants, professionals, and government officials. Rulers and their officials drew on this discourse as they felt their way into more aggressive forms of state power in the sixteenth and seventeenth centuries, backed by more exclusive formations of religious truth. They

13. The burning of a community of Jews, from the *Nuremburg Chronicle* (1493). Courtesy of the Thomas Fisher Rare Book Library, University of Toronto.

could pose as God's servants working against God's enemies. Riots and pogroms had gripped some medieval communities with devastating effect, although even when implicitly or surreptitiously sanctioned by authorities, they were staged as spontaneous outbursts of mass violence [Fig 13]. It is not really surprising that some of the largest officially sanctioned purges of dissidents, heretics, witches, marginals, and outsiders for reasons of communal religious purity and integrity did not take place at the beginning of our period but after a century or two. This was when states began exercising greater powers in pursuit of distinctly national goals, and were drawing on religious rhetoric to legitimize secular goals. What were abstract ambitions for fifteenth and early sixteenth century authorities turned gradually into practical agendas and even obligations for their successors.

The previous chapter set out what some perceived as threats to the *Corpus Christianum*, and this chapter will lay out solutions which were pursued in some areas. It is important to remember that they were not adopted universally. The discourse around reform had initially included many different voices advocating co-existence, negotiation, and compromise. But successive outbreaks of war, exile, and prosecution hardened attitudes. Returning refugees and exiles could be uncompromising hard-liners, and they were influential. Those who fled England as religious refugees in the 1550s and 1640s came back to shape policy from the 1560s and 1660s; the same happened in the Netherlands in the 1560s and 1570s, and in France and Germany throughout their protracted Wars of Religion in the later sixteenth and early seventeenth centuries. In Catholic territories, a series of rulers from the later sixteenth century pursued aggressive programs of 're-Catholicization', inspired and mentored in many cases by Jesuit confessors and teachers whose order was founded as a particularly vigorous proponent of purifying and purgative reform. Rising violence muted opposing voices in the discourse around reform and made violence itself seem normal. It also made negotiation and compromise seem politically weak, strategically unsound, and religiously impious.

Separation, containment, prosecution, and purgation became key characteristics of what has been known as the period of the Reformation. They were not the only realities, and we should not forget that reformers also promoted more distinctly positive values like interior piety, spiritual integrity, common humanity, and justice. Yet as we try to understand why reform took the path that it did, and above all why and how early modern Europe developed a distinctly persecuting character, we need to trace the sharper and more exclusionary themes that reflect a rising emphasis on discipline and purgation. And we need to remember that for many of these reformers, hard discipline began at home: those like Savonarola, Luther, Calvin, and Ignatius who were hard on others were usually even harder on themselves. Many saw intolerance not as the lack of charity, but as an expression of it, or what Alexandra Walsham has called 'charitable hatred'. There was no charity in letting others condemn themselves to hell through their beliefs or actions, so it was better to act harshly in the hope of converting them or at least containing the damage they could cause.

Paradoxical as it seems, it was often through noble and even humane intentions that the religious divisions in Europe gradually hardened. As the discourses around discipline narrowed, that toleration for firm and even violent actions in the home and in society increased. Reformers, authors, and authorities in both state and church worked together and presented their often controversial actions as protecting the truth of God and the lives of believers. Until the end of the seventeenth century and even beyond, many assumed that states and churches had an obligation to preserve sacred community not just in religious institutions like a church or confraternity, but inside the walls of their cities and the borders of their nations. This in turn required disciplining those who did not fit certain standards of purity, piety, or belief.

Separation

Medieval Observance Movements

Some saw the splits within religious orders and the Catholic church at large as rupturing the Body of Christ, but others welcomed them as a necessary purging which would bring spiritual health. The Franciscans fought bitterly over the question of how closely to follow the rule of their founder, but they were not the first or only ones. Centuries earlier, the Cluniac (909) and Cistercian (1098) reforms had aimed to return Benedictine houses to a purer observance of the Rule of St. Benedict. Reform movements emerged in almost every religious order from the late fourteenth through the early sixteenth centuries. They turned inward over the question of how closely the monks, friars, and nuns were observing and following the order or rule that they had vowed to uphold.

Most orders had moderated their strict rules in practice, particularly as members of wealthy and powerful families joined, bringing their influence, expectations, and wealth. Religious orders steadily grew to become increasingly powerful institutions across Europe: they ran many universities and hospitals, they controlled as much as a third of all farmland, their churches were often the largest buildings in the cities, they were patrons of the arts, and regular clergy acted as diplomats, civil servants, teachers, and legal advisors to rulers. Expanding social and political roles could get in the way of following strict religious rules. Reforming monks and friars who advocated strictly following a founder's rule usually emphasized increased attention to devotional exercises; simplicity in clothing, food, and lifestyle; and days centred around manual labour, study, pastoral work, and charity. They forbade exemptions or dispensations from the rule when it came to owning goods or taking up offices outside the religious house. They believed that stricter observance of original rules and statutes would be enough to regenerate the orders, and from this came to be called 'Observants'.

The Fourth Lateran Council of 1215 put a halt to new rules, and Catholic authorities through the fourteenth and fifteenth centuries were reluctant to authorize the creation of new orders. So reformers had to work with existing rules or orders. This usually took the form of separate groupings (or congregations) of religious houses which often followed the example of one reformed house in more strictly observing the founding rule of the order. Benedictines took this route, and throughout the fifteenth century, reformers created separate reformed Benedictine congregations around the houses in Kastl, Melk, and Bursfelde in the Holy Roman Empire; around

Cluny and Chezal-Benoit in France; and around San Giustina, Camaldoli, Vallombrosa, and Subiaco in Italy. The Fourth Lateran ban on new orders also led to more informal religious communities of lay women and men like the northern Beguines, Beghards, and Brethren of the Common Life. Groups of priests called canons gathered in residential communities like monks and friars while devoting their time to offering religious services in local churches. These congregations of canons gathered under many forms, rules, and names, with some of the leading ones being the Lateran Canons in Italy and the canons of Windesheim in northern Europe. So many men and women aimed to live communally following a strict rule and giving themselves over to charity or religious worship, that it is hard to accept claims that the pre-Reformation Catholic Church was drifting or dead spiritually. On the contrary, the sheer number and variety of reform movements show that many challenged the status quo, and many saw reform as an ongoing process that involved frequent dividing and purging.

Among mendicant orders, the Dominicans modelled a generally peaceful Observant reform while the Franciscans were deeply divided. The influential Dominican house in Utrecht reformed itself in 1390, and gathered nine others around it by the 1460s to form a Dutch Observant Province. The same happened in Poland in the 1470s–80s, then in Finland and in Scotland. Bologna's house, where St. Dominic was buried, was a virtual 'mother house' of the order, and when it reformed in 1427 this gave credence to the Dominican Observant thrust across Europe. Yet there were always holdouts. If individual friars resisted the reform, they could move to other houses; alternatively, Observant reformers could build a new house of their own. When all the Dominican friars at Florence's S. Maria Novella resisted reform in the late 1430s, the influential Medici family put up funds for a new Observant Dominican house dedicated to S. Marco. It would develop into a centre of combative reform headed by Girolamo Savonarola – and become a sharp thorn in the Medici's side.

To expand on what was sketched in the last chapter, the Franciscan experience with Observant reform was more acrimonious and divisive. Some reformers like the 'Spirituals' were disbanded, and others like the 'Little Brothers' were hunted as heretics. From 1368 small groups of Italian friars left their houses to live in extreme poverty in hermitages, and it was from these that the Franciscan Observance developed. The friars they left behind in the large and comparably comfortable convents became known as 'Conventuals'. Franciscan Observance movements developed in France from 1390 and in Spain and Portugal from 1403, although without much initial connection to Italian reformers. The Franciscan Order became ever more deeply divided throughout the fifteenth century, but even Observants could not agree on the problems or solution. In 1446, Eugenius IV allowed the Observants to elect their own head, but the communities in France and Iberia refused to submit to him. Governance became so impossible that Pope Leo X formally divided the Franciscan Order into two groups, Observants and Conventuals, in 1517. Within a few years a new group of even more austere Franciscan hermits emerged, taking the name 'Capuchins' from the distinctive hoods (*capucci*) on their long robes, gaining a separate rule in 1529 and developing into a separate order in 1619.

As Observant movements developed in most religious orders, some reformers came to believe that the deeply divided church was so thoroughly compromised or corrupt that the only solution lay in separation or schism. Most orders followed the Dominican path and managed their divisions without extreme acrimony, both because they had stronger administrative systems and because the reforms themselves were less controversial. The Franciscans were less centralized, and their Observant reformers were more deeply driven to reject wealth and power – no small problem when Conventual Franciscans like Sixtus IV and Julius II reached the papacy. But regardless of whether the divisions were peaceful or troubled, the Observant ethos was one of purification through separation and purgation. And that ethos came to define the cutting edge of reform across Europe throughout the fifteenth and into the sixteenth century.

Observant preachers in all orders lashed out at immorality and spiritual laziness, and their stern messages brought them enormous crowds of followers. Franciscan Observants like Bernardino da Siena and Johann Schilling and the Dominican Observant Savonarola held cities spellbound with sermons demanding repentance, purification, and public pursuit of charity and justice. Bernardino's sermons against all forms of luxury and impurity singled out homosexuals and prostitutes, and triggered increased prosecution of those deemed 'deviant' by civic governments. Some of his successors targeted Jews as outsiders whose money lending trapped poor Christians. They promoted charitable pawn banks through virulently anti-Semitic sermons that often triggered communal violence against Jewish families. Preachers' denunciations of immorality were fiery – in the case of Savonarola, quite literally so as the Florentines twice in the 1490s piled up their paintings, books, and playing cards in the city's main square to be torched in dramatic 'Bonfires of the Vanities'. Within a few years, it was Savonarola himself who was burned on the same spot as a heretic. In 1524, the Franciscan Observant Johann Schilling so stirred up Augsburg with denunciations of clerical abuses and sacramental magic that the city magistrates moved to expel him; a crowd of 1800 angry citizens stormed the council chamber demanding his return.

Other Observants exercised influence through writing rather than preaching. Hendrik Herp (d. 1477) served as rector of houses of the Brethren of the Common Life in Delft and Gouda, but turned to the Franciscan Observants after a trip to Rome in 1450. He spent the next decades writing sermons and treatises such as *The Mirror of Perfection*, a text rooted deeply in Netherlandic mystical traditions and emphasizing love, imitation of Christ, and methodical meditation as the means of purification and spiritual ascent to God. Herp was popular and influential without being a firebrand like Savonarola or Schilling, but by the sixteenth century church authorities were uncomfortable with the way in which he framed his ideas on separation from the world and mystic union with God, and so they censored and 'corrected' his work.

Observants also shaped national politics. The Spanish cleric Ximenes de Cisneros (1436–1517) joined the Franciscan Observants at age 48 and within a decade his stern piety won him a position as Queen Isabella's confessor. The queen's influence promoted him to the highest ecclesiastical offices in Spain, where he pushed through a series of controversial and harshly purgative reforms. In 1498, Ximenes purged the Franciscan Order of friars who kept concubines, and a year later he pushed for a series of punitive measures against Granadan Moors who had rebelled. Their failed rebellion in turn allowed Ximenes to push for forced baptisms and mass conversion of the Moors, with results that will be discussed further below. In the years that followed, Ximenes funded and led a successful crusade into North Africa (1505–09) and for various services to King Ferdinand I was appointed Grand Inquisitor in Spain (1507) and cardinal in Rome. Although offices like this were hardly consistent with the Observant ethos, Ximenes used them to promote the Observant agenda in Spain with particular force against Muslims and Jews.

Observance as an Early Modern Ethos

The Observant ethos of separation and purification deeply shaped early Protestantism. When a German law student survived a terrifying storm by vowing to become a monk, he turned naturally to the Observant Augustinians. Martin Luther (1483–1546) would follow the Observant spiritual and physical disciplines to the letter before deciding that the letter of the law undercut the spirit of Christian faith. He gradually converted to a distinct position which he would promote with equal, and characteristically observant, zeal. When Pope Leo X excommunicated him in 1520, and Charles V secured an Imperial Ban declaring him an outlaw a year later, Luther had to face the question of separation in the most immediate and radical way. He moved slowly and deliberately, but ultimately determined that rupture in the Catholic Church was inevitable and even necessary. Yet like many radicals, his rhetoric reversed the blame: that is, it was not that he was separating from the One, Holy, Catholic, and Universal church, but that this church's own leaders had separated themselves from the truth which he continued to uphold.

Luther pulled the ultimate Observant trump card that Protestants would play repeatedly in the high-stakes ecclesiastical and political games that followed. They were not simply returning to observance of an original monastic rule, but to observance of the original sources of Christianity – the Bible and the example of the earliest Christian communities. God, they argued, had intended these as the only rules for the *Corpus Christianum*. Over the centuries both the Catholic and Orthodox Churches had moved away from them, either through laxity or under the devil's influence. Luther drew into the last book of the Bible, known as Revelations or The Apocalypse, and began using its exclusive and judgmental language to tar his opponents. The Pope was no longer simply misguided or mistaken; he was the 'Antichrist', whose arrival signalled that the Last Judgment was near.

Luther used the language of the Antichrist more than any other reformer before him. It was a rhetoric that demanded separation. This was one reason why so few others had used it, although we can find some examples from the tenth century, and Luther himself credited Jan Hus with describing the papacy in this way. Luther's intensive and exclusive language repelled more moderate contemporaries like Erasmus. They recoiled from it, preferring to pursue spiritual reform in ways that would not break the church apart. Yet Luther used it more and more often, extending it from the pope and Catholic hierarchy to broad swathes of other reformers: first the radicals among his followers in Wittenberg, then the peasants in Germany, then a larger number of Anabaptists and spiritualists. Other reformers like Huldrych Zwingli, John Calvin, and Thomas Cranmer followed suit, but it was the Radical reformers who picked up the language of the Antichrist most vigorously. They very quickly divided into a dizzying variety of groups following charismatic leaders like Thomas Muntzer (1489–1525), Melchior Hoffman (1495–1543), Menno Simons (1498–1561), Conrad Grebel (1498–1526), David Joris (1501–56), and others. All were relatively young, most lacked formal theological training, all aimed to re-create the model of the early church, and all believed that separation from the ungodly was a prerequisite for this radical reform. All freely tarred their opponents as servants of the Antichrist. All expected that they were living in the end times before the Last Judgment, and might have to hurry that judgment along by their own actions. All were exiled or eventually executed for their beliefs.

As the century progressed, fewer Protestant churches emerged out of harsh rhetoric about the Antichrist than out of practical political considerations. Swiss, German, and Dutch governments aimed to preserve the traditional cultural autonomy of their local *Corpus Christianum*, while English monarchs aimed to preserve a national dynasty. As we will see in Chapter 4, Calvinist nobility across Europe found that the doctrine of Election confirmed their view of themselves as God's Chosen who could be trusted to govern others as Christian magistrates responsible ultimately to God alone. All these rulers claimed not to be creating new churches, but only to be returning to the older practices of the early Apostolic church. In their own view, they were more observant than any Catholic Observant monk or friar dared contemplate.

The Observant ethos with its drive towards separation and a return to original sources and virtue was not limited to friars and monks and other clergy. Fifteenth-century preachers like Bernardino da Siena and Savonarola worked hard to promote 'observant' disciplines in Catholic lay confraternities, and particularly in Italy their work triggered reforms to existing brotherhoods and formations of new groups. These 'observant' confraternities increased religious observances like daily prayer, frequent confession and communion, and periodic flagellation. They recruited more narrowly and practiced tighter moral discipline of members, regularly expelling members who blasphemed, failed to take communion, quarrelled with others, or took mistresses. They excluded whole groups of people who had joined confraternities before, particularly women, on the grounds that these would be morally contagious. They also turned their backs on traditional forms of confraternal sociability, like annual feasts. Martin Luther dismissed all confraternities as little more than drunken feasting societies, but his reformed Church Orders notably incorporated many traditional confraternal practices, like lay administration, vernacular singing, organized charity, and mutual discipline. In all these ways, reformed confraternities spread Observant practices and the Observant ethos among broad groups of society, and then demonstrated models for the reform of Church Order itself among Protestants. And as we have just seen and will explore further below, Protestants of *all* confessions embraced the self-image that their entire reform was a return to the ultimate and purest Observance – that of the words of Christ in the Bible and the inspiration of the Holy Ghost in the early church.

When the Catholic Church began approving new religious orders again in the sixteenth century, Observant energies moved in that direction, as a new form of separation within the Catholic Church. We can see new orders like the Theatines (1524 male and 1583 female), the Ursulines (1536), the Barnabites (1533), and above all the Jesuits (1540) as the Catholic Reformation's most determined exponents of Observant disciplines and agendas. Of these, the Jesuits would prove most militant and purgative, reflecting in part Loyola's early life as a soldier and his determination that the order and its members must be tools at the pope's disposal in a time of crisis. Jesuits would reject other clerical offices and concentrate on charity, learning, and missions across Europe, Asia, the Americas, and Africa. This determined and focused approach inspired recruits who were thoroughly dedicated to claiming – or reclaiming – lands for the Catholic faith, and from 1000 members at Loyola's death in 1556 the order grew to 13,000 by 1613.

The Jesuits' appeal and influence was based in large part on very effective pastoral and educational programs as developed in the *Spiritual Exercises* (1540) and the *Ratio Studiorum* (1599), respectively. Both incorporated an Observant separation from the world as the first step of spiritual reform. The *Spiritual Exercises* laid out an intense four-week devotional retreat supervised by a Jesuit spiritual director, and was critical to the Jesuits' restoration of Catholic confidence and spirituality after the demoralizing intellectual challenge and doctrinal purgations of Luther, Calvin, and the Radicals. The *Ratio Studiorum* set the curriculum for the network of residential schools which became one of the Jesuits' chief activities from 1548. They believed in separating the child from family and friends from an early age in order to form him more completely through rules, disciplines, and close surveillance; the early Jesuit Francis Xavier famously said, 'Give me the child, and I will form the man.' The free but rigorous Jesuit colleges attracted students from influential families, including even some Protestants, and gave them a strong sense of religious mission together with a solid professional education. Students participated in the Spiritual Exercises, and the Jesuits organized college alumni into a network of lay confraternities which gathered influential professionals, nobles, and scholars as a self-conscious Catholic elite determined to shape public affairs. The Jesuits believed that it was critical to work with social and political leaders in order to steer policy and shape culture, and their missionaries, confessors, teachers, colleges, and confraternities would prove the most effective agents of a broad, aggressive, and often violent program of re-Catholicizing Europe in the late sixteenth and seventeenth centuries. From the first school in Messina in 1548, they assembled a network of 160 colleges by 1615 growing to 800 by the time the order was suppressed in 1773.

In their many forms, and across broad sections of Europe, Observants both Catholic and Protestant proved to be the most dynamic and influential models for religious reform from the fifteenth to the seventeenth centuries. They were determined, divisive, and disruptive; this was the direct consequence of being deeply pious, firmly committed, disciplined, and exclusive. The sprawling, wealthy, and institutionally complex late medieval Catholic Church was a bureaucratic body that reflected the best and worst of its society. Observant reformers aimed to pursue the best, without ever agreeing on what that was. All Observants rejected the idea that there should be anything new in religion; all claimed simply to be returning to some older and purer practice of the faith. All believed that reform could not be individual or personal, but would have to revive and reshape the entire *Corpus Christianum*. And perhaps most importantly, all believed that reform of their own communities and of society generally would require a willingness to separate from and possibly purge whatever was unreformed, no matter how terrible the cost.

Containment

If separation was the key to reform, then who should be separated, and how, and why? From the fifteenth century onwards, reformers of various kinds aimed to create closed residential communities which could be the place for education, reform, and improvement. Some were protective, some were punitive, and most were a bit of both. Monasteries and convents provided an obvious model for this, although in many cases they were no longer as closed as they once had been. As we can see in convents, charitable shelters, and ghettos, stricter enclosure would become one of the common ways that reformers aimed to both build and protect the Christian community from corrupting influences inside and outside the *Corpus Christianum*. At its most ambitious, enclosure in walled and gated ghettos became the way that some cities in the sixteenth century protected themselves from the 'contagion' of the Jews.

Enclosing Nuns

Catholic Observant reform affected many friars, but it affected nuns far more. Within religious orders, it resulted in a far greater emphasis on enclosure through the fifteenth century – that is, keeping nuns isolated within their religious houses with strict rules limiting their own movements and those of visitors. This in turn set expectations for how all women ought to be protected from the world and, perhaps more importantly, how the world ought to be protected from women. Throughout the sixteenth century, laywomen were pushed out of some mixed-gender confraternities, and women needing charity – whether as orphans, prostitutes seeking to leave the profession, or poor widows needing food and shelter – would more often receive it only in an 'enclosed' institution that separated them from the rest of society

Enclosure became an ever more important tool of reform for those obsessed with purity and contagion. Observant clergy and social reformers promoted it as a way of protecting orphans, widows, the poor, and various other needy and vulnerable groups from assault or exploitation. Within secure walls, they could also be trained in the disciplines of work and spirituality. These walls were perhaps even more valuable as a way of protecting those outside from the contagion of those being enclosed, and enclosures made it possible to exploit the labour potential of marginalized groups while still keeping them at arm's length.

Early monasteries provided the first model for physical enclosure, although it was always applied more firmly to women than to men. In 1298, Boniface VIII imposed enclosure as an absolute obligation for all nuns in the decretal *Periculosa*, but in fact many convents remained relatively open, particularly those with upper-class nuns who maintained active ties with their families and properties. Observant reforms targeted both this practice and also 'open convents' where groups of women lived communally offering work, charity, and spiritual disciplines without formal vows. These communities of *beguines*, *pinzochere*, or *tertiaries* multiplied rapidly across fourteenth- and fifteenth-century Europe and became a model for groups of women emerging in the sixteenth century, such as the Ursulines or Sisters of Charity, who aimed to live together and pursue an 'active apostolate' of charity.

Observant reformers thought these open communities were lax and undisciplined, and pushed for stricter enclosure of women's religious communities. Colette of Corbie (1381–1447) established the Colettines as an Observant branch of the Poor Clares, the Franciscan Order for nuns, and her stricter enclosures spread through the Netherlands, Italy, and Germany. Reformers compared open convents to brothels, and given that many young women were sent into orders by families unwilling to dower and marry them, it was inevitable that many nuns felt no strong religious vocation and had little taste for strict spiritual and moral discipline.

Life would get harder for them. Forcing girls into convents at an ever younger age became more common across Catholic Europe, dramatically increasing the number and size of convents in Italy, Spain, and France at precisely the time when the rules enforcing tight enclosure became more strict. The number of convents in Florence rose from forty-two in 1545 to sixty-nine at the end of the seventeenth century, with four times as many women as men entering them. Here, as in Venice, it was largely upper-class girls taking vows. When this phenomenon peaked in the first half of the seventeenth century, between 50 to 60 percent of patrician girls in both cities were enrolled as nuns, a staggering proportion that actually hastened the demographic collapse of the Venetian nobility. French vocations peaked in the 1620s–60s, when the average age at entry dropped from twenty-four to eighteen, and fully half were under seventeen. In its final session in December 1563, the Council of Trent confirmed the three-hundred-year old decretal *Pericolosa*, and in the decades following many bishops worked to implement it so strictly that nuns complained that the promises made to them on entering the convents were being broken. Nuns could no longer employ male music teachers, give public concerts, or regularly visit their families. The open communities of *tertiaries*, Ursulines, *beguines*, and others were to be closed or eliminated 'to avoid scandal'.

There were certainly some Observant nuns, such as Teresa of Avila, who embraced the enclosure ethos passionately. A few bishops in Italy and the Netherlands gave some mobility to nuns, particularly when local families demanded it, while French bishops proved more rigorous in enforcing enclosure. Gender was everything here. Observant reforms in male houses promoted two models of cloistering, one somewhat open and one strictly enclosed, but strict enclosure became routine for all convents and all professed nuns from the late sixteenth into the nineteenth centuries. This is not to say that nuns disappeared from society. On the contrary, as they searched for ways to generate income within the confines of enclosure, some orders, like Angela Merici's Ursulines and Mary Ward's Institutes of the Blessed Virgin Mary, developed convent boarding schools where nuns taught young Catholic girls in a limited curriculum of music, languages, and religion. Others developed small workshops where the nuns made candles or religious mementos, baked hosts, spun silk cocoons, or wove lace. Nuns drawn from the Sisters and Daughters of Charity and the Ursulines ran practically all of the hospitals in France. The Daughters of Charity were founded in 1633 by a wealthy widow together with a priest from peasant stock who had been enslaved by Barbary pirates in his early twenties and who on his escape aimed to find ways of helping other slaves, refugees, and poor. Louise de

Marillac (1591–1660) and Vincent de Paul (1581–1660) both wanted their new group to be active and engaged in helping the sick and poor, and so established the Daughters as a confraternity of young women funded by a parallel confraternity of wealthy women gathered as the Sisters of Charity. Although the Daughters would eventually be forced into more enclosed communities, they managed to retain their public role as nurses in hospitals across France.

By the later seventeenth century more middle- and lower-class women were joining convents as well, drawn in by their vocations rather than being forced in by their parents. Many became extraordinarily active in all forms of education and health care, and in the Netherlands some communities of *beguines* continued to operate as a semiclandestine Catholic network. These unmarried women became a critical force in early modern society, yet strict enclosure was the fundamental condition for their participation, and the walls, gates, and strict uniforms of their convents were the long-term result of Observant efforts to contain and control the open women's communities of the late medieval period.

Enclosing Marginals

A second group affected by the early modern push towards enclosure were those lay people who were orphaned or abandoned, widowed, poor, or simply sick, and who needed to take shelter in charitable institutions. Charitable hospitals run by religious orders, confraternities, artisanal guilds, and city governments had long sheltered pilgrims, the sick, orphans and widows, and the elderly. These hospitals were not just for the sick, but for anyone needing hospitality, usually for a few days at a time. From the fifteenth century, more specialized institutions replaced these general shelters, beginning with foundling homes for abandoned infants. The Paris Couche was taking in 'burdensome strays' in the 1390s and Florence's Innocenti from 1445. Throughout the following century, specialized homes for particular groups of needy poor multiplied rapidly across Europe: orphanages for girls and boys, poorhouses and workhouses for indigent widows and local beggars, shelters for battered women and for prostitutes seeking a new start. Many began as relatively open institutions, but adopted increasingly strict forms of enclosure, adding locks on the doors, bars on the windows, uniforms and badges, and strict rules.

Medieval hospitals might give shelter for a few days, but an early modern orphanage, women's shelter, or paupers' workhouse could have them in residence for months, weeks, or years. The greater obligation made organizers think more about shaping the lives of their residents—and getting something back from them. New charitable enclosures became as conscious about the rhythms and meaning of time as convents and monasteries were. They drew up detailed schedules for prayer, work, meals, and recreation, aiming to fill time productively, and to shape or reshape the characters of those they sheltered. This took discipline, and a young girl, adolescent boy, or abandoned wife who resisted could be punished by losing meal privileges, recreation time, or even the opportunity of leaving. The homes also used work as a way to shape character, train in employable skills, and cover costs. Piece work, above all in low-paying labour-intensive textile industries like silk and lace, expanded to take advantage of the scale of institutions where dozens or even hundreds lived.

Aiming to improve their wards while covering their costs, administrators turned enclosed charitable shelters for children and the poor into Europe's first real factories. When Florence's Silk Guild demanded the right to be the 'sole patrons, defenders, protectors, and supporters' of the Innocenti foundling home in 1421, it was looking out for its members' need for readily available and low-cost labour as much as for the foundlings' need for shelter. Lyon's innovative poor-relief agency, the *Aumône Générale*, put silk training and production at the centre of its operations from its origins in the 1530s, and was a critical factor in expanding the silk industry in that city. From their origins in the 1570s, the orphanages of Amsterdam and Augsburg were important institutional buyers of foodstuffs, clothing, and services, and also important providers of child labour. Once the Augsburg institutions divided on confessional lines after 1648, the Lutheran orphanages became central to the urban economy while the Catholic orphanages dealt more with rural aristocrats and religious houses outside the city. Genoa's *Albergo dei Poveri*, opened in 1666 with a model of funding which assumed that its resident poor would spend their time in manual labour, and by 1694 it had 2,600 residents who were forbidden from leaving either by day or night except in exceptional circumstances.

Enclosure became as much a part of daily life for these abandoned, orphaned, and poor dependents as it did for nuns. This was something new in charitable institutions, and in each case enclosure radically transformed the kind of care offered. Enclosed institutions merged protection, punishment, and productivity under one roof so that it became hard to tell whether they were shelters, factories, or prisons; most were a bit of each. Overcrowded and underfunded, the living conditions could be appalling, particularly in foundling homes. Though 'normal' infant mortality rates ranged between 40 percent and 60 percent, conditions in enclosed foundling homes regularly pushed this higher to 75–90 percent. Religion and morality figured critically in planning all charitable enclosures. Shelters provided a practical way of separating those poor considered worthy of help (e.g., orphans, widows, the disabled, the aged), from those who were not (e.g., younger adults who were physically able to work but who could or would not find jobs). Early shelters of the sixteenth century aimed to bring 'worthy poor' together, give them food, shelter, and work, and offer training that would get them on their feet. In practice, few worthy poor wanted to stay, and so by the seventeenth century shelters started to fill up with those considered lazy or deviant 'unworthy poor', who were sent there as much for punishment as for training. In this way, some of these charitable shelters gradually evolved into virtual prisons.

Enclosing Jews

A third form of enclosure that emerged at this time was larger still: the walled, gated, and guarded ghetto that enclosed whole communities numbering many thousands. Jews had always lived in particular quarters of cities, usually in the centre and close to markets, municipal buildings, and cathedrals. Messina, Palermo, Seville, and Toledo each had at least 2,000 Jewish residents in the fourteenth and fifteenth centuries, and Prague's *Josefov* or Jewish quarter was perhaps the largest in Europe, located in a bend in the Vlatva River and home to 6,000 in 1600. From the mid-fifteenth century, these open quarters began turning into walled enclosures. In 1462, Frankfurt erected walls around its hundred or so Jews, and by the end of the century Kraców did the same. Yet the ghetto that stands out, and that gave the phenomenon its name, was the one established in Venice in 1516 on an island occupied by metal foundries (*geti*). As a military-industrial site, it was already fortified: a local patrician argued, 'send them all to the Ghetto ... which is like a castle, with draw bridges and walls, and with a single gate that can be closed when they are all inside' [Fig 14].

Jews themselves wryly termed it their *get*, from the word for the Hebrew bill of divorce, as a sign of their separation from Christian society. Venetian officials forced all practicing Jews into the ghetto to divert public calls for their expulsion altogether, and the walls, gates, and a night-time curfew were meant to protect Christians from Jewish contagion. Laws forcing Jews to rent houses at above-market rates – they were not allowed to own property – boosted Christian profits as the ghetto expanded in 1541 and 1633 to handle the growing population. The ghetto, however, was more porous than was once thought. By day, Christians could visit the ghetto, and Jews could work

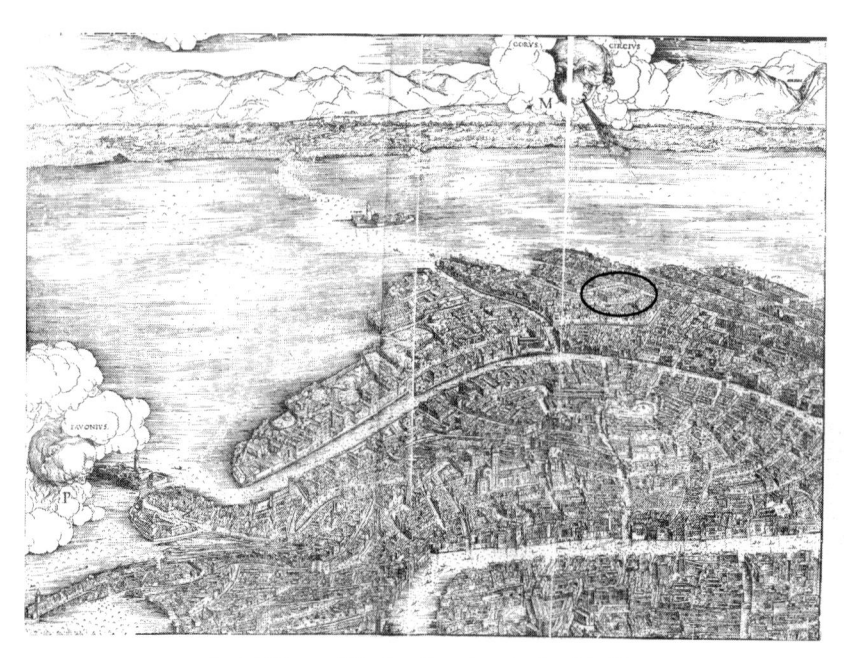

14. Aerial View of Venice Showing the Jewish Ghetto.
Courtesy National Gallery of Art (Washington).

in the city, provided they wore distinctive yellow or red head coverings. Yet we should not let some exceptions make us forget that that Jews were forced to brick up all outward-facing windows and doors, to pay for the guards who manned the gates and patrolled the canals, and to ensure that they and their children were inside when the gates closed at nightfall. There was a duality to this enclosure: meant to protect Christian Venice from Jewish contagion, the ghetto's walls and gates equally protected the Jewish community from the violence of rioting bands of young Christians who in other parts of Europe periodically smashed into synagogues and desecrated the scrolls and other holy objects.

The Venetian ghetto became a model for walled and gated enclosures established in Rome and Bologna (1555), and in Florence and Siena (1570). Each was somewhat different. Roman Jews faced far more pressure to convert, through forced sermons, free dowries, and a hostel known as the 'House of Conversion' just outside the gates. Bolognese Jews had their ghetto established in 1556, then eliminated in 1569, then re-established in 1586 before being done away with for good in 1593. Florentine Jews faced a common insult when their ghetto was established next to the civic brothel. Christians had long linked Jews and prostitutes together as a way of insulting both – often both had to wear the same red or yellow symbols or pieces of clothing or jewellery. Roman authorities organized a race every Carnival time that forced Jewish men, some young and some old, to run naked in competition with prostitutes.

Segregation and enclosure had a profound impact on how these communities governed themselves: life inside the enclosures became ever more disciplined. In the larger and wealthier Jewish communities, merchant elites controlled community councils and worked together with rabbis to enforce strong hierarchical structures. Civic magistrates in Venice, Amsterdam, Hamburg, Surinam, and elsewhere supported these authoritarian communal governments because it simplified their own work while ensuring that Jewish trading networks would continue to benefit their Christian communities. In 1679 the Iberian *converso* Isaac Cardoso described these Jewish communities as 'a separate Republic' because they used many of the same tools that other European governments employed to shape their populations: detailed regulations, interlocking councils and societies, taxes levied internally, bureaucratic structures and ever-expanding sets of records and accounts. Cardoso was thinking particularly of the Amsterdam community, which was perhaps the most organized of all, but others in London, Hamburg, and the Americas aimed to follow its example.

Enclosure as an Early Modern Ethos

Convents, orphanages, workhouses, and ghettos were all quite distinct. Some were for privileged women, others for worthy poor, others for entire communities, and others for those marked off as 'deviants'. Christendom's embrace of enclosure as a form of protection and purification put all these diverse groups behind secure walls. Regardless of the particular group, their enclosures created separate secure spaces for controlling the body and time, for purifying or punishing through discipline, and for protecting those inside and those outside from each other. The economic value of a captive labour force was not lost on merchants and rulers, and some of these enclosures developed into early factories, like Amsterdam's Rasphouse for men and Spinhouse for women. For those unable or unwilling to work, the regime might become more punitive, and some did indeed develop into prisons, as Amsterdam's enclosures certainly did.

Although we have looked at convents, charitable shelters, and ghettos, in other situations enclosure was also a common form of containment aimed sometimes to protect those on the inside and sometimes those on the outside. Some towns around the western Mediterranean had built walled brothel enclosures in the late fourteenth century. Valencia's La Pobla brothel quarter was walled up in 1392 and 1444, with security and regulations very similar to those later imposed on the Jewish ghettos. Many towns had quarantine zones outside the city walls, and from 1485 Venice devoted an entire island, St. Mary of Nazareth (later called the Lazaretto Vecchio), to be the place where plague victims were sent, and where sailors and goods were kept before being given leave to enter the city. Innovative humanist schoolmasters like Vittorino da Feltre, John Colet, Desiderius Erasmus, and Ignatius Loyola thought that an enclosed school was the best laboratory for forming a young mind and character, particularly if the parents were kept at bay.

Enclosures expanded rapidly from the late fifteenth century, becoming a cultural form that we can see used in a host of positive and punitive settings. The French thinker Michel Foucault would term this 'The Great Enclosure' and chart its continuation into the twentieth century. Although he saw it as rising out of Enlightenment views of human perfectibility and the complications of either controlling or hiding those less perfectible, we can see it originating far earlier in the Observant reform ethos. It expanded as many societies aimed to respond more creatively and proactively to increased levels of difference. Difference was not yet seen as a positive thing in itself, and toleration was seen more as a weakness than a strength. Given these values, enclosure became one of the main cultural and political forms for early modern societies to accommodate the ever-larger number of groups deemed 'marginal', 'vulnerable', or possibly 'deviant' while protecting the integrity of the *Corpus Christianum*. Enclosure was meant to help reform, convert, improve, and prepare those inside so that they could be reintegrated into Christian society, but sometimes it did the opposite. Behind their ghetto walls, Jews fashioned a rich and distinctive cultural life, and some residents welcomed the protection from outside influences, even if rioters occasionally broke in to loot and pillage [Fig 15].

Not all early modern enclosures were made of bricks and mortar. Many historians of gender have shown how marriage and the family also became legal enclosures in this period. In France, Germany, and England, law codes were revised according to the classical Roman models found in the *Corpus Juris Civilis* (529–534), and this stripped wives and children of rights they had exercised under earlier common law traditions. Parents generally, and husbands and fathers in particular, were meant to protect the vulnerable women and children in their care. Taking their cue from the Bible and from classical Roman sources that emphasized the father's total authority over everyone in the household, legal reformers reinforced patriarchal legal power in the new law codes. This view of family did not just lock doors

15. Matheus Merian the Elder, *Plundering the Jewish Ghetto in Frankfurt* (1614). Art Resource, New York.

and windows, but could develop into a domestic tyranny that erased the separate legal identity and rights of wives and children. When English women married, their property became their husband's under the legal practice of *feme covert* – the wife was literally covered, or enclosed, under her husband. Common law traditions assumed a mutuality that cast husband and wife as loving partners. Roman law assumed that the family was a physical, moral, and legal place of enclosure where parents protected and prepared their children for life, and that the father was the ultimate or sole authority within it.

Life never follows legal principles exactly, and these legal enclosures had as many cracks as their brick and mortar counterparts. A wife might have a superior status or fortune, a child might flee the household, and a man might be unwilling to fulfil the patriarchal role. Yet all the burgeoning advice literature of the day, all priests, pastors, rabbis, and imams, and all law codes both civil and ecclesiastical took patriarchal authority for granted as the only foundation for a stable society. This too was a cultural form, and one as far-reaching and influential as the enclosures for nuns, orphans, paupers, and Jews.

Prosecution

Not all marginal groups could be kept in protective enclosure. In the case of those who threatened its spiritual integrity, the *Corpus Christianum* had to reply firmly. Tolerating evil did no one any good, because God could lash society with 'natural' disasters as a form of warning, and then consign evildoers to eternal punishment in hell. When evil was collective, as in the case of heresies or witchcraft, all of society had to respond. Because some of the greatest threats came from within the Body, every city, state, and institution in this period developed the codes, policing methods, and courts or tribunals that allowed them to identify and prosecute those whose beliefs and actions were too far from the norm.

Inquisitio, Conversion, and Heresy: The Inquisition

The Catholic Church early on developed institutional tools for identifying and purging sin and heresy. From 1215, individual believers were to go to the priest at least once annually to confess their sins and receive the penitential disciplines and communion which would restore them to spiritual health. Until the late sixteenth century, the sacrament of confession took place in public, and believers were as apt to confess their neighbour's sins as their own, so there was a strong sense of this as a community's purgative ritual and not simply an individual pious practice.

The greater threat of communal heresy demanded a more proactive response, and in 1184 an Inquisition was established in Southern France to deal with the Cathar heresy. It became a permanent body in 1229, and under Gregory IX (1227–41) the Dominicans emerged as the ones most often conducting it, although Franciscans gained control in some localities like Florence. The tribunal took its name from its legal method of '*inquisitio*', by which legally-trained investigators, following rigorous rules of evidence based on Roman Law, systematically examined offenders who had either been denounced by others or who had come forward to confess a fault. In 1376 the Dominican friar Nicholas Eymeric, a combative Inquisitor who managed to be exiled twice from Aragon, published the procedural manual that became most influential over the centuries following, the *Directorium Inquisitorium*. Inquisitorial procedures and rules of evidence were arguably fairer than other forms of legal prosecution then common, above all because they involved more direct examination of crimes and criminals on the basis of evidence, and there were procedures for appeal and review. At the same time, Inquisitions effectively created new categories of crimes, which had hitherto been difficult to prosecute since there were no clear victims. Heresy and witchcraft fit this description. Inquisitors could use torture to gain evidence and confessions, and an individual summoned before them had no idea whether she or he was there as a defendant or a witness. Moreover, defendants had no lawyers. Inquisitors aimed for repentance and conversion more than punishment, but worked together with secular authorities in the event that an unrepentant prisoner required removal from the *Corpus Christianum*. Heresy was treason against God, and the Roman death penalty applied. Church authorities could condemn a soul to hell, but only secular authorities could actually take a life.

Historians often distinguish the medieval inquisitions from their later successors. Inquisitors like Heinrich Kramer pursued witches in mid-fifteenth century Germany, but complained to Pope Innocent VIII that local political rulers were often sceptical and uncooperative. In fact, centrally directed inquisitions declined through the fourteenth century, and the targets and force of prosecution depended on local bishops and inquisitors. Yet others seized the tool. In 1478, the Spanish Inquisition emerged as a national body under political direction, followed by the Portuguese Inquisition in 1536. Both targeted Jews who had publicly converted to Catholicism, particularly after the riots of 1391 in which thousands had died and many synagogues burned. Some of these *conversos* rose to prominent positions, but were suspected of privately being 'crypto-Jews' or 'Judaizers' who continued to follow the Jewish religion or helped others to do so. An Observant Dominican, Tomas de Torquemada (1420–98), himself of *converso* background, convinced King Ferdinand and Queen Isabella of the need to systematically purge Spanish Christendom of Judaizers. Although a series of popes aimed to resist or at least limit the powers of the Spanish Inquisition, strong royal pressure won out. Neighbours launched denunciations, looking for *conversos* who avoided pork, did not work on Saturdays, bought special provisions before Passover, or baptised their children with the names of Old Testament heroes like 'David' rather than New Testament disciples like 'Peter' or saints like 'Mary'.

The first authorized public burning of six *conversos* took place in Seville in 1481, and these ritualized *autos da fe* (acts of faith) would develop into ever more extravagant theatrical re-enactments of the Last Judgment. The Spanish Inquisition executed at least 2,000 heretics in its first fifty years, more than 90 percent of them Jewish *conversos*. In some instances, the bodies of suspect *conversos* who had already died were hauled out of graves for posthumous trial and burning. Inquisitorial pressure led many *conversos* to migrate to new overseas colonies. Although professing Jews and Muslims were formally banned from Spanish and Portuguese colonies in Asia, Africa, and the Americas, authorities often welcomed *conversos* and tacitly ignored their religious practices, in part because few others wished to emigrate. As a result, some colonies like Mexico had sizeable numbers of *converso* settlers. Inevitably some of these Jewish *conversos* returned to discretely practicing their original faith, and just as inevitably the Inquisition sought them out once reports began filtering back to Europe.

The first Inquisitors for the Americas were appointed in 1519, and the first *auto da fe* was held in Mexico City in 1528, executing three *conversos*. The Spanish soon appointed local Inquisitions in all their overseas territories, including Sardinia (1492), Sicily (1511), Mexico (1571), and Peru (first trials 1539; formal office 1570). In Sicily, a local inquisition held the first *auto da fe* in 1513 and, despite intense local opposition, expanded through the 1540s to target *conversos* who had fled there from Spain. Papal Inquisitions had operated in the kingdom of Naples from the middle ages, but Jews, *conversos*, Waldensians, and heretics moved into the kingdom regardless in the late fifteenth century. After the Spanish gained control of Naples in 1504, they aimed to extend their Sicilian Inquisition into the kingdom in 1510 and 1547, but backed down in face of stiff noble resistance; the Roman Inquisition would eventually enter in 1553. The Spanish conquered the Philippines in the late 1560s and conducted the first *auto da fe* there in 1572. Similarly, the Portuguese Inquisition, established in 1536, would develop as a state body aimed primarily at converts in Portugal itself and across the Portuguese Empire in Goa (1562), Brazil (1579), and Angola (1626); African animist, Jewish, Muslim, and Hindu communities first encountered intense pressures to convert and then equally intense prosecutions to purify. In both the Spanish and Portuguese empires, indigenous people were considered to be 'without reason' and as such were not subject to inquisitorial investigation if they deviated from the Catholic faith.

Over time, the Spanish Inquisition turned its attention beyond Jewish *conversos* to *moriscos*, Protestants, and witches, and to sexual 'crimes' like bigamy and sodomy. From 1540 to 1700 there were about 87,000 trials across Spain, with approximately 1,300 executions. The relatively low figure suggests both that the Spanish Inquisition was perhaps not as severe as anti-Spanish propaganda claimed (much of it generated by Dutch and English pamphleteers during their wars with Spain). Yet it also suggests that the Inquisition was generally effective in curbing religious diversity within the Iberian kingdoms. Some heretics were exonerated, while others recanted, converted, or fled and were burned in effigy. Most Inquisitions had periods of more or less intensive activity dependent on local politics and religious reform movements, but it was difficult to predict when these might flare up. Portugal's Inquisition began in 1536, but persecution of *conversos* intensified in a sustained campaign by Catholic clerics forty years later. From 1581 to 1600, the three Portuguese tribunals sentenced 3,000 'Judaizers' in 50 *autos-da-fe*, burning 221 of them. This was a time when the Spanish Inquisition had backed away almost entirely from prosecuting Jewish *conversos*, and so not surprisingly many *conversos* now retraced their ancestors' steps and fled from Portugal back to Spain. This only increased Spanish anxieties and stereotyping, and led the Spanish Inquisition to once again focus on *conversos*, particularly those from Portugal, through the seventeenth century. From 1615 to 1710, a third of those condemned by Castile's Inquisition were Portuguese *conversos*.

In a feature unique to Iberia, new laws identified the threat of difference not only by individual beliefs but by blood. Spanish governments adopted 'pure blood laws' (*limpieza di sangre*) which forbade *conversos* and their descendents to the sixth generation from holding public office, joining guilds, attending university, entering military or religious orders, or marrying Old Christians. These laws took the obsession with blood that we saw in the last chapter out of the realm of metaphor and into daily life. They triggered a Spanish obsession with genealogy, and while they were not always observed, they would not be repealed formally until the 1860s. Some *conversos* went to the Spanish colonies, where the laws were not enforced as firmly, and some went to Italy or the Netherlands where they might make further changes. When the Jesuit Order refused to accept the Spanish *converso* Paulo de Pina because of the pure blood laws, he moved first to Portugal and then to Italy where, after meeting with another *converso* who had returned to Judaism, he made the same step. The would-be Jesuit Father Paulo changed his name to Reuel Jessurun and moved on to Amsterdam where he participated openly in the Sephardic community.

The Iberian pure blood laws forced some *conversos* to go to extreme lengths to hide their Jewish past, and in some cases such as that of the humanist Juan Luis Vives or of the painter Velasquez, it is only in recent years that historians have uncovered their Jewish ancestry. The laws would have excluded some *conversos* who had already gained a reputation as some of the firmest advocates of purgative reform in Spain, such as the first Grand Inquisitor Tomaso de Torquemado (1388–1468). No other action of the period so thoroughly connected purity and blood, and no other religious or ethnic group was singled out in this way. Spain's pure blood laws stand in a long line of actions by European authorities that put blood at the heart of the differences between Jews and Christians, and that would culminate eventually in the race laws and pogroms of the twentieth century.

It is impossible to determine how many *conversos* or religious dissidents like Paulo de Pina migrated 'voluntarily' to avoid prosecution, or how many Catholics simply refused to entertain different ideas altogether out of fear of the possible cost. Of all regions in Europe, Iberia had been the most religiously diverse in the Middle Ages. By the early modern period, it was the most frequently, thoroughly, and successfully purged, and the Spanish Inquisition was a critical tool in that process.

The Spanish and Portuguese Inquisitions operated independently of Rome, and even the medieval inquisitions had often been locally organized. Yet not all so-called heretics were prosecuted though church agencies. Henry VIII, Mary Tudor, and Elizabeth I all prosecuted religious dissidents through state tribunals [Fig 16]. In France, it was the work of the

16. Burning of English religious dissidents (1557) from Foxe's *Actes and Monuments* (1563). Courtesy of the Thomas Fisher Rare Book Library, University of Toronto.

various regional parlements and the monarchy; Kings Francis I and Henri II both believed in a strong state church, and executed approximately 500 heretics from 1523 to 1566. The number pales beside that of Flanders and the Netherlands in roughly the same period, where authorities executed almost three times as many as France (approximately 1,300) even though the region had little more than a tenth of France's population. It was, in fact, the area of Europe with the highest number of executions for heresy. The intensity of the anti-Protestant crusade from the 1520s to 1560 may help explain the ferocity of Protestant iconoclastic riots in the Netherlands in 1567.

By contrast, the Roman Inquisition established in 1542 was a far more centralized bureaucratic body than anything that had preceded it. The pope chaired a committee of six cardinals who met weekly to appoint local inquisitors and conduct business. Over time, local offices were established in Milan, Naples, Florence, and Avignon, while Venice established a separate state body staffed in part by lay members. One historian estimates that the Roman Inquisition prosecuted roughly 50–75,000 cases and sentenced 1,250 to death, or somewhat more than the Spanish Inquisition. And as with Spain, we cannot tell how many fled Italy to avoid arrest. As many as 200 Anabaptists lived in the north Italian towns of Imola and Forli before the Inquisition arrived in 1569, and all of them disappeared within two years, most moving en masse to Moravia. The Italian inquisitions targeted witchcraft, homosexuality, and blasphemy as much as heresy or 'judaizing'. As Christopher Black has noted, their effects go beyond statistics to a cultural legacy. The long imprisonments of Tommaso Campanello and Galileo Galilei fostered a 'narrower-minded Catholicism' which discouraged some forms of theological and intellectual debate, while the steady surveillance fostered skills of evasive storytelling and dissimulation.

Inquisitio *and Community: Communal Discipline*

Protestants did away with the Inquisition, but not with the *inquisitio*. They established, expanded, and formalized the religious tribunals that investigated moral and religious lapses. Admittedly fewer of these directed their attention to heresy, and few imposed death sentences. Calvinist consistories in Geneva, Emden, and the Netherlands almost all began with case loads that focused on those who were violating the new religious rules, either defiantly or unawares, by missing Sunday services, associating with Catholics, posting images of saints, or putting votive candles in their windows. Over a few decades, they saw these replaced with a steady increase in cases of immoral behaviour (drunken-ness, dancing, gambling, violence, blasphemy), sexual misdemeanors (adultery, premarital sex), and interpersonal disputes and anti-social behaviour (gossiping, disobedience to parents). English ecclesiastical courts saw the same trajectory, and moved over time to prosecuting a similarly wide range of moral and social offenses.

Although they had abandoned the practice of confessing to the local priest, Protestant authorities had effectively criminalized immorality. Local church bodies enforced moral codes as though they were civil crimes. These could be so broad ranging that one historian has estimated that a majority of people in Britain would have an encounter with a church court at some time in their lives, most often during adolescence. Consistory procedures were more often conversational than judicial, and the offender might be given a fine or be ordered to attend more sermons. The ecclesiastical courts in state churches were somewhat more formal, and here the penalties could range from fines to stocks to light corporal punishment.

The most serious offenses could trigger excommunication, and Protestants and Catholics alike placed an enormous emphasis on this as the ultimate punishment because it stretched past life and into eternity. Protestant church authorities wanted to control it as a means of establishing obedience to new beliefs and practices. They had to argue with state officials who were reluctant to cede control of church discipline entirely, since excommunication could jeopardize individual's membership in the *Corpus Christianum* and hence their civil and political rights. Control of church discipline thus became a critical point of tension in early Protestantism.

Almost everywhere, state authorities gained at least a say, if not complete control, particularly in the state churches of Scandinavia, Britain, and the Holy Roman Empire. While these states did not have a formal Inquisition, some nonetheless put heretics to death, for reasons sometimes hard to distinguish from treason. Nuremburg executed four people for 'blasphemy' from 1521 to 1560, while Elizabeth I executed 183 Catholics ostensibly for rejecting their queen's religion, but in fact for rejecting their queen. In the Netherlands a reaction set in after the bloodbath of the 1520s–50s: some executions for heresy continued in southern towns like Antwerp that were in the grip of the revolt against Spain (17 from 1561 to 1566), while the northern province of Holland went from having executed 292 in 1531–40 to 3 in 1561–66, and the province of Friesland, which had executed more than 13 in 1531–40, executed none. In a state church, the line between heresy and treason was blurred entirely, and the ambiguous position of the Calvinist state church in the Netherlands from the 1570s may be part of the lingering revulsion against the extraordinarily high level of executions earlier in the century. Although Calvinists in the Netherlands wanted their excommunications to have the force of law, local political officials consistently refused to recognize this, a gap which became the basis for the distinctive Dutch form of religious co-existence.

The Protestants who were perhaps the most extreme in disciplining members were the Radicals. Among the followers of Thomas Muntzer during the Peasant War, and then again in cities like Amsterdam and Munster in the early 1530s, radical millenarians who believed that the Last Judgment was at hand aimed to seize whole cities and expel entirely all those who deviated from their doctrine. They believed that this would create a New Jerusalem populated with true believers that would draw Christ out of heaven in the Second Coming, which they believed would trigger the End Times and the apocalyptic Last Judgment. Less militant or millenarian radicals held so strongly to the idea of forming communities of pure believers that it became vital for them to find an effective means of purging those who deviated from the common doctrine. They feared that someone who had slipped from the faith might betray the rest of the community, a serious problem when they could face death for their beliefs. Their tool of discipline was social rather than political, a form of ostracism known as the 'ban', which could be temporary or extend to permanent excommunication. In both cases, the one under discipline was shunned entirely: friends, neighbours, children, and spouses could not eat or work with, or even talk to the one under the ban. Even as fears of prosecution faded, communities of Mennonites or Amish isolated themselves from 'the world' in self-sufficient agricultural communities in remote parts of Eastern Europe, Russia, and the Ukraine. They survived little changed until the twentieth century, having enclosed themselves with the social tool of the ban to protect themselves from the surrounding cultures.

Jewish communities noted above also developed tighter forms of communal discipline in diaspora. Their forms of self-government included local councils of lay elders known as the *Ma'amad*, regional councils in places like Iberia and Poland that had many local communities, and specialized courts for various cases and offenses set out in medieval law codes. The Sephardic merchant Abraham Pereyara, who was a member of Amsterdam's *ma'amad*, wrote a guide in 1666 which lifted whole passages from the works of Spanish Catholic authors who argued for a powerful Catholic monarchy. Pereyara simply adapted their ideas for strong religious-political discipline to the separate context of the Jewish nation. He argued that although lay syndics should rule, they should obey the rabbis, who were the most skilled interpreters of those divine laws and traditions that undergirded the community. Rabbis could thus best judge how Jewish communities should be taught, supported, and purged, using warnings, fines, reprimands, and expulsions either from worship or from the community as a whole.

Pereyara's advice was indistinguishable from what Catholic and Protestant authorities gave to their rulers, and not all Jewish lay leaders would have agreed with it. In fact, under the conditions of diaspora, tensions between lay and rabbinic leaders grew through the period. Both became steadily more authoritarian, with wealth a key lever of power. They competed for primacy both within their communities and in relations with Christian and Ottoman authorities. Although the local *ma'amad* could not imprison or execute those who violated a community's rituals, codes, or expectations, it could impose a form of social death by putting persons under a ban, or turning them out of the Jewish community entirely, making it virtually impossible for that person to remain in the city.

Inquisitio *and the Devil: Hunting Witches*

Although Catholics and Protestants devised different ways of purging their own faith communities, one threat united them. Witches were the enemies of the Body who faced the most serious penalties from both. Some historians have tried to determine whether Catholics were more likely than Protestants to fear and prosecute witches, or vice versa, and the results are not at all clear. Charges of witchcraft often came bundled together with other crimes that could range from political sorcery to fortune-telling to fertility magic. We do see a steady increase in frightening images and witch hunting texts from the mid-fifteenth century, due in large part to the expansion of the printing press. More to the point, the two waves of prosecution noted earlier, from the 1480s to the 1520s and then from the 1560s to the 1630s corresponded to a general shift towards increased involvement of the state in prosecuting witchcraft as a crime against the social and political order, and not just against God. The Inquisitorial tribunals of the first wave were more willing to see repentance as the end of proceedings: their chief worry was the threat of heresy. As state tribunals expanded their role from the 1560s, punishment took priority over repentance, and so prosecutions increased: state authorities worried less about heresy than about hailstorms destroying crops, murders taking infants, curses leaving people and animals infertile, and conspiracies threatening political authorities.

Of course, we should not distinguish too sharply between church and state prosecutions, since witches supposedly worked with the devil against the community, and this made their sorcery or witchcraft (*maleficium*) at once a religious and a civil crime. In Catholic lands, various Inquisitions investigated and tried those accused of witchcraft before turning them over to the secular arm for punishment: In Protestant lands, state tribunals carried out hunts with the advice of clergy. Because witch-hunts were always local events triggered by local disasters like war, plague, natural disasters, and famine, and above all by the dynamics between local people, we need to play close attention to the geography and chronology of the hunts. Brian Levack notes,

> Most European territories experienced the full force of the European witch-hunt between 1580–1630. Large scale prosecutions involving hundreds of victims occurred through western and central Europe, most notably in the diocese of Trier in the late 1580s and early 1590s, Scotland in 1590 and 1597, Lorraine in the late 1580s and early 1590s, Ellwangen in the 1610s, and Wurzburg and Bamberg during the 1620s. Without complete statistics it is difficult to determine which decade between 1580s and 1630 was the time of most intense witch hunting. The 1580s were especially bad in Switzerland and the Low Countries; in the 1590s in France, the Low Countries and Scotland and many German territories; the 1600s in the Jura region [of Switzerland] and many German states; the 1610s in Spain; and in the 1620s and 1630s in Germany.

Levack notes that common factors in each region included harsh climate changes, famines, economic depression with wages and employment dropping as prices rose; we can also see that the hunts in France, Germany, and Switzerland — where three-quarters of all the hunts took place — also corresponded to periods and regions torn by civil-religious wars. All these factors increased social tensions, and set the stage for hunts.

Legal systems could also govern the intensity of hunts. Roman law put few limits on the power of the investigating magistrate to launch investigations, take private testimony, and use torture to gather evidence; French magistrate Nicholas Remy, author of *Demonolatry* (1595), reputedly sent more than 2,000 to their death as witches. Where appeals courts were weak or absent, the number of executions was far higher. It was the lack of an effective appeals process that gave the Holy Roman Empire the highest level of executions: between 20,000 and 25,000 over roughly two centuries. On the borders of the Holy Roman Empire, Switzerland had 10,000 executions and Lorraine 3,000. Hungary tried 1,500 and executed 450, while the Netherlands had many hunts and trials, and executed 150.

In France there were roughly 3000 prosecutions with about a third resulting in execution. In Britain there were roughly 5,000 trials and 1,500–2,500 executions, though a disproportionate number of these were in Scotland where the 1563 statute gave a mandatory sentence of death. Scandinavian magistrates tried 5,000 and executed 1,700–2,000. Polish records have been lost, but recent estimates suggest 2,000 were executed in a hunt which began and ended later than most others: the last person executed in Europe for the crime of witchcraft died there in 1793. Yet legal systems did not govern everything: In Mediterranean Europe, where witchcraft was associated more with magic than with demonolatry, there were fewer trials and executions: Spain saw 3,500 trials between 1580 and 1650. Italian execution figures range from 400 to 2,500, and recent research suggests that it may not have been as moderate a place as once thought.

The language of witchcraft, like the language of Observant reform, could be spoken by many people and be called up in many circumstances. The fact remains that it was most often spoken by highly educated elite men like Nicholas Remy with the legal, police, or ecclesiastical power to turn words into actions. This is why it makes more sense to root the hunts in elite sociology than in social pathology. It was not a panic or the kind of social pathology that the word 'craze' suggests; if anything, to oppose witches in the period of the most intense hunts (1560s–1630s) was to be enlightened, informed, and politically correct. This helps us see the witch-hunt less as something exceptional and bizarre, and more as an example of the general late medieval and early modern drive to identify and then purge enemies of the *Corpus Christianum*. It was one purgative tool among many, at a time when a wide range of tools were in use, and it took its shape and urgency from deeper fears about the devil and his work in the world. It could be wrapped readily into a compelling narrative of the threats to society, and could explain why local natural, economic, or political life had collapsed, and how the direct action of a few might redeem it.

Many were tried as witches, but fewer executed. Survivors might be saved less because they had been clearly exonerated than because there was not enough judicial evidence to prove their guilt conclusively. Yet the charge itself was so extreme that many would have been marginalized or forced to leave their communities – ostracized, exiled, or 'voluntarily' escaping the cloud of suspicion that now hung over them. The expulsion and migration of thousands, many of them women, were an uncounted and uncountable consequence of the witch-hunt.

Purgation

Expelling the Other: Jews and Muslims

In 1549, Dr. Ludovico Fioravanti was asked to help a Spanish woman who had suffered a stomach ailment for three years. He prescribed his own remedy, a form of mercury oxide he had brewed up and called *Precipitato*. Within hours 'she had vomited an enormous quantity of putrid matter, and among the things she vomited up was a huge clump, as big as a hand, and it was alive! . . . the whole city talked about it and because of it I became very famous.' Fioravanti and his fans knew that the most thorough way to purge threats from any body was by expulsion. A doctor's care of the body might involve amputating a limb or purging bad humours by drawing blood or stimulating vomiting, urination, or bowel movements. So too, it could take radical action to purge the *Corpus Christianum* of what made it sick. This extreme action would become more familiar and more common over time. Europeans would start by expelling those who were religiously alien – the Jews and Muslims – but as they became familiar with the tactic they would move progressively towards expelling other Christians who differed from them over points of doctrine. Alongside forced expulsions were the many who fled on their own, either a step ahead of authorities, or once they had survived a bruising examination or trial. But like Fioravanti's cure or bloodletting, severe purgations could seriously weaken the very bodies they meant to save.

The first Europeans to experience mass expulsion were the Jews. The English crown staged the earliest expulsion of an entire Jewish community in 1290, and in the centuries following this was a form of purgation which governments across Europe adopted. Jews were usually offered the option of converting to Christianity as a way of avoiding expulsion. Yet converts were never entirely accepted, and in many cases suspicions and persecution only increased. Moreover, many expulsions were fundamentally economic or political, targeting Jews as moneylenders. This was certainly the case in England, where King Edward I initially protected the Jews in order to borrow from and tax them, before abandoning and expelling them for political advantage.

In the aftermath of the Black Death of 1346–53, suspicion that Jews had spread the plague or were poisoning city wells triggered local expulsions from parts of France, the Holy Roman Empire, and Hungary. The pattern accelerated through the next century, as individual cities and territories expelled their Jewish communities in two major waves. The first wave from the 1420s to the 1550s saw Jews expelled from many jurisdictions in the Holy Roman Empire: from cities like Vienna (1421), Cologne (1424), Zurich (1436), and Augsburg (1438), and from territories like Bavaria (1442 and 1450) and Moravia (1454). In many of these cities, Jews were forced to abandon homes in the area bounded by the city walls, but were allowed to settle in suburban or rural communities and then continue entering the city by day to work and trade. The bounded sacred space of the city could be a workplace but not a home, since Jews carried out many of their religious rituals in their homes, and a resident community would soon demand a synagogue. In a similar way, most of these cities had long prohibited Jews from being buried within the city walls, but allowed cemeteries just outside them.

Some Jews accepted these restrictions, while others moved across the Alps to Italy where city governments interested in economic development recruited Jewish moneylenders with contracts (*condotta*) granting special privileges, like freedom from the requirement to wear an identifying sign, permission to bring communities of co-religionists with them, and even citizenship. Other Italian communities accepted the transalpine Jewish refugees, but required them to lend money to Christians at fixed lower rates, segregated them in separate areas, and required traditional coloured fabric badges or newer signs, like earrings, that would associate Jews with immorality, luxury, and vanity. These were the terms under which Jews entered Ancona (1427), Padua (1430), Perugia (1432), Florence and Siena (1439), and Assisi (1452). With regulations like these, German and Italian authorities showed that their drive to purify the *Corpus Christianum* by expelling non-Christians did not overcome their desire to keep Jews close by for economic purposes.

The second wave of expulsions occurred from the 1480s to the 1550s, and affected Jews over a far larger area. Some were expelled from the very Italian cities that had only recently recruited them, including Perugia (1485), Parma (1488), Milan (1489), and Florence (1494). In many of these, Observant preachers like Bernardino da Siena, Bernardino da Feltre, and Giacomo della Marca stirred up public opposition with harshly anti-Semitic sermons that claimed that Jewish money lending was feeding wasteful spending on luxuries and driving Christians into debt. Cities and territories of the Holy Roman Empire continued expulsions through this period, including Geneva (1490), Mecklenburg (1492), Halle (1493), Salzburg (1498), Nuremburg (1517), Regensburg (1519), Strasbourg (1520), and many others. Many of these were towns which would adopt Protestant church reforms within a few years or decades, and expel Catholic clergy and liturgies in a second stage of

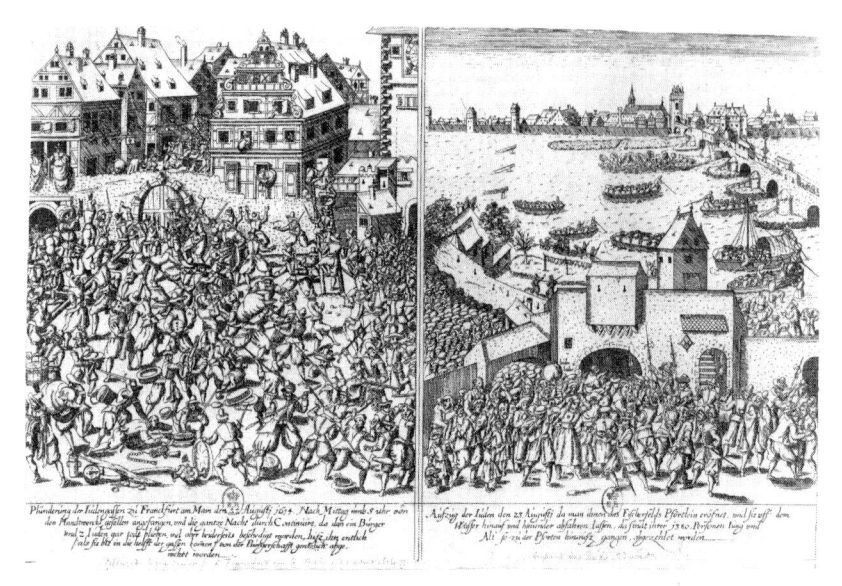

17. Jews Chased Out of Frankfurt (1614). Art Resource, NY.

religious purgation. Hundreds of Jews expelled in this period moved to Prague, centre of Hussite reform and home to one of Europe's largest communities of Jews. The doubling of Prague's Jewish community in the early sixteenth century would trigger periodic reactions and temporary expulsions (1542, 1557, 1561). This pattern repeated in Frankfurt, where rioting mobs chased Jews from the city in 1614 [Fig 17].

Yet the most dramatic and thorough expulsions in this second wave of the late fifteenth century were from Spain and Portugal, home until then to some of the largest and oldest communities of Jews in all of Europe. Violent riots in 1391 and 1415 had led many to convert and some to flee, and placed all Jews under suspicion regardless of their professed religion. 'Old Christians' suspected that the conversions of 'New Christians' were not genuine, but merely a strategy to gain access to the privileges that came with membership in the *Corpus Christianum*. They mocked the New Christians as '*conversos*' or '*marranos*' (pigs), and launched the Inquisition in 1478 specifically to hunt and prosecute false converts. Many Old Christians suspected that Spain's still considerable Jewish community secretly supported *conversos* in the faith of their ancestors, and so pressured for the removal of those who remained. Jews were expelled from Andalusia in 1483. The influential Observant friar, inquisitor, and cardinal, Ximenes de Cisneros, argued for the complete purification of Spain, and three months after conquering the last Moorish kingdom of Granada in 1492, Ferdinand and Isabella issued a decree ordering all Jews who refused to convert and be baptised to leave their kingdoms within four months. Possibly 35,000–40,000 went into exile, most of them leaving for the Ottoman Empire or Italy, while some passed over to Portugal, hoping perhaps that the order might be rescinded. Instead, the Portuguese followed with their own expulsion decree in 1497, and many thousands, reaching one tenth of the population may have left. Navarre then banned its Jews in 1498, completing the purgation of the Iberian peninsula.

The Iberian expulsions were unprecedented in scope and scale. No state had ever expelled this many of its people; by contrast, England's expulsion in 1290 had forced out 2000 Jews. There was no tacit toleration of the kind that had German cities forcing Jews to move outside the walls and settle in nearby suburbs and towns. The Iberian expulsions were national projects, undertaken for ideological reasons and against the economic self-interest of the states forcing the Jews to leave. Ottoman Sultan Beyazid II could hardly believe that Spain would deliberately savage its own economy, and gladly welcomed the refugees into his own territories. There would be more to follow as Spanish authorities extended the expulsion decrees to their territories on the Italian peninsula, including Sicily (1493), the Kingdom of Naples (1542), and Milan (1597).

Spain's purgative actions fell even more heavily on the Muslims. Perhaps half a million lived in the Moorish Kingdom of Granada before it fell in 1492. As many as 100,000 of these died or were enslaved in the military campaign, while 200,000 fled to North Africa. This left another 200,000, most of them gathered in a few enclaves. The mountainous territory of Alpujarras east of the city of Granada remained largely Islamic, and a 1492 treaty allowed Muslims to preserve their mosques, religious institutions, language, laws and customs. The first archbishop of Granada was a moderate, Hernando de Talavera (1428–1507), who promoted the official policy of segregating Christians and Muslims in separate quarters of the city without forcing conversion on the latter. This changed when Ximenes de Cisneros arrived in 1499. He promoted mass conversions and publicly burned 5,000 Arabic religious texts, triggering a rebellion in the Alpujarras which gave Ferdinand and Isabella the pretext to suspend the 1492 treaty. In 1502, Moors in Andalusia and Valencia were given the choice of baptism or exile, and after 1526 this was extended to Catalonia and Aragon as well. Spain's sorry history with the Jewish *conversos* now repeated itself with the Moorish converts, called *moriscos;* many also lived a double life, and soon also came under scrutiny of the Inquisition.

Morisco adherence to Christianity was often rudimentary, and the community preserved its identity through traditional forms of dress and diet, and through *aljamiado,* a form of Spanish written in Arabic characters. This only heightened Old Christian fears of contagion from 'false' and Islamicizing converts. In 1567, King Philip II passed an edict banning the use of Arabic script, and suppressing all Islamic traditions in religion, dress, and customs. This triggered a second rebellion in the Alpujarras (1568–70), during which the Ottomans and North African Berbers offered some military support to their embattled co-religionists. It was all the Spanish needed to justify a horrific response. Don John of Austria led a brutal suppression, slaughtering the entire population of the town of Galera east of Granada and forcing 80,000 Granadan *moriscos* north into Castile. At the same time, Old Christians from northern Spain were settled in Granada.

Complete expulsion of the *moriscos* was first proposed in 1582 in Philip II's council of state as the final solution to the problem of false Catholics in the Iberian *Corpus Christianum.* Many nobles initially opposed it, fearing the loss of farmers and skilled labourers from areas like Valencia where large regions were populated almost entirely by *moriscos.* They were promised *morisco* lands in compensation for the loss of people. At the same time, Archbishop of Valencia Juan de Ribera (1542–1611) who had initially opposed expulsion, gradually came to agree that it was the only way to completely purify and restore the land. Support for expulsion slowly grew. Between 1609 and 1614, King Philip III (r. 1598–1621) issued a series of edicts of expulsion which resulted in the departure of more than 90 percent of Spain's remaining *moriscos,* by then numbering roughly 300,000. The Kingdom of Valencia alone lost a third of its population, and nearly half of its villages were deserted by 1638 [Fig 18].

Since Spain and Portugal were Europe's first truly global empires, these 'national' expulsions extended far beyond Iberia. As we saw above, Jewish *conversos* migrated in relatively large numbers to Spain's territories in the Americas, and may have constituted the largest single group of Spanish citizens there. Yet they were followed there by the Inquisition, which targeted *conversos* in particular and burned a number of them in dramatic *autos da fe.* When the Portuguese landed in Goa, they found a mixed population of Jews, Muslims, Hindus, and Thomist Christians who traced their roots to the apostle Thomas and who used Syriac language and rituals. The Portuguese convinced the Hindu ruler of Goa to force the Jews into a ghetto, and then began systematically attacking Goa's Muslim community, burning mosques and destroying other buildings as an effort to exterminate what they saw as 'Moorish'. The Portuguese missions also targeted the large

18. Vicente Carducho, *Expulsion of the Moors from Valencia* (1627). Art Resource NY.

Hindu community with almost predictable results – 70 percent of inquisitorial activity was among Hindu converts. Yet while the Hindu community was larger, and arguably posed a greater potential threat to Portuguese Christians, the Portuguese rhetoric against Hindus never reached the level or intensity of that against Muslims and Jews.

Expulsions of Jews and Muslims from England, from cities and territories across the Holy Roman Empire, France, and Italy, and from the kingdoms in Iberia all had local triggers and particular characteristics. Different economic and political tensions shaped each one, yet they all shared a common legitimizing discourse framed in religious language. Jews and Muslims were the enemies of God and contagious aliens within the *Corpus Christianum*, and the only way to purify that Body of Christ was to expel them entirely. Some authorities were content to move them just outside the walls, while others pushed them completely offshore. Those who converted to Christianity could avoid expulsion, but in most cases remained under suspicion. This was certainly the case in Iberia, where *conversos* and *moriscos* came under increased suspicion and attack as duplicitous enemies of the faith. Jews encountered the same suspicion in Italy, in part because *conversos* headed to towns like Ancona, Livorno, Ferrara, and Venice and re-connected with

Jewish merchant communities there. Some converts attempted to blend in and reclaim their Jewish faith. Catholics considered this heresy, and in 1555 Pope Paul IV had twenty-five of these 'lapsed' *conversos* who had returned to Judaism burned in Ancona.

Forced conversions did not exactly create eager Christians, and frequent policy reversals only added to the confusion. The group known as Portuguese Jews experienced this clearly over many generations. Portugal replaced its 1497 expulsion decree with a mass campaign of forced baptisms the following year. Yet the 'New Christians' continued to live, marry, and socialize together, observed the Sabbath, Jewish festivals, and dietary laws, and remained essentially Jewish; some saw their merging of Judaism and Christianity as a fulfilment of both and superior to practicing just one or the other. King Manuel I prohibited marriages between New Christians, and until 1532 prohibited them from leaving the country. Portuguese authorities treated the *conversos* as a distinct and suspect group until the mid-eighteenth century, levying special taxes on them, dealing with them through separate community representatives, and singling them out as the primary concern of its Inquisition in 1536. This may have been because some of these *conversos* were doubly 'alien' having arrived in Portugal only after the expulsions from Spain in 1492. Under these circumstances, many had little commitment to either Catholicism or Portugal, and little incentive to develop one. When some returned to Spain in the seventeenth century, suspicions of them were so high that the Spanish Inquisition returned to hunting 'Judaizers', with Portuguese *conversos* as the most suspect group. They were certainly among the first refugees to return to the Jewish religion once they immigrated to countries that allowed it. King Francis I of France gave special protection and extensive autonomy to *converso* 'merchants of the Portuguese nation' who had fled to coastal and border towns in southwest France; some continued practicing Catholicism, some returned to Judaism, and some landed in between. As long as they were discrete in following Judaism or integrating Jewish rituals into their Christian practice, the authorities left them alone. This arrangement carried on to the early eighteenth century. When 'Portuguese' merchants showed up in English plays, Dutch towns, or German roads they were almost always Jewish *conversos*. Authorities might also deliberately turn a blind eye to what religion they practiced in private. Yet those same authorities still upheld the bans on public Jewish worship until the seventeenth century. When Amsterdam magistrates finally allowed the Sephardic community to open its first public synagogue in 1639, it was known as the Portuguese Synagogue.

Expelling the Self: Christian Migrations

Expulsion, exile, and migration became more complicated when Christendom fractured into a host of different confessional groups from the early sixteenth century: Lutherans, Calvinists, Anglicans, Catholics, Anabaptists, and a host of others with no name or fixed catechism challenged the religious unity that was critical to the ideology of the *Corpus Christianum*. The recent experience of secular and ecclesiastical authorities with Jewish 'contagion' shaped authorities' evolving responses to these new groups of Christian 'deviants'. Some religious dissidents were expelled, while the threat of prison or execution forced many more to flee.

As we look at the accelerating purgations that drew tighter religious boundaries across the European map, we have to be careful about definitions, time, and scope. Those on the move might be exiles, religious refugees, or simply migrants caught up in broader movements. They might move temporarily during some crisis and return home in a few months or a year. They might move permanently to a place that suited and supported their religious identity. They might hit the road as individuals, moving from place to place across Europe in search of some degree of religious freedom, or they might migrate in large and organized groups. These distinctions are important, yet also a bit abstract. They do not change the fundamental reality that in this period religious exile and religious refugees gradually expanded to become a mass phenomenon as much for Christians as for Jews and Muslims.

Expulsions of Jews had expanded in two waves through the fifteenth century, and expulsions of Muslims came in two waves at the beginning of the sixteenth and seventeenth centuries; in both cases the second was larger than the first. Expulsions of Christians expanded in three waves from the sixteenth to eighteenth centuries and also steadily grew in size. Beginning on a relatively small scale with some hundreds at a time fleeing in the 1520s–50s, these waves steadily expanded to affect a few thousand refugees and migrants at a time from the 1550s to the 1590s, and then hit their largest size when many thousands and even hundreds of thousands of exiles fled from the 1600s to 1750. Politics and war pushed each wave higher. Monarchs appointed themselves the defenders of particular religious creeds and confessions which were in turn identified with the character and mission of the nation itself. For at least three centuries, rulers and their officials claimed that God had appointed them to defend a national and religious creed against enemies both in and outside the

Corpus Christianum, and that this divine mission both legitimized their own rule and set a standard that their subjects had to obey.

Belief and Exile: 1520s-1550s

It began almost immediately. In traditional accounts of the Reformation, the German friar Martin Luther is seen as the catalyst to broader reform due to his expanding challenge to key Catholic doctrines in a series of wildly popular publications from 1517 to 1520. By 1521, he had fallen under a Holy Roman imperial ban for refusing to retract his views, and with his life in danger he spent almost a year as a refugee hiding in a remote castle under an assumed identity. Many individuals would similarly go into individual exile and travel around Europe seeking refuge in the years following Luther's actions. The earliest groups of refugees were those known as Radicals, Sacramentarians, or Anabaptists. In the 1520s–1540s, they pushed beyond the views of the most widely recognized reformers such as Luther and Huldrych Zwingli (1484–1531) on points having to do with scripture, with the main sacraments of baptism and communion, and with membership in the church. Two of these were Thomas Muntzer (1489–1525) and one of Luther's early allies, Andreas Karlstadt (1486–1541). When they attempted in the early 1520s to move more quickly and radically in reform than Luther wanted, they were dismissed from their positions and expelled. At roughly the same time, the diffuse groups of radical reformers in Switzerland were also forced to flee in order to avoid execution. Throughout the 1530s, many moved to Poland and Transylvania. In the period 1547–51 when Charles V was busy restoring Catholic worship across the Holy Roman Empire, Moravia (between modern-day Poland and Austria) became the destination of choice for south German, Swiss, and Austrian radical reformers. More than 1,600 settled in the town of Nikolsburg alone, though most moved out to isolated rural settlements where they could practice their faith complete with the community of goods.

German radicals were active in the Peasant's Revolt of 1524–1525, while Dutch radicals in the 1530s aimed to seize town governments in Amsterdam and Leeuwarden. Fuelled by apocalyptic rhetoric about Christ's imminent return, 2,000 of them headed to the north German town of Munster in 1534 with the vision of building a pure community. They expelled those who resisted them, but were themselves besieged, betrayed, and executed in a military campaign in 1535. Munster soon became a symbol of the radicals' revolutionary determination to overturn the existing order and usher in a new and purified Kingdom of God. They continued to be targeted as the black sheep of the broader Protestant movement, in large part because their ideas about the purity of the church led them to firmly reject traditional views of the *Corpus Christianum* as a comprehensive merging of church and state.

As the troops of the Holy Roman Empire were besieging Munster, the threat of soldiers at the door had individuals fleeing England and France. In the 1530s, Reginald Pole escaped to Italy to avoid Henry VIII's religious settlement, while John Calvin fled Francis I's crackdown on reformers by heading to a series of towns just over the Rhine River. Both worked hard from exile to shape religious affairs in their homelands. Henry's shifting and very personal policy ensured that he would have opponents across the spectrum, from the very Catholic Pole to the Bible-translating follower of John Wycliffe, Miles Coverdale, and a host in between. Some fled to Strasbourg and Wittenberg, and others to Rome. Pole was involved in a series of plots to unseat the king, and eventually returned to England as archbishop of Canterbury in Queen Mary's failed Catholic restoration of 1553–1558. Calvin followed many individual French exiles to Strasbourg and Basel and by 1541 had settled permanently in Geneva, helping turn it into a shelter that took in refugees and sent out books and missionaries. Italian Protestants began making their way to Switzerland from the 1540s, following some high-profile Italian refugees from the newly established Roman Inquisition like Bernardino Ochino, head of the observant Capuchin group within the Franciscan Order, and Peter Martyr Vermigli, an Augustinian canon from Florence. Both would soon move far beyond Switzerland and its reformers, and end their lives as refugees suspected of heresy by Protestants and Catholics alike. Other Italian refugees who followed the same path included Lelio Sozzino and his nephew Fausto, who would travel between Geneva, Rome, Basel, and Lyon before heading to Transylvania and Poland and shedding more and more standards of orthodox doctrine, above all the idea of the Trinity and Christ's divinity. The Sozzini are considered founders of Unitarianism. Many of the most radical reformers were moving continually in their thinking, and this put them continually on the road avoiding prosecution and seeking shelter.

German refugees arrived in Geneva in the late 1540s, and about 800 English refugees from the Catholic restoration of Queen Mary Tudor arrived throughout the 1550s. These so-called Marian exiles were never formally expelled from England, but simply fled for their lives. Refugee communities more than doubled the population of mid-sixteenth-century Geneva, but few stayed more than a few years, preferring either to return home like the English and Germans, or to move to larger cities in the Holy Roman Empire. There were similar short-lived communities of exiles dotting borders across

Europe, including Emden in northern Germany and the Rhine cities of Cologne, Strasbourg, and Basel. In this early stage of the Reform movement, exile and flight were common but involved relatively small numbers of people who fled for relatively short periods of time. Almost all aimed to return home to shape religious reform there, and those who did often returned with sharper views and a reduced appetite for compromise.

Politics and Exile: 1550s-1600

The numbers of religious migrants grew after the 1550s–1560s as religious identity became more closely tied to political disputes. The Religious Peace of Augsburg in 1555 allowed rulers in the Holy Roman Empire to determine whether their city or territory would be Catholic or Lutheran, but with no provision for either Calvinism or Radicalism. Elizabeth I came to the English throne in 1558 determined to govern a church that would not be subject to the Roman pope, and ruled until 1603. Simmering religious tensions in France broke out into a civil war by 1562, which consumed the country even after formal peace was declared in 1594. The Netherlands moved steadily towards rupture from the Spanish crown in a revolt that began in politics but steadily took on a religious character. In 1579, a group of southern provinces and territories confirmed their loyalty to Catholicism and Spain in the Union of Arras spurring the seven northern provinces to respond with a Protestant Union of Utrecht, which virtually declared their independence from Spain. The conclusion of the Council of Trent in 1563 settled doctrinal directions for the Catholic Church and opened a period of intense missionary and diplomatic activity, which would turn it into what was arguably the first global institution.

After the rapid and chaotic changes of the 1520s–1550s, no one could have predicted that these events in the mid-century would each in their own way set directions that would harden by 1600. In the 1550s, the religious character of each of these states, and indeed of many religious movements, was in flux. By 1600, each was firmly on the way to having a particular religious confession as a central part of its political order and national identity, with a ruling family taking personal responsibility for upholding this distinct and increasingly exclusive character. Each church or religious movement had firmer and more exclusive statements of doctrine, often written by those who had spent some time in exile. They also devised efficient means of promoting and policing these, and closer ties to political authorities. As a result of all these changes, exile was less a matter of individual conscience, and increasingly one of political reality. It also expanded in scale and impact: the numbers increased dramatically, and it was no longer sure that refugees would ever be able to return. In this second period, religious exile for European Christians came to look increasingly like what it had become for Iberian Jews and Muslims: permanent expulsion.

The largest movements came in the Netherlands. In 1566, rioters entered churches and destroyed religious icons like statutes, paintings, and stained glass windows. The so-called iconoclastic fury so terrified local Catholic magistrates that hundreds of them fled over the border into France and Germany. They received a chilly reception in most places, since their flight had essentially opened the way for Protestants to take control of government. The Spanish Crown responded by sending the duke of Alva to subdue the Netherlands in 1567, and his armies succeeded initially in restoring both order and the magistrates. Yet Alva's harshness, and his determination to restore not just Spanish political rule but also Spanish Catholic culture, gave an ever-stronger religious character to what had begun as a purely political and cultural dispute. His opponents claimed that Alva would bring the Spanish Inquisition into the Netherlands to recast the Dutch *Corpus Christianum* in an Iberian mold. Opposition grew from the 1570s. Over the following eighty years an escalating series of military campaigns alternating with treaties and alliances saw the seven northern provinces sever their allegiance to the Spanish king and Catholicism, while the six southern provinces affirmed both. In 1572, the Spanish brutally sacked Antwerp, the largest and wealthiest city in the southern Netherlands and a Protestant stronghold. When they seized it again in 1585, 150,000 refugees fled north in fear to cities controlled by Protestant councils; a smaller number of Catholics fled south. By 1579, the southern provinces had been restored to Spanish control, and within a few years the nine United Provinces to the north had consolidated their anti-Spanish and Protestant alliance. An interim settlement in 1609 and final resolution in 1648 confirmed the religio-political division into two nations, with the Spanish Netherlands having a Catholic state church, and the Dutch Republic a Protestant state church.

France's civil Wars of Religion (1562–98) saw a similar steady escalation of the stakes, although its Protestant population was never as numerous. Later called 'Huguenots', a name of uncertain origin and meaning, French Protestants were concentrated in the south where the Cathar and Waldensian heresies had originated. They included artisans, professionals, and nobles; this was the same demographic that had been drawn to the Cathars in earlier centuries. Through the course of France's sixteenth-century civil wars, the ruling family of the Valois aimed to ally with either the Catholic Guises or Huguenot Navarre family, and after three decades of brutal military campaigns, frustrated alliances, and assassinations, Henry of

19. Francois Dubois, *Massacre of St. Bartholomew Day*. Scala/White Images/Art Resource.

Navarre ended up as the military victor by 1592. His pathway there had included an ill-fated 1572 marriage alliance with the king's sister Margaret of Valois, which was meant to confirm the steady ascent of the Huguenots in city governments across France. Many leading Protestants came to Paris to celebrate the wedding, but the now-ambivalent Valois and the Catholic Guises used the occasion to plot a series of assassinations which triggered massacres of Huguenots in major cities across the country [Fig 19]. The Huguenot duc de Sully thought that 70,000 had died in what has become known as the St. Bartholmew's Day Massacre, but there are no accurate statistics, and most estimates now range from 10,000 up to 30,000. Bells rang in celebration across Catholic Europe, and Pope Gregory XIII declared it a great victory. It certainly fed the fears of Protestants across Europe that Catholic authorities were bent on their utter destruction. St. Bartholomew's Day became one of the most resonant symbols of religious division across Europe, with Catholics considering it a sign of God's favor, and Protestants a sign of Catholic treachery and violence. Henry of Navarre did eventually take the French throne as King Henry IV, but he could not take the country without converting to Catholicism. He aimed for a religious settlement resembling what Elizabeth I was working towards in England: one faith, one monarch, one law. His adoption of Catholicism in 1594 could have triggered a mass Huguenot exodus. In order to prevent this Henry IV passed the Edict of Nantes in 1598, which protected the Protestants' community by granting them about one hundred fortified towns and specific rights to public worship and legal protection.

In England, Elizabeth I came to the throne in 1558 aiming to calm political and religious divisions by restoring her father's Church of England as an institution that preserved many Catholic rituals without submitting to the Catholic pope. She faced challenges from both sides. Vocal and motivated men who had been among the 800 Marian Exiles filled Parliament and key church positions, and many wanted to apply to England the more reformed theology and independent church government that they had just experienced in Geneva, Basel, or Strasbourg. They staged serious political campaigns in 1563, 1572, and 1587 to pass the necessary Parliamentary legislation, and it took all Elizabeth's skills at persuasion, threat, and delay to hold them at bay. Large parts of the country remained firmly but discreetly Catholic. This included significant parts of the North and West, particularly in rural areas, and some key noble families. When Elizabeth's cousin, Mary Queen of Scots, came to England as a refugee after being deposed by Scottish nobles, she became an active focus for plots to restore Catholic rule in both England and Scotland. Elizabeth would finally order her execution in 1587.

Despite Elizabeth's aim for a middle way, England was seen across Europe as fundamentally in the Protestant camp, and Elizabeth's religious policies fed a steady exodus of Catholic families to the continent, where they settled in Douai, Paris, Rome, Rouen, Madrid, and Valladolid. Noble families sometimes sent their young men to Catholic schools and sheltered those who returned to England as covert missionaries. Young women also fled. Twenty-two English convents were founded on the continent from 1598, and approximately 4000 young English women would join them over the next two centuries, the majority of them in the 1610s and 1620s. Most came from families already in continental exile, and most lived in poverty. Catholic refugees supported a series of plots, diplomatic efforts, and military campaigns aimed at returning England to Catholicism. This included efforts to assassinate Elizabeth I and her successor James I; support for Spanish invasions in 1588, 1596, and 1597; and an effort by to blow up Parliament in 1605. Each failed effort increased active prosecution of Catholics in England, and fed a religious nationalism that associated Catholicism with treason and that framed England as a distinctly and exclusively Protestant nation.

In Eastern Europe, the union of Poland and Lithuania in 1569 created a vast Commonwealth which, though ostensibly Catholic, included diverse ethnic settlements of German Lutherans, Swiss, Dutch, and Italian Radicals and anti-Trinitarians, Moravian Brethren, Tartar Muslims, Ashkenazi Jews, and Ukrainian Orthodox. These all lived under the protection of nobles who were significantly more powerful than the king. While increasing numbers of nobles had turned to Protestantism by mid-century, they welcomed religious refugees primarily as a valuable source of settlers and skilled artisans. The Polish-Lithuanian Commonwealth preserved noble freedom of religion and other privileges, yet tensions over religious identity were common, and local outbreaks of violence not unknown, particularly against Radicals and Calvinists. Protestantism had never made serious inroads among the broad mass of the population, and from the 1570s the many religious minorities began fracturing. By the 1580s, Polish Protestantism was clearly in decline. The Jesuits had come to Poland in 1564, quickly establishing colleges and working with some nobles and the king to promote re-Catholicization. King Sigismund III (ruled 1587–1632), who had been raised a Catholic, began appointing only Catholics to high office, and this led many nobles to convert. By 1600, the Polish-Lithuanian Commonwealth still had many hundreds of congregations representing all varieties of Protestantism, and while there were no large-scale expulsions, the community steadily declined over the following centuries.

The map of religious confessions at the end of the sixteenth century shows an incredible variety of religious groups co-existing in large communities across Europe. There were still significant numbers of Muslims in Spain; Protestants and Hussites in Eastern Europe and France; Catholics in England, Holland, and Switzerland; Radicals in Moravia; Unitarians in Poland and Transylvania; and Jews in cities across Europe. All boundaries were blurred. Individual exile and the migrations of groups of religious refugees created a patchwork of religious communities which managed, on the whole, to preserve a practical co-existence. Within a century, the map would change radically as growing concerns about religious identity and national security would trigger Europe's bloodiest wars around dynasty, borders, and religion. With a few notable exceptions, Europe's governments and people would become remarkably less tolerant of religious diversity in the seventeenth century, and the boundaries of religion and nation would converge and become more firm and fixed.

Nation and Exile: 1600–1750s

By the turn of the seventeenth century, religious confession was becoming a fundamental feature of national identity in the states that were forming across Europe. This combination would feed a series of brutal wars over the next half century that would generate hundreds of thousands of refugees. These wars set the stage for an even longer and more deliberate series of religiously defined expulsions in the third wave that carried on to the 1730s and beyond. The drive to purge fed on itself and consumed all of Europe. From the 1590s through to the 1750s, religious leaders mounted determined missions to enforce uniform beliefs in particular regions. European governments would for the first time stage systematic 'religious cleansings' that were as wide ranging and brutal as the 'ethnic cleansings' of the twentieth century. This deliberate collaboration of church and state elites politicized and nationalized religion as never before. It introduced institutional and legal forms of segregation and intolerance that shaped attitudes and actions into the twentieth century.

The expulsions of the Moors and *Moriscos* from Spain in 1609–1614 was the first example of the period's ambitious campaigns of ethnic-religious cleansing. Many small- and large-scale purgations of Catholics and Protestants across the rest of Europe followed as the unfinished business of the Reformation. They were legitimized by discourses of purgation long after politics, security, and economy had replaced religion as the main driver of state policy, and indeed long after many elite men and women had moderated their active faith. Many of those in positions of authority believed on purely practical grounds that religious diversity weakened a nation. As the public square expanded through newspapers, coffee houses, pamphlets, rituals, and festivals, and as public opinion needed to be manipulated rather than ignored, the propaganda around religion and nationality intensified. The traditions being invented and the communities being imagined saw ethnic and religious diversity as a political problem, and not a social good.

French, English, German, and Scandinavian monarchs worked hard to eliminate diversity within their borders while working equally hard to promote it in the territories of their enemies – chiefly the Holy Roman and Spanish Empires. The Thirty Years War of 1618–48 shaped this entire period with rapidly shifting public and secret alliances between all faith groups that made a mockery of the religious causes which first triggered the disputes. A century later, the concerns motivating expulsions were more overtly strategic, but the legitimizations remained the same.

Some of the largest expulsions in this period arose out of explicit state actions which followed long periods of more subtle pressure: Spain's expulsion of Muslims in 1609–14 and France's revocation of the Edict of Nantes in 1685 follow this pattern. Others were the collateral damage or legacy of war, and the Thirty Years War of 1618–48 and England's Civil War (1642–51) are prime examples of this. Given that there were so many, and that they were driven by national concerns, we will divide them politically rather than consider all expulsions in a single chronological narrative.

Holy Roman Empire   The 1555 Religious Peace of Augsburg established the principle that it would be the rulers rather than the people who determined whether a territory would follow Catholic or Lutheran worship. These were the only two options for the over two hundred states within the empire, and the growth of Calvinism among German elites soon complicated matters. Cities with an imperial charter granting them self government, like Augsburg, Nuremburg, or Strasbourg, could allow public worship in both confessions under terms determined locally. This 'religious peace' bore little or no relation to what local populations believed, and it reinforced the power of their rulers significantly since they effectively determined the form of Christianity practiced locally. It also meant that dynastic changes in even the smallest of territories could trigger anxieties and intense negotiations across Europe. The death of a duke or king could easily start a war. Some of the bloodiest wars and harshest expulsions of the period came as part of the Thirty Years War, which was sparked by a change of monarchs in Bohemia, before sucking in virtually every European nation and devastating much of Central Europe. What began as a dispute between Protestants and Catholics in the Holy Roman Empire would develop into a much broader struggle about the balance of power between all the leading nations on the continent.

Minor violations of the Augsburg religious peace agreement accumulated through the later sixteenth century and started becoming major issues. Since Calvinism was not recognized in the Augsburg treaty, it was not clear whether a ruler who embraced Calvinism could impose this on his territory. When the Catholic archbishop of Cologne converted to Calvinism in 1583 it triggered a war because he was one of the seven electors of the Holy Roman Emperor. Since the three secular electors of the Palatinate, Saxony, and Brandenburg had already abandoned the Catholic faith, his fourth vote could potentially turn the entire empire over to the Protestant cause. Catholic rulers were particularly vigilant at protecting their religion. When the Lutheran majority in the imperial free city of Donauwurth blocked a Catholic religious procession in 1606, the Catholic duke Maximilian of Bavaria paid a rather violent visit to restore Catholic privileges.

War seemed inevitable. Protestant rulers in the Holy Roman Empire formed a protective Protestant Union (1608), and Catholics responded with the Catholic League (1609). The spark which blew everything apart landed in the large eastern territory of Bohemia, where nobles and people still defended the separate religious settlement first launched by Jan Hus 200 years before. A series of Hapsburg rulers, who had at one and the same time worn crowns as kings of Bohemia and as emperors of the Holy Roman Empire, had tolerated this in order to keep the Bohemian crown on their head and the Bohemian nation in their empire. In 1617, Ferdinand II of Austria, trained by Jesuits and determined to restore Catholicism across the Empire, was elected king of Bohemia and moved immediately to limit Protestant worship. Bohemian nobles who had already feared what policies he might follow now challenged his right to rule. In the negotiations that followed, they threw Ferdinand's representatives out of the window of Prague Castle, and instead elected as their king the Calvinist Frederick V, ruler of the territory of the Palatinate along the Rhine River. Although only twenty-two years old, Frederick V was as close to being the leader of German Protestantism as one could hope to find. He was one of the seven imperial electors, the head of the Protestant Union, and son-in-law of King James I of England. His decision to accept the Bohemian crown in 1619 triggered the war that everyone had been dreading. It was guaranteed to be violent when Ferdinand II, the man he replaced, was elected Holy Roman Emperor only three days later. Unable to get support from other Protestant rulers, Frederick now forged an alliance with the Ottomans. Turkish troops would defend the Calvinist ruler of Hussite Bohemia from Catholic soldiers. Yet before this head-scratching paradox could play out, the Holy Roman emperor's armies invaded and soundly defeated the Bohemians in the 1620 Battle of White Mountain on the outskirts of Prague.

The new king and queen barely escaped from Prague. More than 80 percent of Bohemian nobles soon followed them into exile, forfeiting their lands in the process. Bohemia went from being an elective monarchy to a hereditary Hapsburg possession. In 1621, King-Emperor Ferdinand II ordered all Calvinists to convert or leave Bohemia in three days, and in 1622 he extended this decree to Lutherans. By some accounts, over one-third of a population of three million went into exile. Spanish troops later overran even Frederick V's hereditary territory of the Palatinate, and he too died in exile. Emperor Ferdinand II went on to carry out a prolonged campaign of forced reconversion to Catholicism in Austria and Hungary, assisted by the Jesuits. With both older and newly appointed nobles, they used the strategies of selective patronage or ostracism that French and English monarchs had employed so skilfully and successfully. With the common people they combined discipline and more effective local pastoral work, including greater attention to religious exercises, rituals, and shrines. The re-Catholicization campaign would continue on to the eighteenth century and eventually turn Austria, which had a majority Protestant population in the late sixteenth century, into a strongly Catholic state. Hungary, by contrast, retained significant numbers of Calvinists and anti-Trinitarian radicals, due in part to the fact that the Ottomans favored Protestants in those parts of Hungary that they occupied.

The events in Bohemia may have triggered the Thirty Years War, but deeper political divisions fuelled its destructive path back and forth across Germany. Over the next three decades, troops and funds from Denmark, Sweden, France, Spain, England, the Netherlands, and the Ottoman Empire poured into the Holy Roman Empire, ranging widely and wreaking devastation everywhere. Catholics and Protestants fought on both sides. Alliances shifted frequently over questions of property and advantage – Ferdinand II passed an Edict of Restitution in 1629 restoring all Catholic properties seized by Protestants since 1555, but had to back down within a few years when major Protestant territories abandoned him. Yet the Thirty Years War pushed the process of re-Catholicization in the southern and eastern cities and territories of the Holy Roman Empire, both through the forced conversions of nobles, and by the forced removal of those Protestants of all classes who refused to convert. War, famine, and plague killed many, while untold numbers fled in advance of troops: 60 percent of the population of Wurttemberg disappeared, half that of Brandenburg, and a third of Bohemia. It is difficult to work out how many died and how many fled from any particular territory, but the population of the Holy Roman Empire fell by a quarter from 21 to 16 million, with the greatest collapses in the northeast and southwest where war was most intense. About two-thirds of the empire was seriously damaged socially and economically. Typhus, plague, and dysentery did their work in war-ravaged lands, but some rulers willingly depopulated particular regions in order to build what they thought would be a more coherent, unified, and loyal state.

England In the seventeenth century, England began using refugees and migrants in order to secure and develop new and troubled areas in Ireland and the Americas. In the course of that century's protracted Civil War, marked by the execution of one king and the exile of another, the monarchs were forced to accept Anglican Protestantism as a condition of rule.

Ireland was chief of the troubled areas secured by refugees and religious migrants. From the 1560s successive English governments had aimed to expand control by bringing English settlers into what were called 'plantations' that had been cleared of their Gaelic population. Settlements planted by force did not always grow, and some notable reversals included the southern province of Munster in the 1560s. The Catholic monarchs Mary and Philip had first authorized plantations in the 1550s, but from 1606 religion became a bigger factor in what had until then been a cultural fight between English settlers and the Gaelic/Celtic nobility, particularly in the northeastern province of Ulster, which the English had never controlled. In a determined push, about 125,000 settlers were shipped over to Ireland in the space of a few decades, with 80,000 sent to Ulster alone.

The native Irish rebelled in 1641. Perhaps 4–12,000 of the Protestant settlers were killed in Ulster, a figure quickly inflated to 100,000 by propagandists. Oliver Cromwell led a bloody reconquest from 1649 to 1653, and the war and punitive peace completely reshaped Ireland. Famine, plague, and war casualties killed as many as 600,000 out of a population of 1.4 million and a further 50,000 were deported. Catholic landowners and soldiers were dispossessed and fled as refugees. English, Scottish, and Welsh Protestants were settled in larger numbers, including thousands of soldiers who were given land in place of wages. Before the 1641 Rebellion, Irish Catholics had owned 60 percent of the land, but Cromwell's changes cut this to 8 percent. His controversial policies of ethnic-religious cleansing are seen by some as an early example of genocide, and the political and social ramifications reverberated for centuries.

Ireland was the closest, but not the only battlefield for England's ongoing religious civil wars. Through the sixteenth century, governments pressured Catholics into accepting the middle way settlement, but in the seventeenth they also turned against a wide range of Protestant groups who for one reason or another rejected the Church of England's privileged powers and hence were called Dissenters or Non-Conformists. Some aimed for a Genevan-style organization of religion, complete with more Calvinist doctrines and lay governance (Presbyterians); in Scotland, these signed a solemn 'Covenant' to resist Anglican forms of worship and church government. Others picked up parts of the older Radical reform tradition with its emphasis on adult baptism (Baptists), or developed new forms of Christianity which downplayed the role of clergy, abstract theology, and formal churches (Quakers). Many rejected what they considered to be continuing elements of Catholicism in the Church of England's organization, doctrine, or rituals, picking up on criticisms raised by Puritans ever since the 1560s. The English Civil War marked the high point of their influence, and particularly the period of the Commonwealth and Protectorate (1649–60) when the Church of England lost its bishops, its service book and creed, and above all its monopoly on protestant worship. The fact that the various Protestant Dissenters shared common enemies in both Catholicism and Anglicanism did not generate much toleration between them, and they joined in repressive campaigns against each other. From the 1650s to the 1680s, early Quakers like George Fox, Margaret Fell, and William Penn were widely seen as threatening, treasonous, and anarchic. They rejected church buildings, marriage ceremonies, oath-taking, and visible forms of status and hierarchy. They allowed women to preach, and the sermons of male and female Quakers were full of apocalyptic warnings that the Day of God's Judgment was coming. Under Cromwell's government, Quakers were chained in underground cells, tortured, and executed.

The tide began to turn when Cromwell died in 1658, and King Charles II was restored to the throne in 1660. The king brought back the Church of England's bishops, its Book of Common Prayer, and its Thirty-Nine Articles, while bending slightly on its monopoly. Both Charles II and his brother and successor James II were willing to tolerate some Dissenters if it meant that they could also extend toleration to Catholics. This was a purely strategic and very limited toleration: the Stuart kings rejected Puritan and Presbyterian efforts to push for more Calvinist forms of church organization and worship. They actually struck particularly hard at a rebellion among these groups in Scotland, since they blamed the Calvinist Scots for the execution of their father Charles I. In 1685, the Privy Council authorized summary execution of those rebel 'Covenanters' who refused to acknowledge the king. While relatively few were actually executed, their deaths were dramatic, including a man shot in front of his children for refusing to acknowledge any king but Jesus, and two women tied to stakes in the Solway Channel to be drowned slowly by the rising tides. The suppression triggered a new wave of religious dissenters migrating to the American colonies who kept alive the story of British religious persecution. An eighteenth-century account of the suppression in Scotland described it as 'The Killing Time' and this became – and remains – the central event in Covenanter martyrology. The British government was in fact willing to allow a degree of toleration in America in order to promote settlements there. As a result, particular religious groups promoted settlement of particular areas and gave them a distinct religious character from the beginning that tended to be reinforced by later migrations. The Massachusetts Bay colonies became attractive to Calvinist Puritans; while Pennsylvania drew Quakers, German Mennonites, Amish, and Moravian Brethren; Catholics, Jews, and Quakers settled in Rhode Island, and Catholics moved to Maryland.

The idea that many of America's founders and early settlers came in search of religious freedom is largely an invented tradition. Distinctions between religious refugees and migrants quickly blurred in these colonies, and indeed most settlers had mixed motives for immigrating. Perhaps 21,000 had moved to the New England colonies in the first stage of Puritan migration from 1620 to 1640 when Charles I and the Church of England were making life difficult for Dissenters in England. Yet even more migrants were moving at the same time to colonies in the Caribbean and along the southern seaboard like Virginia. As new settlements opened up along the Atlantic seaboard, such as Delaware (1638), New Jersey (1660), the Carolinas (1653, 1670), and Pennsylvania (1682), settlers sought both religious toleration and economic stability. In some cases, the intolerance that they fought against was that of other religious refugees in America: New Hampshire began as a refuge from the religious intolerance of early settlers in Massachusetts Bay.

For two hundred years, Ireland and America would be the destination of most of Britain's religious migrants. As England's imperial reach expanded throughout this period, the tensions between the monarchs and the aristocracy came to be framed in particularly religious terms, with ongoing geopolitical results. The extended civil-religious war that had sent English puritans overseas from the 1620s to the 1640s, continued smouldering underground after the deaths of Charles I (1649) and Oliver Cromwell (1658). It complicated the Restoration of Charles II in 1660, and burst back into open flame in the 1670s and 1680s. King James II had converted to Catholicism long before his accession to the throne, and in 1688 his Catholic wife gave birth to a male heir. All too well aware of what had happened to their continental counterparts when powerful Catholic kings curbed noble privileges, some of England's most powerful aristocrats engineered a palace coup. They sent the king into exile and installed as queen and king his daughter Mary from an earlier marriage together with her husband William of Orange, the titular head of the Dutch Republic. In the 1690 Battle of the Boyne north of Dublin, William of Orange successfully repulsed James II's effort to return, and gave Ulster's Protestants the hero and holiday that Orangemen would turn into a powerful emblem in the nineteenth and twentieth centuries. Recently exiled French Huguenots were prominent among the officers in King William's army and among the pastors and bishops that he installed in Ireland in the years following his victory. They argued hard for suppressing Catholic worship and stripping Catholics of their lands and offices. They demonstrated no desire to bridge the confessional difference or the tensions generated through over a century of forced deportations, plantations, and civil war, and the legacy of their actions helped keep Ireland's religious divisions raw until today.

The so-called Glorious Revolution that deposed Catholic James II in favour of Protestant William and Mary was justified by supporters as necessary to protect 'liberty' in politics and religion. It included strict laws reinforcing the social and political status of the Church of England. No one could sit in parliament, graduate from Oxford or Cambridge, or enjoy various other privileges without being a full member of the Church of England. Monarchs were prohibited from marrying Catholics, a rule not lifted until the twenty-first century. An intense educational and propaganda effort followed. Babies learned from their nursery rhymes ('Rock a Bye Baby' commented on the male heir born to James II) and adults from their prints, popular songs, and commemorative teacups that England was a decidedly Protestant nation. The campaign was as intense and successful as the re-Catholicization campaigns then underway in Poland, Austria, and France, and turned England's Protestantism from a political position to cornerstone of popular patriotism.

It would not be easy to maintain this Protestant dynastic identity over the following decades, particularly when Mary and her sister Anne, who followed her as monarch, both died without heirs. Rather than allow James II's male heir to succeed, the British government looked to the continent for a new king and dynasty. The most eligible Protestant dynasty in Europe was in the German territory of Hanover, where Elizabeth, daughter of James I and widow of Frederick II, the short-lived king of Bohemia, had finally settled. It was stretching imagination to assert that the foreign and German-speaking George I was a more legitimate king of England than James Francis Edward Stuart, son of the deposed James II, and so the propaganda campaign emphasized Protestant purity over royal genealogy. James's son, Bonnie Prince Charlie, led an unsuccessful revolt from Scotland in 1745 and remained active in plots after that time.

Ongoing anxiety in London over the Stuart threat and Catholic loyalty became a factor leading to the last large religiously influenced expulsion of our period. From 1755 to 1760, more than 11,000 Acadians from the modern Canadian Maritime provinces were deported to other British colonies or to England, France, and French Louisiana. Acadians had fought with the French against the British in their protracted American wars, and the British believed that deportation was the only way to handle a group which, for ethnic and religious reasons, would not assimilate into the British Empire. This made the Acadians the last of the long line of Reformation refugees. By 1760, the

British forced the French out of Quebec, and the decision to grant a significant degree of self-government and religious toleration to the 70,000 Quebecois marked the start of a new British policy of handling ethno-religious difference within the Empire.

France When Henry IV converted to Catholicism, he was well positioned to use privileges and legal guarantees to bring Huguenots and Catholics together in a single French state religion. After he was assassinated by a Catholic priest in 1610, French Huguenots began worrying about the fate of the 1598 Edict of Nantes by which he had guaranteed their security. His widow and son soon began a process of re-Catholicization, pushing the Huguenots into open rebellion by 1620. A string of defeats ended in the 1628 loss of their main port city of La Rochelle after a fourteen-month siege that had left it with only a fifth of its earlier population. King Louis XIII and his chief advisor Cardinal Richelieu claimed that with the rebellion the Huguenots had forfeited their right to have separate fortified towns and armies, and they moved to further curb the anomaly of a separate and protected Huguenot state within the French nation. A small but steady number of Huguenots aimed to follow the example of English Puritans and voluntarily emigrated either to French colonies or to other parts of Europe. For a while a disproportionate number of settlers in New France were Huguenot, but the French Crown feared for their loyalty, and so tried to prevent their further immigration. It banned public Huguenot worship altogether in New France in 1627 and 1659.

Throughout the course of the seventeenth century, French kings followed the example of England, Austria, and Poland, and shut out nobles and professionals who failed to follow the monarch's religion. This led many ambitious Huguenots to convert and/or marry into Catholic families, thereby robbing the minority community of its political and intellectual leadership. After decades of steadily limiting Huguenot civil rights and pressuring for conversions, Louis XIV formally revoked the Edict of Nantes in 1685. This abolished all the rights guaranteed by Henry IV, gave Huguenot clergy two weeks to leave France (though without children over age seven), required that all Huguenot schools be dissolved and churches destroyed, prohibited Huguenots from gathering on pain of confiscation of goods by the state, and forced Catholic baptism on all newborns. It also prohibited Huguenots from emigrating, although in fact anywhere from 150,000 of a total Huguenot population of about 730,000 did leave France over the next few years, moving mainly to Switzerland, the Netherlands, England, German territories, the Americas, and South Africa. Huguenot watchmakers turned up in Geneva, glassmakers in Denmark, silk weavers and financiers in London, and army officers in England and Prussia. Persecution of Huguenots in France carried on for century, including a military crusade against isolated communities in the southern Cevennes Mountains (1702–05), until Louis XVI again granted toleration in 1787. Protestants only gained formal equal rights as French citizens in the 1789 Declaration of the Rights of Man and of the Citizen.

Hungary and Transylvania   After their victory at Mohacs in 1526, the Ottomans took the central part of Hungary, leaving a small Hapsburg client kingdom bordering Austria to the north, and a larger Transylvanian Principality with its own Diet to the east. Despite some early anti-Protestant legislation, the Hungarian Diets of 1557 and 1572 allowed toleration of Lutheran, Catholic, Calvinist, Unitarian, and Orthodox worship in a rare example of legal confessional pluralism. By the end of the sixteenth century, both Transylvania and lower Austria were about 70–80 percent Protestant, with a political class and intelligentsia oriented towards Calvinism. The strong Saxon community remained Lutheran, but the Ottomans favored Calvinists in part because both shared a common enemy in the Hapsburg Emperors. Under Ottoman supremacy, followers of different confessions sometimes shared single church buildings, and in 1639 the town council of Kosice (where three Jesuits had been killed two decades earlier) forbade religious debates in order to foster co-existence.

Imperial politics brought an end to this formal co-existence while also preventing full confessionalization. From the early seventeenth century, the noble Esterhazy family pushed a re-Catholicization campaign that targeted all opponents and denounced toleration itself as heretical. They worked primarily with the Jesuits and particularly with Peter Pazmany, a compelling missionary and former Calvinist noble who had converted to Catholicism and then joined the Society of Jesus. The Transylvanian vassal princes were able to play off various sides throughout the Thirty Years War and so increase their practical independence, but Ottoman control tightened again after the 1648 Peace of Westphalia. The Ottomans failed to take Vienna in a siege of 1683, and by the end of the century they had been forced out of Southern Hungary and Transylvania. In 1692, the Habsburgs closed Calvinist churches, banned Calvinist catechisms, and sent Protestant clergy to prison or the galleys. Yet the intensity of their re-Catholicization campaign triggered a Hungarian uprising in 1705–1711. Though they were able to regain control, the Hapsburgs then scaled back the campaign and allowed some discrete toleration until a formal Decree of Toleration in 1781.

20. Anonymous, *Expulsion of the Jews from Vienna* (1670). Art Resource NY

Austria Seventeenth-century Austria had a sizeable Protestant population, but a series of monarchs like the Hapsburg emperor Ferdinand II were determined to re-Catholicize their ancestral territory. Forms of coexistence emerged in some major cities like Vienna, where from 1577 Lutheran believers could walk outside the city walls to worship in a church which a group of nobles had purchased. In Salzburg, the archbishop held both spiritual power as a cleric and secular power as a prince, but the area that he ruled over was occupied by many thousands of Lutheran peasants. As many as 100,000 Protestants were displaced from Austria generally in the first decade of the Thirty Years War, and after the 1648 Peace of Westphalia the Jesuits mobilized a re-Catholicization campaign in the Salzburg area. Vienna's Jews were expelled in 1670 [Fig 20]. Missionary pressure led some Protestants to outwardly conform while continuing secretly to practice their own faith. Jesuit priests went on house-to-house visits to find and burn Protestant books, and there were a few small-scale expulsions in the 1680s. At this time they also began to expand the number of confraternities in the region, and particularly those promoting public processions or the use of outward signs of Catholic devotion, like the rosary (a string of beads used to order cycles of personal prayer) or the scapulary (two rectangular pieces of cloth joined to be worn like a cape on the chest and back). The confraternities were used to find and expose secret Protestants, triggering sharp responses like the peasant who declared openly, 'I shit on the scapulary.'

At the lay level, both sides had accommodated each other for practical reasons for a long time, and some even migrated back and forth. Some of the Protestants even blended Catholic rituals like the rosary into their own religious practice. Yet authorities found this intolerable, and more intense investigations to root out Protestants began in 1727. Local Catholic shopkeepers and artisans protested without success that this was bad for business. In 1731, the archbishop of Salzburg gave the Protestants six months to leave, and over the next three years 20,000 exiles moved north through Germany to settle in Prussia, where they were welcomed by the Calvinist duke-elector. It was a Protestant cause célèbre, with more than 300 works published in Germany in 1732–1733 alone denouncing the archbishop's action. Propagandists predictably exaggerated the situation, with many comparisons to the Exodus of the Israelites from Egypt. Yet the refugees did have to leave practically everything behind, and their departure left whole districts around Salzburg virtually deserted. They could take barely a tenth of their belongings, which were estimated at 2.5 million thalers. This windfall may help explain some of the motivations behind the last major religious expulsion to occur in continental Europe.

The sense of community and threat that developed through the fifteenth and sixteenth centuries resulted in a wide range of responses. The four responses considered here – separation, enclosure, prosecution, and purgation – were driven by mixed motives but shared a common religious legitimizing discourse. These four responses underscore the intensity of their sense of the *Corpus Christianum* and the depths of their fears of the enemy and the alien. Yet they do not exhaust the forms and meaning of the Reformation – it was far richer and more varied. Others have written of the Reformation's more positive legacies in the form of representative political systems, spiritual and social psychological developments, and artistic innovations. To explore the more restrictive and negative sides of it here is not to suggest that the Reformation was itself entirely restrictive and negative, but rather to seek some means of understanding the question we started out with: why does religious exile become a mass phenomenon in this period? Why are so many individuals turned into refugees or involuntary migrants on account of religion?

Exploring the complicated dynamics driving religious exile and expulsion also underscores three central realities. First, these expulsions were most often the results of strategic actions by small elites working for their immediate advantage. They seldom reflected broadly held animosities, at least at the beginning of our period. Second, although religious differences motivated the expulsions, it was governments who carried them out. Third, the expulsions and forced migrations did not decline in scale and scope over time, but grew. Tens of thousands at a time were being exiled in the 1490s, the 1570s, the 1610s, the 1680s, the 1730s, and the 1750s. There was no steady progress of religious toleration from the Reformation into the Enlightenment. If anything, the experiences of early refugees were refracted and expanded over the decades. They became part of invented traditions, legal settlements, and political campaigns that led to much larger expulsions of hundreds of thousands at a time. We may be right to be sceptical about the numbers, which propagandists regularly inflated. And we may question how intensely the late seventeenth- and eighteenth-century elites behind the expulsions actually felt about the religious issues of the sixteenth century. At a certain critical level, the *Corpus Christianum* was evolving into the body politic of the nation-state. Yet the fact remains that religious language remained a powerful touchstone which authorities drew on deliberately and effectively. Well into the eighteenth century, authorities made this language central to their rhetoric and propaganda. They used arguments of religious purity, identity, and contagion to legitimate the purgative expulsion of populations on a major scale. It is sobering to realize that contemporaries often knew that the purgations would immediately and demonstrably harm the national economy, yet they persisted in undertaking this radical surgery on the social body.

Forced migration was a fundamental reality of the late medieval and early modern periods. But what other realities did it spawn? How did it shape people, and the places they were forced to?

3

DIVIDING THE BODY: PEOPLE AND PLACES

RELIGIOUSLY DRIVEN EXILE MAY HAVE EMERGED AS A MASS phenomenon in the early modern period, but how did individuals experience it? What was it like to look at the world from the position of the religious refugee? By comparing the experiences of a range of individuals from across different faiths, we can begin to put a human face on what was often an inhuman tragedy. Some weathered this better than others, and all were deeply marked by it. In many cases, removal was not a one-time thing. Some moved frequently in search of a place that would allow them to build a community. Others found that community and turned it into a test case for ideas and an incubator for missionary activity. Some were in constant motion physically because they were in constant motion intellectually, moving from one creed to another in search of something that reflected their deepest convictions. Women often had less freedom to move, and so it is important to consider the experience of those who did not manage to escape, particularly since their followers later wrote powerful accounts turning them into martyrs for the cause.

Refugees and exiles needed shelter, and after having considered some of those who fled, we will look at a range of the places that they travelled to. Some of these places were relatively open, but others quite closed. In most cases their own recent history shaped the way these cities or territories responded to the waves of exiles and refugees who appeared at their gates. Cities with a history of accepting strangers continued absorbing these new groups, though usually with some effort to control where and how they would live. Other cities and territories became shelters for a particular group, and slowly turned into fortresses of that group's orthodoxy – their own exile past did not prevent them from expelling others in turn. Some refugee cities adopted rules without rigorously enforcing them, and so developed gradually into open, international, and often quite prosperous centers.

Both the refugees and their refuges were fundamentally changed by the dynamics of religiously driven exile. It was the key factor shaping the ideas of some of the most influential thinkers of the early modern period, and it would also direct the political and economic development of cities around the Mediterranean, in continental Europe, and in America.

People

Migration was a common and expected experience for many thinkers and writers, who often needed to travel for education and for professional work. As religious tensions sharpened from the late fifteenth century, some of these migrations became a way to preserve life and not just pursue opportunity. Almost all of the major thinkers who shaped Christian theology in the period were themselves shaped in some way by a period of forced migration or exile. For some, like Martin Luther, it was a brief episode of a few months. For many like John Calvin it was a permanent relocation to a different city. For yet others like Menno Simons, it became a way of life, as they spent the rest of their lives being chased from one refuge to another. Experiences like this profoundly shaped their ideas about purity and purgation, and their biographies inspired generations of followers. In this context, it is worth also considering those who did not make it – that is, those whose execution for heresy made them both a cautionary example and also an inspiration. Some Muslim writers were forced suddenly into exile, while most Jewish thinkers had for centuries been forced to accept migration as an almost permanent condition.

In order to explore the refugee experience comparatively, we will look at how forced migration affected a few individuals from different faith communities, either through expulsion and exile, or as refugees, or through execution. Isaac and Judah Leon Abravanel were wealthy secularized Jewish exiles from Spain, while Juan Luis Vives was a Catholic humanist who carefully hid his *converso* identity and refused numerous invitations to return to Spain. Al-Hasan Ibn Muhammad al-Wazan al-Fasi was an Andalusian aristocrat who moved around Africa and the Mediterranean and between Islam and Christianity. Luther and Calvin highlighted purity and purgation in their thinking in ways which we might trace back to their exile experience. Mary Ward was influential less for her writings than her actions, as were Elizabeth Dirks, Janneken Munstdorp, Joan Waste, and Rose Allyn, women who chose martyrdom rather than flight and whose choices and experiences shaped the worldview of many of their co-religionists. Adam Neuser was a pastor who began travelling as his thinking about purity moved from Calvinism to Radical anti-Trinitarianism to Islam.

This is not meant to be a comprehensive review of ideas, but rather a selective singling out of themes related to forced migration and the refugee experience in the lives of a diverse group of people: how might we see these experiences, and the ideas of purgation, in their work and lives? Coming from many backgrounds and experiences, through words and actions, in treatises, poems, and travel accounts, we can see how exile profoundly shaped the lives of early modern people. Some embraced purgation, some rejected it, and some travelled along a path of perpetually purging themselves.

Isaac (1437–1508) and Judah Leon (1460–1535) Abravanel: Jewish Exiles

When Jews in Salonika repeated the Ladino proverb 'it is sufficient that my name is Abravanel' they signalled the continuing prominence of an Iberian Jewish family that claimed descent from the ancient Israelite king David. Abravanels had been prominent Iberian tax collectors, financiers, and royal treasurers since the thirteenth century. Their forced migrations around and beyond the Mediterranean from the fourteenth to the seventeenth centuries track the experiences of many Jews from the peninsula. The Andalusian royal treasurer Samuel Abravanel was forcibly converted in the anti-Jewish riots of 1391, but his son Judah fled to Portugal where he returned to Judaism and filled a series of important financial positions. Judah's son Isaac was born in Lisbon but eventually moved to Castile where he handled finances for Ferdinand and Isabella until 1492, when he was swept up in what he later described as 'the bitter and hasty exile and forced conversions when we were exiled from Spain'. With his three sons, Isaac moved first to Naples, then Sicily and Corfu before settling in Venice in 1503.

Exile freed Isaac Abravanel to study Torah and to write, and also gave a sharp Messianic thrust to his pen: the sufferings that God visited on the Jews through forced conversions and expulsions only sharpened his sense of the Jews' divine destiny. In a series of influential works and scriptural commentaries, Isaac criticized those who gave in to their own despair or to the Catholic priests who promised peace through the water of Christian baptism. He called on the Jews in diaspora to remain true to their faith and to the hope of a Messiah who would come soon to save his people. The Messianic tradition would prove particularly strong among Sephardic Jews who, like many Christian and Muslim exiles, saw their dispersal in communities across the Mediterranean basin as a sign of judgment, a test of faith, and a source of hope.

Isaac's writings circulated largely within the Jewish diaspora, while Judah's reached a Christian audience as well. The father is sometimes considered the last of the great medieval Jewish commentators, and the son as one of the first of the early modern Jewish philosophers. Known to Italians as Leone Ebreo, or 'Leo the Jew', Judah Leon had been a doctor to Ferdinand and Isabella before being caught up in the 1492 deportations. Hearing of a plot to hold his infant son hostage and force the family's conversion, he quickly dispatched the boy to Lisbon, but the child was seized and forcibly baptized. Robbed of his son, Judah Leon left for Naples with the rest of his family, and then moved around Italy to Genoa, Venice, Tuscany, and possibly Rome. There was nothing abstract about his suffering, which he expressed in sharp poetry haunted with the loss of his infant son:

> Time with his pointed shafts has hit my heart
> and split my guts, laid open my entrails,
> landed me a blow that will not heal
> knocked me down, left me in lasting pain . . .
> He did not stop at whirling me around,
> exiling me while yet my days were green
> sending me stumbling, drunk, to roam the world . . .
> He scattered everyone I care for northward,
> eastward, or to the west, so that
> I have no rest from constant thinking, planning—
> and never a moment's peace, for all my plans.

Exile led Isaac Abravanel to write of hope, and it led his son Judah Leon to write of love; both resisted despair. Judah Leon's major work, the *Dialogues of Love* brings together a mature male philosopher Philo and a female student of philosophy Sophia to discuss love as both a cosmic and a sensual principle. Their engagement is intellectual and witty, and Philo clearly hopes that it will be fulfilled physically. Judah Leon may also have written a now-lost text *On the Harmony of the Spheres* and dedicated it to Pico della Mirandola, a well-known advocate of syncretism. He had clearly absorbed both the dialogic form and neo-Platonic values of late Renaissance Italian humanism. While his father's commentaries preserved traditional Jewish wisdom, Judah Leon's neo-Platonic dialogues suggested a greater open-ness to the idea of a perennial wisdom which incorporated and transcended all particular theological and philosophical schools – the very project that many Renaissance humanists like Pico della Mirandola and Marsilio Ficino advocated, and that thinkers of the seventeenth and eighteenth centuries would offer as a challenge to narrower definitions of religious purity.

Judah Leon aimed to demonstrate that Jewish ideas could be found at the source of later western traditions, and he challenged the tendency of many Catholic commentators to find prophecies or foreshadowings of Christ in Old Testament scripture. He cast the universe as a living and dynamic organism through which the Creator allowed some to encounter divine love and beauty. The world and humanity were not defined by how far they fell short of divine perfection, but rather by how much they themselves could be paths towards it. It would be hard to find a more complete repudiation of the contemporary ethic which emphasized purity through purgation, and aimed to protect communities from "polluting" natural or human phenomena. Judah Leon's vision distanced him from many contemporary Jewish and Christian thinkers, including his own father. Yet we know from the many vernacular translations of the *Dialogues of Love* that he had admiring readers across Europe. Elements of his thinking can be found in the natural philosophers of the seventeenth century, and in the Amsterdam *converso* Baruch Spinoza, who owned a copy of Judah's *Dialogues*.

Juan Luis Vives (1493–1540) Converso *Humanist*

A homeland should be 'where life passes quietly and peacefully ... where justice, peace, and concord are revered'. But what happens if it is 'where one citizen harasses another or a newcomer; where one curious or trouble-making neighbor annoys another; where one's spirit is disturbed by a relative, a friend, a slight acquaintance, or an utter stranger, and one is torn from his repose. It is not only impossible to endure this; to see it is so revolting that many prefer to abandon their houses and their homeland, which have also been those of their forefathers, and to go away to distant lands.'

The man who wrote this left his hometown of Valencia at age sixteen to study in Paris. Although he became a leading European intellectual and was frequently invited to return home to take up a university position, he never felt it safe to travel to Spain. And no wonder: his father was burned by the Inquisition as a heretic in 1524, and his mother's bones were dug up four years later and burned as well. His brother likewise fled Spain for a career as a prominent diplomat and courtier with Holy Roman Emperor Charles V, but even that strong family connection provided no protection. It was not Vives' humanist ideas that caused a problem, but rather his Jewish ancestry.

Juan Luis Vives was one of the leading humanists of the early sixteenth century, a friend and equal of Erasmus and Thomas More. Like them, Vives wrote many works on education, literature, theology, and social philosophy that combined humanist methods and values with Christian theology in order to shape a new and reformed Catholicism. He sharply criticised Aristotelian dialectics and metaphysics, and any scholastic theology that was built with them. Like many humanist reformers, he found Plato and the Stoics more in keeping with a Christian morality that blended the natural inclination to goodness and truth with fundamental gospel truths. Not surprisingly, he argued for a philosophy that was clear and direct, leading to practical moral knowledge. For this reason, he favored history as a practical guide for reforming individuals and society. His writings circulated widely, and many moderate Catholic reformers picked up his ideas and methods through the course of the sixteenth century.

Vives' scholarship won him an invitation to a professorship at the University of Alcalá, where he could have ended up teaching a young Ignatius Loyola. Yet the invitation came as the Inquisition was investigating his father, and Juan Luis was afraid to go. Vives' parents were Jewish *conversos*, his mother having converted only a year before the expulsion of the Jews from Spain, which was also the year when he was born. Although his parents raised Vives as a Catholic, they retained a deep attachment to Judaism, and his father was arrested and investigated a few times as a suspected 'Judaizer', that is, a Catholic convert who secretly practiced and promoted Judaism. Some Spanish Catholics thought that converts should repudiate their Jewish past, but many *conversos* resisted this. Some continued practicing Jewish rituals secretly, while others simply believed that their Jewishness gave them a stronger direct link to Christ.

Tensions between the Old Catholic and *converso* communities were higher or lower in different parts of Spain, and triggered different responses. Many *conversos* fled when they learned that the Inquisition was about to be introduced locally, with the result that even the high percentage of *conversos* prosecuted in particular cities during Vives' youth – more than 90 percent in Barcelona and Valencia – underestimates the real impact. Laws from the same time enforcing 'purity of the blood' (*limpieza de sangre*) kept those who had even distant Jewish ancestors out of public office, the nobility, the church, and government. Authorities did not always enforce these pure blood laws strictly. The Royal Council rejected an effort by the archbishop of Toledo to adopt one in his cathedral in 1547, and the University of Salamanca refused to adopt the laws in 1562. At the same time, the purity laws set a chill across Spain, and the climate of fear led many into reluctant exile or deep denial. Vives covered up his own *converso* heritage so thoroughly that it remained unknown until the twentieth century.

Vives never returned to Spain or to Judaism, but he did keep up his expatriate connections. He married a *converso* woman in Bruges, maintained close contacts with other Iberian and *converso* exile theologians across Europe, and wrote *Instruction of a Christian Woman* (1523) for Henry VIII's Spanish wife, Katherine of Aragon, as a guide to training the young princess Mary. He supported Katherine when Henry VIII was negotiating for an annulment, and this led to his being arrested and then expelled from England in 1528. He later wrote a passionate denunciation of war (*On Concord and Discord in Humankind*, 1529), a thorough discussion of educational reform (*On the Disciplines*, 1531), and a systematic account of his theological views that was published three years after his death (*On the Truth of the Christian Faith*, 1543). Vives advocated social and religious reform in these works, following a moderate Catholic line that emphasized piety, morality, and the coherence of the *Corpus Christianum* – all things he looked for in his ideal homeland.

Although Vives did not advocate purgative or schismatic reform in church matters, he was the first influential advocate of enclosure as the means of disciplining and reforming the poor. His most widely influential work was a short piece proposing more rational and humane ways by which cities could care for their poor. *On Assistance to the Poor* (1526) argued that city magistrates should systematically survey the urban poor, organize alms collection, and then shape relief according to the particular needs of poor individuals and families. Protective enclosures could shelter and educate orphans, while enclosed workhouses could get the older poor working towards their own maintenance and the city's economic profit. As we will see in Chapter 4, Vives' plan to enclose the poor and force them to work echoed Thomas More's *Utopia* (1516), but his plan was more practical and became particularly influential because it was published at a time when poverty was increasing due to economic stagnation, population increase, and increased migration. Vives wrote his plan for the magistrates of the Flemish towns of Bruges and Ypres in 1526, but translations into French, Italian, Spanish, Latin, and German quickly appeared, and versions of the plan were adopted in Lyon in 1534 and Bologna in 1563. Civic plans for poor relief multiplied rapidly in Europe throughout the sixteenth century, and most followed Vives' prescriptions for expelling foreigners and enclosing locals, particularly orphans and women. Enclosure became the new and progressive method for effectively handling abandoned boys and girls, single poor women, prostitutes, and others. Vives gave it a protective and educative side that reflected his humanist and moderate Catholic beliefs. He believed that poverty was a form of deviance which could be solved by character-shaping discipline. It is ironic and puzzling that an exile like Vives would propose expelling foreigners who had fallen on hard times, but as we will see below, this is not the only paradox that we confront among those who were forcibly converted or exiled.

Al-Hasan Ibn Muhammad al-Wazan al-Fasi (c.1494–c.1554): Muslim Aristocrat and Catholic Convert

Al-Hasan al-Wazan migrated often and far, beginning shortly after his birth. Some of his travels were voluntary but most were not. Perhaps appropriately, his final travels took him completely out of the historical record – we simply do not know where he went or when he died. He was born in Granada shortly after the Spanish conquest, and by some accounts his mother was a Jewish convert to Islam. The family soon joined the diaspora that saw many thousands of Granadan Muslims cross to North Africa. They relocated to Fez, where an uncle served in the sultan's court. His uncle's influence secured a university education and a place in court for al-Hasan al-Wazan, and when barely a teenager he travelled with the uncle on diplomatic missions into the Maghreb to Timbuktu. At twenty-one he went on his own to the Ottoman court in Istanbul. He witnessed the Ottoman conquest of Mamluke Egypt in 1517, and travelled further into Egypt and into Arabia before turning for home in 1518. He never arrived. Catholic corsair pirates working with the crusading Order of St. John out of the island of Rhodes seized the ship and imprisoned its passengers. When they realized that the twenty-four-year-old boy was a university-educated diplomat from a prominent Moorish family, they bundled him off to Rome where, after a short stay in the papal prison of Castel San Angelo he was presented to Pope Leo X.

The next stage of al-Hasan al-Wazan's life is the most dramatic and certainly the best documented, though at the same time the most puzzling. In 1520 al-Hasan al-Wazan converted to Catholicism and was baptized by Pope Leo X himself with the Latin name of Joannes Leo de Medici; most people in Rome referred to him simply as Giovanni Leone. His baptismal name combined the pope's birth name and papal name, and signified that he was Leo X's personal project. He certainly was famous: a contemporary Italian portrait of a humanist is taken by some to be an image of him, although this cannot be confirmed [Fig 21]. More than simply a convert to Catholicism, he was a potential intelligence asset at a time when the pope feared that the Ottomans would attack Italy from their new territories along the North African coast.

What the name and Catholicism as a whole signified to al-Hasan al-Wazan is anyone's guess. He translated the epistles of St. Paul into Arabic in 1521, although his later writings and actions make it clear that his 'conversion' was a strategic and not a spiritual act. Conversion freed him from prison and opened doors across Italy. It also set the stage for his most

21. Sebastiano del Piombo, *Portrait of a Humanist* (reputedly Al-Hazan al-Wazzan) (1520). Courtesy National Gallery of Art (Washington).

famous work, the *Description of Africa* (*Della descrittione dell'Africa et delle cose notabili che lui sono*), whose popularity led many to call him 'Leo Africanus'. Al-Hasan al-Wazan wrote this after a few years of travelling around Italy, during which he lived with a family of Jewish Iberian exiles in Bologna and wrote some other works on Arabic medicine and grammar. He returned to Rome in 1526, where Giulio de' Medici had taken the papal throne as Clement VII. He completed the *Description of Africa* under Pope Clement's patronage, though it would only be published in Venice in 1550. It was republished frequently and quickly translated into Latin, French, English, Dutch – all nations that negotiated and traded heavily with North African rulers.

Europeans could read many ancient Romans and medieval travellers on Africa, but there were few contemporary studies of the interior apart from some Portuguese travel accounts. Leo Africanus wrote mainly about Morocco, Fez, and Sudan. He focused on geography, history, ethnography, and politics, and his account of Timbuktu as a fabulously wealthy but remote and inaccessible city fed European imaginations into the nineteenth century. The *Description of Africa* conveyed both his diplomatic travels across North Africa, and also his earlier literary training in Fez, and in this way also conveyed to Europeans some earlier Islamic learning. It is hard to tell how much invention frames the facts, although Al-Hazan al-Wazzan had absorbed the lessons of European travel writers ranging from Marco Polo to the legendary John Mandeville. He was certainly aware that his exotic novelty as a prisoner and convert drew fame and readers. In the text he emphasizes that his roots are in Granada and Fez, and European readers took the book as an account by one of those rarest of prizes: a Muslim convert to Christianity. This undoubtedly increased his book's appeal.

Al-Hazan al-Wazzan disappeared just before some of Charles V's unpaid and restless German mercenaries sacked Rome in 1527. Although some later authorities claimed that he remained in Rome, contemporary correspondence suggests that he most likely returned to Tunis and Islam. He may later have journeyed to Fez, although there is no record of him in either place, or anywhere else for that matter. His seems not to have realized his oft-stated goal of writing an account of Europe for Muslims.

Martin Luther (1483–1546): Observant Reformer

The time that Martin Luther spent as a refugee was relatively brief – a little under a year following the 1521 Diet of Worms, where he had been placed under an Imperial ban for refusing to recant his writings. And his was a protective exile. Luther's ruler Elector Frederick of Saxony hustled him to the remote Wartburg Castle, where Luther took on the identity of a knight. Luther was a refugee, but not in any real danger, and when he felt compelled to return to Wittenberg, he was free to go. He left because he feared that the more radical reforms being pursued in his absence by Andreas Karlstadt would jeopardize the entire reform movement. It was purging time again, although this time it would be his own lieutenant that he would force into exile.

Luther began as an Observant and kept to that ethos even after he broke with the Catholic Church. His initial conversion came out of fears that his sins would send him to hell and that he needed to follow the rules of the Catholic faith more purely. Abandoning his legal studies and joining an Augustinian Observant monastery in Wittenberg was a personal purging of sorts, and one that allowed him to get a fresh start on life by undergoing ordination. Luther could have joined any one of a number of religious orders, and he was no doubt drawn to the Observants because of their strong emphasis on personal and social purgation. He followed the Observance movement's bodily purges with such extreme fasting and vigils that he likely damaged his health permanently. Yet Luther began to believe that the problem was not his alone: the whole Body of Christ was sick, and it needed an even more radical purging. The rules, rituals, and institutions of the Catholic faith were just so much waste needing to be flushed away. From this point, he was an Observant about the means, but not the ends, of reform.

Two themes stand out in Luther's early theology: one was a purgative impulse, and the other was the dynamic of Freedom and Captivity. These are not doctrines, but intellectual themes and rhetorical strategies that come up repeatedly in his works. We can certainly trace the purgative impulse in almost everything he writes, from the early purging of indulgences, on to the progressive purging of the status and powers of the clergy up to and including the pope, to the elimination of most of the sacraments from the rituals of faith, and the removal of the Latin language from the mass. Although he rejected violent iconoclasm, even the saints were effectively exiled by his reforms, stripped of their role as patrons of believers and go-betweens with God, and left only as spiritual models.

Unlike many Catholic Observants, but together with most Protestant reformers ranging from Karlstadt to Calvin to Menno, Luther believed that indulgences, clerical privileges, rituals, and icons were not a sign of corruption but a sign of evil. The answer was not to correct details, but to purge the entire theological apparatus. In the first decade of his polemical writings, when his books and pamphlets comprised up to half and more of *all* titles sold in Germany, Luther was busy purging the Catholic Church in the most radical simplification of Christian faith possible. The key to it all, and the most powerful purgative in Dr. Luther's medical bag, was his doctrine of *Sola Scriptura*, or Scripture Alone, as the final authority for faith and practice.

This was a bold and absolute position to take, and it may have helped that Luther was not the first one to take it. Reformers since Wycliffe and Hus a century earlier had emphasized scripture pure and simple, and advocated vernacular translations that would allow common laypeople to bypass the clergy and absorb the Word of God directly. Humanists across Europe similarly emphasized returning to ancient and purer texts for their wisdom. Some favoured the writings of Livy and Cicero, others the works of Church Fathers Origen and Jerome, and yet others the Prophecies of Jeremiah and Letters of Paul. It took no particular boldness to argue for a return to classical sources, and in fact anyone who did not advocate it in some way would have been seen as a bit of a dullard and behind the times.

Luther's purgative radicalism lay in the adjective 'alone'. Arguing for Scripture Alone cut cleanly through centuries of Catholic theology, history, and doctrinal discussion and rendered their results beside the point – whether those results were a celibate clergy, a plenary indulgence, or a powerful pope. Scripture Alone demands an intellectual leap back to the first years of the church, when all that mattered was the gospel or 'evangel'; hence Luther and his followers embraced the term 'Evangelical' with a passion. What they took from scripture were the allied doctrines of Grace Alone and Faith Alone. Grace Alone means that only Christ's forgiveness (grace) can wipe out sins and restore a relationship with God. Faith Alone means a believer can never earn this forgiveness through any kind of ritual observances or heroic personal efforts of endurance or self-denial like fasting, pilgrimages, or prayer vigils, but only by having faith in Jesus Christ.

The dynamic of Freedom and Captivity is another recurring theme of Luther's early sermons and writings. It shapes three famous tracts of 1520 that sketched his basic ideas. In *The Babylonian Captivity of the Church*, Luther condemns the clergy for holding the church and believers hostage with their claim that the seven sacraments (baptism, confirmation, confession, communion, marriage, ordination, and last rites) provided the only access to grace, and that the clergy themselves are the only ones who can provide access to these sacraments. In *An Address to the Christian Nobility of the German Nation*, Luther appeals to the experience and ambition of the nobles by claiming that they must batter down the three theological walls that clergy have built to protect their privileges. This first is the claim that the church's spiritual power is greater than rulers' temporal power, the second is the claim that only the pope can interpret scripture with authority, and the third is the claim that only the pope can call a council to reform the church. Luther argues that scripture provides no shred of support for any of these walls, and so nobles must tear down all three in order to free both the Christian religion and Christian believers. In *The Freedom of the Christian*, he argues for the paradox that true spiritual freedom lies in surrendering oneself completely in order to follow Christ. In the upside down world of faith, freedom lay in captivity. A 1520 image by the famous artist Lucas Cranach depicts Luther as a monk, but with these three tracts he was moving beyond simple Observantism and purging Catholicism beyond recognition [Fig 22].

Luther lived another twenty-five years after he was effectively sentenced to death at the Diet of Worms, and would develop his ideas at considerable length and sophistication. Yet it was his early works, written when he was essentially under the threat of exile and execution, which captured the greatest readership and had the most dramatic effects. So dramatic in fact, that within a decade of being banned at Worms, Luther felt compelled to turn purgation against those who had considered themselves his followers. His early follower Andreas Karlstadt was exiled from Wittenberg for

22. Lucas Cranach the Elder, Martin Luther as an Augustinian Monk (1520). Erich Lessing/Art Resource.

moving too far, too fast, and too violently. The extent and pace of plans by Karlstadt and other radical reformers like Thomas Muntzer to purge images, statues, liturgies, clerical training and robes, and even celibacy alarmed him, even though he had provided both these reformers with their inspiration. Similarly, Luther would soon disown those peasants and townsmen who cited him in the manifestos they wrote as part of the great Peasants Revolt in 1524 and 1525; Luther condemned rebels as contagious rabid dogs fit for slaughter. He dismissed Radicals as a pollution. Erasmus he tossed off as yesterday's man, and other influential civic reformers like Huldrych Zwingli and Johannes Oecolampadius he rejected as though they were heretics. By 1543, Luther was arguing that Jews who refused to embrace his evangelical gospel message should have their synagogues, homes, and books burned, their rabbis executed, and their money confiscated, and then be sent to rural labour.

Some see Luther's turning on old allies and sharp attack on critics or enemies as signs that he was either a hypocrite or a canny strategist who always sensed which way the wind was blowing and quickly tacked towards the authorities who would promote him. Those motivations may have existed to some degree, although Luther could be an appallingly bad strategist. His virulent purgative rhetoric became more extreme towards the end of his life when fears and frustrations began to mount, yet Luther's last battles reflected some early fundamental convictions. Believers are caught between good and evil, God and the devil, and the choices that they face are black and white – and ultimate.

Elizabeth Dirks (d. 1549), Janneken Munstdorp (d. 1573), Joan Waste (d. 1557), and Rose Allyn (d. 1558): Female Martyrs

No religious confession offered a serious public role to women, although local crises might give one or another exceptional woman a voice and a hearing. Protestantism deliberately removed almost all distinctly female elements from faith and practice, such as the community of female saints and the network of female convents. St. Margaret had guided women through pregnancy, St. Mary Magdalen guaranteed that mis-steps early in life could be remedied, and St. Anne, mother of the Virgin Mary was revered by Christians and Muslims alike for her mystic spirituality and the hope she offered that even older women could bear children. Although not all women entered convents voluntarily or on equal terms, these religious communities offered opportunities for study, writing, administrative work, and collective charitable activity with other women, duties that few could carry out if they were married and raising children under a husband's authority. Patrician abbesses like Caritas Pirckheimer (1467–1532), abbess of Nuremburg's St. Clara convent, controlled large estates and resources, while Italian nuns like Lucrezia Orsina Vizzana and Maria Clemente Ruoti had the freedom within convent walls to develop their gifts as composers and dramatists. While they disagreed on many things, Protestants were united in removing any special role for these saints and nuns.

Judaism, Islam, and Protestantism brought women's religious and cultural expression more exclusively into the domestic household. This made women vitally responsible for maintaining important religious traditions and rituals. Among families forced into exile or conversion, women's domestic activities were critical to survival. When a Jewish or Muslim mother cooked food, made clothes, lit candles, and ritually cleaned the house before major holy days, she was preserving and transmitting the family's culture and religious identity. If the mother was *converso* or *morisco*, the stakes were even higher, and the challenge of passing on the rituals of faith was even more vital. Mothers could merge Christian identity with Jewish or Muslim, or submerge it under them. Having a domestic rather than a public role did not eliminate women's influence, but it did reduce the ways in which they could serve as inspirations, guides, and mentors to other women and to men.

The circumstances of persecution offered an exception, which the printing press made the most of. From the mid-sixteenth century, Protestant authors in particular began publishing lengthy martyrologies which dramatized the pious lives and holy deaths of women and men who had been drowned, burned, or beheaded for their beliefs. Unlike Catholic saints, these martyrs could not intercede or answer prayers, but they could and did inspire. And many were women: a woman dying for her faith was more exceptional since women were considered to be weak and inconstant. Similarly, killing a woman for her faith was considered exceptionally cowardly and treacherous, a side to the story that martyrologies never failed to emphasize.

Elizabeth Dirks was a Frisian girl sent to a convent by her noble family. Hearing of the execution of a local Anabaptist, she began studying the Latin New Testament and was drawn to radicalism. A year in convent prison failed to shake her convictions, and she fled disguised as a milkmaid, taking shelter with an Anabaptist family. She worked and taught with Menno Simons, and may have been the first Mennonite deaconess; those who captured her in January 1549 took her to be Menno's wife. The arrest launched months of interrogation. As reported in *The Bloody Theater or Martyr's Mirror* (1660) by Thieleman van Braght (1625–64), Elizabeth parried firmly and intelligently with her interrogators, and their exchanges show a woman with a sure grasp on scripture and doctrine, calmly confident, firmly pacifist, and not in the least intimidated by their power and authority. Failing to convince her, they turned to torture in order to get the names of her accomplices. The thumbscrews tightened till the blood squirted out of her fingers, but she never betrayed her faith or fellow believers. After two months she was executed in the fashion that some authorities reserved for those radicals, like Elizabeth, who had been re-baptized: she was sewn alive into a sack and thrown into the river – the so-called third baptism of drowning.

Janneken Munstdorp's story also appears in the *Martyr's Mirror*, told not in a recreation of her interrogation but in the form of letters she wrote to her infant daughter, her parents, and her sister in 1573 while awaiting execution. The daughter had saved her life, or at least prevented the pregnant Janneken from being burned together with her husband Hans (whose letter to his wife also forms part of the corpus). Janneken wrote of the lessons of Christ, the words of the New Testament, and the example of the martyrs of the early church. She urged her daughter to remain true to God's truth and will until death: 'always join those that seek to fear the Lord from the heart, and be not conformed to the world, to do as she does, nor walk in any improper course of life ... nor have fellowship with the unfruitful works of darkness.' Being faithful to God and to the example of her martyred parents Hans and Janneken would be the surest way to be reunited with them: 'flesh and blood must remain on the posts and on the stake... do you also follow us my dear lamb, that you too may come where we shall be, and that we may find one another here.... Let it be your glory that we did not die for any evil doing, and strive to do likewise, though they should also seek to kill you ... adieu my dearest upon earth; adieu and nothing more; adieu, follow me; adieu and farewell.'

Another famous martyrology was John Foxe's *Book of Martyrs*, which appeared in a series of editions from 1559 and included many stories of women executed for their faith. Though born blind, Joan Waste of Derby earned enough by knitting to buy a New Testament, and then went to find others who could read it to her, paying them if necessary. She memorized large sections, and from scriptures and daily sermons became a committed Protestant. Only nineteen when Queen Mary restored Catholic worship in England, Joan's absence from the mass caught the attention of church authorities who arrested and questioned her. Through five weeks of interrogation, she turned the tables on the examining clerics with a defense that played on the stereotype of women being weak and ignorant. She offered to agree to their position on the sacrament of communion if they would prove it from scriptures, and also promise to take on her punishment at the Last Judgment should their position be wrong. They refused and had her burned.

Foxe also wrote of Rose Allyn, whose parents William and Anne Munt were visited by officials bent on asking why the family was not attending Catholic worship, and above all the mass. One of the officials stopped the twenty-year old Rose as she was bringing a candle and a pitcher of water to her ill mother. Taking the candle and gripping her wrist tightly, he began interrogating her while holding the candle to her hand, burning the flesh 'till the very sinews cracked asunder' and yelling, 'why whore, wilt thou not cry?' Rose took this calmly but firmly, neither striking the official nor renouncing her faith, but taunting him, 'if ye think it good, begin at the feet and burn the head also.' This is precisely what the officials did, burning Rose, her father and mother, and seven others in a single day in the town of Colchester. Early editions of Foxe's *Book of Martyrs* included a woodcut of the scene, complete with an image of the martyrs being burned in the background [Fig 23].

Martyrologies catechized, inspired, and gave a script to follow. They could empower women with examples, words, and sheer indignation. Like the earlier saints' lives, they might invent narratives rather than record actual events, although Reformation authors went to great pains to emphasize that

23. Rose Allyn from Foxe's *Actes and Monuments* (1563).
Courtesy of the Thomas Fisher Rare Book Library, University of Toronto.

they were writing histories and not holy legends. Their biographies lacked the kinds of miracles which instructed Catholic readers of the *Golden Legend* that St. Anne, or St. Lucy, or St. Margaret had God's favor and God's ear and would be able to act in response to a woman's prayer. Protestant martyrologies often featured women acting courageously both in and outside of domestic contexts – they defied unbelieving husbands, comforted those in prison for the faith, and upbraided Catholic priests. In that sense, their example of placing faith ahead of patriarchy disrupted social norms as much as early Catholic martyrs did. Yet the martyrologies also modelled the appropriate uses and limits of disruptive behaviour: Dirks, Munstdorp, Waste, and Allyn demonstrated that the great learning of holy Protestant women did not bring pride. They remained respectful, calm, and confident. They submitted to authority even to the point of death, secure in the belief that they were obeying God's higher authority, and never responding violently even when provoked. This rhetoric of the calm response was a script for other women to follow. It was a lesson not only for women, but also for those men who might argue that educating women only led them to get puffed up, abrasive, and rebellious.

John Calvin (1509–1564): Legal Thinker and Reluctant Refugee

Unlike Luther, John Calvin spent most of his life as an exile or refugee. It clearly had a profound impact on his thought and practice. Like Luther, he had an early legal training and was part of a community of reformers in Paris that included some prominent figures like the University of Paris rector, Nicholas Cop. The group scattered when royal persecution picked up in 1533, and Calvin headed just over the border to Strasbourg and then Basel where communities of educated religious refugees could be found. In Basel, he completed and published the first edition of the *Institution of Christian Religion* (usually known simply as the *Institutes*), a short book that he would expand through seven subsequent editions over the coming two decades. These later volumes of the *Institutes* tracked the evolution of his thinking as he read and studied and also as he lived the life of an exile responsible for the wellbeing of other exiles.

Always an exile, Calvin never moved far from the borders of France or took his eyes off that kingdom. Drawn to Geneva in 1536 by the prospect of steering its budding reform movement, he was expelled two years later when his proposed Church Order proved more purgative than the Genevans could stomach. Three years later in 1541 they called him back, knowing now what strong medicine was in store. He did not lack for serious enemies locally, at least until 1555, and this may have shaped his disinclination to compromise.

If Luther comes back so often to the theme of purgation, Calvin instead frames his thinking around the experience of the exile. The historian Heiko Oberman saw him as a refugee theologian above all, and many of his key doctrines resonate with this experience. The doctrine most associated with Calvin is the doctrine of predestination, which Calvin preferred to think of as a doctrine of election, or being 'chosen' by God. This distinction may seem too subtle and rhetorical, but Calvin was not arguing abstractly that some individuals win an eternal lottery before they even draw breath. He wrote pastorally to give confidence that God chooses and protects his people. Election gives no guarantee of a happy life free of difficulty on earth, but it does offer confidence that God is ultimately in charge and that the chosen will enjoy eternal life in heaven. God's promise ensures that a believer cannot 'lose' salvation. Many of these themes are familiar from Judaism, and Calvin saw election as the extension of the Jewish idea of having a covenant relationship with God. Given the allied idea that God disciplines the ones he loves, election pretty much guaranteed a difficult life; Jewish thinkers certainly made the same point. Later Calvinists framed this even more securely: the grace of God that selected believers was irresistible, and a believer once safely in the refuge of the elect could not be harmed or thrown out again, but would persevere. This was more than most refugees could count on in their lives on earth, Calvin himself included, but it was what they certainly hoped for and took comfort in when things got difficult.

To emphasize Calvin's pastoral intent behind election is not to claim that he was equally sensitive in exploring its implications. He criticised those who avoided persecution and exile by going underground or by living a life of outward conformity to religious doctrines that they did not believe in. Drawing an image from the story of the Jewish religious leader Nicodemus who came to talk with Jesus under cover of night, he dismissed such people as 'Nicodemites'. The reality of religious dissimulation could be found across the religious spectrum at this time, from *conversos* and *moriscos* in Iberia to closet Catholics in England under Elizabeth, and discretely transalpine Protestant students attending universities across France and Italy. For all of these people, persecution was a real and present threat, and Calvin was not particularly sympathetic to their difficulties in balancing faith and life.

The Nicodemite charge is the pungent point of a broader reality that could come with the doctrine of election. Once you believe yourself to be Chosen, it is hard to think that you might be seriously wrong on other details of faith and life. This was true to some extent of Calvin himself. Yet the Calvinist reputation for self-righteousness and inflexibility arises more from the actions of Calvinist communities that developed across Europe, the Americas, and in South Africa than from Calvin himself who, admittedly, was not as colourful or human a character as Luther.

The exile reality emerges in Calvin's emphasis on the order and self-sufficiency of the Christian community. As we will see below, his *Ecclesiastical Ordinances*, with their stiff discipline exercised by a consistory determined to mould believers, shaped Geneva and went on to provide models for Calvinist diasporic churches (often called 'Stranger Churches') in London, Berlin, Amsterdam, and elsewhere. Calvin's legal training and appreciation for a political order may have been a factor here, since he was building through the *Ecclesiastical Ordinances* a church which could survive apart from government support and involvement. Order was centred in the consistory, which contained within itself the human resources for preaching (pastors), education (teachers), discipline (elders), and charity (deacons). This independence from the oversight of a council, duke, or king made Calvinism a hard sell in territories where a strong government organized, protected, and ultimately controlled a state church. Yet it did provide a model of separation, self-government, and social discipline which fit the needs of refugee groups, migrant communities, or the many Calvinist congregations in France,

Hungary, Poland, England or Scotland that existed as minorities in tension or at war with their monarchs.

It was in most places a minority creed. Omitted from the 1555 Religious Peace of Augsburg, rejected by Elizabeth I as a model for her rejuvenated Church of England, feared, defeated, and eventually suppressed by a series of French monarchs and Holy Roman Emperors, and a particular target of re-Catholicization campaigns in Poland, Hungary, and Transylvania, Calvinism was the form of Protestantism which paradoxically had perhaps the greatest respect for political order and yet the greatest difficulty winning political acceptance. In the Netherlands and Switzerland, the existence of Calvinist state churches, *de jure* or *de facto*, was offset by decentralized political regimes. Only in Scotland, South Africa, and parts of America did Calvinism gain significant political or cultural dominance, and in these places the elements of Calvin's thinking that arose out of the exile reality – election, separation, purity, and purgation – shaped regimes which sometimes created many refugees, exiles, or separated and marginalized communities of their own.

Mary Ward (1585–1645): Active Apostle

Being a Catholic forced Mary Ward out of England as a child, and then brought her back again in the last years of her life. In the years between, she negotiated her place within the Catholic Church as a female and a refugee, both fulfilling and also falling foul of the church's more determined approach to religious reform and particularly its effort to purify itself by enclosing nuns more tightly in convents. Catholic authorities would prove even more vigilant than English Protestants in aiming to curb or eliminate Ward's female communities. Yet the women who worked with Ward persisted despite repeated bouts of exile and migration, and eventually won approval for an order dedicated to helping the marginalized, outcast, and persecuted.

Ward's family suffered persecution in England, and had their house burned down around them by a Protestant mob. Yet she only left England at age twenty-one, heading to a convent of Poor Clares in France. A few years later in 1609, she led a group of young nuns out of the enclosure and into a new model of religious community based around a school for girls. Taking the Society of Jesus as her model, Ward established Institutes of the Blessed Virgin Mary, which gathered women who wished to exercise charity in communities that were free of enclosure, religious habits, and the frequent singing of religious offices. Like the Jesuits, they opened schools to train young people in a humanist and Catholic curriculum. They also practiced the intense set of prayers, meditations, and Spiritual Exercises framed by

Ignatius Loyola in 1522–1524, and which spread through print and schools to revolutionize lay spirituality in the Catholic Church. Ward opened Institutes in Flanders, Austria, Italy, and Bavaria, with significant help from local state and church authorities.

Young women and older widows living in informal communities had long offered charity through direct action on city streets. Beguines in Flanders, the *pinzochere* in Italy, and the first Ursulines in Italy and France all expressed many Catholic women's desires to be active and public missionaries. Authorities in all religious confessions were suspicious of such 'independent women' and aimed to force them into marriage or more strictly regulated and enclosed communities. These sixteenth century developments cast a shadow over Mary Ward's Institutes. Few at the time shared Ward's conviction that women were the spiritual and intellectual equals of men. The Jesuits did not return Ward's open appreciation for their work. The fact that many called her 'the Jesuitess' only irked the Society of Jesus, which unlike the Franciscans and Dominicans had quite strenuously resisted establishing any female order at all. Ward was summoned to Rome in 1629 to defend her work, and a year later was ordered to shut down the relatively 'open' Institutes.

Did this feel like another expulsion? Ward remained in Rome through the 1630s, and then decided to return to England in 1639, armed with a letter from Pope Urban VIII to Charles I's Catholic Queen, Henrietta Maria. It was perhaps the worst time to move home: England was poised on the edge of two decades of chaos that would include a bloody civil war, the execution of Charles I, elimination of the British monarchy, and a widespread flowering of Protestant radicalism. The chaos led many to think that they were living through the apocalyptic end times before the Last Judgment. A woman on the margins of a society in chaos had some practical freedom to operate, but as London became increasingly dangerous, Ward moved her community north to York in 1642. When she died a few years later, she was buried in a rural Anglican church where 'the vicar was honest enough to be bribed.' The coyly vague epitaph on her tomb summed up an ecumenical mission which had won her support even from some local Protestants: *To love the poor / presever in the same / live, dy and rise with / them was all the ayme / of Mary Ward.*

The execution of Charles I in 1649 and establishment of a firmly Protestant Commonwealth pushed the members of Ward's Institute to Paris by 1650. Some migrated elsewhere in Europe, where they came to be known as the 'English Ladies'. The restoration of monarchy under Charles II in 1660 would eventually allow a group to return to London in 1669 to open a school, and a few then moved to York in 1686 to open the Bar Convent. Their work in promoting Catholic education and charity in the context of

Ignatian spirituality would eventually be accepted when Pope Clement IX approved the group and Mary Ward's original rule in 1703. Yet because her work had been formally suppressed by Catholic authorities in 1631, they had to operate under another name and without formal recognition of Ward as the founder until 1909.

Adam Neuser (ca. 1530–1576): Towards Islam

Conversions to Islam were not uncommon among Catholics and Protestants, though the circumstances were often telling. Sailors and passengers captured by Barbary pirates in the Mediterranean were encouraged to convert in order to win their freedom. Some did, and many of these so-called renegades then went on to build and sail pirate ships out of Algiers or Tunis to prey on French, Italian, or English boats. Christian women captured in the Balkans or Greece sometimes married their captors and, while Islamic law and Ottoman practice required the husband to allow his wife to continue practicing her religion, her conditions improved if she converted. Yet not all conversions were opportunistic or forced in this way, and a steady stream of Protestant refugees found their way to Islam and usually to Istanbul.

It was most often religious radicals who took this route, and they usually took it after they had begun doubting the central Christian doctrine of the Trinity. Was Jesus both a human being and God? Asking this question brought them to the very borders of the Christian faith. Intense persecution by civic and religious authorities then forced them to the borders of Christendom as well. Protestants may have been particularly vigorous in prosecuting anti-Trinitarianism because it frequently arose within reform groups. Yet there was a longer humanist tradition of it as well that was active in Catholic circles. Some refugees like Bernardino Ochino, Michael Servetus, or Giordano Bruno who fled Italy or Spain found little attraction or welcome in cities like Geneva or Protestant territories such as England, usually because they had begun questioning Trinitarian orthodoxy. For a time in the mid-sixteenth century, anti-Trinitarians could find a degree of toleration only in some parts of Eastern Europe. Fausto and Lelio Sozzino, who gave the name of 'Socinianism' to what later became known as Unitarianism, moved from Siena in Italy north through Geneva, and on towards Poland and Transylvania. Being on the fringes of the Christian faith and on the fringes of Christendom, some anti-Trinitarians stepped over the borders and into the world of Islam as the only way of escaping an inevitable death sentence.

'If I had not been a Calvinist, I should never have come to this.' Adam Neuser was a popular preacher in the important Calvinist city of Heidelberg whose path to Islam led through prison and the threat of execution. He was in Heidelberg during the 1560s when groups representing Lutheran, Zwinglian, and Calvinist confessions were fighting over theological differences. Among these was the Swiss doctor and university professor Thomas Erastus, who promoted Zwingli's ideas on the sacraments and Church Order. Neuser became persuaded by Erastus' view that the state should take a major role in running the church, including matters of discipline. Both of them argued against local Calvinists who wanted a Genevan-style church order in which a consistory of pastors and elders would closely probe the personal convictions of their flock for heresy, and withhold sacraments from those who strayed from formally adopted Confessions. The Heidelberg Calvinists won this fight, and quickly charged both Erastus and Neuser with denying the Trinity. Erastus denied the accusation, while Neuser and another pastor, Johann Sylvan, could not. Sylvan in particular had already been moving in this direction, helped in part by studying the works of Jewish scholars. In 1570, he removed all doubt about his views by publishing a work with the provocative title, *The Ancient Faith of the One True God ... Against the Three-Person Idol and Two-Natured False Deity of the Antichrist*.

Neuser and Sylvan attempted to flee east to Transylvania, but their letters seeking refuge were intercepted, and they were imprisoned. The Heidelberg magistrates beheaded Sylvan in the city marketplace, but Neuser escaped prison twice, very likely thanks to some sympathetic collaborators. On the second escape, he managed to make it to Transylvania. By 1572 he had crossed the border to Istanbul and Islam. His route is difficult to follow since it is obscured by the claims of later historians who may have invented documents to build a case against him. Some argue that he went to Istanbul as a spy, others that he was forced to convert there out of self-preservation, like those captured by Barbary pirates. Others claimed that this destination was the natural outcome for a renegade who had preached heresy in Germany, plotted with Polish anti-Trinitarians against the Holy Roman Empire, and written to Ottoman Sultan Selim II seeking refuge.

Our clearest account of Neuser's path comes from Stephen Gerlach, a Lutheran pastor to an Austrian diplomat in Istanbul from 1573 to 1578. Gerlach's diary describes a large circle of German converts to Islam in the city, with Neuser as their very active leader. Some served as go-betweens and interpreters between Ottoman authorities and Hapsburg diplomats and traders. Gerlach repeats Neuser's comment about Calvinism having led him to Islam, and certainly its emphasis on God's absolute sovereignty could have opened this route. That was the accusation made by many later anti-Calvinists who picked up on the monotheism implicit in Calvin's emphasis on the Covenant, and who claimed that Calvin was reviving the fourth-century anti-Trinitarian Arian heresy.

But Calvinism was not the only route to Islam. Another member of Istanbul's circle of central European expatriates was Murad b. Abdullah, who wrote more openly about his own conversion. Raised a Protestant in Hungary, he described conversion to Islam as a rational process based on deep study of the scriptures that convinced him both that God was one and not a Trinity, and that at least some Protestants obscured this truth when translating the Bible into their vernaculars. Murad was drawn to the idea of God's supreme one-ness and Christ's complete humanity, and also to the conviction that scriptures should never be translated but only studied in their original tongue. He came to believe that the Ottomans marked the culmination of God's divine plan of universal history. The Ottoman Empire rather than the Holy Roman Empire was the true successor to the ancient Roman Empire, which was itself the fourth of the four monarchies prophesied in the Old Testament book of Daniel. Service to the Ottoman Empire and its sultan was thus service to the One True God in fulfilment of the ultimate World Empire.

In a landscape of shifting religious and political boundaries, it is not farfetched that the Rev. Adam Neuser would have found a similar route to Islam. He died in Istanbul in 1576 after a serious illness, which some claimed was divine judgment on his apostasy. It is telling that civic and religious authorities in the Holy Roman Empire used his premature death, together with some forged letters, to discredit Neuser and paint anti-Trinitarianism not as simply one theological position among many, but as dangerous heresy and treason.

As we compare these individuals we see that for all their differences, the common thing holding them together is an experience of exile which shapes fundamentally how they see the world. Some like Judah Leon Abravanel, Al-Hasan al-Wazan, and Adam Neuser balance multiple possibilities or evolve in their thinking. For some, like Juan Luis Vives or Martin Luther, exile is a reality which exists as a historical event in their background and gives a particular character to their way of dealing with later challenges in life. Vives remains very cautious and even defensive, while Luther becomes ever more radically purgative. For others like Isaac Abravanel, John Calvin, and Mary Ward, exile defines the horizon of their experience and sets the limits of the possible – their entire lives are devoted to working within its limitations and working out its possibilities. Some of those considered here never get the chance to flee. The kinds of unorthodox or unacceptable beliefs which sent the others into exile are the beliefs which send Elizabeth Dirks, Janneken Munstdorp, Joan Waste, and Rose Allyn to their deaths.

Places

Exiles, refugees, and migrants needed a place to go. They typically headed for a town or city to find allies, anonymity, or a community to blend into. Most of their chosen destinations were on a border or coast or river that made them easy to reach. In many cases, recent wars or upheavals had overturned older power structures and traditions in these places. At the same time, no place became a destination for refugees without political authorities approving it, either directly or tacitly. Some refuge centers were highly developed, and others were practically bare ground. By looking briefly at nine of them, we can compare some of the different dynamics at work. In Salonika, Istanbul, and Algiers, Ottoman authorities welcomed refugees and integrated them into their traditional forms of governing different ethnic and religious groups. In Venice, Basel, and Amsterdam, tensions between local government and outside state and church powers broke down usual restraints and allowed an opening that the local authorities then fostered. In Munster, Geneva, and the Massachusetts Bay Colony, refugees themselves pushed hard to implement their own vision for a new society, sometimes overwhelming local communities, and creating new waves of refugees by their own firm determination to purify and purge.

Salonika and Istanbul

Some cities became refugee centers because political authorities deliberately steered exiles towards them. This was the case with Salonika (also known as Thessaloniki), a major port on the northern coast of the Aegean Sea. Founded by the Macedonians in the fourth century BCE, it was well located for both trade and agriculture, and prospered under the Romans. Its early Jewish community included some who converted to Christianity and then sheltered the Apostle Paul after he had been thrown out of Philippi. The Ottomans took it without a fight in 1387 before briefly losing control again to the Byzantine emperor. Sultan Murad II mounted a siege in 1422, and while many in the city were quite willing to surrender a second time, the Orthodox archbishop organized resistance. When Murad II finally broke through in 1430, his troops completely sacked the city and enslaved its inhabitants as a lesson to others. Some Greeks returned over the decades that followed, but Murad II moved in large numbers of Muslims from Anatolia to rebuild and repopulate the city. This followed the longstanding Ottoman practice of *sürgün*, which transferred whole populations to designated cities to repopulate them or provide border security, usually after a war or conquest.

The Muslim colonists rebuilt the devastated city as an Islamic center, with mosques, minarets, schools, and charitable institutions. By the late fifteenth century, the population of 10,000 was perhaps a quarter of what it had been before Murad II's siege, and was divided evenly between Muslims and Christians. This rapidly changed after Jewish exiles arrived from Spanish crown territories in Iberia, Sicily, Sardinia, and the kingdom of Naples in the 1490s. Sultan Bayezid II invited them to enter the Ottoman Empire, and directed them specifically to Salonika, Istanbul, and Izmir under the policy of *sürgün*. Within a couple of decades, Salonika tripled in size to 30,000 with Iberian Sephardim comprising fully half the population. Jews expelled from Provence and Navarre soon followed. The refugees moved into streets and homes that had been abandoned since the siege of 1430, and within a couple of decades built two dozen synagogues. The three faith communities occupied distinct spaces within the city. Muslims took the neighbourhoods on the hills, Greeks concentrated in the western end of the city, and Jews occupied the tight and congested spaces of the Old Town. Arriving with significant capital and trading connections, the Jewish community transformed Salonika into a wealthy port, which became a key centre of Mediterranean trade and a critical source of taxes for the Ottomans.

Arriving en masse and in such dominant numbers, the Sephardim held on to their Spanish customs, language, and rituals. Some considered Salonika a new promised land, and saw themselves as divinely chosen to settle and shape it, completely outnumbering both the small existing Jewish population and the Ashkenazim who arrived later. Children learned a form of Spanish using Hebrew characters (known as *ladino* or *judezmo*) that had been common among Iberian Jews, and religious and scholarly texts were translated into it. While Jewish traders, artisans, and sailors used this common *ladino* vernacular as a working lingua franca incorporating Turkish, Greek, Arabic and other influences, there was great pride among Sephardic elites in also speaking a pure Castilian that amazed Spanish visitors centuries later.

The Ottomans governed minority religious groups like the Jews and Greek Christians according to the *millet* system. The sultan recognized a single head over the community, often drawn from the ranks of its religious leaders, and charged him with overseeing justice, tax collection, and religious affairs. As in other parts of Europe, sumptuary laws reinforced ethnic, religious, and cultural distinctions. Under Ottoman rule, Jews wore yellow turbans, Christians blue, and Muslims white. So long as they paid their taxes, kept a low profile, deferred to Muslim officials, and never did anything that might be seen as an insult to Muslims or Islam generally, members of other religious groups could govern themselves. Salonika's Sephardim seem not to have had a single leader, or at least not for long, and the community was completely fractured along the lines of its two dozen synagogues. Each synagogue took care of its own, although from 1565 the rabbis collectively were designated as the group that represented the Jews as a whole. The *millet* system in general, and even its fractured form in Salonika, put significant power into the hands of the rabbis that increased their authority within their congregations.

Muslim authorities certainly favored their own, but they did not try actively to turn Jews and Christians towards Islam. As a result, the Jewish communities of the Ottoman empire experienced a degree of autonomy not found in most other parts of Europe. They soon faced a challenge over relations with Jews whose ancestors had converted to Christianity generations earlier in Spain, and who now wished to return to Judaism. Many of these *conversos* and their descendents were caught between two faiths whose rituals had become the rhythms of their life. When they tried to maintain both these rituals and rhythms, as some did, they were treated by both Jewish and Christian communities as suspicious, dangerous, and apostate.

The religious co-existence that the Ottomans exercised through the *millet* system almost guaranteed that boundaries would be blurred, and in Salonika above all. If some *converso* Jews held on to Christian rituals they had learned as children, others moved closer to Islam. Perhaps the most notorious group were the Sabbateans, disciples of the charismatic rabbi Sabbatai Zevi (1626–76) who was proclaimed as the Messiah and for a period in the 1650s and 1660s drew support from Jewish followers in Salonika, Safed, and Cairo and attracted delegations from northern Europe and Persia. Zevi went to Istanbul in 1665 to overthrow the sultan, but on being arrested he converted to Islam, gaining the name Aziz Mehmed Efendi and a state pension. Most followers abandoned him, but some suspected a cunning strategy by which the Messiah meant to convert the Turks to Judaism, and the Sabbatean movement carried on for centuries. Salonika later also became the centre of a small group of Judeo-Spanish Muslim converts known as *Ma'min* (the Faithful) or *Dönme* (converts). Intensely mystical and deeply schismatic, this collection of small groups continues to exist as a distinct ethnic subgroup in modern Turkey.

Refugees completely transformed Salonika economically and culturally, but they made a less dramatic impact on Istanbul, six hundred miles to the east, where Sephardic Jews also arrived in large numbers after 1492 [Fig 24].

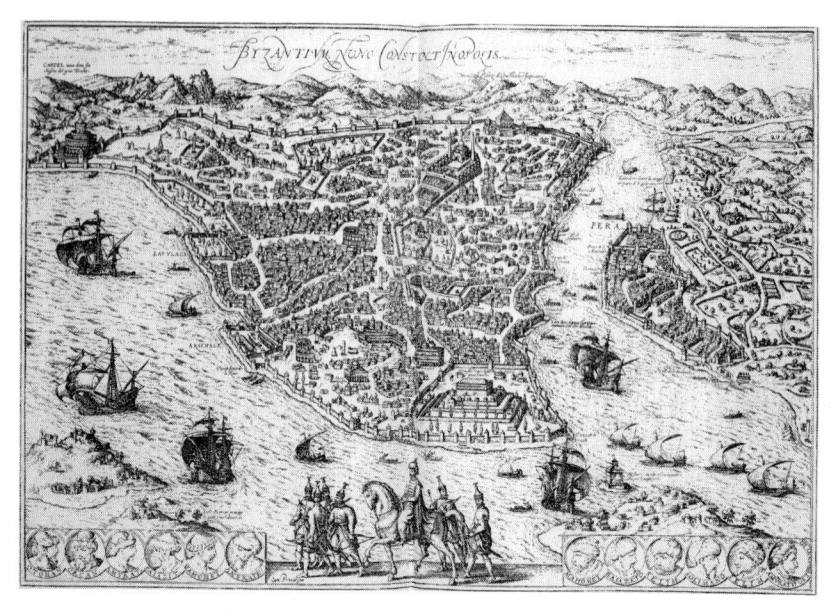

24. Istanbul, Braun & Hogenberg, *Civitates orbis terrarum* (1572).
Courtesy of the Thomas Fisher Rare Book Library, University of Toronto.

While the community included many doctors, merchants, and wealthy bankers like the Mendes family, they were greatly outnumbered by Muslims and Greek Orthodox. One of the Mendes nonetheless rose to the position of duke of Naxos, and helped fund Sultan Selim II's conquest of Cyprus in 1571. Protestant refugees began arriving in Istanbul after the 1530s, and the Ottoman wars against the Hapsburgs meant that many East European Protestant nobles, particularly Polish and Hungarian Calvinists, would find refuge here by the end of the century. Although small in number, the Calvinists gained Ottoman favor for worshipping with a minimum of ritual and sensory imagery, and for being more determined opponents of the Catholic Hapsburgs than Orthodox, Lutheran, or Radical Christians. Most Protestant exiles in Istanbul were temporary refugees from upper-class families who enjoyed considerable freedom of worship, sometimes with co-religionists in Istanbul on diplomatic missions like the Lutheran chaplain Stephen Gerlach who we encountered earlier. In 1572, Istanbul's Huguenots were permitted to stage a protest against the St. Bartholomew's Day massacre. Many Protestants worked as interpreters or traders for European states or trading companies and either disappeared into the broad community of dragomans (interpreters and translators between European and Ottoman authorities), or came under the authority of their national ambassadors after the 1648 Treaty of Westphalia.

Venice

Some cities became refugee centers because of longstanding economic and political practices. The more they took in diverse groups of migrants, the more they became open and attractive to refugees. It was appropriate that Venice should emerge as one of early modern Europe's leading refugee centers because it was originally settled in the fifth century by coastal fishermen fleeing Huns and Goths. Venice developed into a frontier outpost of the Byzantine Empire, and then saw its own fortunes expand as that empire declined. It carved out a commercial empire of coastal and island trading posts scattered around the eastern shores of the Mediterranean and the Black Sea in competition with both Genoa and Constantinople. Venice then began expanding ambitiously on the Italian mainland from the early fifteenth century in order to secure trade routes, territory, and food supplies.

Although it was the only major city in Europe without a circle of walls, Venice defined and defended itself fiercely as a particular *Corpus Christianum*. An elaborate set of rituals and extensive networks of confraternities defined a civic religion that positioned the city very self-consciously between the Orthodoxy of Constantinople and the Catholicism of Rome, and it ran its own Inquisition as a civic magistracy. Venetians refused to submit to Roman authority in matters religious, and so suffered repeated papal interdicts (1482, 1509–10, 1606–07). Lutheran and Anabaptist communities flourished for a period in the mid-sixteenth century, and the city sheltered such a diversity of religious groups that many Protestants in the later sixteenth century hoped that it would convert to the Protestant cause. But Venice was always distinctly Venetian. Under the titular leadership of a Doge, it operated as an oligarchic republic with power in the hands of a closed group of a few thousand nobles. Through a complicated series of magistracies and colleges, and with frequent commissions overseas as military leaders or governors, this class of nobles matured into what was paradoxically the most closed and yet the most cosmopolitan group of rulers in Renaissance Europe, as much at home in commerce as in governing.

The French ambassador Philippe de Commynes noted in the late fifteenth century, 'most of their people are foreigners'. Venice was famous for its international polyglot character, and this together with the city's wealth and trading connections drew in many printers, artists, and writers, making it a leading city of printing and art in the sixteenth century. The bulk of Venice's creative class were émigrés, including the printer Aldus Manutius, the painters Titian, Veronese, and Bassano, the architect Jacopo Sansovino, the composers Adrian Willaert and Claudio Monteverdi. Many economic migrants came from towns in the sea or land empire, and tended to gather in particular areas of the city where networks of shops and landlords drew the communities tightly together. Each group also outfitted itself with social institutions like confraternities, which they used, as the Venetians did, to care for their poor, honour their local saints, socialize their young, and make a civic splash with large buildings and long processions.

Venice had strong political, cultural, and economic ties across the Mediterranean, Northern Europe, and the Italian mainland. Fifteenth- and sixteenth-century developments in each of these areas made it a magnet for religious refugees. As Ottoman Turks rolled back the borders of the Byzantine Empire, Orthodox Christians moved to Venice. Scholars and merchants came after the conquest of Constantinople in 1453, and a wider variety came after Turks seized the Venetian outposts of Negroponte and Lemnos (1470–79), Cyprus (1570–73), and Crete (1645–69). In 1494, Venice permitted the Greeks to establish their own confraternity, the School of St. Nicholas of the Greeks, followed four decades later by a church dedicated to St. George of the Greeks. The confraternity and church allowed Greek Orthodox to worship publicly in Venice for the first time. They also gave the refugee community the tools it needed to care for its own sick, poor, young, and widows. The forty-member confraternity council elected by the Greek community became a form of self-government, even though it was ultimately responsible to Venetian magistrates.

The Greek district was clearly demarcated without any walls to mark its boundaries. As we saw in Chapter 2, however, the first ethno-religious district enclosed by brick walls and restrictive laws developed in Venice. Jews expelled from German and French towns had moved to Italian cities and towns throughout the fifteenth century. Venetian authorities allowed Jews to trade by day in the city but ordered them to return at night to homes on the mainland. When war brought papal, French, Holy Roman, and Spanish troops to the very shores of the lagoon in 1510–11, these Jews appealed for refuge on the islands. Venetian authorities relented, and Jews found homes where space and wealth allowed. Yet this triggered sharp reactions, and as the military threat receded there was increasing talk of the Jews as a contagion or pollution which had to be flushed out of the Venetian lagoon. As we saw earlier, authorities nervous about the loss of Jewish capital found an alternative in the tight enclosure of the entire community on a small island out by the northern edge of the city. It was the only one of Venice's over sixty islands without a consecrated church, and the idea of using a whole island to quarantine Venice from a 'dangerous contagion' was backed up by the established practice of forcing all international traders arriving by ship to pass through the quarantine island of St. Mary of Nazareth. On March 29, 1516, authorities ordered the city's 700 Jews to move to the island, which would become Venice's quarantine against Judaism, paying a premium to their landlords and paying the cost of the Christian guards who would man its two gates and patrol its encircling canals. Jews arriving from Germany, Spain, the Levant, France, and Italy pushed the ghetto population to a peak of 5–6,000 by the seventeenth century and forced expansion onto adjoining islands in 1541 and 1633. The ghetto had the tallest buildings in the city, as landlords added floors in order to house successive waves of newcomers. Each of the national communities established their own synagogues, charitable confraternities, and benevolent societies (*gemilut hasidim*), and traded actively with their homelands.

Beyond the local quarantine island, Venice's new Jewish ghetto also borrowed from familiar commercial models found across Europe and the Mediterranean. When merchants travelled overseas, they frequently lived in similar walled and self-governing communities; Venetians had one of their own in Mamluke Alexandria, there was another for Italians generally in Barcelona, and among the most famous in Europe was the Hanseatic League's Steelyard on the Thames in London. These walled merchant communities protected traders from periodic rioting mobs while also protecting local communities from the often riotous traders, most of them young men in their twenties on the hunt for taverns, prostitutes, and action.

Quarters like this balanced commercial opportunity, political necessity, and ethno-religious anxiety, and Venice had already opened one in the thirteenth century to house traders from Germany. Merchants arriving from Augsburg, Nuremburg, and other Imperial cities were directed to the combination hostel/warehouse known as the *Fondaco dei Tedeschi* (Storehouse of the Germans), at the foot of the Rialto Bridge in the commercial centre of town. Venice rebuilt the *Fondaco* (from an Arabic word for storehouse) from 1505 with four floors of warehouse, offices, market space, and sleeping quarters for about 160 around a central courtyard, and a few years later Giorgione and Titian frescoed the exterior walls facing the Grand Canal. Merchants were required to stay either at the *Fondaco* or in a series of hostels in the area, but had relatively free rein inside their enclosure. It was convenient for the merchants, and allowed Venetian authorities to keep an eye on them. When Protestant merchants came from the 1530s, they brought Lutheran preachers with them and then opened the doors so that those outside would be able to hear the sermons – providing they understood German. Venetian authorities opened a parallel *Fondaco dei Turchi* (Storehouse of the Turks) in an old palace further up the Grand Canal in 1621. Like the *Fondaco dei Tedeschi*, it was both hostel, warehouse, and market for merchants arriving with wax, oil, and wool from the Ottoman Empire – some of them Muslims and some Jews. Unlike its German counterpart, the windows facing the city were sealed up, and its guards were more vigilant in keeping the doors closed and keeping traffic in and out to a minimum.

The bounds of the Jewish ghetto were protective but also porous. Jewish merchants and bankers worked in the city by day, and Christians visited and even lived and worked in the ghetto; Christian builders constructed each of the synagogues. Members of Venice's large Iberian *converso* community were under no obligation to live in the ghetto, but they both drew on and enriched the cultural life within it. A steady number converted back to Judaism through the seventeenth century, including some whose families had lived as *conversos* for four generations or more. A number had studied medicine, law, and theology, and some had been professors, jurists, monks, and clergymen. They shared their Sephardic cultural traditions, while learning more about Judaism from the ghetto's rabbis. Schools, stores, printing workshops, and coffee houses made the Venetian ghetto a centre of Jewish cultural life and civil society that had few equals in Europe. Jewish merchants plied Venice's far-flung trading routes, sometimes living as *conversos* in one place and as Jews in another. This plasticity of identity was not unique to Jews and *conversos*, but characterized many families which had for centuries worked between Venice and Constantinople/Istanbul with loyalties in both, turning them into what Natalie Rothman has called 'trans-imperial subjects'.

As a result, the ghetto walls protected Jewish Venice as much as Christian Venice. Venetian Jews gained a secure space for the community's life and did not need to fear Christian youths invading to vandalize houses and desecrate synagogues as they did in many other communities, particularly during Holy Week. Some preachers and politicians continued to call for their expulsion, but the Venetian Senate voted definitively against that in 1571. Until Napoleon destroyed the ghetto gates in 1797 as a sign of liberation, the protected space of the ghetto drew in thousands of refugees and migrants to Venice.

Venice sheltered Greek Orthodox, Jewish, and Turkish refugees and migrants for mixed historical, economic, and political reasons, according to differing models, and with mixed results. Christian migrants moving to the city could live anywhere but might cluster in particular neighbourhoods. Travelling merchants, Muslims, and Jews got tighter control in isolated enclaves that were either free-standing enclosed buildings like a convent or orphanage, or the isolated ghetto like a quarantine station. The Venetian approach emphasised boundaries and walls between communities, and even if these might be breached from time to time, they made insiders and outsiders alike feel more secure. Venice's distinctive way of handling migrants drew in many thousands who in turn expanded the city, its culture, and its economy. The Venetian press was one of the largest in Europe due in part to large numbers of Greek and Hebrew printers who had arrived as refugees; and Greek and *converso* merchants kept trading internationally long after Venetian patricians shifted more of their capital and energies to mainland estates.

Basel

Salonika, Istanbul, and Venice took in whole communities numbering hundreds and thousands of refugees, but other cities attracted single individuals or very small groups. Wealthy merchants and magistrates might seek a place with markets or political protectors, but humanists and theologians sought out cities with a university and many printing presses. Both kinds of exiles could be found along the Rhine River, which was both a major trade and transportation route and also a boundary zone between France, the Netherlands, and the Holy Roman Empire. This allowed many refugees to escape to safety in a new jurisdiction simply by crossing the river. Large cities like Cologne, Freiburg, Mühlhausen, and Strasbourg had the cultural, political, and ecclesiastical resources to attract many of these individual and itinerant migrants.

Basel was one such city on the upper Rhine [Fig 25]. Its location attracted many traders, including a Jewish community that settled there in the twelfth century and helped pay for a new bridge over the Rhine in the thirteenth. The Jewish community came under suspicion in the aftermath of the Black Death, and at the urging of local guilds some Jews were tortured and killed and the rest expelled in 1349 and then again in 1398. As in many contemporary Rhineland cities, some of these moved no further than one of the surrounding rural villages.

Basel gained prominence throughout the fifteenth century as the site of the conciliarist Council of Basel (1431–49), which deposed Pope Eugenius IV and elected the duke of Savoy as Pope Felix V. Felix V held his papal court in Basel until 1448, and his resignation the following year brought a formal end to both the schism and the council. The city opened a university in 1460, which in turn attracted students, important printing presses like that of Johan Froben, and a growing number of major itinerant scholars like Erasmus. These helped turn Basel into the intellectual and cultural centre of the emerging Swiss Confederation, even though its population was only about 8–10,000. Basel joined the Swiss Confederation in 1501, as one of a series of political moves by which the city council supplanted the ruling bishop. By

25. Basel, Braun & Hogenberg, *Civitates orbis terrarum* (1572).
Courtesy of the Thomas Fisher Rare Book Library, University of Toronto.

the 1520s, broader religious controversies were swirling around the Swiss Confederation, pushed in large part by the humanist preachers Huldrych Zwingli in Zurich and Johannes Oecolampadius in Basel. Oecolampadius and Zwingli led a 1528 public disputation in Bern which led that city's council to abolish the mass and embrace evangelical preaching.

The emerging reform movement began straining the Swiss Confederation, particularly as iconoclastic violence broke out. Erasmus described two days of iconoclastic rioting in Basel in February, 'the smiths and workmen removed the pictures from the churches, and heaped … insults on the images of the saints and the crucifix itself. . . . Not a statue was left either in the churches, or the vestibules, or the porches, or the monasteries. The frescoes would were obliterated by means of a coating of lime; whatever would burn was thrown into the fire, and the rest pounded into fragments.' Basel's council abolished the mass by April, leading the bishop, Erasmus, and a number of other scholars to quit the city.

Both Zwingli and Oecolampadius died in 1531, and from that point Basel's council took a firmer hand and moderated the pace of the evangelical reform. That, together with the university, the printing presses, and the wealth of an established patriciate, attracted many educated reformers to Basel. Martin Luther's early ally Andreas Karlstadt, in flight from Wittenberg after the two fell out, arrived in Basel in 1534 and served as a professor of Hebrew and dean of the University until he died of plague in 1541. Erasmus, who had never cut his ties to the university, returned in 1535. He may have had the chance to see a copy of the first edition of the young John Calvin's *Institutes of the Christian Religion*, published just a few months before he died in August 1536. Calvin had arrived after fleeing Paris in 1533, and would only stay a few months longer before heading to Strasbourg by way of Geneva. For his part, Erasmus left a legacy which would bring many more exiles and refugees to Basel. He died a surprisingly wealthy man, and in his will established a foundation to distribute funds to refugees, exiles, travelling students, and the local poor. The trustees distributed more than 10,000 small and large subsidies from 1538 to 1600, with more than a quarter going to religious exiles – including Protestants, Catholics, Jews, and Orthodox – who were seeking funds to come and study in Basel. While most came from Germany, refugees from Italy, England, the Netherlands, and France all gained living subsidies, scholarship funds, and fellowships from the Erasmus Foundation.

Calvin's short sojourn was typical of many who started turning to Basel at this time, some of them Radicals who were determined to keep their identities hidden. The refugees arriving from the 1540s were largely Protestants fleeing emerging Protestant regimes. They included Sebastian Franck (1499–1543) an early follower of Luther who came to increasing trouble as his thinking moved away from churches and strict doctrines towards a form of open spiritualism. Franck arrived in 1539 after having been banished from Strasbourg and Ulm, and worked as a printer in Basel before dying there in 1543. The Dutch Spiritualist David Joris, described by Gary Waite as 'the most hated man in Europe' arrived the following year under an assumed name after having worn out his welcome in Antwerp, Delft, and Strasbourg. With funds and housing provided by wealthy patrons, this glass painter passed as a patrician merchant and Protestant refugee, while still secretly writing radical tracts, part of a lifetime oeuvre of more than 200 with compelling titles like *Hear, Hear, Hear, Good News, Good News, Good News* conveying the urgency of his message. A hundred of his followers, including his own mother, were executed in the international search for Joris, but they never betrayed him, and he died peacefully in Basel in 1556. Three years later, his true identity was betrayed to Basel authorities. They responded by opening the grave and burning Joris' corpse on the charge of heresy.

One of those who may have witnessed this posthumous burning was John Foxe, who at that point was a refugee from Mary Tudor's Catholic restoration. Foxe was working for printers in Basel while preparing the first edition of his *Actes and Monuments*, the official title of what is commonly known as *Foxe's Book of Martyrs*; it was published in Basel a few months later in August 1559. The burning of Joris's corpse would likely have been the first burning of a heretic that Foxe ever witnessed. Since he had barely begun on the passages dealing with the Marian Martyrs, it would have been very much on his mind as he began describing the deaths of Thomas Cranmer, Nicholas Ridley, and others. Finally, Sebastian Castellio (1515–63) an early ally of Calvin who was forced to leave Geneva when the two fell out, arrived in 1553 with help from the Erasmus Foundation before gaining a position at the university. His strong critiques of Protestant theocracy and works in favor of religious toleration became particularly pointed after Geneva burned Michael Servetus for heresy, and his corpse too was dug up and burned after he died.

Burning the exhumed corpses of those who called for religious toleration reminds us that the discourses around purification and purgation were not about words alone. The burnings came out of the sharp struggles to define the direction of the Swiss city reforms, and by century's end Basel was becoming increasingly Calvinist and exclusive. Huguenot exiles arrived in the later sixteenth century, but few other refugees came to Basel after the 1590s. Even the Erasmus Foundation gradually wound up its activities. The university distributed its scholarship funds from 1586, and Basel's welfare office took over its small gifts to poor artisans, widows, and marrying couples from 1614.

Munster

As seen in Basel, many refugees of the 1520s and 1530 were reformers expelled by other reformers. Radical Anabaptists frequently called for an immediate, thorough, and mandatory abandonment of all Catholic practices, and their firm plans triggered sharp reactions – few others wanted follow their regimes based on a literal reading of the Old or New Testament, and so the Radicals had to flee. The Radicals sought places of refuge that were open to the experiment of building a completely new *Corpus Christianum*, but few places fit this description.

They were in a hurry. Many of the first generation of Anabaptist radicals were 'millenarians', believing that Christ would soon be returning to earth in order to inaugurate a 1000-year golden age of peace before the Last

Judgment. Christ's Second Coming was only a short time away – a few years at most, and likely only months or even weeks. Some believed that he would establish a New Jerusalem in whatever place his followers were already implementing his teaching, giving more urgency to their drive to find a place where they could put their ideas into practice. One of the most charismatic radicals, the furrier Melchior Hoffman (1495–1543), targeted Strasbourg, but was arrested for baptising adults soon after arriving there in 1530. Leadership then fell to some of his younger followers, including a Haarlem baker Jan Matthys (1500–34) and a tailor Jan of Leiden (1509–36), who believed that the budding reformation in the North German town of Munster came closest to the millenarian ideal. Matthys arrived in Munster in January 1534, declaring it the New Jerusalem and promising that Christ would return there barely three months later on Easter Sunday. With the help of a local pastor and some leading citizens, the radicals started a rapid and far-reaching reform campaign, taking over the town government and throwing out the existing magistrates. The choice given to Munster's citizens was the same one given earlier to Jews across Europe: be (re)baptized or leave the *Corpus Christianum*.

Events moved quickly. Perhaps a thousand Munsterites were rebaptized in the first few weeks, while hundreds were expelled from the city of about 10,000. Hundreds of radicals who were themselves refugees on the run began moving to Munster from across Northern Europe in order to greet Christ when he returned. Using the example of both the Old Testament law and the New Testament early church, they aimed to institute a radical theocracy. At an early stage, they began instituting the community of goods as described in the New Testament book of Acts. Munster's exiled Catholic bishop returned with troops in late February to besiege the city and purge the radicals from it. A month later, Matthys ordered that all books except the Bible be burned in order to purify the city. A few weeks later on Easter Sunday, Matthys charged out of the gates with thirty men, following the example of the Old Testament leader Gideon who had beaten a mighty army of Israel's enemies with a small band of soldiers and God's help. Matthys and his thirty men clearly thought that their bold faith would bring God into the battle. All were quickly killed.

Jan of Leiden now assumed control over the city and accelerated Matthys's efforts to establish a New Jerusalem in Munster. Barely twenty-five years old, he took the name and powers of King David in the Old Testament, expanding the community of goods, and instituting polygamy in July 1534. He cited divine visions, but was also looking to practical needs and opportunities. Munster was an increasingly desperate and starving city under siege from which many of the native men had been expelled. Following a common arrangement for exiles across Europe, most had left their wives behind to protect the family property. As a result, women made up as much as 75 percent of the population, but many were hostile to the radicals. Aiming to put these women under closer male radical authority while also increasing Munster's population, Jan of Leiden declared all existing marriages void, and then ordered that the wives of Munster exiles be remarried. He barely suppressed an internal revolt and executed its leaders, and perhaps the greatest surprise is that it then took almost a year before some of those inside Munster found a way to open the gates to the besieging troops. After being publicly tortured and executed, the bodies of Jan and two of his closest associates were put in cages that were hoisted up the Munster cathedral steeple. Their bones were eventually removed, but the cages still remain.

Munster's experiment in radical theocracy had a profound impact. For almost a year and a half, it had been a magnet for radical refugees and exiles who were aiming to shape a *Corpus Christianum* along the strictest biblical lines, and who expelled any who refused to be rebaptised and accept their new order. Some of the more apocalyptic radicals had been working for this kind of total change since the Revolt of the Common Man or earlier. They had the kind of burning zeal found in Thomas Muntzer's staccato call to the people of Allstedt in 1525 'go to it, go to it, go to it. The time has come, the evildoers are running like scared dogs ... pay no attention to the cries of the godless ... they will whimper and wheedle like children. Show no pity, as God has commanded. . . . As long as they live it is impossible for you to rid yourselves of the fear of men. . . . Go to it, go to it, while it is day. God goes before you, follow, follow.' Yet millenarian radicalism quickly fractured, its leaders' prophecies went unfilled, and the theocratic vision descended into parody and pariah through force, violence, and enforced polygamy.

Although most Anabaptists remained attached to the idea of a community of goods, many now aimed to realize this without force or violence but in small, self-sufficient, voluntary rural communities. These would not seek out cities of refuge, but would disperse in large numbers across Moravia, Poland, and eventually Russia and the Ukraine, where nobles with large estates were willing to grant a degree of religious toleration to groups of farmers who would develop the land and wanted only to keep to themselves in what were virtually self-policing enclosures. Although small segments of the radical community remained wedded to polygamy and even to violence, the main streams of Mennonites, Hutterites, Amish, and Moravian Brethren adopted even stronger commitments to pacifism, traditional family structures, and isolation from the world. Their commitment to purity and even purgation through devices like the ban and excommunication remained as strong as ever, but these would be spiritual disciplines that they would apply within their communities and not force on others.

Geneva

If Munster was the radical experiment, Geneva was its opposite: a Calvinist laboratory which Scottish reformer John Knox (1514–72) declared 'the most perfect school of Christ'. Like Munster and Basel, it was caught between competing forces, and the fight between the city council, the local bishop, and the duchy of Savoy created a political and religious instability that opened an opportunity for radically new approaches.

Geneva's grand council was a political body established in 1457 which had gradually assumed considerable authority over religious life, expelling the Jews in 1488 (who had gained permission to live in a separate quarter of the city only in 1428), appointing the bishop from 1490, and eventually banning the mass in 1528. Geneva's drift towards Reformation had much to do with the fact that many of its clergy had allied with Savoy through the 1510s and '20s, when dukes of Savoy were working hard to subdue the city. The grand council responded by forging a defensive alliance with the Swiss Federation in 1526, and Bernese troops helped keep the Savoyards at bay on condition that Geneva welcome Protestant pastors. The local Catholic clergy left the city in protest, essentially leaving it open to being shaped by outsiders.

The first Protestant refugees arrived from France in 1523. Yet no one could have predicted how much the city's history would be shaped by the twenty-seven-year-old former law student who arrived in 1536, was exiled two years later for trying to push reform too far, and then returned in 1541 to lead the city's church until his death in 1564. John Calvin would face considerable opposition from members of the grand council until 1555, but the city nonetheless became his laboratory and international staging ground. His publications, letters, church organization, and school for pastors attracted thousands of refugees from France, England, Italy, and Germany who by 1557 had than doubled the size of the city to about 14,000.

Tensions grew as the refugees began outnumbering the native Genevans. What drew them? Calvin's writings certainly appealed to the class of professionals and artisans who dominated among refugees. Printers, pharmacists, doctors, and merchants could also more readily work here than in cities with more highly-developed and tightly-regulated economies. And Calvin's form of church organization, the source of early fights with Geneva's Council, allowed refugees a degree of self-governance seldom found elsewhere. A single civic consistory made up of pastors and lay elders governed the civic church and disciplined its members, often by requiring more frequent attendance at the hour-long sermons that Calvin preached many times during the week and twice on Sunday. The separate national exile communities had their own congregations with their own boards of deacons to oversee charity within their communities. Most exiles hoped to return to their homelands, and so prepared themselves for preaching and missionary work. Others, like a group of Italian exiles from Lucca, remained in Geneva as an important but distinct community. Genevan translators produced vernacular bibles in English (1560), Italian (1603), and French (1644), while its presses printed these and numerous pamphlets and theological texts in different languages. Geneva's Academy would become an important seminary, while its Company of Pastors effectively apprenticed many missionaries who then circulated elsewhere in Europe.

Calvin, too, kept his eyes on his French homeland but also corresponded widely in Latin to reformers across Europe. His intellectual standing attracted many individuals who were searching and curious, and many came to Geneva to see the experiment unfolding there and to discuss or debate with Calvin. Many, like the Italians Bernardino Ochino and Pier Martire Vermigli, and the French Sebastiano Casellio (1515–63) left voluntarily or were forced out, since Calvin's experiment did not involve much toleration for different points of view. One who learned this the hard way was Michael Servetus (1509–53), a Spanish theologian and humanist of *converso* background on his mother's side. At age twenty-two, Servetus had published a book denouncing Trinitarian theology, and the uproar forced him to go underground in France, change his name, and become a physician. Two decades later in 1553, he was arrested by the Inquisition after further publications, but escaped and inexplicably fled to Geneva, even though he had been sharply criticizing Calvin for years. Here he was arrested and a little more than two months later was burned outside the city walls as a heretic for rejecting both the Trinity and Infant Baptism.

Servetus's execution broadcast the limits of John Calvin's reform as effectively as support for the harsh suppression of the Peasant's Revolt had marked the limits of Martin Luther's. Both men appeared to supporters and critics alike as the advocates of a pure orthodoxy which might differ from Catholicism in this or that doctrinal detail, but which was to be defended just as firmly. Knox's 'perfect school of Christ' was a place of pure doctrine and purgation. Calvinist doctrines were particularly well suited to refugee communities and the refugee experience for reasons we will return to below. While Geneva's refugee communities would eventually either dwindle or assimilate, the intensity of the Genevan experiment and the social, political, and literary influence of those who lived there even relatively briefly had a profound impact in spreading Calvin's ideas in France, the Netherlands, Scotland, England, Hungary, and Poland. Throughout the 1540s, the north German town of Emden served a similar function as a haven for Dutch refugees, led by a Polish cleric Jan Laski who would later lead refugee churches in London and Brandenburg before returning to lead reform efforts in Poland. Colonial enterprises and the exiling of Calvinist Puritans from England in the seventeenth century would then spread Genevan theology and model of church government to South Africa and North America.

Amsterdam

War, trade, and civic traditions led refugees towards Amsterdam in the later sixteenth century just as they had earlier drawn migrants to Venice [Fig 26]. Spanish military pressure in the Lowlands from the 1560s, and most notably the devastating Sack of Antwerp in 1585, triggered an exodus of Protestant and *converso* refugees. Amsterdam's deep cultural traditions of co-existence and co-operation rooted in the *Corpus Christianum* made it more welcoming to these migrant communities and others that followed in their wake. A city council oriented to trade and internally divided on matters of religion allowed

26. Amsterdam, Braun & Hogenberg, *Civitates orbis terrarum* (1572). Courtesy of the Thomas Fisher Rare Book Library, University of Toronto.

a range of religious groups to settle there on the understanding that they would maintain a low public profile and keep their places of worship hidden in attics or courtyards. Tacit toleration encouraged the growth of large communities of refugee Catholics, Jews, and Radical Anabaptists who would gradually come out of their attics and shape the city's economy and culture through the seventeenth century.

Amsterdam's early experience with radical religious exclusivism may have shaped later attitudes. Luther's ideas were discussed in the 1520s, and the city council hired four 'evangelically-minded' priests in the 1530s. Yet the Radicals were already a growing presence. They argued for radical breaks with both Luther and the Catholics on things like the Real Presence and the mass. Melchior Hoffman was active in the Netherlands in 1530 spreading millenarian hopes and mobilizing local radicals. While Munster was descending into chaos, a group of radicals seized Amsterdam's City Hall with a plan to establish an exclusive New Jerusalem. A group of sixteen burned their clothing and ran naked into the street in order to proclaim the new order, while others resorted to violence. They were quickly suppressed, and sixty-two were executed. The traumatic episode forced the Radicals underground or to Emden, London, and elsewhere, and entrenched a Catholic ruling faction on the city council for the next four decades.

Missionary activity and growing dissatisfaction with the conservative city council led to a gradual expansion of evangelical preaching and some iconoclastic riots in 1566. But it was ironically the Spanish who did most to promote the Dutch Reformation, with the duke of Alva its most effective missionary. Amsterdam was traditionally loyal to the Spanish monarch, but when King Philip II sent Alva to restore royal control after rebellions in 1567, he fuelled the opposition. Alva's punitive regime merged Catholicism and Spanish imperialism in the eyes of many, and propagandists exploited this to stir up the moderate and indifferent. In 1578 a new council banned the mass, closed the convents, and expelled Catholics. Within a decade, a third of Amsterdam's population was made up of Protestant refugees from across the Netherlands, and Iberian *conversos*, Lutherans, and pacifist Mennonites soon followed. Many Catholics remained and worshipped discretely.

Economic opportunity was a great or greater draw, and the city council recognized the contribution wealthy migrants and refugee traders could make. Local magistrates officially banned Catholicism, but some took bribes to turn a blind eye to priests who surreptitiously led masses and administered sacraments. Amsterdam's council passed laws against Catholic worship, but also cracked down on officials who enforced them too rigorously. The council even reprimanded a sheriff for disrupting an illegal Catholic funeral and insulting the widow, and then dismissed the priest's fine. If Catholics did not advertise their presence publicly, officials would not prosecute them privately. Hidden churches (*schuilkerken*) proliferated in private houses and attics, often exuberantly baroque on the inside, but bland and invisible from the street. One house church built in 1661–63 which still exists as a museum under the name 'Our Dear Lord in the Attic' (*Onze lieve Heer op Kelder*) held 150 in a third-floor nave with two galleries above. Amsterdam had twenty such Catholic churches by 1700, and they were not alone. Mennonites alone had six churches 'hidden' in courtyards, while four more sheltered other groups. These were in addition to the officially recognized and publically funded French Walloon (1586), German Lutheran (1588; 1633), and English (1607) 'stranger' churches that gathered religious refugees from across Europe. The Walloon church was one of fifteen across the Dutch Republic that gathered French Calvinist refugees from 1571 to 1590, while the English church attracted mainly Dissenters from the Church of England. It made Amsterdam a prominent way-station in the large Puritan diaspora that settled New England in the mid-seventeenth century.

The first Jewish refugees arrived as *converso* Catholics fleeing Antwerp in the 1580s. As in England, Germany, and other parts of northern Europe, they were known as 'Portuguese', even though many were on extended migrations over the generations that had begun with expulsion from Spain and moved out of Iberia altogether after the Portuguese Inquisition began its work in 1531. Since so many Amsterdamers saw Spain as a formidable and aggressive enemy, it was more politic to pass as Portuguese. The first *conversos* lived initially as Catholics but slowly returned to Judaism as they acclimatized to the local terms of covert co-existence. Authorities allowed the public practice of Judaism in 1603, and three Sephardic congregations emerged over the next decade and a half. Worshipping initially in hidden spaces like Catholics and Anabaptists, they merged to build a large public synagogue in 1639. By this point they had already been helping Ashkenazi Jews, many of them destitute and dislocated by the Thirty Years War in the Holy Roman Empire. Rabbis from Venice and the Ottoman Empire assisted in a return to Judaism, which was sometimes marked by serious tensions and disputes; at one point, Amsterdam's secular magistrates had to encourage the governing council of *parnassim* to ease up on its excommunication of Jewish members.

As the Jewish community grew, the internal social and economic distinctions found in places like Salonika and Istanbul emerged in Amsterdam as well. The Ashkenazim tended to be poor labourers speaking largely Yiddish, wearing traditional clothing, and isolated from Dutch civic life. The

Sephardim included more merchants and financiers whose activities extended to the Ottoman Empire and along the routes of Dutch trade into the Caribbean, North Africa, and the Americas. They spoke Spanish, Portuguese, and Dutch, dressed and acted more like locals, and moved more readily in Dutch society. By 1674, as many as 5,000 Ashkenazic and 2,500 Sephardic Jews lived in Amsterdam, and in this same decade each community built its own enormous synagogue on opposite sides of a single square in a new district that officials had marked out as a Jewish quarter. Growth begat growth, and as the Jewish community of Amsterdam expanded, the city emerged as a major centre of Jewish cultural life and publishing.

Not all former *conversos* returned to Judaism, and individual families might include a mix of religious confessions. One of the pillars of the Sephardic community was Isaac Israel Suasso, born Antonio Lopes Suasso, and son of an Iberian *converso* doctor who had become a professor of medicine at the University of Bordeaux. Three of his brothers married Catholics and publicly professed that faith in Southern Europe. Isaac together with another brother and all four sisters moved to northern Europe, married into Jewish merchant families, and returned to Judaism. After converting to Judaism, Isaac took a prominent role in Amsterdam's Sephardic community. He was one of those who excommunicated Baruch Spinoza (1632–77), the young philosopher who doubted traditional views of God and the Bible, who appreciated the work of Judah Leon Abravanel, and whose own writings would become central to Enlightenment rationalist thought.

Amsterdam's magistrates cultivated co-existence much as their Venetian counterparts did, though without enclosed ghettos or *fondaco* hostel-warehouses. They held off a religious establishment that wanted more purification and purgation. Vigorous Calvinists protested the presence of Radicals, Catholics, and Jews and wanted all of these groups – and especially the Jews – expelled for their 'abominable lack of faith'. Yet neither the Reformed nor the refugees ever constituted a majority. The Reformed Church exercised a disproportionate influence culturally, but was too consumed by internal debates to unite effectively against the new groups of outsiders. Even more critically, the Netherlands had no monarch calling for 'one king, one faith, one law' as in France, and its ruling oligarchies were too divided. The de facto toleration of Amsterdam was not an open acceptance and celebration of different understandings of truth, but a form of practical co-existence. A 1607 municipal plan actually envisioned designating distinct districts of the city for particular ethnic-religious groups like Huguenots and Jews, giving each space for a market, a public square, and a place of worship.

As in Venice, Amsterdam authorities knew the value of a relatively open publishing industry, a vibrant economy, and a prolific artistic scene. So, while some clergy and magistrates may have yearned for a pure and exclusive Calvinist society, others recognized the extraordinary economic and cultural contribution of Catholics, Jews, and Mennonites to what would develop as a seventeenth-century Golden Age.

Algiers

North Mediterranean ports like Salonika and Venice had long histories predating the refugee migrations of the fifteenth and sixteenth century, and their trading links together with state policies drew refugees to them. By contrast, Algiers' population, economy, and formidable military presence were all direct consequences of the Iberian expulsions and Spain's effort to push its anti-Islamic Reconquista crusade on to the North African coast [Fig 27].

Algiers had been a relatively minor centre of Mediterranean trade under the Phoenicians and Romans, and various European and Arabic armies occupied the port through the Middle Ages. The series of Iberian expulsions of both Jews and Muslims in the 1490s, 1520s, 1560s, 1580s, and then finally

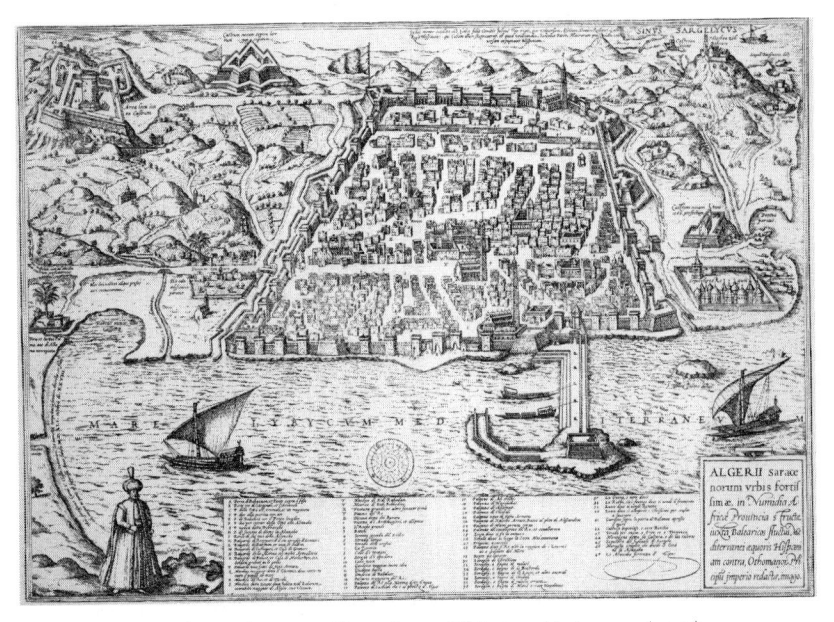

27. Algiers, Braun & Hogenberg, *Civitates orbis terrarum* (1572). Courtesy of the Thomas Fisher Rare Book Library, University of Toronto.

from 1609 to 1614 brought a flood of refugees and turned Algiers into a major port from the sixteenth through the early nineteenth centuries. The port city was essentially on the front lines of a war between the Spanish and the Ottomans for control of the North African coast from the 1510s through to the final defeat of Charles V's crusading army of 30,000 in 1541. By this point, Süleyman I the Magnificent had already taken Algiers into the Ottoman Empire, and this increased the geo-political stakes of the war. Algiers became one of the principal naval bases of the western Mediterranean, and a key centre of trade and piracy. By 1570, it had a population of around 120,000, putting it in the same league as Venice and Istanbul, and ten times larger than Basel, Munster, or Geneva.

Throughout the centuries of corsair piracy, as many as a million Europeans were seized from ships or French and Italian coastal towns to serve time as slaves on corsair galleys, in shipyards, on farms, or in households on the shore. Unlike the Atlantic slave trade, Mediterranean slaves were usually imprisoned for only a few years until a ransom was paid. A steady stream of books and pamphlets written by those who escaped or bought their freedom put Algiers very vividly into the European imagination as a lawless frontier city made all the more dangerous by the most exotic racial and religious mixing. The European Muslims and Jews in Algiers were most often refugees, while the Christians were involuntary migrants. Religion defined where and how every inhabitant lived, but religion here was different from almost anywhere else because so many traditions came together in Algiers. Iberian Moors and Ottoman Turks competed with North African Berbers, and this Muslim population became even more varied over time because Algiers was also the place where many Christians and Jews cast off their faith and converted to Islam. Conversion freed a slave and could set him on a path to becoming a ship captain or public official. Arabic and European Jews lived uneasily together, and even Christians had their own marketplace, churches, and public services.

The Ottomans assumed a relatively loose control of this dynamic multi-ethnic port, following the *millet* system under which religious communities lived separately and ordered themselves. An early account of it comes from a Portuguese priest, Antonio de Sosa, who was captured by pirates in 1577 and spent the next four years as a slave. De Sosa was fascinated by the religiously polyglot city and described closely the divisions of powers, layering of customs, and crossing of boundaries that made it unlike anything he had ever experienced. His owner, Mohammed, was a Jewish refugee who had converted first to Islam, then later to Christianity when captured and enslaved in Genoa, and then back to Islam when he returned to Algiers.

The existing community of Arabic-speaking Jews had been overwhelmed both by the Sephardic influx after 1492 and also by small groups of refugees from France, Italy, and various Mediterranean islands. De Sosa estimated that the community as a whole numbered about 150 households, or about 1500 people 'so ill treated by all Turks, Moors, and Christians that it is something incredible to see . . . and for this reason, many Jews turn Turk every day.' The different groups lived uneasily together, with the newcomers founding their own synagogues and following different traditions, yet they combined to elect a single governing *parnassim* or council and a single rabbi represented them to the Ottoman governor.

Even more complicated rifts divided the Muslim community. Local Berbers and Bedouins had sheltered the Moorish refugees from Granada, Valencia, and Aragon, but found their customs strange and did not know what to make of those Catholic *moriscos* who now wished to return to Islam. Power lay in the hands of the Turks, but following long-standing Ottoman practice, it was often converts or so-called renegades who took the most important positions in government and the military. Converts came from around the world – De Sosa names at least fifty distinct groups including Mexicans, Brazilians, and South Asians, and many different Europeans 'of Christian blood and parentage who have turned Turk of their own free will, impiously renouncing and spurning their God and creator'. By the 1570s, there were already 8–10,000 Iberian moors and *moriscos* and perhaps as many Turks and Berbers, but many more converts from Christianity – the 'renegades' made up over half the population of Algiers, and were found everywhere. Those Christians who did not convert lived either in the homes of their owners or in one of a few large prison-like enclosures called *bagnos*. The largest in Algiers was Bagno Beyliç, housing hundreds of slaves and organized as a series of cells, offices, warehouses, hospital, and chapel built around a central courtyard. Slaves had some mobility, in part because they were expected to work off their ransoms. One historian estimates that from 1580 to 1680 there were regularly about 35,000 slaves being held in the city's homes and *bagnos*.

In this way, Algiers was not unlike Salonika, Munster, and Geneva. A small local community found itself outnumbered by many distinct groups of refugees who together took over political and religious life, reshaped the economy, and gave it an international prominence that it had never had before. As in Amsterdam, there was de facto toleration for those who kept a low profile. While many Christians effectively lived in custody, they had more opportunity to engage openly with Jews and Muslims in Algiers than in any city north of the Mediterranean.

Massachusetts Bay Colony

Like Munster and Geneva, the Massachusetts Bay Colony was both a refuge and an ambitious experiment in creating a new and pure *Corpus Christianum*. In all three of these refugee centres, the very intensity of the experiment in building a pure and disciplined society according to a very strict set of theological doctrines soon generated opposition and further exiles. Yet much had changed in the century since the older cities in Europe had become refugee centers in the 1530s. On a certain level, the Massachusetts Bay Colony reflected Munster and Geneva less than it did the rural settlements founded by the radicals, Anabaptists, and anti-Trinitarians who had fled those self-styled New Jerusalems. The Puritan refugees of the 1630s were looking for virgin territory or a blank slate where they could establish their city without negotiation or compromise. Largely disregarding the native aboriginal peoples, they found their promised land on the opposite side of the Atlantic. Here they instituted regimes as uncompromising as those which had forced them to flee their own homelands.

Prosecution of English Protestants who wanted a more Calvinist doctrine and Church Order within the Church of England became particularly intense through the 1610s and 1620s. Some fled to the Netherlands, which was closer than Geneva and allowed independent English congregations. Others aimed to capitalize on England's interest in developing the territories it claimed across the Atlantic, and gained charters to establish new colonies there. The Massachusetts Bay Colony was one of the first successful ones. Shortly after its founding in 1628, Charles I's deepening struggle with Parliament triggered a wave of predominantly Nonconformist Protestants to leave England in what was known as the Great Migration. From 1620 to 1640, about 80,000 moved to Ireland, the West Indies, the Netherlands, and the emerging North American colonies. Many were economic migrants, but those heading to Massachusetts Bay were intent on constructing what their first governor, John Winthrop, described as 'A City on A Hill'. His use of familiar biblical language emphasized the goal that so many Protestant refugees from Munster radicals to Genevan Calvinists shared. They were not building pure societies for themselves alone, but as models for the world.

Settlers in the string of small coastal villages farmed nearby plots and met for worship and community events in the kind of simple multi-purpose meeting halls that French Huguenots favored. They wrote a new legal code, the 1641 Massachusetts Body of Liberties, based largely on their reading of the Bible. Puritan refugees tended to come as families rather than individuals, and were often relatively well educated and prosperous. Ministers led many of the groups, and their theological education and rhetoric shaped the laws and language of the settlements. These Puritans were not desperate refugees fleeing for safety, but self-sacrificing architects of a new society, and they were determined to keep control over it. Unusual terms in their royal charter allowed the Colony's administrators to limit the right to vote to those who were church members in good standing. About 10,000 migrated here until England's Civil War broke out, giving Puritans more hope for a new regime at home and so less incentive to set sail for America. Many returned home.

The Puritans' high ambitions and strict regime in Massachusetts left little space for newer groups of Protestants like Baptists and Quakers, whose theologies were more Anabaptist and Radical than Calvinist. As early as 1636, settlers began moving south to the newer and more open Rhode Island and Connecticut Colonies or north to the New Hampshire Colony in search both of land and, ironically, greater religious freedom. Quakers pushed out of England by Cromwell in the 1650s settled initially around Boston, but the Puritan government there was even stricter than Cromwell in prosecuting them as heretics. Puritans were self-sacrificing, but expected others to sacrifice too. Some non-Puritans were imprisoned, others whipped out of the colony, and four who later came to be known as the Boston Martyrs were executed from 1659 to 1661.

When news reached England that Puritans had hanged Quakers, newly restored King Charles II had the pretext he needed to regain and expand control over the American colonies. Colonial commercial and political interests were complicated by fights against the Dutch, the French, and the Indians, but colonists continued to frame their disputes in religious language. Massachusetts stiffly resisted England's new Navigation Acts (1660 and 1663) that channelled all trade between colonies back through England, and rejected imposition of an established Church of England like that found in the Mother Country. The English crown responded by cancelling the colony's royal charter in 1684. Yet the efforts to control all the New England colonies directly from London fell apart within a few years when James II was expelled in the Glorious Revolution. The new King William III approved a new charter for Massachusetts Bay in 1691, but deliberately ended Puritan dominance in order to build a broader Protestant coalition, which the monarchy could rely on to fend off challenges from the deposed Stuarts and their many Catholic allies in Europe and the Americas.

Like Munster and Geneva, the Massachusetts Bay Colony showed that many religious refugees were not seeking religious toleration, but the opportunity to build a new and pure society which could be as exclusive and intolerant as any found in Europe. Those in Massachusetts Bay were among the first of a new class of religious migrants who were driven by strong beliefs and utopian visions to migrate without being absolutely forced. Many similar groups of idealists would form communities across the Americas well into the nineteenth century, including eighteenth-century Moravians and Shakers and nineteenth-century industrial Socialists, Mormons, and free thinkers. Religious refugees could be as repressive as those who had forced their own migration, and in this way they generated new waves of exiles and refugees from the pure religious communities they were building. Despite their many differences, they would come to define a central strand in American civic life: the idea of America as exceptional – a promised land blessed by God, and given a duty and destiny to be a model for the world. Under this ideology, immigrant dreams were understood as divine visions. A strong commitment to personal freedom of faith and conscience, a sense of collective righteous purpose, and the missionary zeal to defend and export this with violence if necessary, was one of the most abiding – and ambivalent – legacies of the Puritan exiles and refugees to New England.

Exiles and refugees profoundly shaped the economic and cultural life of the places they fled to. Migrants developed new industries and trading links, and gave a higher international profile to what had often been small backwaters. Yet the effects were not the same everywhere. The reception that cities offered to refugees and exiles determined the impact these migrants could have on their new homes and the kind of growth and development that would result.

Wars and simmering disputes with church or state authorities beyond their boundaries often created the first opening for refugees to settle. Sometimes these upheavals cleared a space for refugees geographically, socially, and politically. Sometimes they created a context of insecurity or outright threat that quickly transformed the refugees into defenders of their new homes. The ongoing Mediterranean wars between the Ottomans and Christian Europe influenced the influx of refugees and exiles to Venice, Algiers, Salonika, and Istanbul, and the role that they would play there. Broader European dynastic and colonial struggles were the context for framing policy in other centers: Amsterdam grew against the backdrop of the protracted Dutch Wars with Spain, Geneva faced continual pressure from Savoy, and the Massachusetts Bay Colony could not escape the ongoing effects of civil-religious disputes in England.

Authorities in each of these centers responded quite differently to the influxes of migrants, and the role they allowed refugees to play inevitably shaped the longer-term effects these newcomers had. Almost all of the cities considered here were initially reluctant to take in refugees, and almost all put the earliest arrivals under tight restrictions. One group of cities aimed to become a monocultural ideal paradise. Basel, Munster, Geneva, and the Massachusetts Bay Colony stuck closest to the old idea of a *Corpus Christianum*. In their efforts to build a pure city around a single ideology, they tried to control new refugees or even to close the doors on them. These cities were left with smaller populations and economies, and a narrower range of influence. A second group like Venice and Algiers practiced disciplined or closed co-existence. They were willing to take in new groups, but segregated and controlled them, and restricted the public profile that these migrants could display. As a result, the migrants seldom considered themselves part of urban civil society, and these two cities did not expand much through the seventeenth and eighteenth centuries. A third group, including Salonika and Amsterdam, practiced a discrete and increasingly open co-existence. They allowed distinct ethno-cultural and religious groups a significant degree of independence and an expanding public role in civic life. They gave exile communities the greatest degree of security, mobility, self-government, and integration. Perhaps not surprisingly, these cities prospered the most and developed increasingly complex international economies through the early modern period.

4

MIND AND BODY

THE SOCIAL BODY HAD A MIND, BUT WAS NEVER OF ONE MIND. Its many members had varying physical needs, and no single way of meeting them. Thus far we have seen how tensions of the late medieval period began to complicate Europeans' understandings of what it meant to be a *Corpus Christianum*, or Body of Christ. In this chapter, we will see how ways of thinking and ways of acting began to diverge in that Body, and tear it apart. We have already seen how anxieties about external and internal threats gripped Europeans from the fifteenth century, and how they responded with strategies to separate, contain, prosecute, and purge these threats. The result was a flood of religious exiles and refugees that poured out of particular nations and cities and washed around Europe and across the globe from the fourteenth through the eighteenth centuries. It was because of these late medieval and Renaissance-era tensions that the religious refugee and exile emerged as mass phenomena in the early modern period. We have also looked at the paths that some individuals took in their thinking and with their feet when they were separated, prosecuted, or purged. Their mental and physical migrations took them across Europe, the Mediterranean, and the Atlantic, and transformed the places where they settled. The migrations of religious refugees and exiles fundamentally shaped early modern political, economic, and cultural life.

Religious doctrines lay at the heart of both the threats and the strategies, and thus far we have sketched only some of the main differences between Jews, Christians, and Muslims, and between Catholics, Lutherans, Radicals, Calvinists, and others within Christendom. A thorough comparative discussion of the theologies of the Reformation is beyond the scope of this book. Yet it is helpful to look briefly at a few of the doctrines that were most contentious and were most often used to mark and divide. We will then see how religious communities worked to put their beliefs into action through different forms of charity. Many religious refugees and migrants needed it, and many religious communities thought that help to the poor and needy was the best measure of true faith.

The first half of this chapter will consider three themes that were litmus tests for purity both in formal doctrine and in popular piety. All became critical tools used to define, to convert, or to purge. We can think of them as questions. First, how do believers join a community (Initiation)? Second, how is God present in that community (Presence)? Third, how and through whom does God speak to that community (Authority)? All three questions ask how God relates to and is present among communities of believers. Christians, Muslims, and Jews of the late medieval and early modern period all reconsidered their views as a result of religious, social, and political developments. Initiation, Presence, and Authority were at the root of the most controversial theological points dividing Catholics from Protestants, and Protestants from each other; Muslims and Jews in Europe were also forced into rethinking these points by the reform movements that were remaking Christendom.

The theme of Initiation involves rituals like circumcision and baptism, and concerns about how the community polices its boundaries and conducts its sacraments. The theme of Presence involves the ritual of communion, and expresses the ways in which God may or may not be present among believers. The theme of Authority brings these together around the fundamental issue of scriptures, and how God speaks to believers. It raises further questions about who interprets God's revelation and the role of clergy as the instructors, guardians, and main ritual actors in the community. Religious authorities had debated and developed these issues for centuries and would continue to do so. A relatively short survey like this one cannot convey the subtle differences within and between distinct religious confessions. Although we will distinguish Lutheran, Calvinist, Radical, and other views where appropriate, the emphasis will often be on much broader distinctions like those between Protestants and Catholics, Jews, and Muslims

The second half of the chapter will turn to look at changes in how Christians, Muslims, and Jews aimed to put their faith into action, above all through charity to various groups of the needy. The purgations that rolled through one community after another added many to the ranks of the needy, and made charity a very immediate concern. Beyond that, it was often through charity that communities marked their boundaries and disciplined their own members. When we move from theological doctrines to religious charity, we are moving from what people thought and believed to how they put their thoughts and beliefs into action. Changes to charity in the early modern period show how ideas of purity, purgation, and protection affected not just priests, pastors, merchants, and lawyers, but also orphans, abandoned children, widows, the sick, and the poor. The poor and needy were on a battleground, and sometimes it was hard to know whether they were being saved or sacrificed in the cause.

Ways of Thinking: Purity of Thought

Initiation

When faith communities welcome a new member, they mark the event – and sometimes mark the member – in a ceremony of initiation. Jews circumcised infant males soon after birth to show that they had joined the agreement or 'covenant' that God had made with Abraham naming him and his descendents as God's uniquely chosen people. Circumcising baby boys showed that this covenant passed through households, and that membership in the Jewish nation came in the first instance through family bloodlines and parental initiative. The boy then signaled his own acceptance of the covenant and gained entry as an adult into the local community of worshippers in the ceremony of bar mitzvah. Muslims also traced their origins to Abraham and also circumcised males as a sign of initiation into the faith, although they waited until age six or seven or even older. Muslims often celebrated circumcisions in festive public ceremonies that might initiate dozens of boys at a time. The Muslim boy was not being initiated into a select community, but onto a path that an entire community shared, and there was no later ceremony like the Jewish bar mitzvah to signal his own acceptance of the faith. There were no initiation ceremonies bringing Jewish or Muslim girls into the faith in the early modern period, and the *bat mitzvah* only emerged in the late nineteenth century.

From its very beginnings, Christianity adopted a different form of initiation into the faith: baptism. The ritual involved either sprinkling a little water over an initiate, or immersion into a larger pool or a flowing stream or river. It was performed on babies, or on early adolescents or young adults. Unlike circumcision, baptism was a form of initiation used with both males and females. It was a way of bringing everyone into the *Corpus Christianum*, whether or voluntarily or not.

Since baptism was often the first ritual performed on a Christian, we can use it as a way into understanding the broader range of rituals by which the faith was understood and practiced. And since it became one of the most controversial rituals of the early modern period – forced on Jewish and Muslim converts, and the lightening rod for fights between Radical Anabaptists and other Christians about who belonged in the *Corpus Christianum* – we need to understand it well in order to understand the broader dynamics around purity, purgation, and exile.

In the most common medieval forms of baptism, the priest marked the infant's forehead with water and oil as a sign that the child had entered the *Corpus Christianum*. The Catholic Church held that faith was not purely personal or purely individual – there would be little purpose for the church itself if it were. All members of the Body of Christ were to help each other through life and beyond death in the common goal of reaching heaven. The Judeo-Christian Bible provided the broad narrative that explained this path from the birth of the world to the final judgment at the end of time. Each believer's task in life was to repair the relationship with God that had first been broken when Adam and Eve, the original parents of the human race, disobeyed God's explicit command not to eat the fruit of a particular tree in the Garden of Eden where they lived. To disobey God was to 'sin', and this first act of disobedience by humanity's first parents was the 'original sin' that now disrupted every human being's relationship with God. In Genesis, the first book of the Judeo-Christian Bible, God had promised Adam and Eve that death would interrupt their relationship with him if they disobeyed. The Jewish scriptures (known to Christians as the Old Testament) included later references to a Messiah who would repair the broken relationship, and in Christian scriptures (i.e., the New Testament) this was interpreted this as the promise that God himself would come to earth in human form and take on the death penalty that he had imposed. Christianity emerged out of the conviction that the Jewish religious teacher Jesus Christ, condemned and executed just outside of Jerusalem by Roman authorities under the Emperor Tiberius, was indeed the promised Messiah who fulfilled the promise made to Adam and Eve. Jews and Muslims recognized Jesus as a historical religious teacher or prophet, but categorically rejected the idea that he had been God in human form, much less that the Messiah would have to suffer a humiliating death.

Judaism and Islam understood the original rupture of the relationship with God in much the same way as Christians did, and also emphasized that repairing the relationship came through membership in the community of the faithful. Christianity elaborated on this further by emphasizing that believers had to take the additional step of identifying directly and individually with the work, teaching, and death of Jesus. Through the Middle Ages, the mainline position was that the church was God's only vehicle on earth for doing this, and that it was necessary to be initiated into it. Repairing the broken relationship with God, what Christianity called 'salvation', could only take place in the community of other Christians gathered in the church, using the wide range of spiritual tools that God had given and continued to give. The influential fourth-century theologian St. Augustine held that it was God who initiated this process of repairing the relationship with believers, and that Jesus and the church were among his gifts of 'grace', which allowed that repair to happen. Just as Jews and Muslims believed that they represented the only true faith and way to God, Catholic and Orthodox Christians held that there was no salvation outside the church. Only the tools that God had given the church would in turn give believers the grace needed to heal the relationship with God and so bring them to heaven after death.

The Catholic Church's chief tools were seven rituals called 'sacraments' that marked the stages and set the rhythms of life: baptism, confirmation, penance, communion, marriage, ordination, and last rites. Receiving them brought you into an extended network of family and friends with whom you negotiated life's tensions and trials. It reshaped your natural inclinations around models set by Christ and his saints. More to the point, the sacraments were 'visible signs of invisible grace', and a continuing reminder that God's grace was a gift that had to be received and acted on. They provided a way into the world. John Bossy called the sacraments the 'skeleton of the social body', since they were not just theological abstractions but spiritual forms that shaped broader social relationships and realities. The five pillars of Islam that shaped a believer's life around almsgiving, prayer, and pilgrimage, and the set of dietary laws and holidays in Judaism served the same function of knitting the individual's life together with community. All three Abrahamic religions shared this same conviction that in order to enter heaven after death, you had to formally enter the religious community after birth.

It was baptism that brought you into the church. Of all the sacraments, it most clearly expresses the Catholic view of the church as a protective, purifying, and exclusive community. The rituals of baptism first cleared you of any evil spirits and then gave you the marks that identified you as a member of the *Corpus Christianum*: your personal names, your spiritual kin (godparents), and your saintly protectors. Catholics across late medieval Europe followed a host of local forms rooted in early Christian rituals and elaborated through the pronouncements of local councils, clergy, and rulers. Protestants quickly adopted new and distinctive ritual forms, but Catholics would make no effort to impose standardized forms in the Catholic Church until after the Council of Trent, and even then local traditions continued for centuries. Yet through all this diversity, a few constants remained, many of them resonant with lessons from the gospels.

Catholic baptism began with an exorcism. Whether infant or adult, the unbaptized one was thought to be firmly in the devil's grip. The priest first had to break this hold with special prayers and condemnations made at the door into the church. The celebrants then moved to a large container of consecrated water, called the font. The priest put some salt on the recipient's tongue, explained as preparing for the 'taste' of faith, and also touched the eyes, ears, nose, and heart (sometimes with spittle, following the example of Christ who had healed the blind and deaf in this way) to open the way to regeneration. After this, the godparents who were bringing a child forward (or, in cases of adult converts, the baptisands themselves) recited a few words renouncing Satan and his works. Godparents were the spiritual kin chosen by the parents to train and look out for the child, and they passed the child's name or names to the priest: possibly one name to signal the infant's blood kin and another to identify its patron saint. The ritual continued with water and oil, which were both signs of cleansing. Traditions around the water varied: some communities immersed their baptisands in a bath or river, others dipped them three times into a font, and others sprinkled their foreheads with water. The priest then made a sign of the cross with oil on the forehead. The baptisand was then dressed in a white robe to signify liberation, innocence, and purity, and given a lit candle to signal the light of faith.

The Catholic Church taught that the sacrament of baptism was not just a *sign* of grace but that it actually *gave* that grace. It was an extraordinarily powerful ritual and, in the eyes of some, an extraordinarily magical one. Parents brought ailing infants for baptism as early as they could, because they feared both that devil's grip was making their child physically ill, and also that a child who died unbaptized could never make it to heaven but would spend eternity in limbo. Those fears were strong enough to make baptism the only sacrament that a layperson or a woman could perform. In extreme cases with a newborn on the point of death, the midwife could administer baptism. This was an extraordinary concession, since the official Catholic position was that only those men who had been formally sanctioned and appointed by the church as priests through a ceremony known as ordination could perform the sacraments.

Baptism's power to cure, heal, purify and prepare for heaven was one of the key reasons why so many early Christians had fought over it. Their biggest disagreement was whether it should be performed on infants or on adults. The fourth-century emperor Constantine weighed the odds and chose to be baptised shortly before his death, as he believed that this would clean his soul of sin at the very point when he needed it most in order to move rapidly to heaven. Similar calculations led others to seek rebaptism late in life. The Catholic Church eventually ordered that believers should be baptized once only, and early at that. The sacrament was to initiate you to life and not prepare you for death. Since multiple baptisms would degrade the sacrament into a magical trick, any *re*baptism later in life was declared heresy.

Converts were the only exception. Early missionaries to Germanic tribes used baptism not only as a sign of conversion but also as the very means of it. Early modern missionaries to the Americas and Asia would do this as well. Some asked few questions before simply applying the water and oil. They were counting on baptism's power to break the hold of the devil, open the heart, purify the soul, and so achieve regeneration. Clergy who thought this way were making a logical extension from the fact that in Catholic theology the effectiveness of any sacrament, and hence also of baptism's power to purify and regenerate a soul, lay in their hands. The Catholic Church taught that it was the *action* of the priest that gave the sacrament its saving power, and not the spiritual state of either the recipient or the priest. The priest was not a magician, but simply an agent empowered by ordination. Ordination made him a conduit for God's grace, and that grace flowed by virtue of the ritual alone (expressed in the Latin term *ex opere operato,* or 'by the work worked'), rather than by the priest's personal power or character (*ex opera operantis,* or 'by the work of the one working'). This assured believers that the sacraments they received from their local priest were valid even if he was ignorant, inept, or immoral, as he frequently might be.

Given the common belief that baptism could purge the soul and complete the purifying process of conversion, it is not surprising that authorities used it when delivering ultimatums to Jews or Muslims: either be baptized or be exiled. We saw earlier that it was King Edward I who first gave this choice to England's miniscule Jewish community in 1290. French authorities repeated the ultimatum to Jews in the fourteenth century. Cities of the Holy Roman Empire did the same in the fifteenth, and Iberian kingdoms in 1391, 1492, and 1496. Iberian Moors would face the same choice in 1499–1502, repeatedly through the sixteenth century, and again in 1608–14. Carved reliefs from the Royal Chapel of the cathedral in Granada show separate mass baptisms of *morisco* men and women [Fig 28a & 28b]. Those who were baptized were spared exile, but not much else. Particularly in Iberia, both the Jewish *conversos* and the Moorish *moriscos* were marginalized, scrutinized, and treated with extreme suspicion as possibly false converts who secretly maintained their ancestral faith behind a facade of Catholic observance. When Al-Hazan al-Wazzan converted, Pope Leo had him closely questioned by his chamberlain and two bishops before agreeing to undertake the baptism. The ceremony took place in St. Peter's on the Feast of the Epiphany (January 6), with three cardinals who were all well known as enemies of Islam acting as godfathers.

28(a). Mass baptism of *Morisco* men in Granada. Art Resource NY. 28(b). Mass baptism of *Morisca* women in Granada. Art Resource NY

The larger complicating reality was the fact that many *conversos* and *moriscos* developed hybrid theologies that combined their old religious traditions with Christian beliefs. The Catholic Church had long embraced some degree of diversity in its rituals and spiritual practices, but integrating large groups of those raised as Jews or Muslims tested the limits of this diversity. Some Iberian *conversos* believed that they were now doubly chosen by God, by virtue both of circumcision and baptism. They believed that this made them superior to the Old Christians around them, and that they should integrate as many Jewish customs and rituals into Catholicism as possible. Similarly, many *moriscos* saw their own hybrid of Catholicism and Islam as orthodox because they had grown up learning that Islam integrated some elements of the Jewish and Christian narratives, and that it had superseded both. Iberian inquisitors did not agree, and deeply feared any inter-confessional mixing. They emphasized that Judaism and Islam were alien, and they fought for a very exclusive form of Catholicism built on purging heresy and framing the pure faith in abstract terms. They were so afraid of hybridity that they kept *conversos, moriscos,* and other converts out of the ranks of the clergy altogether, out of suspicion that these would subvert the Catholic faith from within. Spain's pure blood laws would prove a blunt but effective instrument for this.

Catholics believed that baptism triggered a process of regeneration that turned 'heathen' converts into complete Christians. Most people at the time considered conversion not as a one-time dramatic event that turned an individual around, but as a slow process of learning, adaptation, and acculturation to the rhythms of the new faith. And it was not just Christians who believed this. Muslims also thought that conversion was a journey rather than an event, and tracing the slow process of movement to the true faith was common in the memoirs of early modern converts to Islam like the Hungarian Catholic Murad b. Abdullah, the Greek Orthodox Mehmed, and the Jewish Yusuf b. Abi Abdudeyyan. When Islamic authorities staged public celebrations to mark the circumcision of converts and gave gifts like outfits of new clothing, they were signalling publically that a process of lifelong maturing had now begun. But what if the process never ended?

This was the fear that gnawed at Iberian Catholicism. Some authorities suspected *conversos* of secretly maintaining Judaism and *moriscos* of covertly practicing Islam for generations after the first conversion in a family. This was apostasy or heresy. Did these same authorities recognize their own anxieties as a sign that baptism's purgative and regenerative powers might be quite limited? Apparently not, for they continued the practice in spite of their fears. The Catholic Church certainly taught that the recipient had to be spiritually receptive for any sacrament to have validity and for it to work its power. Numerous popes had fought against the forced baptisms carried out on Iberian Jews because they believed it perverted the sacrament. The Council of Trent confirmed both the theology and liturgy of baptism in one of its earliest sessions in March 1547, and did not support using baptism as a tool to impose Christianity on unwilling forced converts. Yet the fact that Catholics across Europe continued with forced baptisms demonstrates that many were prepared to place their hopes in its magical powers ahead of theologians' careful formulations about the working of grace in the sacraments. Iberian missionaries, who would have been more familiar than most with the spotted record of baptism in perfecting conversion, expanded their ambitious baptizing campaigns among American aboriginals, African slaves, Indian Hindus, and others. Of course, they also expanded the Inquisition.

Baptism's 'failure' to reshape converts did strike a chord in another part of Europe. From Martin Luther onwards, Protestants retained baptism as a sacrament and as the main form of initiation into the Christian church. Until the eighteenth century, they did far less mission work outside Europe than Catholics did, and they seldom engaged in any forced conversions. Despite the many differences separating Protestant groups, they agreed on a number of points regarding baptism. They radically simplified it by abandoning three of the critical features that had fed Catholic expectations of its miraculous power to purify and regenerate. First, Protestants were united in believing that baptism did not give grace but was more modestly a sign of grace received; it confirmed but did not confer grace. Second, receiving that grace came only if the believer had faith. Third, any sacrament received in faith did not transform the believer's actual state, but only God's view of him or her – believers continued to *be* sinful, but God no longer *counted* their sins against them. These three changes effectively reversed the spiritual power in the sacraments: for Protestants, that power now lay in the faith of the believer and not in the hands of the priest. Baptizing Jews or Muslims against their will would not make them Christians; it would only make them wet.

Baptism was just one instance of a larger shift underway among Protestants as they rejected the idea that rituals and priests had special spiritual powers that made them intermediaries between believers and God. *'Ex opere operato'* was a dead letter for them, and not just in baptism, but in all the sacraments—and indeed in the processes of faith generally. Protestant reformers switched the focus from the officiant to the recipient of the sacrament, or from the priest to the believer. They still shied away from making this entirely subjective: as Luther put it, 'My faith does not make the baptism, but receives the baptism.'

Protestants' more limited view of what baptism did reflected their more limited view of what the church generally could do, or even had to do. For Catholics, baptism started a process of purification. Protestants believed there could be no such process because believers could never purify themselves – they were just too far gone in sin. Catholics could not accept the extravagant statements of absolute human sinfulness that Protestants frequently indulged in, thinking instead that God must have left humans with at least some capacity to do good even after the fall into sin. Humans could and must act on that capacity as they purified themselves over the course of their lives. Yet Luther and Calvin emphasized how terribly, totally, and absolutely cripplingly sinful human beings are because they considered this as just the first act in a two-act drama. The first act would bring despair, and the second act would then see a complete reversal as Christ covered over that mountain of sin in a single stroke, and so allowed the believer to pass directly into heaven as though personally pure.

Contrasting absolute sin and absolute grace in this way was using rhetoric and psychology to shape theology. It put an end to the church's larger role as the divinely appointed agency which alone could offer the tools that allowed you slowly to find your way to heaven. There was, in fact, salvation outside the church. Most reformers abandoned the Catholic view of the church as a protective, purifying, and exclusive institution. Most rejected the idea of advertising its great spiritual powers by building elaborately decorated churches rich in sights and smells, appointing powerful clerics in lavish robes, and recruiting armies of diplomats, soldiers, and judges to negotiate with friends and enemies across the globe. They replaced it with the far more modest idea of the church as the simple gathering of believers. Their radical simplification of the church and of Christianity itself had wide implications for everything churches and believers did, beginning with baptism.

After some initial hesitation, Luther simplified the baptismal ritual itself, removing the exorcism, the spittle, the anointing oil, the white robe, and the candle. Luther called these 'externals', and he could not find any of them in the Bible. Other Protestants followed suit, although they did not agree on whether the recipient should receive a sprinkling of water from a font, or full immersion in a river, stream, or pool. Protestant baptisms became very short affairs with hardly any ceremony attached. Calvin wanted them to take place within the ordinary worship service to emphasize that a new believer was joining the existing body of believers. The modest ceremony reinforced the fact that the *real* initiation was into the community of God's elect, and no one could really know whether they were in or out. That underlying conviction may have given Calvinists less comfort in the baptism ritual and less incentive to make much of it.

Yet in simplifying one aspect of baptism, these reformers complicated another. Rooting the sacraments in the faith of the believer made sense on one level, and reflected some lessons of the Bible. The Book of Acts, which Protestants asserted was the literal model for their ideas about faith and the church, had numerous examples of dramatic conversions marked by baptism: the Roman centurion Cornelius, the un-named jailers of Peter, Paul, and Silas, and most notably Paul himself. Conversions in the Bible were sudden, dramatic, and life-changing, and a baptism always confirmed the revolutionary change. Yet many Protestant reformers wanted to keep baptism as a sacrament performed on infants to usher them into the church. What infant had faith? The cool logic broke down a bit here, and efforts to fix the gap seemed inevitably to undermine the position that it was the believer's faith that turned a bath into a baptism.

Luther, Zwingli, and Calvin all argued that it was God who initiated salvation and that baptism is more a promise of God than an action of humans. They claimed that baptism was simply God's way of replacing the Old Testament Jewish ritual of circumcision with a more expansive New Testament ritual that broke open earlier boundaries of gender and race or family. Both were actions to be performed on infants as a sign of their membership in the Elect and Covenant people. Some argued that in keeping with the idea of a Covenant people, the faith which really mattered was God's faithfulness to his people, and the faith of parents who promised to raise their child as a believer. Some reached to metaphor and compared the water of baptism to Old Testament stories when God had quite literally saved his people from drowning, as during Noah's flood or the safe passage of the Israelites through the Red Sea.

Mainline reformers had fewer difficulties with these theological gymnastics than with what could have been the most elegant and logical solution to the problem: if it was the faith of the believer that made baptism, then only baptize the one who had a self-conscious grasp on faith. This would mean abandoning infant baptism and embracing adult baptism instead, although in practice the 'adult' here could be as young as twelve or fourteen. This was in fact the position taken by many Radical reformers, and it was so important to them that their broad corpus of doctrines was reduced by their enemies to one insulting tag line: 'anabaptists'. The Greek prefix 'ana' signified 'again', and so the insult meant that they were 'rebaptizers'. This of course only held for converts to Anabaptism who celebrated their new views with a new baptism, and not those who were raised by Radical/Anabaptist parents. Modern scholarship tends to prefer the term 'radicals' and to group these reformers with the Protestants, though that reflects later realities more than sixteenth-century attitudes. In the early sixteenth century, one of the few things that both Catholics and mainline Protestants could agree on was that the so-called Anabaptists were dangerous heretics who ought to be prosecuted.

If the mainline Protestant reworking of baptism implied a changed view of sacraments, the clergy, and faith, then the Anabaptist reworking of it implied a very different view of the church itself. While other Protestants still wanted an inclusive church on the old model of the *Corpus Christianum*, the Anabaptists believed that the church had to be a more selective body of true believers. Protestants generally, and Calvinists in particular, equated circumcision and baptism as the old and new signs of initiating infants into the community of God's Chosen People. Anabaptists made a sharp break here, and emphasized the church as a new, select, and adult people of God who had to break with the old 'Jewish' past. Baptism *replaced* circumcision. Anabaptists initiated each other into small and highly selective communities, not into a broader *Corpus Christianum*. It was an individual's personal faith that mattered, and not any broader social networks of spiritual kin. For those still shaped by earlier views of baptism, the Anabaptist refusal to baptize their infants meant that whole towns were now vulnerable to the contagion posed by these un-exorcised and unprotected children. In some parts of the Netherlands, Radical and Anabaptist families were more subject to accusations of witchcraft as a result.

No group of reformers had a more exclusive view of the church. Radicals continued to view the church as protective, purifying, and exclusive, but this was not the old *Corpus Christianum*. As we will see below, many Radicals adopted a highly literal view of the Bible, while others matched this with visions and revelations through which they believed God continued speaking in the present to his followers. Focusing on the model of the New Testament communities of believers, they believed the church had to remain outside political power structures and should even be ready to oppose them. It was not just that power would corrupt believers. Radicals believed that they were meant to demonstrate a purer order of social relationships beyond power and politics. This would work only if churches were extremely careful about whom they initiated, and extremely vigilant about removing those who failed to continue living by a high standard. Lose the faith, and you lost membership. The church must be pure, and in order to protect its purity, it had to be ready to exclude or ban those who repeatedly failed to meet its standards of perfection.

As we saw earlier, some radicals fought to destroy violently the current sinful order. Apocalyptic millenarians emerged in the context of the Peasant Wars, the Munster experiment, the English Civil War, and the European Thirty Years War. Other radicals embraced pacifism, deciding not to fight the sinful world but simply to withdraw from it and live in self-sufficient rural communities to demonstrate the new spiritual order with the primitive communism of the early Christian church: these moved to Moravia and Poland. Some who were less absolute in their pursuit of purity, lived discretely in Dutch towns, and cities and gradually gained the right to live openly, like the Waterland Mennonites.

Baptismal practices began to vary widely among Europe's Christian confessions by the late sixteenth century. This reflected their different views of how and through whom God worked in the world, and of how and by whom the church was constituted. Even the place and rituals demonstrated this. Many Catholic towns in France and Italy had separate baptisteries, some dating back to the fifth and sixth century, where every infant born within the walls was brought by godparents to be initiated with salt, water, and oil. The small octagonal baptisteries found in Poitiers, Aix, and Riez, are among the oldest surviving buildings in France, while the monumental baptisteries in Rome, Pisa, and Florence show how central the ritual was in medieval cities. Most Protestant churches had only a small baptismal font in the local church, where the priest or pastor sprinkled water on an infant's head. Fearing that Anabaptist parents and their unbaptized children would be physically and spiritually contagious, Protestant and Catholic authorities alike became more vigilant about keeping written baptismal registers that allowed them to track who was baptizing their infant children. Zurich adopted the register as a practical and legal necessity shortly after its city council declared in 1526 that both rebaptism and baptism by a layperson would be punishable with death by drowning. Not all cities were quite so harsh, but they could impose strict penalties. Genevan mother Ameyd Darnex failed to baptize her child until age six, and so in 1542 was thrown in prison and forced to make a public apology. Lutheran and Calvinist authorities also aimed to stop the exorcisms that had long been the first step in the baptismal ritual, but they encountered stiff opposition from parents who still feared the devil's grip on their child. One Dresden butcher threatened a pastor with a cleaver to ensure that his infant daughter would get her exorcism, while in other cities parents were delaying baptisms or crossing over borders to find a priest who would perform the rite.

The Protestant mainstream rejected the idea that baptism had purifying and purgative powers, and with that they rejected the Catholic practice of using baptism as a tool to achieve conversion and not just to mark it. Perhaps because they had stripped the sacrament of this power, Protestants did not pursue forced conversion on the mass scale of Iberian Catholics. Some Anabaptist Radicals continued treating baptism as a purifying and purgative agent, though it was less to purge others than to purify themselves. This emphasis on cleansing was one reason why early Radicals like Conrad Grebel preferred to perform baptism in a flowing stream or river, as Christ had received it from John the Baptist. Later Mennonites and Baptists imitated the large bath-like pools of the early church, which more dramatically demonstrated baptism's full washing away of sin.

Regardless of these wide variations in popular understanding and ritual performance, it is worth noting that baptism remained everywhere a key sacrament marking initiation into the Christian community. And the belief common to all confessions was that the sacrament which marked inclusion in the community had by necessity a deeply exclusive side to it.

Rituals of initiation became more important in the early modern period because of the number of forced baptisms of Jews and Muslims, and the intense battles between different Christian groups. They took on a special resonance in Islam and Judaism as these communities had to determine how to re-integrate people who had been forcibly converted to Catholicism in an earlier age or generation and who now wished to return to the ancestral faith.

In the Arabic formularies of the ritual, adult male converts to Islam were seen as 'surrendering' or 'submitting' to Allah. Dressed in Ottoman or North African dress, the convert was led on horseback in procession to a shrine where, in the presence of a holy man and with his index finger raised to heaven, he spoke the Muslim confession (*shahada*) three times: 'I bear witness that there is no god but Allah, and I bear witness that Mohammed is the

Messenger of God.' He was immediately circumcised and received a gift of new white clothing just as young Muslim boys did. In major cities like Istanbul and Algiers, the conversions of Christians to Islam became important acts of diplomatic propaganda that highlighted Islam's claim to be the superior faith. The Ottomans began keeping records of major public ceremonies in 1609, and developed specific public rituals in which officials gave sets of new clothing, and scribes recorded both the convert's new name and the gifts and pensions that he received. The more lavish public ceremony was meant to underscore the fact that in Islam as in Christendom, the convert was taking on an entire political order and identity together with the new religion.

The situation was more complicated for Jewish communities, due not to geopolitical rivalries but rather to the long history of forced conversions of Jews to Catholicism. In Islam, the context of piracy and conquest meant that there were many 'strategic' converts who were interested in gaining some political or economic power. By contrast, conversion to Judaism brought few if any political or economic benefits. Most of those seeking to convert to Judaism were *conversos* returning to the ancestral faith after a few generations of living as Catholics. Catholic authorities saw the return of *conversos* to Judaism as heresy, and Jewish authorities were caught between welcoming and also suspecting converts for whom Judaism might mean little beyond a few domestic rituals and some favourite foods. Their anxieties increased as *conversos* moved to major refugee cities like Salonika, Venice, and Amsterdam, and began doing business with Jewish merchants, connecting with families, and participating in cultural activities. Catholic fears that *conversos* would be drawn back into their ancestral religion if they were not closely monitored drove the Iberian Inquisition into Spanish and Portuguese colonies and led Inquisitors to ramp up their efforts any time large groups of Jews migrated. But Jewish rabbis and councils in Venice, Salonika, and Amsterdam worried just as much that the *conversos*' relative indifference to some of the Jewish laws deriving from the Torah, Talmud, and rabbinic law and known as *halakha* might have a corrosive influence on practicing Jews. As a result, they too put more emphasis on teaching the traditions and rituals and on disciplining those who failed to follow them.

In fact, just as some *conversos* had brought Jewish traditions into their Catholic practice, so now many of those reconverting to Judaism remained attached to some Christian traditions and understandings, to the point that some historians speak of them as 'divided souls'. Some *conversos* believed that they had never ceased being members of the 'Jewish Nation' by virtue of their ancestry and beliefs, and that this was more important than any forced public conversion to Catholicism that they had made to avoid exile or death.

For them it was enough to believe in the Law of Moses without actually following the difficult and sometimes puzzling commandments of *halakha* in detail. Beliefs like this challenged Jewish communities. Some of them developed new ceremonies and rituals around key rites of passage that would be familiar and appealing to *conversos* raised in Catholicism. The Amsterdam synagogues developed elaborate circumcision ceremonies to celebrate and initiate returning *conversos*. Yet these new ceremonies and the looser views of the 'divided souls' pushed some other Jews to opposed compromises, and to push for more exclusive definition of who comprised the Jewish Nation and how they had to demonstrate this.

Presence (Communion)

Many Christian sacraments were important, but only one brought God directly and physically down to earth. In the New Testament account of the last meal that Jesus shared with his disciples before his trial and crucifixion, which was the Jewish Festival of Passover, he referred to the bread and wine they were sharing as his body and blood. Jesus commanded that his followers repeat the meal in the future to mark his sacrificial death, and the ritual steadily moved to become the centre of Christian worship in the form of communion. But how could Christians balance physical reality and metaphor when bread became body and wine became blood? It was to outsiders the most puzzling and even offensive religious ritual. Some early Roman critics accused Christians of cannibalism, while Luther lampooned Catholics for worshipping a 'God of Dough'. Muslims scratched their heads: how could this man be the All-Powerful God when he could not even prevent a colonial governor and some common soldiers from killing him? Why would Christians choose to commemorate a humiliating execution? Jews and Muslims rejected the very idea that God would take physical form at all, and even some Christians like the medieval Cathars and early modern anti-Trinitarians rejected the concept of 'incarnation'. It was his embarrassing death even more than his tawdry birth that made Jesus' humanity so offensive and improbable to many, and that made the ritual celebrating it so repellent. What must Al-Hazan al-Wazzan or any other forced converts have thought when first taking a communion wafer?

Making God physically present on earth was a central feature of Catholicism. It happened in communion, and three late-medieval developments in doctrine and ritual forms shaped later controversies around this sacrament. First, the Dominican theologian Thomas Aquinas used Aristotle's metaphysics to frame a more sophisticated explanation of how two common foodstuffs like bread and wine could become human flesh and blood while never changing their shape or taste. Very few Christians could be expected to understand his explanation of transubstantiation. Yet they did know one thing: it meant that every time a priest celebrating mass raised the small round wafer called a 'host', Christ bodily joined the *Corpus Christianum* gathered near the altar. This was highly abstract. A second and far more concrete and powerful development were the miracles that came soon after, in which a consecrated host dripped real blood that stained altar cloths red. Miracles helped expand a new devotion around the host that had first emerged from a community of women in Liege in 1246. Called Corpus Christi or Corpus Domini, this feast a little more than eight weeks after Easter soon became one of the most important on the Catholic calendar. Thomas Aquinas wrote the liturgy, but whole communities took it to the streets. And this was the third critical development, since Corpus Christi processions brought all the guilds, confraternities, and clergy marching together through the streets of the community in company with Christ himself, really present among them in the form of a consecrated host.

The Real Presence of Christ was awesome and electric. It was the most powerful physical expression imaginable of the three meanings of 'the body of Christ' that we saw in Chapter 1 – the person of Jesus, the bread of the sacrament, and community of believers all together in one. *This* was what you converted to and for, and one of the main 'powers of the host' was precisely its ability to change hearts. The Real Presence turned the host into a talisman, and elevated the role of the priest, who alone could perform the ritual magic of consecration. At that central moment in the mass a tinkling bell silenced conversation and focused everyone's attention as the priest raised the host and triggered the miracle. This re-enacted Christ's sacrifice on the cross. It brought blood into the sacrament in a deeply resonant form that illustrated Christ's ultimate sacrifice while also explaining for Christians the demonic evil of some of their enemies. In the legends that soon spun and grew, Jews and witches thirsted for that blood. They clearly did not want to drink it as Christians remembering that Christ's sacrifice was their salvation. They wanted to spill, desecrate, and destroy it. Stories, songs, and woodcuts about Jews stabbing or burning consecrated hosts they had stolen or bought, or of witches offering hosts to the devil served as a kind of backhanded confirmation of transubstantiation. If even Christ's enemies recognized the presence and power of Jesus' blood in the wine and bread, what business did Christ's followers have in doubting it? So great was the belief in the wine as Christ's physical blood, that there were real fears that the laity might desecrate that body with their slurping and spilling. As a result, from the thirteenth century, lay communicants were given the bread alone (usually placed not in their hand but directly on their tongue by the priest), and only clergy could take communion in the 'two kinds' of bread and wine.

Eucharistic piety was at the center of popular devotions and popular fears throughout the fifteenth century. The devout took communion often, hurrying around churches to witness the moment of consecration, and jostling for position in Corpus Christi processions. They marvelled at and commissioned ever-more-ornate communion cups and plates glistening for their parish, guild, or confraternity altars – royal tableware for the king of Heaven. They left legacies for masses to be said on their behalf after they died, with the result that some priests worked all day long fulfilling these vows, and anyone entering a church would have seen priests saying mass at altars with no one else present.

Believers also heard stories, sang songs, and saw broadsheets illustrating how Jews and witches desecrated the host. In these popular media that exploded with the spread of printing, Christ's enemies soon took their hunt for blood further into the *Corpus Christianum*, seeking even the blood of Christ's followers, and particularly children. It is unlikely that this broader 'blood libel' against Jews and witches would have emerged initially or become so profound or powerful were it not for the increased emphasis on Christ's Real Presence – that is, Christ's physical body and blood – in the communion host. Earlier propaganda about Jews had focused more around the fear that they spread plague. So it is also no surprise that the theology and rituals around communion would become a lightning rod for other issues like the role of the clergy and their relation to laity, and the very nature of the *Corpus Christianum*.

The Hussite and Lollard movements of the late fourteenth and early fifteenth movements both allowed laity to once more drink from the communion cup. It was a powerful symbol of how to curb the privileged position of the clergy and to emphasize that all believers were equal within the *Corpus Christianum*. Each reform movement and each so-called heretical movement of the next two hundred years would hammer on the same point. There was fundamental equality in the Body of Christ and full access to communion was a potent demonstration of it. This was all the more central a marker of identity because everyone understood the implications immediately: Hussite leaders posted a large communion cup on the facade of the late Gothic Tyn church that towered over the Old Town Square in Prague; they were commonly known as 'utraquists', adapting a Latin term for 'both kinds'. Yet even the most vigilant Catholic reformers took up the image. In a particularly heated sermon in 1493, Savonarola thundered 'in the primitive church we had chalices of wood and prelates of gold, and in these days the church has chalices of gold and prelates of wood!'

Reformers of the early sixteenth century seized on this image. Huldrych Zwingli very deliberately replaced the elaborate golden communion chalice in Zurich's Great church with a simple wooden beaker. This was the visible sign of another and far more controversial replacement: Zwingli rejected outright the very concept of the Real Presence, and all that had grown up around it in Catholicism. In his view, when Christ said, 'This is my body' and 'This is my blood,' he was only speaking metaphorically. Trained as a humanist, Zwingli looked at Christ's words as a rhetorical statement and not a physical fact. As a result, there was in Zurich no re-enactment of Christ's sacrifice, no transubstantiation of bread and wine into flesh and blood, no physical entry of Christ into the community of believers gathered around the altar. For that matter, there was no altar: Zwingli replaced this with a simple table, the better to signal that communion was not some species of ritual magic staged by a priest, but rather that it was a meal shared by equals in memory of and thanks for Christ's death and resurrection. Zwingli – and all Protestants after him – chose not to re-enact Christ's death, but rather to re-enact and embody the community of the early church. They called it the 'Lord's Supper' to commemorate the final Passover meal that Jesus had shared with his disciples when he first offered bread and wine as a memorial of his coming sacrifice. To further emphasize that communion happened in the local community of believers, Protestant pastors used common everyday language rather than Latin in their communion services.

Zwingli's complete purging of the Real Presence from communion was one of his most radical acts, and a profound and unsettling departure that few could follow – the Hussites and Lollards had not gone this far. Luther and Calvin would also balk at it and aim to find a less radical linguistic solution to the problem. Because they did see a problem here. The Real Presence had generated within Catholicism a florid and expensive material culture of gold and silver communion ware, processions, and masses being said in a continuous loop in otherwise empty shrines. The commercialization of communion threatened to overwhelm its spiritual meaning. It solidified the privileged position of the priests – Luther himself identified the priests' decision to withhold the cup from the laity as one of the 'walls' with which clergy protected their claims to a special character, power, and position in the church. It fed magical superstitions and manipulations of the host. In 1558, a Tournai weaver rushed up to the altar, seized the consecrated host, and yelled 'deceived people, do you believe this is the King, Jesus Christ, the true God and Saviour? Look!' He then crumbled it in his hands and ran away. It was fear of the host's power that lay behind blood libels against Jews and witches, though neither Luther nor Calvin pointed this out as a specific problem. They wanted to move beyond the host as a talisman and magical object and emphasize instead communion as a community meal in which bread and wine fed believers' faith. They rejected the idea of masses celebrated by a priest alone to fulfil a donor's legacy or vow as though hard cash could buy holy magic. Communion could only happen when a community was present to receive Christ.

Protestants agreed that communion did not involve some kind of re-sacrificing of Christ, but they divided on the question of whether and how Christ was present in the bread and wine of communion. Radicals and Anabaptists held to positions like Zwingli's and saw rituals as no more than symbolic reminders of a spiritual truth. Their purging of all Real Presences and their emphasis on the purely spiritual content of the sacraments earned them the tag 'spiritualists' or 'sacramentarians'. Erasmus and many others who came to religious reform out of the humanist movement held to similar views, both because of their appreciation of the richness of language and their aversion to more literal or material readings that could feed superstition and magical practices. Peter Riedemann claimed that individual believers were like the many grains of wheat united in a single loaf of bread, and that the miracle of communion lay in Christ's uniting scattered bodies and divided minds into that one loaf. Yet such metaphors earned Radicals the intense opposition of more mainline Protestants who rejected their theological formulations even as they gradually adopted many of their more simplified ritual practices.

Luther was most vehement in rejecting radical spiritualism. When debating Zwingli in the town of Marburg, he wrote Christ's words 'Hoc est corpus meum' ('This is my body') on a table top in chalk (some claimed he carved it with a penknife). Yet Luther's solution to the problem played with rhetoric and language as much as Zwingli's. He claimed that the bread and wine never ceased to be foodstuffs even as they miraculously became Christ's body and blood – the two substances simply co-existed ('consubstantiation'). Luther's striking image of red hot iron – which he described as being both entirely iron and entirely fire at the same time – picked up on a different side of Aristotelian physics to explain the paradox. Calvin's heart was with Lutheran imagery, but his mind tended towards Zwinglian metaphor. In his formulation, believers received Christ's body and blood 'truly and spiritually', while unbelievers and Catholics ate and drank judgment on themselves because of their superstitions. On this point, as with predestination, Calvin resolved the intellectual difficulty by claiming that limited human understanding could not comprehend all the mysteries of faith. More importantly, his followers reduced communion in practice to an infrequent ritual of purely symbolic importance. Lutherans and members of the Church of England continued taking communion weekly as a spiritual obligation, while most Calvinists and Radicals took it once every few months as a doctrinal statement.

This was critical. Doctrinal formulations were important, but the real texture of differences came in what lay believers experienced when they entered a church. When a city council or a duke or king decided to change religious practice, the most critical step was banning the mass. Nuremberg did this in 1524–1525, Bern in 1528, Geneva in 1535, Augsburg in 1537. No other action came close to matching the significance of this move: not the Strasbourg city council ordering evangelical preaching, not a Munster mass baptism, not a Basel mob smashing images, not a Saxon duke or English king closing monasteries and convents. Banning the mass expelled Christ physically from worship – at least in the eyes of those deeply steeped in Catholic spirituality. Banning the mass and stripping the altars was a highly political move, which signalled that a community was abandoning Catholicism. It could be so traumatic that many attempted to cushion the blow: the artful and sometimes obscure expressions of Luther's 1526 German mass and Cranmer's 1552 Church of England communion liturgy are evidence of this. So too are the frequent efforts in localities across the Protestant world to evade the new rules. Some English parishes responded by burying their communion cups and plates in the hope that the tides would eventually turn.

Catholics were not idle as Protestants battled over communion. Some moderate Catholic reformers like Erasmus or Augsburg's Johann Schilling criticised eucharistic piety, and there were intense debates at the Council of Trent over whether to give the cup to the laity. Yet in the end, Trent would confirm all the fundamental points of Catholic tradition. It confirmed that the mass was a re-sacrifice of a Christ really present. It confirmed Latin as the language of the mass, without ruling out vernaculars, and it still held back the cup. The ability to make Christ present in the here and now became the most profoundly distinctive element of Catholic spirituality. It was a powerfully direct challenge to Protestant claims to have shortened the distance between believers and God. Existing devotions like frequent communion became more common. Processions like Corpus Christi that brought the host along city streets and into neighborhood churches became longer and more dramatic, often taking place by torchlight in the evening. Each parish gained a Holy Sacrament confraternity to organize these and other eucharistic devotions and help the parish priest as he policed observance. Authorities placed greater emphasis on the sacrament of confirmation, which allowed a child to take communion. Some early church authorities had set this at age one or three, even though the general notion was that it should be at the 'age of discretion' when the child had a clearer sense of what communion entailed. Both before, but particularly after, the Council of Trent, adult volunteers began teaching Catholic beliefs in rudimentary Sunday Schools called 'Schools of Christian Doctrine', with an eye to seeing children through confirmation and into the Catholic Church before early adolescence. Poorhouse and orphanage censuses now noted clearly which children had reached the age of confirmation.

There were also new devotions. At some point in the 1520s or 1530s, lay members of a Milanese Catholic confraternity began praying in shifts for forty hours continuously before a consecrated host. Within a couple of years, Pope Paul III endorsed the new devotion, claiming that it would turn back God's anger at Christian sins and halt the expansion of the Turks. Forty hours corresponded to the time that Christ had spent in the tomb after his crucifixion, and so this new pious exercise emphasized his death and resurrection. Confraternities and religious orders, the Jesuits above all, spread the Forty Hours devotion widely through the sixteenth century, and almost always as a direct challenge to Protestant claims to have made Christ more present in the lives of ordinary believers.

Communion was about community, and what you believed about whether or not Christ was physically present in the celebration had many implications for what you thought about authority in the community generally. As with baptism, how and where communion took place said a great deal about what it meant. The Catholic Church promoted frequent communion according to a uniform ritual with lavish cups and plates worthy of the King of Heaven. One significant problem faced by colonial missionaries was how to keep wine and wheat from spoiling, since there could be no substitutions. Anglicans and Lutherans retained more of the liturgical rituals and elaborate dress and furnishings of Catholicism in their weekly communion services, while Calvinists and particularly Radicals eliminated most forms that might suggest clerical magic and emphasized with communal tables that this was fundamentally just a meal.

Clergy used communion to sharpen confessional lines, and political authorities both Catholic and Protestant made it a critical marker of obedience. In later years, Scottish Presbyterian and French Huguenot elders would visit congregation members in the week before communion, distributing tokens which gave those in good standing admission to the communion table. Few other churches used markers in this way, but all practiced forms of 'closed communion' that made sure only members got the host. Catholics in particular went out of their way to ensure that *all* took it. Catholic priests brought the host into public streets and private homes in ways at once pastoral and provocative, since it could be a way to identify dissidents. A priest's visit to the home of a sick or dying individual to administer communion showed deep faith in the power of the sacrament to heal body and soul, but also rooted out closet Protestants who might be aiming to evade detection by avoiding public mass. Since the host he brought had already been consecrated, those whom the priest passed en route to the private home were expected to remove their hats and bow or kneel in honour to Christ. In some divided cities in Spain, France, and Germany where Jews, Muslims, Protestants, and Catholics lived side by side this could prove contentious. An Andalusian Muslim in fifteenth-century Valencia who failed to kneel when a priest passed by with the consecrated host risked death. A Huguenot in sixteenth-century France who failed to at least remove his hat risked being beaten up. While some quickly scurried down a side street to avoid the encounter, priests were known to go out of their way to bring the host through Protestant neighbourhoods, to surprise them in markets and squares, and even to chase them, as happened to a Protestant maid in Bordeaux called Toinette who was convicted for failing to honour the host even though others testified that the priest had pursued her 'purposefully and maliciously'.

Toinette was charged in 1646. We may think that religious differences were less significant by that time, but in fact they were hardening. Communion was indeed about community, and what you believed about it could be the single most critical test determining whether you were part of a community or not. Soon after Catholic troops routed the Bohemians in the 1620 Battle of the White Mountain, Holy Roman Emperor Ferdinand II had the Hussite chalice removed from the facade of the Tyn church and melted down to create a halo for the statue of the Virgin Mary that would replace it. Half a century later, as England was emerging from the Civil War and Commonwealth, Charles II had Parliament pass a Corporation Act (1661) requiring that all members of civil and political corporations, including Parliament, had to take communion in the Church of England or face dismissal. The later Test Act (1673), 'For Preventing the Dangers which may Happen from Popish Recusants' required all civil and military officers to publicly declare, 'I do believe that there is not any transubstantiation in the sacrament of the Lord's Supper, or in the elements of the bread and the wine, or after the consecration thereof by any person whatsoever.' A third act in 1678 required all members of the House of Lords and House of Commons to declare publicly against the mass, transubstantiation, and the invocation of saints.

As we will see further below, through the course of the seventeenth and right through the eighteenth century, many churches were built close to borders across the Holy Roman Empire so that people of a banned religion living in one territory could commute across the border in order to worship and take communion in another. When William III of Orange began attempting to force conversion on the Catholic majority in Lingen by restricting their civil rights and forcing them to attend Calvinist services, they responded by travelling to Catholic churches built specifically for them over the border in Munster and Osnabruck. A few years later, the duke of Wurttemberg sheltered Huguenots who left France after the Revocation of the Edict of Nantes, but required that they worship outside his territory, thus forcing them into colonies close to the border. Lutherans in Catholic Silesia began travelling to a series of churches built just over the border in Saxony shortly after the 1648 Peace of Westphalia, and when their Hapsburg rulers aimed to stop the practice it took Swedish intervention to negotiate an agreement in 1707. Thanks to tightly enforced political restrictions on religious worship, residence and faith no longer formed a single *Corpus Christianum*.

On one level, the Catholic Restoration in Bohemia, the Corporation and Test Acts in England, the border churches across the Holy Roman Empire, prosecutions of servant girls like Toinette, and even Presbyterian communion tokens were just crude power plays meant to marginalize religious dissidents. Yet they signal two critical points. In any state church, whether Catholic or Protestant, points of religious belief were critical points of political obedience, and they remained so into the eighteenth century. The single most deeply held, most definitive, and most divisive point of religious belief had to do with how Christ was present in worship and in the community, not least because it was about far more than religious doctrine. The Catholic doctrine of the Real Presence suspended time, since mass repeated Christ's actual sacrifice and underscored the immediate and ongoing presence of the sacred in the world, and the sacramental power of church and clergy. By contrast, the Protestant emphasis on symbolic presence and memorialisation demonstrated a more linear and chronological view of time, with Christ's sacrifice an unrepeatable historical event that all believers could remember, publicly or privately, and that clergy evoked more in sermon lessons than by ritual magic.

Authority (Scripture)

Most religious traditions assume that God speaks to his followers, either through some set of written sacred scriptures (the Torah, the Qur'an, the Bible), which become fixed over time, or through dreams and visions that come in times of crisis. These are not necessarily opposed: scriptures often include written accounts of dreams or prophecies, and those proposing new interpretations of the written scripture will often claim to have received a vision directly from God. Yet with either writings or visions, questions of authenticity and authority arise immediately: who decides on the written scriptures? How do believers interpret one or the other? How can anyone be confident that it is God speaking? How can communities protect themselves and their traditions from fraudsters, heretics, or the power hungry? These were the most urgent questions dividing Christendom in our period, and they were at the bottom of the some of the fiercest fights.

It may seem that Protestants very easily swept away centuries of Catholic tradition on the sacraments of baptism and communion. As we look more closely, we see that they were not simply changing this or that doctrine. They were engaged in a wholesale purgation and radical simplification of Christian theology. They based this on a radical re-thinking of authority and scripture. Yet their complete rejection of traditional Catholic restraints on interpreting scripture left them open to the endless series of disputes and divisions over doctrine which led Protestantism to fracture into ever-smaller groups with no central authority.

There was a common principle behind the different Protestant purgations. Any religious idea or spiritual practice or clerical office or authority which could not be found in the Bible – the New Testament particularly, but for some the Old as well – had to go. The Bible was not simply the main authority for faith and practice, it was the *only* authority. What Luther described with the Latin term *sola scriptura* (scripture alone) became perhaps the single doctrine that Protestants could most agree on in principle. Of course, as a result it became the one they most diverged on in practice. Protestants' allied conviction was that the Bible had to be translated out of Latin, Greek, and Hebrew into the vernacular languages that people spoke daily. Christians of all confessions described scripture as God's 'Word', picking up on a term found in the Bible itself. Protestants took this a step further: God would speak his Word to ordinary believers in their ordinary languages. Moreover, believers were expected not just to hear it in church services, but to read it themselves, using sermons and catechisms to guide their reading.

In June 1523, Bern's city councillors passed a law requiring preachers to preach only from the scripture. Constance, Kitzingen, and Memmingen followed suit in 1524. In 1525, after a city council debate on preaching, Nuremberg forbade Catholic preachers from mounting the pulpit. These so-called scripture mandates were promoted as moderate compromises to calm restless cities. Yet they were political endorsements of *sola scriptura*, and indeed each of these cities subsequently banned the mass, changed the baptismal order, closed monasteries and convents, and expelled or expropriated Catholic clergy and institutions. As Protestantism developed, scriptural preaching no longer had to be mandated by authorities because it was a given. Luther's Bible commentaries trained Lutheran pastors for preaching and teaching, Calvin's many thousand sermons moved systematically through all books of the Bible, and each of England's pulpits was provided with an Authorized Version of the Bible in the language of the common people.

Bible translation was one of the first activities that reformers undertook, in part so as to ensure that passages would say what the reformers wanted or needed them to say. Henry VIII banned Tyndale's 1525 English translation, but commissioned his own Great Bible (largely a purged and 'corrected' version of Tyndale's) in 1539. The Marian exiles responded with a Genevan Bible (1557–60), which restored much of Tyndale and became so much more popular than Henry's Great Bible that Elizabeth I sanctioned the Bishops' Bible (1568) as a translation less offensive to Catholics and moderate Anglicans [Fig 29a, 29b, 29c]. James I finally stepped in with an Authorized Version of 1611 which again trimmed the more radical – now Calvinist – shadings in this or that passage and ensured that the Bible on the pulpit and in

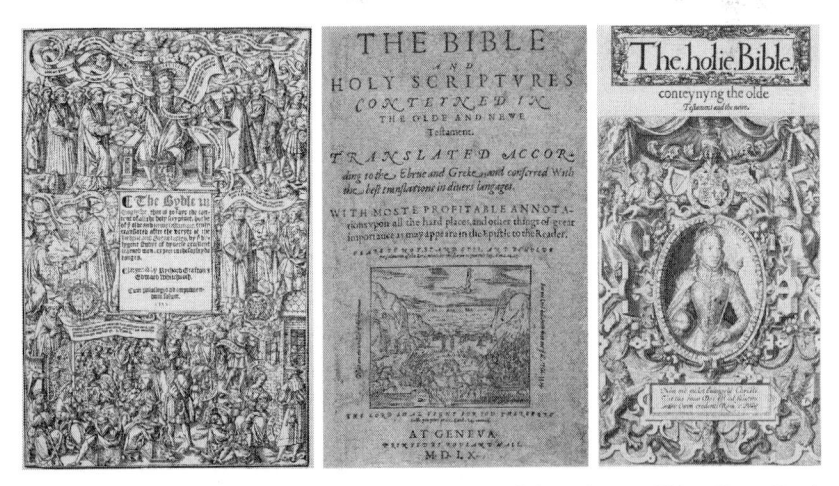

29(a). Henry VIII's Great Bible (1539). Courtesy of the Thomas Fisher Rare Book Library, University of Toronto. 29(b) Geneva Bible (1560). Courtesy of the Thomas Fisher Rare Book Library, University of Toronto. 29(c) Elizabeth I's Bishops' Bible. Courtesy of the Thomas Fisher Rare Book Library, University of Toronto.

the pews fully upheld the Church of England and the monarch who was its Supreme Governor. Calvin similarly rejected Sebastiano Castellio's French translation in favor of one done in 1535 by his cousin, Pierre Olivetan. Five years after Calvin's death, a team of Geneva's pastors and professors began revising this translation and after almost two decades produced the French Geneva Bible (1588) that remained the authoritative version for over a hundred years. Many early vernacular translations were the work of one energetic individual, but as concerns over orthodoxy increased, so too did the number of scholars collaborating together and the time they took producing it.

If we think of churches as 'imagined communities' that identify themselves by a few key convictions, then *sola scriptura* would have to be the one most central to Protestant identity as the religion of the common believer. Protestantism would eventually generate doctrinally bound institutions and state churches that competed to outdo Rome in the extravagance of their architecture, liturgy, and claims to truth, but *sola scriptura* spoke to Protestants' most cherished conviction that, unlike Catholics, they followed a simple form of Christianity in which God spoke directly to his believers and they spoke directly back. It was the doctrine which most empowered the laity, because it was the one which most thoroughly purged the Catholic concept of the church with its clergy and rituals guarding access to God. Every special office or power, every gold chalice or incense-filled censer, every indulgence, decretal, and ban, every patron saint demanding prayers or priest demanding alms could be swept aside. *Sola scriptura* was the most powerful purgative in the Protestant arsenal, and every layman, woman, and child knew it.

The question was 'how does God speak, and to whom?' *Sola scriptura* assumed that the Bible was transparent and accessible and that the clergy were delegated and accountable to the laity generally or to particular lay rulers and authorities. Catholic authorities resisted this on many grounds, and not only in order to protect the privileged position of the clergy as Luther so powerfully charged in early popular writings like the *Address to the Christian Nobility* and *Freedom of the Christian*. Nor was it because they did not appreciate scripture or want to keep all vernacular translations out of the hands of the laity. Catholic laity had been reading vernacular Bibles for well over a century. The 1229 Synod of Toulouse indeed made it illegal for laity to own scripture, Pope Gregory XI banned vernacular religious books in 1375, and English bishop Thomas Arundel (later also Archbishop of York, Canterbury, and a number of smaller sees) banned vernacular translations of the Bible in 1409; the archbishop of Mainz in Germany followed suit in

1485. But Luther was inventing tradition when he claimed that the Bible lay 'under the bench and in dust, disregarded by theologians, unreadable for believers'. Twenty-two German translations of all or part of the Bible appeared before Luther's New Testament in 1522, and in the 1470s alone Bibles appeared in French, Italian, German, Dutch, Spanish, and Czech. Biblical study was a standard of the Flemish *devotio moderna* and hence taken for granted by Dutch reformers like Erasmus. Short collections of psalms and gospel passages, called 'little flowers' (*fioretti*) in Italian, were widely popular, and Italian confraternities stocked up on gospel harmonies as these became more widely available in print through the fifteenth century. The Bible was not absent from Catholic homes or pulpits.

Ecclesiastical authorities were more anxious about whole vernacular Bibles than about edited selections, and they worried about heterodox marginalia above all. Catholic resistance to making the Bible widely available was rooted in the conviction that it was a potentially dangerous text, not at all transparent and accessible. For every comforting psalm or simple gospel story, there were dozens of perplexing prophecies and scorching judgmental tirades. Misunderstanding passages like this could lead to heresy and send countless souls to hell; it had certainly happened often enough in the past, at least in the eyes of Catholic authorities. Given the stakes involved in handling this revelation from God, interpretation of the Bible was something best left to trained professionals. These had the skills to consult earlier debates, broader doctrines, and past theologians. They could peel back at least four different layers of meaning in the text: the literal, the prophetic (known to medieval theologians as the 'anagogical' meaning), the allegorical ('typological'), and the moral ('tropological'). In case of disagreement on some fundamental matter, the church's army of theologians could weigh in, and the pope could arbitrate. This was at least as self-evident and as rational as *sola scriptura*: Luther would not trust the health of his body to anyone but a trained doctor or surgeon, so why trust the fate of his soul to an uneducated ploughman or the corner butcher? In fact, he would not, as his response to the Peasants' Revolt amply demonstrated. The laity were fine in principle, but in the flesh they tended to be less compelling. What seemed simple was anything but.

It was not reading the Bible that was radical and purgative, but the Bible *alone*. The intellectual movement towards *sola scriptura* emerged from the emphasis within humanist scholarship on reading classical sources in their entirety, in original languages, and without the distraction of commentaries and interpretive sidebars called 'glosses' that sometimes overwhelmed the text. The Venetian printer Aldus Manutius dropped marginal commentaries from the texts he published for economic reasons – he could sell texts by Aristotle or Cicero for far less when there were fewer pages to print. Yet his economic decision underscored a deeper intellectual reality: the highly trained humanist scholars of the fifteenth century preferred to encounter ancient texts directly, and often found the ideas of twelfth and thirteenth century interpreters to be misleading or absurd. Publishing the text alone with few if any glosses was itself a purifying act. *Sola scriptura* would have been inconceivable without the humanist drive *ad fontes* – to the sources – both because of this new orientation to the past, and also because one of the texts that humanists worked to improve with their scholarship was the Bible. The early fifteenth-century Italian Lorenzo Valla prepared a guide to scriptural translation which Desiderius Erasmus used when preparing his Greek and Latin Bible translation of 1516 – a project he rushed to completion in order to beat out a competing Spanish version spearheaded by the Observant theologian and Cardinal Ximenes de Cisneros. Produced at the Complutense University outside Madrid, this Spanish version gave Hebrew, Greek, Latin, and Aramaic in parallel columns, and was published in six volumes in 1522. Martin Luther took Erasmus's version with him into his short exile in the Wartburg and used it as the basis for his 1522 German translation of the New Testament. Luther's new German translation became the basis for later translations into Danish (1524), Swedish (1526), and Swiss-German (1530).

The floodgates were opening. Humanist *ad fontes* biblical scholarship, and Erasmus's edition in particular, was the choice of early translators into French (1523), English (1526), Italian (1532), Hungarian (1541), and Spanish (1543). That scholarship had opened a way for co-operation with other groups through the fifteenth century. Greek Orthodox refugees from Byzantium and Jewish refugees from Germany and Iberia taught and translated the ancient languages for Christians. Controversies around Jewish translators in particular divided German opinion in the late fifteenth century, particularly when a recent Jewish convert Johannes Pfefferkorn (1469–1523) argued that all Jewish books should be destroyed in order to hasten the conversion of Jews to Christianity; he won the Dominicans to his side. A leading humanist scholar, Johannes Reuchlin (1455–1522), opposed this proposed purgation and earned an Inquisitorial trial for his troubles. Most humanists took Reuchlin's side in the resulting pamphlet debate, but it is noteworthy that over the course of the following century, most Protestant seminaries training pastors soon relieved themselves of the need to call on Jewish scholars for Hebrew language training by employing Christian Hebraists instead. As a result, from the later sixteenth century onwards, few Protestant pastors ever encountered Jews in the course of their theological studies.

Humanist Greek, Hebrew, and Latin scholarship exposed numerous flaws in the fourth-century Latin Bible translation by the church father Jerome which the Catholic Church held to be authoritative. The Council of Trent faced a call to revise and translate Jerome's Vulgate in its first session in 1546, but soon deadlocked as German, Polish, and Italian delegates favored the plan, while the Spanish and French resisted it. Pope Pius V agreed to commission a corrected version of the Vulgate only in 1570. And when English Catholics published translations of the New (1582) and Old (1609) Testaments, some passages remained so close to the Vulgate's Latin style and diction as to be almost unreadable. Ironically, the clearest passages in the authorized English Catholic translation drew heavily on Tyndale's Bible, and later revisions would even reach over to the King James Version. Yet few English Catholics read it, both because of its difficulty and because the Bible's centrality to Protestant identity made it somehow suspect to embattled Catholics. The Catholic Church's own ambivalence only deepened this prejudice. In areas like Italy where vernacular Bibles had proliferated, the Catholic Church acted more decisively to curb vernacular Bibles after the Council of Trent: censors prevented their publication, the Inquisition prevented their sale, and bishops' agents purged them from confraternity libraries.

The Bible *was* a dangerous purgative. It was also anything but transparent. As interpretations multiplied, reformers of all stripes had to reconsider what *sola scriptura* meant in practice. For Zwingli it was quite obvious that Jesus was speaking metaphorically when he said the bread and wine was his body and blood. For Luther wielding his chalk or knife at the Marburg Colloquy, it was just as clear that Christ was speaking literally. They never resolved their dispute, and thanks to this single point the two were unable to ally. But Luther's chalk stayed in his pocket when faced with radical reformers who argued for adult baptism from the New Testament example. Or when they argued that Jesus' own words in the New Testament gospels did not support the idea of the Trinity, a complicated view of God that could only be found in the New Testament letters of the apostle Paul. Things became even more complicated politically when Radicals drew out of the Old Testament and the New some thunderous passages against unjust rulers and turned them against the German princes of their own day in the Peasants' Revolt. Or when they claimed to receive the visions and prophecies that both Old and New Testaments predicted as a sign that the Last Judgment was coming. They found it absolutely transparent that God's Word would speak to their immediate situation, and soon some, like Thomas Muntzer, were arguing that God's word was too powerful to be limited to the pages of a book – they mocked Luther for following a 'God of Paper' just as savagely as Luther mocked Catholics for their 'God of Dough'.

Luther countered fiercely that sticking closely to the written books of scripture was the only way to test the validity of visions and prophecies. Yet this begged the question of what those books actually were. It had been generally recognized from at least the time of the fourth-century theologian Jerome that certain books in the Old Testament were not actually part of the 'canon', that is, the authoritative revelation of God. Jerome identified some popular books like Tobit, Judith, the Books of the Maccabees, and Esdras as being 'apocryphal', that is, edifying but not authoritative. They continued appearing in Bibles nonetheless, and Gutenberg certainly included them when producing his Bible of 1455. Luther gathered them together and placed them together between the Old and New Testaments in his 1534 German Bible, as did the Geneva and King James Bibles; the 1530 Zurich Bible put them in an appendix. Yet from the mid-seventeenth century Protestants began removing the apocryphal books from their printed Bibles, a sign of how much of a talisman the Bible had become. Purgation began with the Bible itself. From this point the quickest way to tell whether one was holding a 'Protestant' or 'Catholic' Bible was to check whether it included the Apocrypha. Later Protestants who developed the idea of the Bible being completely 'inerrant' were following the logic of their printed Bibles. Having already expunged the edifying apocryphal fiction from between the covers of this most powerful book, it was a short step to assuming that what remained was free of any error – a view that few Catholics found equally compelling.

Christian debates about scripture opened up new exchanges with Islam, which had its own questions about the centrality of scripture, the writings that comprised it, and who should read it and how. Muslim rulers learned of the widening divide in Christendom from ambassadors and others, and in the first century after the fall of Constantinople, a number of them fashioned themselves as the coming rulers of a new empire which would unite many religions and peoples. Muslims had long held that Christians had suppressed a fifth gospel which made clear that Jesus – called Isa in the Qur'an – was a human being and that he acknowledged the superiority of Mohammed. At the same time, Qur'anic prophecy held that it would be Isa and not Mohammed who would return at the time of final judgment. All this could be found in a 'Gospel of Barnabas' that emerged from convert circles (likely North African *moriscos*) in the late sixteenth century and circulated around the Mediterranean in Italian, Spanish, Arabic, and Ottoman Turkish copies. Believed by some to be an authentic ancient text, it was most likely a late-sixteenth-century forgery, and a sign of how some *moriscos* were aiming to merge Christianity and Islam. The supposed gospel cites Mohammed and rejects the Trinity and crucifixion, following instead the Qur'an's assertion that Jesus was simply a prophet who rose directly to heaven and that Judas was crucified in his place. Yet to many early modern readers it was *scripture*, and as such an authoritative guide which pointed to bridges between the faiths.

A surprising number of people aimed to travel back and forth on these bridges, particularly in the middle decades of the sixteenth century, when Ottoman Sultan Süleyman I was promoting himself as the universal world emperor. In 1534 he even planned to call a council bringing the pope and Martin Luther together to settle their differences. Muslim scholars were intrigued by the debates dividing Europe. In 1527, Molla Kabiz was executed in Istanbul for claiming, on the basis of both the Qur'an and the Bible, that Isa was superior to Mohammed; others with the same message were executed in 1537, 1561, and 1573. The Ottomans gave a warmer reception to anti-Trinitarian radicals like Adam Neuser, who led a large circle of German converts to Islam, and the Hungarian convert Murad b. Abdullah, who had received his earliest education among Christian humanists in Vienna. Istanbul's convert community was so active that there were briefly plans in the 1570s to publish radical anti-Trinitarian works in Istanbul for circulation to the rest of Europe.

Anti-Trinitarianism was the intellectual path that most Christian converts took as they moved towards seeing Islam as the fulfilment of the Christian message. They were deeply shaped by the humanist *ad fontes* ideal of close philological study of scripture in original languages, and some at least were aware of Protestant and Catholic scriptural scholarship. Yet many also came to reject vernacular translations of scripture, whether Old or New Testament or the Qur'an, as a perversion of God's original revelation. Their views were as closely tied to contemporary Ottoman ambitions as to classical religious texts. They held that just as the Qur'an completed the Jewish and Christian scriptures, so the Ottoman Empire would fulfil the prophecy common to all Mediterranean religions of the coming of a new universal monarchy.

The twin emphases on vernacular translation and printing became common across the Christian world, even if they differed on questions of who should buy and read the Bible. By contrast, Muslims were reluctant to see not only the translation, but even the printing of the Qur'an. The first printed text appeared only in Venice in 1537/38. Meant for export to the Ottoman Empire, its numerous errors and shabby appearance cost it this market, and Ottoman authorities destroyed all but a couple of copies; another European edition would not appear until 1694 in Hamburg. Yet many Catholic and

Protestant scholars shared the ambition of translating and printing Islamic sacred texts, and in this period they were able to act. The oldest Latin translation of the Qur'an, prepared for Abbot Peter the Venerable of Cluny in 1143, was finally published in Basel in 1543. It sold so quickly that a second printing followed in 1550, providing the basis for later translations into German, Italian, and Dutch.

The large Jewish communities of Salonica, Venice, and Amsterdam all supported many presses, and these produced distinct copies of the Torah for scholarly and ritual purposes. Readers in synagogues used only the hand-lettered scrolls known as Sefer Torah, which were produced, read, and stored according to strict guidelines. Printed and bound versions that were produced for personal and scholarly use added vowels and accent marks for the ritual chanting of the text. Known as Humash, the first editions with parts of the Torah began emerging from Italian presses in the 1470s and 1480s. The first edition of the entire Torah was again produced in Venice in 1516/17 by the Antwerp-born publisher Daniel Bomberg (d. 1549) soon after he moved to the city. Like Aldus Manutius, Bomberg secured an early dominant market position by developing distinctive typefaces and responding to shifting markets around the Mediterranean and across Europe. He would go on to produce roughly 230 Hebrew books. Other editions of the Torah emerged from presses in Istanbul (1522), Paris (1539–44), and Hamburg (1587), demonstrating that both Jewish and Christian readers were fuelling a high level of demand. Jews also produced vernacular scripture translations, particularly into Spanish. A Spanish translation of the Old and New Testaments produced by refugees in Ferrara in 1553 became the most authoritative and widely used among Iberian *conversos*, and particularly with those whose views evolved as a hybrid of sorts between Christianity and Judaism. Some believed that it was faith in the Torah that saved them more than faith in Jesus, and they used the Ferrara Bible because it was free of the Catholic or Protestant influences that marked all other vernacular translations.

Tensions around conversion also helped drive the development of Jewish lives of Jesus which circulated as a kind of anti-gospel parody. Known as the *Toledot Yeshu*, these late antique collections of stories about Jesus expanded in the eleventh and twelfth centuries in Islamic areas like Yemen, Spain, Galicia, and Afghanistan where Christians and Jews competed for privilege and position. Some Christian theologians knew of the *Toledot Yeshu* through a thirteenth-century Latin translation, and Martin Luther was able to quote it in a German version, but it really expanded in the seventeenth century. Various versions painted Jesus as a bastard conceived while Mary was menstruating. He was smart but proud and disrespectful, and he became a charlatan who exploited the gullible with magic tricks and sorcery until Jewish religious leaders finally confronted him and purified Israel by securing his execution. Authorities hanged him on a cabbage stalk, and his body was later dragged through Jerusalem to disprove the claims of his followers that he had ascended into heaven. He was never anything more than 'the hanged one' and a *mazmer*, or 'son of a whore'.

Strategically inverting the Christian gospel allowed communities to use the *Toledot Yeshu* to bring converts back to the Jewish faith (one of its common uses in Iberian and German territories), and to instruct Jewish children made curious about Christianity by what they heard and saw around them while living in a Christian town. It was part of a broader tradition of resistance that included anti-Christian prayers and polemics, mockery of Christian holidays and ceremonies, and scatalogical stories about Jesus crawling through the latrines and sewers on Christmas night on the hunt for Jewish children; this was the literature that the German Jewish convert Johannes Pfefferkorn had wanted to destroy. The increasing volume of these materials produced from the sixteenth through the eighteenth century suggests both that Jewish communities thought the message of mockery and resistance was more pressing in the period of expulsions, migrations, and conversions, and also that they were more confident in delivering it. While the Islamic Gospel of Barnabas emphasized respect for Isa as a prophet before Mohammed, the satirical counter-gospel *Toledot Yeshu* taught Jews that Christ was a fraud and that Christians (and by extension Muslims too) were more to be pitied than feared. The fact that both took the literary form of a gospel underscores the continuing importance across the Abrahamic traditions of scriptural texts as the primary vehicles for religious authority.

Scripture was the sixteenth-century touchstone for *all* religious traditions. It animated warring peasants, radical millenarians, and anti-Trinitarians, some of whom aimed to move beyond its limits into deeper forms of revelation or broader kingdoms of God. It remained incontrovertible and compelling to Protestants as the single most important justification for their rejection of Catholic theology, liturgy, and ecclesiology. It was the single most important source for the alternative forms they devised. What may seem odd is that Catholics also came eventually to connect the Bible more directly to Protestants than to their own tradition. The Council of Trent never condemned vernacular Bibles, never enshrined Jerome's Vulgate, and never recognized as authoritative any 'traditions' that were other than biblical or apostolic. To say it did, as many Protestants and Catholics do, reflects later developments in both churches, and particularly the invented traditions around which both confessions began defining themselves as early as the seventeenth century.

Some *conversos* who were returning to Judaism brought these sensibilities with them and aimed to cast their recovered religious identity more around adherence to the Torah as a text and symbol than around *Halakhic* rituals as a discipline. This was particularly the case with Iberian Sephardim, and it spurred the communities of Sephardic rabbis and syndics to emphasize and enforce ritual practices more sharply and to promote Torah study in both Hebrew and the vernaculars. Divisions like this were less common among *moriscos* aiming to reconvert to Islam, due largely to Islam's emphasis that both the physical text and the Arabic language of the Qur'an were holy and untranslatable. We might say that Christian converts to Islam took the talismanic impulse behind *sola scriptura* to the furthest extreme by arguing that the true believer had to bend to Allah's language and not the other way around.

The fundamental question about scripture – how God spoke and to whom – was as much a matter of form as of content for early modern believers of all confessions. All took scripture as the main measure of authority, and appealed to it in order to handle numerous practical questions around purity and purgation. But authority rested on radically different assumptions about accessibility or remoteness, and these in turn spoke directly to issues of Initiation and Presence. When religious communities argued with others and each other about the physical form scripture should take, the language it should appear in, and whether it should even be widely distributed, they signalled their broader beliefs about who constituted the social body of faith, and how God addressed them.

Ways of Living: Purity of Action

Religious communities saw charity as the obligation and outgrowth of their distinctive doctrinal positions. While they emphasized their differences, common features marked their efforts. Medieval Catholicism had shaped charity around a set of concrete actions described in one of Christ's parables as recorded in the New Testament book of Matthew: feed the hungry, give drink to the thirsty, provide clothes to the naked, care for widows and orphans, heal the sick, visit prisoners. With the later addition of 'bury the dead', these became the seven works of charity, and a guideline to immediate personal and collective action. Judaism and Islam similarly emphasized concrete relief of practical needs. Through the early modern period, religious communities across Europe moved from giving this kind of episodic and short-term relief to experimenting with 'solutions' which involved supporting more poor individuals for a longer time. They aimed to address the whole of the poor person, arguing that charity should discipline and improve recipients, not just keep them fed, clothed, and sheltered. True charity should address the poverty of the body by addressing the poverty of the spirit, and in this way it could purify the character of society's most needy members. This was a deeply humanist idea, which Catholic and Protestant reformers absorbed in their separate ways, and it moved Christian poor relief to emphasize receivers over givers, an emphasis less evident in Muslim and Jewish charity.

Because they aimed ultimately to purify the recipient and the community, reformers often gave charitable relief a disciplinary edge that emphasized conditions for receiving aid and that raised boundaries between insiders and outsiders in particular groups, parishes, or towns. This fed into a deeper suspicion of poor strangers, who increasingly came to be seen as vagrants, deviants, and possibly even criminals, and this was another common feature that shaped poor relief for refugees and migrants. For them, as for many other groups of poor, much of early modern poor relief was about marking geographic, religious, and moral boundaries with new institutions and new bureaucratic forms.

Poverty and Community

When Raphael Hythloday, the intrepid explorer and narrator of Thomas More's *Utopia*, travels around that fictional no-where island, he is particularly impressed with the many public hospitals sheltering the sick, the aged, and dying:

> These are so roomy as to be comparable as to many small towns.... [They] are very well furnished and equipped with everything conducive to health. Besides, such tender and careful treatment and such constant attendance of expert physicians are provided that, though no one is sent to them against his will, there is hardly anyone in the whole city who, when suffering from illness, does not prefer to be nursed there than at home.

Every Utopian town had four hospitals like this. As a result, no Utopian experienced the fear, common in Europe, that if a working man fell sick or died, his entire family could be pitched into poverty and worse as they wrestled with his care, his lost wages, and eventually his corpse. The great majority of Europeans lived in poverty – some when they were children in a struggling family or when they themselves were too old to earn much by working, some when work dried up or famine and plague overturned their town's economy, some when husbands died leaving them with many children and few opportunities, and some because they lacked skills, connections, or health.

Gender, age, and health were the key predictors of poverty. Every authority in every society everywhere faced poverty as a primary challenge. To govern justly as a Christian, Muslim, or Jew, you had to ensure that the poor were cared for. To fail at that basic challenge undermined the legitimacy of a town council, a Jewish *parnassim*, a Catholic king or Lutheran prince or Muslim sultan. As a result, authorities regardless of religion or geography often learned from each other how best to handle the challenge of poverty.

More's Utopians managed their health system without any particular religion, even though Thomas More himself was a firm and partisan Catholic. Did religion make a difference? Catholics claimed that Protestants lacked much motivation towards charity, since their emphasis on salvation by Faith Alone without spiritual works took away the incentive to give the alms or establish the hospitals that would win God's favor and hence the donor's place in heaven. Protestants responded that the most effective answer to poverty lay with faithful earthly communities rather than with fruitless efforts to buy one's way into heaven. They busied themselves in organizing more systematic, more secular, and often more efficient methods of collecting and distributing charity within towns and cities. Throughout the 1520s, small towns like Leisnig, Kitzingen, and Windsheim and even larger centres like Strasbourg and Nuremberg brought in new laws regarding poverty *before* they brought in new laws regarding Protestant theology and worship. Charity was where abstract religious doctrines hit fixed social realities, and in fact all religious confessions aimed to become more systematic, efficient, and effective in their poor relief. All clearly took lessons from their religious opponents as much as from their religious allies. The needs were too great to do anything else.

It had long been this way. Medieval Catholic monks and friars had established hospices on the model of the Byzantine *xenodochium*, where a resident community of regular clergy provided care to both local poor and travellers. Crusading soldiers and merchant traders travelling the Mediterranean encountered the Muslim *waqf*, an institution which could include hostels, schools, hospitals, and soup kitchens alongside a mosque, and which relied less on resident clerical communities than on endowments and secular administrators. *Waqfs* multiplied across the Muslim world from the tenth century, and later one of the largest would be the Süleymaniye, built from 1550 to 1558 on the highest hill in the centre of Istanbul where it still dominates the skyline. Its huge dome and towering minarets rested not just on Sultan Süleyman the Magnificent's generous endowment, but also on dozens of shops rented out for income to feed and educate the poor. From the twelfth century, merchants and rulers established similar civic hospitals across Europe, with endowments and rental properties funding facilities for the poor, sick, and orphans, and with control vested ultimately in lay authorities rather than clergy. Florence's Folco Portinari established the S. Maria Nuova hospital in 1288, which England's Henry VII later used as a model for his Savoy Hospital in 1505, and which Martin Luther praised when passing through Florence on his trip to Rome in 1510–11 (and which may have inspired Luther's later proposals for poor law ordinances in German towns). Burgundian chancellor Nicolas Rolin with his wife Guigone de Salins established the Grand Hospice in Beaune in 1443 to shelter paupers, distribute bread, and offer medical care. In Seville, Don Fadrique Enriquez de Ribera left a legacy in 1539 to construct the massive Hospital de las Cinco Llagas around ten courtyards. Jewish communities were generally too small to support hospitals on this scale, but exiles arriving in Italy from Iberia soon developed charitable confraternities which mobilized the men and women of their community to distribute a more mobile charity of food and clothing to the needy, medicines to the sick, small loans to the poor, and education and socialization for the young – all activities that they saw the Catholic brotherhoods providing.

The civic hospital, the *xenodochium*, the *waqf*, and the monastic hospice were all critical vehicles for exercising charity. Whether operated by guilds, confraternities, civic governments, lay boards, family trusts, or religious orders, they expressed both the care offered within particular groups that we saw earlier in the ideas of *misericordia*, and also the broader scope of the civic *Corpus Christianum*. But charity took many more forms: individuals gave alms at the door or on the street; employers left legacies to former servants; parishes organized suppers to raise funds for needy members; beggars occupied street corners, clustered at church doors, or trolled through markets with hands outstretched; guild members and godparents took in orphaned children when their colleagues or friends died. Institutions leave records and memories, but no institutions could do enough to help all the local poor. Most charity was face-to-face or at least person-to-person: neighbors, friends, family, guild and confraternity brothers all were the first source of help for those in need, and a poor person had to piece them all together in what one historian called an 'economy of makeshifts' in order to survive.

This was the pattern across Christian, Jewish and Muslim communities. All religious traditions held that God required believers to exercise charity, and made it an absolutely central obligation. Jews and Catholics knew from scripture that they had to devote 10 percent of what they earned as a *tithe* to support kin or clients, and this paralleled the 2.5 or 5 percent that Muslims had to give as *zakat*. Similarly, the general philanthropy within the community that a Catholic knew as *misericordia* was like Islamic *sadaqa,* and also sometimes functioned as a form of mutual assistance or insurance offered through hospitals and *waqfs*. Tithes and *zakat* reinforced vertical social relationships, while *misericordia* and *sadaq* built up horizontal ones, but they worked together in emphasizing that the one giving alms was connected to the poor on one hand and to God on the other. All traditions made charity a reciprocal personal relationship in which the poor recipient prayed for the donor's soul. Christianity went a step further when Christ claimed (in Matthew 25) that helping or ignoring a poor person was helping or ignoring Christ himself, who might be physically present and posing as the needy one. Hence, in a very direct way, believers might encounter Christ's Real Presence not just in the communion host, but in the beggar, the widow, and the orphan. They knew that he would help into heaven only those who helped these so-called poor of Christ.

By the fifteenth and sixteenth centuries sheer need was overwhelming these medieval forms and traditions. Many believed that their communities had enough resources, and that the problem lay not in generating funds but in organizing them rationally and distributing them fairly. Sultans and other wealthy patrons built larger *waqfs* in those Ottoman cities that were growing most rapidly, aiming to make a political, social, and religious statement about the empire's capacity and legitimacy. Jewish communities erected more confraternities to handle daily life in the diaspora, including organizing worship, schooling young boys, and assisting young couples and older widows. Men ran most of these, like Modena's *Gemilut Hassadim* (acts of loving kindness), and *Rahamim* (mercy), but in others like the later *Soed Holim* (to benefit the sick), women came together to help other women. From this period, city governments in Italy, Spain, and France began taking more direct control of hospitals in response to increasing need. Sometimes they also consolidated many small guild and family institutions into a single Great Hospital, expropriating a monastery or building a new monumental building to underscore its importance: Siena's S. Maria della Scala, Milan's Ospedale Maggiore (1456), Paris' Hôtel Dieu (1505), London's St. Bartholomews (1546–47), and Seville's Hospital de la Santa Caridad (1678) were among the most famous. Sometimes authorities focused a hospital's activity on a particular group of poor like foundlings, orphans, syphilitics, beggars, or battered women who might require specialized care. More importantly, poor relief expanded in scope as many reformers and some governments aimed to draw hospitals, parish relief, individual alms-giving, confraternal and guild aid, and all the rest into a coherent and organized municipal system. This would inevitably require governments to get even more directly involved.

Poverty of Body and Poverty of Spirit: Charity as Formation and Purification

There were two drivers behind changes to poor relief. The first was escalating need. As we saw earlier, the Black Death had cut Europe's population by at least a third, to 55–60 million, but it recovered to almost 70 million by 1550 and 80 million by 1600. Growing populations and static food supplies resulted in recurring famines, which got progressively worse through the sixteenth and seventeenth centuries as plague, war, and economic collapse followed. Thousands died in cities across Europe in the 1520s, 1550s, 1570s, 1590s, and 1630s, leaving urban authorities with dozens or hundreds of suddenly widowed parents and suddenly orphaned children to provide for. The numbers fleeing pogroms, war, or plague escalated. Neighbours and friends helping each other was still the most common way that charity circulated, but this informal help could not cope with the new forms of poverty or the sheer numbers of the poor. As a result, hospitals, confraternities, religious orders, and civic governments expanded institutional forms of help.

A second and perhaps greater driver of change was rooted in the drive for purification. There was a growing sense that it was not enough to passively shelter the needy when there was an opportunity and even a demand to actively educate, train, and *shape* them. This conviction led *waqfs* to expand their charitable schools, and Jewish communities to put more resources into educational confraternities for young boys. Christian communities followed suit, but broader questions and suspicions informed their charitable work. Were the poor just lazy? Were they frauds or thieves or travelling vagrants? Reformers believed that not all those with their hands out were worthy people who were truly unable to help themselves and so deserved charity. Orphans certainly were, as were the blind, injured, sick, or very old. Widows needed to be considered cautiously, particularly if they were young or had originally come from elsewhere. Young men who were physically fit were definitely off the list, while young women posed a different problem, since refusing to help them might force them into prostitution. There was great suspicion of travelling paupers, or vagrants, and not much sympathy for people born beyond the locality. One early impulse in poor relief was to force vagrants to keep moving, sometimes back to where they had been born, and to force locals to settle down in enclosures. Helping the poor did not just mean feeding and sheltering them all in the same way. To really help them, you had to think about their past and plan to shape their future – whether they liked it or not.

Thomas More certainly had this in mind with *Utopia*, which, apart from everything else, was an extraordinary experiment in behavior modification [Fig 30]. Utopian children wore jewels, slaves chafed in golden chains, and everyone shat into golden chamber pots to teach the worthlessness of these supposedly precious goods. Utopia was a meritocracy with no private ownership or wealth, where everyone worked and developed their natural skills, living modest and sober lives in large households and eating in common dining halls. Ordered lives grew in an ordered society. Utopia's authorities monitored the size of communities, and shipped people off or on the island to keep the fifty-four cities fixed at 6,000 souls each. Theft, adultery, and travelling the island without a passport could get one slapped into the golden chains of slavery for a few years. We are accustomed to thinking of Utopia as an ideal society, yet the forced relocations, behaviour modification, and purges to purify citizens and build a communal society are uncomfortably totalitarian tools not unlike those used in twentieth-century Cambodia and China. While there is some question whether More was being serious or satirical, he was not the only humanist to argue that firm discipline could improve individuals and whole societies. And *Utopia* found some imitators who aimed to adopt it in whole or part, and whose own writings and example triggered further imitation across Europe. These other plans combined a political practicality with the same drive shared by humanists and theologians to use charity to shape and improve – and to make poverty history.

Vasco de Quiroga (ca. 1478–1565) translated More's *Utopia* into Spanish, and aimed to translate it into practice as bishop of Michoacan on the Pacific Coast of central Mexico. In the 1530s he founded two hospital complexes outside Santa Fe and Pátzcuaro as safe sites where Nahuatl Indians could get food, medical care, artisanal instruction, and religious instruction; these were meant to rebuild and above all convert to Catholicism the indigenous communities that had been ravaged by Spanish conquistadors. De Quiroga adopted More's guidelines on work and even tried to implement Utopia's political structure. His hopes that these conversion hospitals would be a model for others in New Spain were not realized, but another reformer was more successful. Thomas More had begun writing *Utopia* in Flanders, but only came into contact with the *converso* humanist Juan Luis Vives a few years later in 1519. Yet he supported Vives' annual visits to England through the time that the latter was writing *On Assistance to the Poor* (*De Subventione Pauperum*, 1526) on commission from the civic magistrates of Bruges, and the two scholars must have shared ideas on the common humanist topic of how best to order society.

Vives did not attempt to translate More into action quite as systematically as Vasco de Quiroga, and some of their common policies go back to medieval or biblical models. Yet both expressed the newer approaches being worked out by sixteenth-century humanists and reformers as a way to not only assist but also to improve or purify the poor. They saw poor relief as a state responsibility; shared a trust in rational bureaucracy to assess needs; proposed systematic collection and delivery of aid; believed begging in the street should be banned; relied on centralized facilities for feeding, sheltering, and training the poor; and established work as the reward and discipline that would lift the next generation out of lives of poverty. Both also believed that those who refused to be lifted up by work should be forced into it. This was one reason why the enclosed shelters offering charity to orphans or the poor could so readily develop into prisons. Work did not simply generate income to keep food on the table and sheets on the beds. It acted with religious education to correct morals and shape character – work disciplined, reformed, and purified the poor.

Character-building discipline was the keystone in the humanists' overarching system of civic welfare, and it also figures in the poor laws that Martin Luther proposed for Wittenberg (1522) and Leisnig (1523). Luther also took charity out of the priests' control and put it in the hands of lay leaders, although he proposed boards elected annually by townspeople. He placed less emphasis on work to generate income and more on community-wide forms of fund raising that worked like taxes or obligatory almsgiving to share the financial burden equally. Taken together, these constituted the Community Chest, a local resource that combined all the legacies given to parish churches and monasteries in the past and all the tithes (which could be coins, firewood, or food) donated by believers in the present. Lay boards multiplied across Germany to direct the funds in these Chests towards help for the poor, low-cost loans to artisans, payments for pastors, and subsidies for schools. Luther's merging of alms, education, and pastors' salaries in the Community Chest emphasizes his conviction that the sacred and secular spheres worked together in something very like Catholic *misericordia* in the old *Corpus Christianum*, although with lay leaders now firmly in control. In the 1520s and 1530s, many were optimistic that the local Chests contained enough resources to help the local poor, and that funds simply had to be distributed more efficiently. Past shortfalls could be blamed on priests skimming off too great a share for themselves, beggars from other towns jostling out the local poor, and a few people getting alms who didn't need or deserve them. Hard-nosed laymen would have the experience, business sense, and determination to use discipline to govern priests, pupils, and the poor, and to regulate the lazy poor in particular. The poor could work, or they could starve; one thing they could not do was publicly beg.

It would soon become clear to Augsburg magistrates, Saxon princes, and English members of Parliament that in fact there was not enough money in local Chests and endowments, and that obligatory taxes and fees might need to supplement voluntary legacies and alms. The rich would need to be disciplined as much as the poor.

The problem was not only that funds were contracting, but that expectations were expanding. Traditional forms of charity had addressed immediate physical needs: Christ in Matthew 25 had taught that giving food, drink, clothing, and shelter, and visiting the sick and prisoners would secure a place in heaven; Catholics added burial of the dead to what were called the bodily (or corporal) works of mercy. In the sixteenth century, Catholics began emphasizing a second parallel list of spiritual works of mercy that show how seriously they took personal purification: teaching, counselling doubters and comforting the hurting, condemning immorality, being patient and forgiving, and praying for the living and dead. If the bodily works of mercy provided an agenda for hospitals and confraternities, the spiritual works could perhaps best be brought together in schools and reformatory charitable enclosures. Protestants explicitly rejected both bodily and spiritual 'works of mercy' as ways to heaven, but they implicitly followed them as ways that a Christian community should order itself and form, or reform, its weaker members. So whether it was in Seville, Regensburg, Dijon, Venice, or Amsterdam, civil and ecclesiastical authorities began thinking about how to extend charity beyond food, drink, and shelter, and into education and character formation.

Charity was the driving force behind many of the new confraternities and new religious orders that the Observant reforms were multiplying across the Catholic world from the sixteenth century onwards. Confraternities known as 'Schools of Christian Doctrine' marshalled hundreds of lay men and women to teach reading, writing, and Catholic catechism to thousands of working children in Sunday Schools. The Sisters of Charity in France, Oratorians (began 1497, approved 1612) in Italy, and Ursulines (began 1535, approved 1566) in Italy, France, and the Spanish Netherlands staffed hospitals. The English Institutes of the Blessed Virgin Mary opened elite girls' schools across Europe, while the Society of Jesus developed a network of elite boys' schools that began in Italy and spread through Europe, Asia, and the Americas. The Piarists (1617) emphasized teaching poor children, and the French Oratorians (1611) emphasized training priests. As tighter enclosure forced nuns to give up their more public income-generating activities, they realized that teaching girls in residential convent schools could fill the gap. Disciplined 'formation' was even more critical in some of the new charitable enclosures that aimed to convert prostitutes from their profession, the poor from their laziness, and Jews and Muslims from their religion than it was in schools. Who was better placed to provide this formative discipline than those male and female clergy who had vowed themselves to the religious life? Jesuits were among the first to organize and run some of these enclosures, and they multiplied across the globe. The fact that Catholic religious orders set up schools, orphanages, and other 'formative' enclosures as they followed Spanish, French, and Portuguese explorers to Asia and the Americas is one of the key reasons why we can see the Catholic Church as perhaps the first truly global institution of the early modern world.

Protestants worked more locally and generally: in the absence of globe-spanning religious orders with hundreds of missionaries, it was laypeople, and most often magistrates, who took charge. Yet they too used charity to build new and more disciplined social orders. Schools were an early priority, both for social and political reasons, and because proclaiming *sola scriptura* obliged them to find ways of teaching people how to read. German magistrates who established free schools for the children of artisans and merchants were building social support for their changes to Church Order, and they frequently adopted new School Orders together with the new Church Orders, borrowing from each other and updating them regularly. Philip Melancthon's School Order for Saxony (1528) influenced those in Schleswig-Holstein (1542) and Hessen (1537), and Wurttemberg's 1569 School Order influenced Braunschweig (1569) and a later reformed Saxon order in 1580. Religious schools taught doctrine through grammar lessons and taught children to take their place in a continuum of order stretching from their parents, through the teacher and pastor (sometimes the same individual), to the prince, and on to God. This practice of merging religious and educational discipline closely together carried on for centuries, and certainly shapes the reformed Prussian Order of 1763. Some parents resisted when compulsory schooling took their children from the fields or when they had to start paying fees, and so to the great annoyance of Luther and many local reformers they either sent their children only for a few winter months or sometimes not at all.

It was all simpler when parents were out of the way. Foundling homes and orphanages offered the opportunity to shape children without parental interference, and they proliferated across Europe in the sixteenth century. One of the first things the Protestant magistrates did upon taking control in Amsterdam in 1578 was expropriate a monastery, convent, and church and turn the three adjoining properties into a single civil orphanage for burgher children. In 1560, Nuremberg magistrates merged separate girls and boys orphanages into a single institution within the former Franciscan cloister; the magistrates who claimed ultimate responsibility for the local church also approved applications to the 'Findel'. Both orphanages trained girls and boys to be productive and Protestant citizens.

While Protestant nations like England, the Dutch Republic, and Sweden all launched colonial enterprises, their distinct state churches did not pretend to be universal like the Catholic Church, and their religious outreach overseas was more modest. Protestants had no religious orders to launch missions, open charitable institutions, or funnel orphans overseas, though they would expand this radically in the nineteenth century. Through the early modern period, they sent preachers across the globe, and opened schools like Harvard (1636) in Cambridge and William and Mary (1693) in Virginia to train even more, but they established relatively few colonial orphanages or formative enclosures.

Charitable enclosures, both Catholic and Protestant, used the family household as their administrative and linguistic model. The wards of the institution called their supervisors 'father' or 'mother', and knew each other as brothers and sisters. This was not just a friendly term or polite metaphor. Constructing fictional families socialized these orphaned and abandoned children in some critical patriarchal norms. First, as we saw earlier, the domestic household itself was treated as an enclosure, secured with the authority of the father. Most women who married entered a legal enclosure where they merged their individual identity and property in a single patriarchal household. Second, the kinship language used in institutional households gave the children the legal identity and social network that they may have lost or, if illegitimate, never had. Legal codes based on Roman law, like that adopted by Henry II in France in 1556, formally forbade legal adoption of illegitimates because they would become like thieves stealing the property of legitimate family members. Illegitimates were alien presences that had to be expelled but, through a charitable institution, they could gain a surrogate family of their own.

Discussing foundling homes for illegitimate children, John Boswell observed that northern Europeans in their terminology emphasized these children's status as having been 'found' (*enfant trouvé*, foundling, *Findelkkind*), while southern Europeans in their language emphasized how they'd been 'lost': exposed, abandoned, or thrown away (*esposto, abbandonato, gettatello*). So Nuremberg had its 'Findel' and London its 'Foundling' Hospital, while Florence had its 'Abbandonati' and Bologna its 'Esposti' (exposed). Terms like the latter were used almost universally in Italy precisely because they reflected the children's' ambiguous legal status outside the family networks that were so central to the patriarchal Roman law used as local common law (*ius commune*). This may in turn explain why it was symbolic kinship groups like confraternities and guilds that ran so many of the small homes in Italian towns, deliberately creating surrogate families for those who had no blood kin, and using enclosure to duplicate familial discipline. By contrast, it may be that Germanic common law shaped the tendency of northern cities to have single, large communal institutions run by civic governments that underscored the children's status as the common obligation of the entire civic community, and that emphasized setting all of them, male and female alike, on the path to an independent life by late adolescence. When comparing statistics, we find that relative to overall population far more children were 'lost' in southern Europe than were ever 'found' in the north, a fact that may also explain why charitable enclosures proliferated earlier and more broadly in the south.

Waqfs gave an institutional structure for charity in Muslim lands by combining prayer spaces with schools, orphanages, hostels, soup kitchens, and other services. Iberian refugees founded *waqfs* throughout the North African and Ottoman diaspora to help community members, but they relied less on the forms of enclosure and indoctrination that were common across Europe. *Waqf* revenues generally went more often to food and water than to shelter, and they built on a long and critical tradition of securing a food supply for the poor in places like Cairo. Governments from the time of the pharaohs had stockpiled and distributed grain in order to even out the disruptions of famine, and the *waqfs* simply continued this practice with their soup kitchens and wells. Those donating to the endowments were looking to secure not just fame and prayers, but also to foster urban development and protect their estates from taxation since, as in Christian lands, they could single out their heirs as privileged beneficiaries. Yet *waqfs* were not always self-serving in this way: the capitulation signed by Granadan Muslims with Isabella and Ferdinand in 1501 established that the *waqfs* would not be confiscated, but would continue to support local communities by feeding the poor, ransoming captives, and repairing roads. The common stipulation that *waqfs* feed the poor and shelter travellers certainly helped those refugees who were forced north to Castile and Valencia after the Granadan uprising of 1567–1571, and Iberian exiles shipped to North Africa and the Ottoman Empire after the expulsions of 1609–1614.

Charity as Boundary Marking

Vives and Luther were among the most influential writers on poor relief, and their short texts circulated widely in Latin and many vernaculars. In spite of profound differences in theological framework, the most radical ideas were practical ones that Catholics and Protestants shared. Even more importantly, civic magistrates across Europe compared notes and shared the sets of regulations that they were drawing up for their own towns and cities. They adapted humanist and theological writings to local circumstances, waged sometimes intense debates with religious authorities who were upset that charity was being distanced from theological considerations and church control, and they found ways to direct poor relief to the needs of new industries or to struggles between political factions. All used charity to support the self-discipline and social discipline that were fundamental to the goal of fashioning a purer and holier society, and all came to rely on the familiar tools of separation, containment, prosecution, and purgation to advance these goals.

One of the earliest and most influential civic plans was the *Aumône-Générale* developed in Lyon from 1530 to 1534; by 1539 Genoa was aiming to imitate it, using an Italian copy of its regulations. Florentine and Venetian authorities looked closely at Bologna's *Opera dei Mendicanti*, whose enormous poorhouse (opened 1563) was widely known and copied. The only effective national system emerged in England, where a series of parliamentary Poor Laws set out common procedures for assessing needs, raising funds, and disciplining recipients. London's Bridewell poorhouse (opened 1556) took in some of those whom the new laws now defined as either needy or deviant. Each of these new systems built on previous institutions. Each also used the occasion of reform to set up new boundaries around geography, religion, and morality, and to expand the bureaucratic means of marking and policing them.

Many of the ambitious local systems failed after a few years or had to change radically to survive chronic financial difficulties. They often responded by tightening the forms of geographic boundary marking. The earliest versions of English Poor Laws, going back at least to 1495, focused first of all on excluding outsiders and punishing vagrants, with threats of whipping, branding, and even execution for those who tried to beg outside of their 'home' parish. English Parliaments then passed Poor Laws in 1530, 1547, 1552, 1563,

1572, and 1598 before framing a consolidated act in 1601, which remained in force until 1834. Through all the local changes and adaptations a few features remained constant across Europe. They helped locals (and preferably the locally born) first of all and treated travelling beggars ('vagrants') like criminals. They aimed to make the collection and distribution of aid more rational, comprehensive, and fair, banning all begging or allowing it only to a licensed few. They distinguished 'worthy' from 'unworthy' poor. They used institutions like hospitals to address particular needy groups, who often had to prove that there was no other community help available for them.

Many magistrates dreamed of large enclosures like Bologna's, but balked at the cost. It was usually easier and cheaper to try and keep people in their own homes and help them there, and this became an efficient way of helping the 'worthy' poor like widows, the elderly, and the infirm, and an effective way of restricting aid to locals. Paying a Norwich widow to foster some of the community's orphans, or giving food or a small allowance to a Nuremberg family with a blind father or an invalid child was cheap and flexible. 'Unworthy' poor included any young adults who were not physically or mentally injured, any vagrants or outsiders not known to locals, or those who were thought to be either too lazy to work or who seemed to be professional beggars.

Exiles and refugees fell victim to the general resentment, and even fear, of outsiders. When iconoclastic rioters rampaged through some Dutch cities in the 1566 and 1572, high-born Catholics fled across the borders to France and the Holy Roman Empire. Yet they got a very chilly welcome in Cologne, Douai, and Antwerp, and even those sheltering them complained about these foreigners effectively draining local alms. Iberian Jews and Muslims encountered similar resentment when they landed in North Africa in the 1490s and again in the 1610s. In this case, the cultural and linguistic differences were so great that some North Africans treated them as Iberian invaders rather than as exiled co-religious refugees.

Religious groups and particularly exile communities were often expected or forced to care for their own. Charity as a religious boundary-marking exercise was rooted in the communal ethos we saw in the Chapter 1. The unprecedented numbers of people fleeing or expelled from their traditional communities, in the interests of religious purgation and purification, only reinforced this ethos. Catholics visualized community with images of the Madonna della Misericordia spreading her cloak. Protestants removed the Madonna and re-framed *misericordia* with biblical language and imagery that was adapted to the new realities of their religious divisions. Jews and Muslims emphasized the fundamental obligation of individual believers and communities to tax themselves regularly in order to generate funds for the poor.

Catholics, Protestants, Muslims, and Jews all helped the poor of their own communities first, and often counted on clergy to judge need and worth. This was one reason why religious tests and training sometimes became a prerequisite for receiving aid. Catholic poor might have to win approval of the priest or, in larger towns, of a review board that might mix laity and clergy. Lutheran poor had to pass the moral and doctrinal scrutiny of the elected lay boards that ran the Community Chest. Calvinist consistories included deacons, the lay religious officers responsible for distributing charity, so that they could learn about and act on any cases of church discipline involving the poor that they assisted. In major Calvinist refugee centres like Geneva and Emden, the English, Italian, Dutch, and French communities all had their own deacons to collect and distribute help within their national communities. Cities like London and Amsterdam allowed so-called Stranger Churches the freedom to preach and follow another liturgy, be it Lutheran or Calvinist, but coupled this with the obligation to register and assist other expatriates. As Amsterdam expanded its practical toleration for Jewish, Catholic, and Anabaptist communities, this obligation became paramount. Of all the reform groups, the Anabaptists and Radicals who practiced a 'community of goods' came closest to utopian communism, taking the idea not from Thomas More but from the early church. When a member fell under the disciplinary ban, she or he was put out of the community and so immediately fell into poverty. The same thing happened in Amsterdam's large and influential Jewish community, where lay leaders examined applicants for poor relief closely and kept meticulous records of who received what and why. Confraternities of men and women in Jewish communities in Modena and Venice gave food and medicine, lent small sums, and provided dowries in order to help their own poor survive. Did many of the poor stay within their religious community and follow its theological and moral codes less out of conviction than out of fear of being destitute? We cannot know, but we do know that in every community where these disciplines existed, religious authorities willingly used charity in order to secure obedience.

After the 1555 Peace of Augsburg, some cities within the Holy Roman Empire could become bi-confessional. This immediately challenged both the old unitary conception of the *Corpus Christianum*, and also the straightforward separation of Catholics from Protestants. They sometimes collaborated and shared charitable institutions and even church buildings, but only under compulsion and protest. Most preferred to guard the religious boundaries. Augsburg, one of the wealthiest of these cities, had a couple of examples. From 1514 to 1523, the wealthy merchant Jacob Fugger constructed a walled and gated community of houses and apartments for 'worthy poor' families – initially those who had lived in the city for at least two years and were poor but debt-free. The 'Fuggerei' added a Catholic Church to the enclosure in 1582 and limited admission to confessing Catholics as well. Augsburg experimented from 1572 to 1648 with having alternating teams of Protestant and Catholic administrators look after its bi-confessional civic orphanage. During the Thirty Years War, this became problematic. When a Catholic warden replaced a Lutheran in 1629, he forced the Lutheran children to memorize the Catholic catechism, follow Catholic rituals, and convert to the Catholic faith. These tensions and more led Augsburgers to abandon the experiment in 1653 in favor of two parallel homes, one by and for the Catholic community, and the other for Protestants.

Marking the boundaries between Christians and Jews had a longer history, but in this period two new boundary-marking forms of Catholic charity that had Jews as their specific target emerged in Italy. The first were pawn banks called *Monte di Pietà* (Mountain of Compassion) offering small loans to worthy artisans and labourers in order to keep them away from Jewish moneylenders. These pawn banks first emerged around the late 1450s and early 1460s in central Italy, and spread rapidly up and down the peninsula with local banks in Ascoli Picena (1458), Perugia (1462), Bologna (1473, 1507), Genoa (1483), Parma (1488), and Florence (1496); there were forty in operation by 1470, and the number grew steadily. They were promoted by Observant Franciscan preachers who sometimes resorted to the most extreme anti-Semitic rhetoric as they aimed to stir up political support and motivate donors or lenders of capital. Most were run by confraternities and eventually developed into banks, some of which are still operating today. Borrowers pawned old clothing, kitchen goods, furniture, and sometimes tools in return for small sums intended to buy medicine or tide a family through some domestic crisis. They could not use the money to gamble, visit prostitutes, or buy tools, though we have records of all three happening. A variation in rural areas was the *Monte Frumentari* or *Monte di Paschi* that helped poor farmers buy seed or livestock.

Many of the Jewish moneylenders targeted by preachers were recent refugees and exiles from German cities. Italian civic authorities had recruited them in the 1420s–1430s to expand lending to merchants and professionals. Within a few decades, the Franciscan preachers were charging that Jewish lending tempted good Christians to rack up debts and spend more than they should on luxuries, to the danger of wallet and soul together. If civic authorities would not expel the moneylenders, these preachers wanted them to at least limit the Jews from lending to the poor or force them to wear stigmatizing signs of luxury like earrings, which should be forbidden to Christians. This was a bit like Thomas More's idea of using gold for slaves' chains and chamber pots, and it backfired badly when Christian women decided that they liked the look of the earrings and started imitating this Jewish fashion. The preachers were not deterred, and they presented charitable assistance to the poor and purgative expulsion of the Jews as two sides of the single coin that was Christian devotion. Their rhetoric was powerful, exclusive, and sometimes effective: Jewish moneylenders arrived in Lucca in 1452 and left in 1493 when a *Monte* was founded. Lucca was a place of serious religious ferment. It would be a hotbed of Protestant reform activity in the sixteenth century, and the largest single source of Italian religious refugees to Geneva. Yet most Italian civic authorities were more ambivalent and pragmatic. Like those German towns that had pushed Jews outside the walls while allowing them to remain close enough to remain active in the local economy, Italian authorities typically chose to regulate rather than eliminate Jewish moneylenders, either forcing them to lend to the poor at a fixed lower rate (as in Venice) or allowing them to rent only to those of means.

Conversion provided the critical context for a second form of boundary-marking charity targeted at Jews, and to a lesser extent Muslims, that treated them as potential beneficiaries. Just outside the ghetto gates in Rome and Venice, Jews could find a shelter known as the House of Catechumens. Since the ghetto community would expel a convert to Christianity, Catholic authorities opened these hostels to serve as halfway houses into the Christian world. Food, lodging, and catechetical instruction were the main offerings in these enclosures, which also aimed to provide work and sometimes even the prospect of a dowry and a spouse in order to lure some young Jews into converting. A former Jew or Muslim had severed kin and household ties when crossing over to Christianity, and the conversion house aimed, much like the foundling home, to create new social kinship ties, which would integrate the convert into the Christian faith and civil society. The Jesuits opened the first catechumen house in Rome in Rome in 1543, and the city of Venice followed with a civic home in 1557; 1300 would enter the Venetian home from 1590 to 1670. In 1577, Gregory XIII opened a college in Rome where young men who had converted from Judaism or Islam could be trained in how to convert others. By 1634, it moved into massive new quarters as a concrete sign of the importance of the work of conversion to the global mission of the church.

One reason why Amsterdam's Sephardic community kept such meticulous records of the charity that it dispensed was because much of it went to *converso* refugees who had fled from Spain and Portugal, and who were now considering whether or not to abandon Catholicism and return to the faith and community of their ancestors. As we saw earlier, Muslim authorities in Algiers also won converts among their Christian and Jewish slaves by promising liberation, an occupation, and integration by marriage into the local Muslim community. The boundary-crossing charity provided by Catholic catechumen houses, Jewish synagogues, and Muslim authorities did not reflect any ambivalence about the boundaries themselves. On the contrary, charity reinforced those boundaries. Authorities believed that they would be able to draw in more converts if the boundaries dividing majority and minority populations became firmer, and if life on the outside of the boundary became harder.

Another boundary was moral. It emerged in all communities that used charity to preserve and promote religious character. Boundaries between 'worthy' and 'unworthy' poor were at once some of the most imprecise but also the most important ones marked by charity – they began as moral boundaries, but from the sixteenth century many cities marked them with walls, bars, and gates. As we saw, age, gender, physical fitness, and parentage all played a part in determining whether a poor woman or man deserved to get aid in the first place. And aid always came with moral expectations. The poor relief systems of Lyon, Geneva, and many German and English towns all had strict regulations: no drinking, no gambling, no improper sexual activity, no cursing, and no avoiding church. Paupers who broke these rules could expect to lose their alms, or be forced into an enclosed institution where authorities could keep a closer eye on them. When authorities and citizens began considering the 'unworthy' poor immoral, deviant or even criminal, then they began modelling the shelters that housed them not on hospitals but on monasteries, convents, and even prisons. In Amsterdam, Nuremberg, Bologna, and many other cities both Catholic and Protestant, civic authorities actually expropriated abandoned monasteries or convents because their layout of cells and courtyards, large communal eating facilities, high walls, gated doors, and barred windows made them the most secure place in the city to enclose and discipline large numbers of poor adults and children.

And so the circle turned. As they came to look more like prisons, more of these charitable institutions began focusing exclusively on the 'unworthy' poor, and particularly those who had sunk into poverty through their own perceived immorality or that of their families. In the process, they adopted forms of separation, containment, prosecution, and purgation that we earlier saw mobilized against the perceived enemies of the *Corpus Christianum*. Poorhouses and workhouses, which had been opened by humane reformers as protective shelters, became increasingly punitive prisons. London's Bridewell had been built as a palace for Henry VIII in 1515–1523, and queens, cardinals, and ambassadors had walked its halls. Its twin courtyards and long hall would have still have been extraordinarily grand when Edward VI gave it to city officials in 1553. When they chose to house both homeless children and 'disorderly women', it quickly deteriorated into a grim workhouse-prison. Amsterdam's workhouse actually developed secure wards to incarcerate those who had broken one or another of the laws that criminalized traditional pauper behavior like public begging. It was known to many as the 'rasphouse' because those incarcerated there were put to work sawing logs of brazil wood into powder that was used for dyeing cloth. Throughout the first decade of Bologna's Mendicanti poorhouse in a former monastery outside the city, the poor schemed so cleverly on ways to get *in* that authorities tightened the regulations on who might be admitted. By the end of the sixteenth century, the poor aimed to stay *out* of what was turning into a sterner workhouse, and to avoid wearing the uniforms whose large letter 'M' marked them publicly as poor beggars. All these cities, and many others, employed beggar catchers to arrest those begging without a license and bring them to the poorhouses for reform.

As stigma and security steadily recast poorhouses and workhouses through the later sixteenth and seventeenth century, they also emerged in other new charitable shelters for worthy and unworthy poor alike. Most agreed that orphans and widows generally topped the list of the most worthy. The historian Olwen Hufton once noted that southern Europeans tended to prioritize *institutional* care around orphans while sheltering the aged in private homes, while northern Europeans reversed this and focused institutional care around the aged while keeping children in private homes. This reflected their different conceptions of how best to preserve families and households, and who best to trust as moral recipients of community help. As we saw above, foundling homes and orphanages steadily became more tightly enclosed and disciplinary, particularly in those instances where they sheltered illegitimate children.

Shelters for the aged were less tightly enclosed, but did use charity to emphasize boundaries. Elderly Italian men and women sometimes deeded their properties to larger hospitals and then joined a residential community organized somewhat like a convent or monastery. Special robes and a distinct rule marked them off as being like the regular clergy, and they prepared meals, bathed patients, and distributed medications until they themselves became patients rather than caregivers. There were only a few institutions like the semi-enclosed Orbatello home in Florence that from 1372 housed more than 100 'respectable' widows and their young children in their own apartments arranged on two levels behind an encircling wall with a central gate. Many Dutch towns created small courtyard communities with private homes like Amsterdam's Begijnhof (1346) where widows could save on costs by living in semi-communal and semi-enclosed cloisters. Parishes across England built small groups of four to ten almshouses near their churches where old men and women approved by the parish or town council received a private dwelling, an obligatory uniform, and an allowance of food and wood. When Henry VIII's church reforms closed some monastic hospitals, parish authorities felt more pressure to provide institutional shelter to the aged. By some estimates, England had 617 hospitals and almshouses sheltering 4,900–6,400 when Thomas More was writing *Utopia*. This would drop to 500 institutions sheltering no more than 5,300 by the 1590s. Elderly poor had to prove that they were local, moral, and indigent to gain a house or apartment, but officials took little for granted, imposing strict regulations and sometimes expelling violators.

What of those who were neither very young or very old? Many new institutions opened in the early modern period as shelters to protect beaten wives, half-way houses to help prostitutes leave the profession, and asylums to keep the daughters of prostitutes from following their mother's profession. These homes aimed deliberately to help young and middle-aged women negotiate the line from unworthy to worthy (or immoral to moral) poverty, and this reformatory purpose made the discipline tighter. Those in Catholic countries drew heavily on the model of the convent and the image of St. Mary Magdalen, a close disciple of Christ who in some accounts had started out as a prostitute before turning her life around, and who became the highest symbol of moral conversion. The bishop of Paris had established a shelter in the early thirteenth century where prostitutes aiming to leave the profession could live while earning a dowry, and at its peak in the fourteenth century it had 260 residents. Temporary homes and convents named after Mary Magdalen and dedicated to sheltering former prostitutes multiplied across Europe, though some of the women carried on their earlier profession regardless, and others seemed little interested in conversion. In 1430, Sister Beatrice de Monyons was hauled up by the St. Mary Madgalen home in Perpignan for discipline after assaulting other sisters. She rubbed excrement in the hair of one, hit others with her fists, a hoe, or a club, instigated rebellion against the mother superior, uttered violent threats ('I'll make your guts come out of your mouth') and brought a priest and other men into the home at night. Sister Beatrice was an extreme but not completely unusual example of the kind of woman who could be locked up in a Magdalen home against her will, and others like her sometimes tried to flee. She survived the discipline and within a few decades had risen to become second in command of the convent.

Magdalen shelters often began as charitable refuges which recognized women's vulnerability in strongly patriarchal societies, yet in many cases proved to be where their very vulnerability was exploited and worsened. Italian 'conversion houses' or 'Magdalen houses' sometimes became a place where husbands lodged disobedient wives or pimps enrolled rebellious prostitutes for periods of a few weeks or months. These males enrolled women not to get them *out* of a difficult situation or profession, but to make them more pliable and obedient *in* it. The Dublin Magdalen Asylum, which opened in 1765, became the template for a system of 'Magdalen laundries' developed across Ireland under the control of nuns for young women who had given birth out of wedlock. The government mandated these institutions and entrusted them to convents that essentially incarcerated the women for periods of years. They put the young mothers to forced labour, and it was later revealed that they sent some children out for adoption without the mother's consent, and buried the bodies of babies who had died in mass graves without a funeral. The last of Ireland's Magdalen laundries closed in 1996.

It is not novel or unusual that communities would look out for their own members, whether by location or creed, or that they would set high moral and religious expectations. What *was* new, however, was the array of new bureaucratic boundary-marking tools to track, police, discipline, and above all purify the poor. Three stand out in particular. First, new laws criminalized age-old activities like begging and categorized travelling beggars as vagrant, deviant, and even contagious. Second, new and specialized enclosures took those newly defined deviant poor who could not be expelled and incarcerated them behind gates and barred windows. Third, new material forms publicly marked status and recorded the identity of the poor. Beggars' licences, badges, special cloaks or whole uniforms, and even brands burned on the cheek were all physical signs that beggars had to carry or wear publicly if they wanted to avoid arrest. They were eerily like More's system of internal passports to control movement in Utopia, although they were targeted directly at 'deviants' as a means of making sure that everyone in the community could keep an eye on them and share in disciplining them.

Parish registers were less public but more universal and effective ways of tracking communal identity. Registers maintained by church authorities gave both governments and churches an efficient system for recording births, confirmations, marriages, and deaths. They became far more systematic across Europe as these authorities aimed to identify what a poor person's 'home' parish was, what faith they had confirmed or married in to, and what cemetery would take their corpse. Parish registers in England and across the Protestant states of the Holy Roman Empire became effectively a record of citizenship, determining whether individuals could hold public office. Similar parochial registers spread across the Catholic world as a way of making good on the Tridentine goal of activating the parish and diocese as the primary home of the good Catholic who, in the past, had likely identified far more strongly with a confraternity or mendicant house. When Roman authorities asked for reports of those being helped in Bologna's workhouse for the poor, they specifically asked how many of the children had taken the sacrament of confirmation. You needed to be in the right register to get a place in Augsburg's Fuggerei or Stratford's Council Almshouses: Protestants need not apply to the former, nor Catholics to the latter, and Jews and Muslims could save themselves the time and effort of even trying. Registers defended the boundaries that made sure a community would help its own and only its own.

The early modern period fixated on reform as purification. In reviewing how people of the time thought and acted, we can see some parallels around the new moral expectations, religious forms, and laws by which they aimed to purify and improve society. All religious confessions began to see certain ways of thinking and certain forms of poverty as somehow deviant, and began to wrestle with how they ought to respond as a community. Working with the broad categories of Initiation, Presence, and Authority, we can see that throughout the fifteenth and sixteenth centuries Europeans diverged fundamentally in their understanding of how individual believers and whole societies should understand their relation to God and how they should aim to repair the broken relationship. Every religious community aimed to better police its boundaries. While some continued using forms of Initiation as a means of drawing members and converts in, many began concentrating instead on how to keep aliens and deviants out. Questions of Presence were critical because these communities were not just differing over words – what they were policing was a very particular relationship with God, accompanied always by the fear that God would punish those who did not take or steward the relationship seriously. Questions of Authority undergirded these other differences, particularly for Protestants who used a very particular way of reading scripture to reject large parts of Catholic tradition, above all those parts dealing with Initiation and Presence. Despite their many and often intense mutual differences, Lutherans, Radicals,

Calvinists, and Anglicans all adopted this distinctly purgative view of scripture, and made it a common point of identity. As we can see throughout, the debates going on among the major Christian confessions had resonances in Muslim and Jewish communities as well, not least because the questions of Initiation, Presence, and Authority also affected them.

At least one implication of these changed ways of thinking was that reformers of all confessions began to accept that they had a responsibility for both the body and the soul of the poor. They not only had to feed and shelter the pauper, they also had to improve her or him by discipline and education in the true faith – whatever that might be. The tools they used drew on milder forms of separation, containment, prosecution, and purgation that we saw mobilized from the fourteenth and fifteenth century against those seen as the enemies of the Body. Most civic governments began by separating worthy from unworthy poor in a step meant both to control costs and help in purifying society. Charity was a tool to prod the unworthy to either work for their subsistence or leave town. Authorities then reached towards types of enclosure as a means both to further access to charity and to improve results. The best and most enlightened minds of the day prodded them in this direction. More, Vives, and Luther had thought primarily in terms of a formative discipline. A century later, the poor relief systems that they had inspired or planned were practicing a punitive discipline. Thanks to corruption, financial straits, a growing punitive ethos, and even the law of unintended consequences, the charitable solutions quickly become worse than the problem of poverty – both of body and of soul – that they had meant to correct. The paradox was almost universal, and almost all enclosures inevitably fell into it. They began with a positive charitable and formative purpose, and within a few decades they descended into a punitive and exploitative shadow of the founders' hopes. Migrants, exiles, and religious refugees were often the most needy of the poor but, as outsiders, they were also among the most resented and feared. They had to find their own way, and this reinforced some of the many boundaries that tightly restricted charity. Purification of thought and action was a serious business. What could not be purified or purged ought to be enclosed, which was much the same thing in the end.

5

RE-FORMING THE BODY: THE WORLD THE REFUGEES MADE

THE DRIVE TO PROTECT, PURGE, AND PURIFY RADICALLY reshaped European society over the course of the early modern period. We can see its effects in politics, the economy, migration, law, and social life, as well as in religious institutions, rituals, and thought. It is striking that definitions become sharper and differences between religious communities more bitter over this period. The number of religious exiles and refugees grows throughout the seventeenth century, and purgative spasms recur in the eighteenth century when we might think that Europe had put all of that behind it as religious faith supposedly began to wane. Instead, Louis XV launched a crusade against Huguenots in the Cevennes Mountains in 1702, the archbishop of Salzburg forced 20,000 Lutherans into exile in Prussia in 1732, and the British loaded more than 11,000 Catholic Acadians onto boats and shipped them overseas in the later 1750s. Religious purgation was alive and well in the Age of Reason.

In order to understand why, we need to look more closely at how the innovations and actions of the fifteenth and sixteenth centuries became the norms and customs of the seventeenth. For that we need to look at how Christians of all confessions, and Jews and Muslims too, began rethinking and reforming the tools, personnel, spaces, and creative life of their religious communities. Refugees and exiles were frequently the most committed and best connected members of their religious communities. They were authors, artists, lawyers, teachers, and bureaucrats, and they worked directly and indirectly for change using the most advanced means available. New forms of technology, particularly printing, allowed texts and images to be used more creatively. New schools, curriculum, and pedagogy coming out of the humanist movement fed a drive to improve the training and raise the professional standards for clergy. New ideas about how communities should relate to God or conduct ritual life changed the spaces, furnishings, and liturgies of worship. The experience of purgation, exile, or forced migration led all communities to look again at their own traditions, at the heroes who populated their collective imagination, and at how they communicated their story to their own children. What is perhaps most telling here is that Jewish and Muslim communities picked up on many of the same changes to tools, personnel, spaces, and creative life, and used them to firm up their own traditions and identities.

The metaphor of the communal Body was re-forming to accommodate emerging boundaries of nation, empire, church, and people and the newly potent conceptions of community. The rhetoric was reactive and exclusionary, even when communities actually drew on each other's traditions, responded to each other's initiatives, and incorporated converts from other faiths. Changes to tools, personnel, spaces, and creative life fed the imagined histories and shaped the invented traditions that were the abiding legacy of this period. They underplayed, ignored, or denied many examples of inter-communal co-existence, and so widened the gap between what many Catholics, Protestants, Jews, and Muslims claimed and what they actually practiced.

Tools

Texts, Tracts, and Polemic

The new technological tool that revolutionized all debates was the printing press. Like most 'new' inventions, it actually combined a few innovations. Johann Gutenberg's big press with moveable metal type would have meant little if reasonably cheap paper and stable ink had not also been available by the mid-fifteenth century. It is commonly claimed that the printing press made the Protestant Reformation, but we could just as easily reverse the equation. With so many authors jostling to declare, protest, argue, and influence the course of events, it was in some ways boisterous reformation – that broader process of purification, purgation, and propaganda that began spreading through the fifteenth century – that made the printing press.

Printing was a commercial activity, not primarily an intellectual pursuit, and printers responded to market demand. Printers printed for the market, so what they printed can tell us a great deal about the reading public. Across Europe, readers bought books dealing not only with religious controversies, but also with the natural world (anatomy, herbals, botanicals, geography), technical skills (mining, agriculture, medicine), self-help (how to write letters, how to conduct cases, how to make wine or beer, or teach yourself Latin), and chivalric moral quests (novels, songs, poems, plays).

Catholics commonly complained that it was the greed of printers that pushed the Reformation forward, but we should not forget that the first printed book in Europe was a Latin Psalter (Mainz, 1457), and the first datable bit of English print is an indulgence (1476). Heinrich Kramer knew how to use the printing press to spread his witch-hunting manual the *Malleus Maleficarum* (1486) to an international audience. The largest concentration of printers – ninety-two – in sixteenth-century Germany was in Cologne, the centre of Catholic power. Yet Catholic printers did little for Catholic propaganda in the first half of the sixteenth century when Luther's treatises were landing like bombshells across Germany. This was in large part because Catholic authorities were opposed *in principle* to popular, public, and vernacular discussions of complex theological issues. Printing would change the notion of what the public square was, who occupied it, and what they could discuss.

Not many printers were strongly Protestant, despite what Catholics thought. Luther's Wittenberg had 38 printers. In mid-sixteenth century Germany, Protestant cities tended to have more presses than Catholic ones, like Nuremberg (62), Strasbourg (57), and Basel (54). Geneva became a major publishing centre when printers flocked there from Italy and Lyon in the 1550s. Yet the largest publishing centres in sixteenth century Europe by far remained the Catholic cities of Venice, Paris, and Cologne.

Looking at almost 6,000 books produced in Strasbourg from 1480 to 1599, Miriam Chrisman traced five stages in lay print culture which demonstrate constantly shifting demand and remind us that most printers pursued profits rather than ideology. From 1480 to 1499 liturgical texts for the church dominated, with almost no popular religious books apart from a few saints' lives. There were also some early practical manuals on how to write letters, make wine, or improve health. From 1500 to 1519, these manuals and handbooks continued expanding in popularity, extending to law, food, medicine, writing, voyages, and travel accounts. Vernacular religious literature also began to pick up, with saints' lives and an illustrated passion book becoming a real hit. Then in 1520–29, a tsunami of popular religious titles swept the presses. The number of books published skyrocketed, and almost 90 percent were religious (383 religious to 43 scientific/literary/practical titles). These were overwhelmingly by Luther, and were overwhelmingly polemical: attacks on Catholic doctrine, on priests, on the mass, on monasticism. Reformers and printers allied to revolutionize Europe.

Yet as we look closer, the picture becomes more complicated. One particular printer, Johann Schott, was an early publisher of polemical pamphlets by Luther, Ulrich von Hutten, and others. These constituted 90 percent of his output from 1521 to 1523, and 100 percent in 1524–25 at the height of the Peasants' Revolt. They disappeared suddenly with the end of the revolt, and from 1526 to 1529 Schott published more conventional sermons and texts by Luther and other leading reformers, with a few medical texts and almanacs on the side. After 1530, he shifted towards publishing medical texts almost exclusively. And he was not alone. From 1530 to 1570 religious books were declining and changing – there were fewer explosive tracts and treatises, and more sermons and catechisms. Bibles were steady sellers, although whole Bibles were bulky and expensive, so most people bought only a New Testament and Psalter. Technical, scientific, medical, practical, and literary works also expanded steadily through these years and on to the last stage of 1571–99. Religious works made a comeback, but no longer as vernacular rabble-rousing tracts by laymen. Clergy and professors wrote confessional and catechetical works to protect and promote orthodoxy, and these won the ever-profitable textbook market.

When we think of printing, we may think first of large treatises and major works. We saw earlier that the powerful purgative of *sola scriptura* unleashed a steady stream of vernacular New Testaments and whole Bibles thanks to intense jostling and debate around questions of religious authority. The Bible was certainly the object of a scholarly project, but it was even more importantly an object of popular culture. Complete Bibles appeared in Dutch (1526), French (1530, 1535), Czech (1533), German (1534), English (1535), Swedish (1541), Danish (1550), Polish (1561, 1563), Spanish (1569), and Hungarian (1590, 1626). It is hard to know how profitable they were, although contemporaries clearly thought that there was money to be made. When Genevan translators finished their new French Bible in 1588, the Geneva consistory published it under its own imprint and ordered that all profits go to help the city's religious refugees.

Confessional disputes only increased Bible publishing, as we saw in Chapter 4. Scholars, reformers, and publishers often claimed to be pursuing scholarly accuracy when producing one translation after another, but it was really ideological purity that they were after. Polish Catholics produced a translation in 1561, and the Calvinists responded with one of their own in 1563. In Hungary, a Calvinist translation of 1590 triggered a Catholic one in 1626. We have already seen that many Jewish converts preferred the 1553 Spanish translation produced in Ferrara because it bypassed these Christian confessional debates. Even in Protestant England, each Bible printed through the sixteenth and into the seventeenth century aimed deliberately to 'correct' the one before it. As we saw in the Chapter 5, Tyndale's New Testament (1526) provoked Henry VIII's Great Bible (1539), which pushed the more Calvinist Geneva Bible (1560), which

30. *Utopia*, from the 1563 Basel Edition.
Courtesy of the Thomas Fisher Rare Book Library, University of Toronto.

triggered Elizabeth I's Bishops' Bible (1568), and finally led to King James's Authorized Version (1611) [Fig 29]. One scholar has estimated that from 1520 to 1649, 1,342,500 whole Bibles and New Testaments were published in England, enough to put one in every household. More than a third were Geneva Bibles – Elizabeth I, James I, and their bishops knew what they risked losing if they did not get into the game. At a time when the English population numbered only 3 million, about 7.5 million 'major religious works' were printed in England as opposed to 1.6 million secular plays, poems, and like materials.

Every English household may have had a Bible, but not every English householder could or would read it. For some, the family Bible was a talisman that sanctified the domestic space and confirmed identity. Parents recorded births, marriages, and deaths on the endpapers as it passed down the generations, turning it into a domestic household register. Dutch households gave similar pride of place to the States Bible (*Statenbijbel*), a fresh translation from ancient languages that the Dutch States General commissioned and paid for at the request of the Synod of Dort (1618–19) and in imitation of England's King James Bible. The States Bible was similarly 'authorized' by the States General in 1637, selling steadily and becoming a fixture of Dutch Protestant households into the twentieth century.

Yet printers needed a steadier business, and controversies drove the market for more ephemeral pieces like tracts and woodcuts. We can see this in Germany in the 1520s, the decade of most dramatic controversy. Luther absolutely dominated a fast-expanding market, selling 22 percent of all German titles in 1518, 45 percent in 1519, and 64 percent in 1520. In 1523, he published 30 percent more titles but with more books flooding off of more presses, his percentage of the total market fell to 36 percent. People were buying tracts rather than treatises. Pamphlets of 16–32 pages were easy to produce and sold cheaply for about 4–8 pennies when a journeyman's daily wage was 24 pennies. A tract like this cost about the same as a hen, a kilogram of beef, a wooden pitchfork, or a pound of wax; woodcuts were even cheaper and often more pungently polemical. Publishers produced about 10,000 different pamphlets between 1500 and 1530, three-quarters of them from 1520 to 1526. More to the point, some sources estimate that there were about 6 million copies in circulation, at a time when the whole German population was only about 13 million, and only a fraction could read – perhaps 4 percent of those in rural areas and 10 percent of city dwellers. Reading aloud in taverns, markets, and homes was the norm, and smart polemicists kept their message brief, simple, and vivid. They knew that only a small fraction of their readers would be pondering a text silently at home, and that their words would have to compete with the noise and distraction of a public space. Ample woodcut illustrations helped drive their messages home in the most basic black and white terms.

The statistics from 1520s in Germany are significant because most of these texts were extremely polemical. This was Luther at his most pugnacious and purgative. His sharp rhetoric called out a host of imitators and respondents, and this encouraged a flood of printers to set up shop. Most pamphlet writers claimed to be 'poor, unlearned, god-fearing laymen', even if they were actually clerics, lawyers, or civil servants. Their messages of judgment, purgation, and purification accelerated in the lead up to the Peasants' Revolt in the mid-1520s. The nobles did not need Luther's injunction that they treat rebellious peasants like rabid dogs, and 'smite, slay, and kill' them in the name of God, but they certainly benefited from what looked like his strong support. Yet Luther's own fortunes turned around. Every graph of his market share shows it collapsing after the Revolt. Although he continued publishing until his death in 1546, three-quarters of all that Luther published in his lifetime appeared before 1530. The collapse of the pamphlet market sent many printers into bankruptcy and forced others to look for new markets beyond religious controversies. Strasbourg printer Johan Schott's shift to medical texts and almanacs was one possibility, while other printers switched to broadsheets, ballads, advice literature, and less polemical religious literature.

As just noted, tracts were read aloud in taverns and market squares. Their accompanying woodcuts reduced an already simplified message into the bluntest black and white terms: the papacy was the Whore of Babylon, the pope was the Antichrist, Catholic clergy were ravenous wolves. Tracts were also the vehicles for debates over Initiation, Presence, and above all Authority. They were vital to reformers, but not new to printers. The sharply anti-Catholic tracts and woodcuts of the early sixteenth century followed the anti-Jewish tracts and woodcuts of the later fifteenth, and presaged the anti-witch tracts, woodcuts, and engravings of the later sixteenth. Regardless of the subject, woodcuts always expressed critiques, condemnations, and fears far more effectively than anything constructive, and so they multiplied when crises broke, and seemed in some eyes to stir up crises further.

Similar floods of cheap and popular polemical washed over France and England during their protracted civil wars of religion in the sixteenth and seventeenth centuries, offering critique, commentary and prophecies. Tessa Watt has emphasized that much of this 'cheap print' was actually relatively conservative, and worked more to confirm than to change attitudes. This did little to reduce the number of tracts and woodcuts produced. Bearing out the observation that it may have been religious controversy that made the press rather than the other way around, publications began to pour off French presses from the mid-sixteenth century as tensions were rising. Alongside almanacs and romantic stories, most titles dealt with religious controversies, including short catechisms, tracts on the sacraments, the clergy, or theological controversies, and enormous numbers of miracle tales and saints lives written like novels and published in cheap blue paper covers as the *bibliothèque bleue* which remained a standard of French publishing well into the twentieth century. While Protestant authors had dominated the market in 1520s Germany, it was Catholics who set the pace in France from the 1560s through the 1590s. An even more sophisticated propaganda machine would come into play in England a century later to make the case for the aristocratic coup that saw James II replaced by his daughter Mary and her husband William in 1688–89. As we saw earlier, no detail was too small in a propaganda campaign that used tracts, woodcuts, teacups, popular songs, and nursery rhymes to underscore that it was God who had stage-managed the so-called Glorious Revolution sending a Protestant Wind to blow William's navy across the channel for the invasion, and engineering the decisive defeat of James II's Catholic troops at the Battle of the Boyne in Ireland in 1690. There would always be an England, and an evolving popular media asserted that it would be The Most Protestant of Nations.

Confessions, Catechisms, and Identity

The Bible was an expensive Protestant icon while pamphlets and woodcuts were cheap bits of ephemeral polemic. Was there anything in between? After the dust of the 1520s settled, printing presses both Catholic and Protestant produced two forms of literature that were less iconic or polemical but that would prove more divisive in the long term: the confession and the catechism. Confessions and catechisms spelled out each religious community's official positions on Initiation, Presence, Authority, and a great deal more. Printing did not create these genres, but it did turn them into a new early modern cultural phenomenon: the detailed but accessible religious text that became a public document setting the boundaries for citizenship.

Confessions (or creeds) had always been critical boundary markers establishing standards for pure and orthodox doctrine, but they had usually been written by and for clergy. From the time of the early church, church and state authorities had used them to suppress particular heresies or divisions. One of the first, the Apostles Creed, was a basic statement of the work of Christ that first emerged in the second century; its twelve statements of faith were widely (though incorrectly) believed to have been written by the original twelve apostles. The Nicene Creed of 325 CE affirmed the divinity of Christ, while the later Athanasian Creed expanded on the doctrine of the Trinity. While these first two were authoritative across all Christian churches, sometimes with strategic variations in wording, the last was not widely accepted among the Orthodox churches. Confessions more often divided than united churches, and that would only increase in the sixteenth and seventeenth centuries.

Some of the early confessions from the 1520s and 1530s looked for common ground among all reformers. At the 1530 Diet of Augsburg, Charles V aimed to establish religious unity in the Holy Roman Empire and so invited statements of faith for discussion. Luther's circle produced the most influential of these, later to be known as the Augsburg Confession, but Zurich and a group of four other cities each produced their own. The Diet rejected them all. As some German cities and rulers started endorsing the Augsburg Confession through the coming decades, it gradually became the leading Lutheran statement of faith. This status was confirmed politically when the 1555 Religious Peace of Augsburg established the Augsburg Confession as the only authorized alternative to Catholic doctrine in the Holy Roman Empire. Differences emerging among Lutherans in the next few decades threatened this political position, so theologians and rulers devised a thirteen-point Formula of Concord in 1577 to highlight their common agreement and emphasize their distinction from both Calvinists and Radicals. Elector Augustus of Saxony (ruled 1553–86) directed his theologians to produce the Book of Concord, and forced pastors, teachers, and professors to endorse it on pain of dismissal. Many dukes and princes, 35 cities, and more than 8,000 pastors signed it, turning the Book of Concord into the most critical document for Lutheran identity within the Holy Roman Empire, even though some Lutheran state churches within the empire and all of those outside it declined to adopt it.

Politics drove more than just the Lutheran Formula of Concord. As England was consumed in the religio-political debates stemming from Henry VIII's changes to the Church of England in the 1530s, officials produced first Ten Articles (1536), then Six Articles (1539), then Forty-Two Articles (1553), and finally Thirty-Nine Articles (1563); each set expressed a different effort to balance constantly shifting political and religious interests. In Switzerland, separate confessions in Basel (1534), Zurich (1536), and Geneva (1536) reflected local politics, and were also superseded as Calvin's influence grew internationally. Calvin's followers in different parts of Europe wrote confessions that responded to their own situations and aspirations. The Hungarian (1557), Gallican (1559), Belgic (1561) Helvetic (1566), and Bohemian (1575) confessions aimed to unite those who to some extent followed Calvin's ideas, while emphasizing their difference from both Catholics and other Protestants. They sealed the process when delegates from across Europe met in a major doctrine-setting synod in the Dutch island city of Dordrecht (or Dort) in 1618–19, approving ninety-three canons in what became one of Calvinism's most critical confessional documents. A few decades later, an English Parliament dominated by Puritans commissioned a new statement of faith for the recently disestablished Church of England. The 1646 Westminster Confession took its name from the palace where Parliament met, and it briefly gave England a Calvinistic theology and church structure, with representative assemblies replacing bishops. Charles II reversed these changes in 1660 when he restored the Thirty-Nine Articles as the creed and the bishops as the leaders of the Church of England. Yet the Westminster Confession remained influential among other British Protestants, particularly those Presbyterians, Baptists, and Congregationalists whose refusal to conform to the Church of England's confession earned them the collective title of Nonconformists.

Radicals had less use for confessions, which many took to be too fixed and confining for Christians who professed to follow the inspiration of the Holy Spirit wherever it might lead. More tellingly, Radicals had no privileged political position to defend, no political enemies to marginalize, and few formal ecclesiastical structures to organize communal life until later in the seventeenth century. One early statement often taken as a Radical creed is the so-called Schleitheim Confession written by Michael Sattler in 1527. Sattler's seven articles convey typical radical ideas on baptism, the ban, communion, separation from the world, and clergy, but were never adopted as authoritative by any ecclesiastical body.

Considering themselves to be the standard from which an increasing number of fractious heretics were peeling away, Catholics initially felt less need to define themselves with new confessions. Pope Pius IV issued a Profession of Faith in 1564 that summed up the responses by the Council of Trent to the issues dividing the once-universal church. It reduced the often lengthy and nuanced debates at the council to short black and white statements that all priests and teachers had to affirm by oath. The council had left significant ambiguity and unfinished business, but this was absent from the simplified and dogmatic affirmations that Catholics 'professed' when taking the oath, as they would into the twentieth century.

It was politically and intellectually inevitable that confessions would grow longer and longer. Within any particular church, succeeding confessions tended to become ever longer and more specific as the number of errors to be rejected and enemies to be anathematized grew. The Augsburg Confession of 1530 was the length of a tract, with twenty-one affirmations and seven denunciations, while the Lutheran Book of Concord added ten further items including Luther's Smaller and Larger Catechisms in order to create a hefty and highly detailed tome. The Westminster Confession of 1646 was twice as long as the Thirty-Nine Articles of 1563, and the second Helvetic Confession of 1566 was ten times as long as the first Helvetic

Confession of 1536. The Radicals remained shy of extensive statements, and the 1632 Dordrecht Confession, a key Mennonite document into the twentieth century, was only half again longer than Sattler's Schleitheim Confession of a century earlier. By the seventeenth century, all governments placed greater political weight on their particular confessions as documents that established political rights and duties. This made it necessary to be ever more specific, particularly as minor disputes and major treatises by professional theologians widened the gaps between particular religious groups. Calvin was not the only reformer trained as a lawyer, and there is a strong legal strain informing this drive for specificity and clarity.

Confessions were supposed to be statements of spirituality, but everywhere they became standards of citizenship. Oaths and public professions to ever more specific and dogmatic statements of religious faith became the norm across Christendom. They were the standard of membership not just in this or that particular church, but in civil society generally. A fifteenth-century graphic representation of the political order of the *Corpus Christianum* had put pope and emperor on equal footing; the seventeenth-century equivalent from Thomas Hobbes's *Leviathan* showed a single towering crowned monarch who incorporated all the citizenry and, armed with sword and bishop's crozier, ruled over church and state together [Fig 31a & 31b]. In Protestant state churches and many Catholic countries, students, politicians, bureaucrats, guildsmen, and even paupers seeking welfare had to swear an oath to uphold the Christian faith as it was laid out in the locally approved confession. Some of those taking the oaths may actually have been ignorant of or indifferent to the theological doctrines they were swearing to uphold. Others may have sworn publicly while keeping what were known as 'mental reservations', particularly given the political stakes involved. As for the rest, how did oath takers know what they were swearing to?

That was the purpose of catechisms.

Catechisms began as relatively short statements of religious belief adapted from creeds and confessions. They were like textbooks, using simpler language and sometimes a question-and-answer format that made them easier to memorize. Reducing complex theologies in this way reduced ambiguity, but also increased expectations that true faith – and true citizenship – hinged on assent to a few clear statements. Many early catechisms used traditional creeds (particularly the Apostles Creed) or familiar parts of the Bible (like the Ten Commandments of the Judeo-Christian Bible) to structure the lessons. Catholic catechisms, which start appearing in the fifteenth century, did not initially use question-and-answer format, but built lessons around numerical devices to aid memorization: the

31(a). Pope and emperor over the *Corpus Christianum*, from the Nuremberg Chronicle (1493). Courtesy of the Thomas Fisher Rare Book Library, University of Toronto.

31(b). The Monarch as Leviathan over State and Church. Courtesy of the Thomas Fisher Rare Book Library, University of Toronto.

seven mortal sins, the seven sacraments, the seven works of bodily or spiritual charity, the five wounds of Christ, and so forth. Catechisms were tools for teaching. When Bologna's Bishop Niccolò Albergati wrote one of the first formal catechisms in 1423, he intended it as a text for the teenage boys of his newly formed confraternity of St. Jerome. The boys could use it to firm up their own knowledge of the Catholic faith before going to teach it to even younger children in the city.

A century later, Italian lay confraternal Schools of Christian Doctrine developed catechisms to teach ritual observances like the rosary and the sign of the cross and the main points of faith and doctrine with a distinct focus on Jesus and on the Catholic Church. These question-and-answer catechisms were oriented to very young working boys and girls, and more generally to any 'good lay person who is knowledgeable and is willing to endure the fatigue of teaching them for the love of God'. Paul Grendler has noted that the 'goal was to teach Christian identity' and teachers also used the small booklets to teach literacy and numeracy. There was a big market for these small texts, often printed in a tiny format that a six- or seven-year-old could easily handle. Ignatius Loyola developed a catechism for his early Jesuits, which emphasized confession, personal responsibility, and obedience to the church. His Dutch colleague Peter Canisius (1521–97) wrote another in 1555 that Jesuits took in many languages across Europe and around the world. By the end of the century there were 130 reprintings of the main text and of the adaptations for young children (1556) and adolescents (1559). Soon after this, the authorized Roman Catechism (1566) gave a systematic review of Catholic doctrine as confirmed by the Council of Trent. It was not used to teach children or even laity, but used mainly to train and test priests.

Catechisms had to address the separate needs of both teachers and students, and while Catholic authors sometimes wrote separate catechisms for each, Protestants seldom followed. Martin Luther's plan to have German fathers teach religious doctrine to their children required workable textbooks, so he wrote two in 1528–29: a Shorter Catechism for children to memorize, and a Longer Catechism as the teacher's guide. The Shorter opened with:

The First Commandment: You shall have no other Gods.

Q: What does this mean?
A: That we should fear, love, and trust in God above all things.

Both of Luther's catechisms got less use around family dinner tables than in Lutheran school rooms and church schools.

Few Protestant churches followed Luther's example of writing separate catechisms, and most seem to have assumed that what worked for children could work for adults. Throughout the sixteenth century, the lines between catechism and confession began to blur, and the opportunities for 'teaching' expanded. While Calvin wrote a catechism for adults in 1536, it was superseded by the Heidelberg Catechism commissioned by the Calvinist elector Friedrich III for his Palatinate schools and churches and published in 1563. It used 129 questions and answers backed up with hundreds of scriptural references to work systematically through the truths and errors of the faith, opening with a short section on Sin and Misery before turning to longer sections on Redemption and Gratitude. Approved by Calvinist synods in 1568, 1571, 1578, and 1586, it was authorized by the Synod of Dort (1618–19) as one of three Forms of Unity (together with the 1561 Belgic Confession and Dort's own ninety-three canons) that functioned for Calvinists much as the Book of Concord did for Lutherans. It became the most widely used catechism in Reformed or Calvinist churches. The Heidelberg Catechism was later subdivided into fifty-two sections, and preachers were obliged to use it to work systematically through an entire course of theology in a year of weekly sermons. The sermon became one of the key opportunities in Protestant churches for teaching large numbers of people at one time, and this altered significantly how worship was organized, how pastors were trained, and even how they dressed.

Many of the later sixteenth century catechisms aimed for encyclopaedic scope and systematic rigour without losing pastoral focus. The Heidelberg Catechism opened with:

Q: What is your only comfort in life and in death?
A: That I, both in body and soul, both in life and in death am not my own but belong to my faithful saviour Jesus Christ; who with his precious blood has fully satisfied for all my sins, and delivered me from the power of the devil; and so preserves me that without the will of my heavenly Father, not a hair can fall from my head; yea that all things must be subservient to my salvation, and therefore, by his Holy Spirit, He assures me of eternal life, and makes me sincerely willing and ready, henceforth, to live unto him.

The Westminster, like Luther's Shorter Catechism, opened more simply with:

Q: Q: What is the chief end of Man?
A: Man's chief end is to glorify God, and to enjoy him forever.
Q: What rule hath God given to direct us how we may glorify and enjoy him?
A: The Word of God which is contained in the Scriptures of the Old and New Testaments, is the only rule to direct us how we may glorify and enjoy him.

Catechisms became far more critical to the many Protestant denominations than they ever were to the Roman Catholic Church. They were the chief ways of teaching identity and difference. They re-introduced forms of ritual and discipline for Protestants who had largely done away with the processions, Latin liturgies, icons, statues, and shrines that shaped a Catholic's sense of identity and religious practice from a young age. On the one hand, Protestants had aimed to replace these traditional church disciplines with personal or domestic ones like mealtime prayer and Bible reading. Yet on the other, Protestants from an early point set young people to memorizing their catechisms in whole or part as a short course in theology, and the practice carried on into the twentieth century. Did Protestant children develop the deep theological literacy that their pastors and parents were aiming for? It is certainly possible to memorize something without absorbing its meaning, yet the discipline was as critical as the content. Memorization of catechisms reinforced for these children their difference from Catholics, just as memorization of the rosary emphasized for Catholic children how much they differed from Protestants. Jewish and Muslim children similarly learned at a very young age the prayers that they would say daily or weekly until they died. What made Protestant practice different was the context. Protestants sharply criticized Catholic and Jewish ritual disciplines for being mindless drills, rote learning, and forms of 'works righteousness' that aimed to earn God's favor by hard effort. Yet memorizing and reciting the catechism became a drill and ritual, a form of rote learning, a test of orthodoxy and sign of righteousness, and even a prerequisite for full church membership.

Jewish and Islamic Confessionalism

Jewish communities did not write confessions or catechisms as such, and it was law and ritual practice more than doctrine that distinguished particular groups. Yosef Kaplan has noted that a 'Jewish Bookshelf' nonetheless emerged among western Sephardic Jews that aimed to inform and train young people and help adults who were reconverting back to Judaism. From the 1620s, Amsterdam presses issued a series of Spanish or Portuguese translations of basic Jewish texts, guides to ritual practice and festive observance, discussions of rabbinic law, and 'Treasuries of Commandments'. These were oriented, as Christian catechisms were, to providing a survey of the faith for a non-specialist audience in diasporic communities across Europe and overseas. The Jewish bookshelf also featured sharp anti-Christian polemics and parodies like the *Toledot Yeshu*, many written by former *conversos*.

Kaplan sees all these books as critical to a larger process of Jewish 'confessionalism' directed to distinguishing between Judaism and its ideological opponents, just as Catholic and Protestant confessions did. Jewish confessionalism used strict doctrine and firm discipline to wean *conversos* away from Catholicism. At the same time, it acknowledged and sometimes even adapted certain ritual forms and ceremonies that *conversos* had learned over generations of Catholic practice. In European diasporic communities like Amsterdam and Venice where former *conversos* made up a significant part of the Jewish population, they developed religious and ceremonial practices that were inevitably influenced both by medieval Catholic traditions around ritual and space, and also by the ecclesiastical reforms reshaping their host societies. By contrast, those who settled in Ottoman centres like Salonika and Algiers retained a more distinctly Iberian and ladino Jewish culture.

Conversion also set the context for Islamic confessional literature in the Ottoman Empire. For over a century after the fall of Constantinople, the Ottomans saw themselves as competing with both the Catholic Hapsburgs and the Persian Safavids to be the dominant world empire and indeed the universal monarchy ruling over the broader European-Mediterranean sphere. They welcomed converts as signs that their empire and Islamic religion were superior to all others, and converts seeking court patronage knew that this was the note to strike in their memoirs and other writings. A long series of texts by Jewish, Catholic, Protestant, and Orthodox converts dating back to the twelfth century provided early models, but from the mid-sixteenth into the seventeenth centuries the number rose, and the tone changed markedly. Tijana Krstic has shown that many of these later convert authors were former Christian priests and pastors raised in the violently polemical literature of Christian confessionalism, and this coloured their use of the genre. They brought the same sharp purgative temperament, exclusionary rhetoric, and mixing of religion and national identity into the religious and political texts they wrote for an Ottoman audience. Their statements about Initiation, Presence, and Authority were more specifically anti-Christian thanks to their early training with Christian catechisms.

There was a distinctly comparative and forward-looking element to Muslim confessionalism. The authors were writing at a time when millenarian and apocalyptic thinking was widespread across both the Christian and Islamic worlds, and when many rulers fashioned themselves as the ultimate universal monarchs whose coming had been predicted by prophets many centuries earlier. Süleyman II the Magnificent had asserted these claims against Catholic and Hapsburg rivals, but as he worked to incorporate the Mamluke Empire while also controlling more of the North African coast and challenging the Safavids, his focus became more distinctly Islamic and more specifically Sunni. The confessionalism he promoted came to emphasize the superiority of Ottoman Sunni Islam over Safavid Shia Islam, in part to legitimate his assertion of the title of Caliph, the unofficial but widely recognized spiritual leader of Islam traditionally based in Cairo. As in Europe, when empires aimed to legitimate their territorial fights with others of the same faith, they reached to religious rhetoric and emphasized the exclusive truth of their particular creed and cause.

Muslim convert authors were particularly adept at confessional polemic, though the Ottomans were already quite familiar with the genre from their own close observations of European politics. From the sixteenth into the seventeenth century, more of these works appeared. The former Protestant Murad b. Abdullah's *Guide for One's Turning towards God* (1556–57), and the anonymous *Priest's Story* written by a former Greek Orthodox priest in the mid-seventeenth century circulated widely across the Ottoman empire and into Europe. The genre gained a boost when a Transylvanian Unitarian convert who took the name of Ibrahaim Müteferrika (1674–1724) established the first Ottoman printing press. In his *Treatise on Islam* (ca. 1710) he picked up the familiar theme, predicting the collapse of the European Christian monarchies and Ottoman world domination, not least because the former were religiously fractured while the latter upheld the one pure monotheistic religion. Muslim confessionalism was an intense but always comparatively marginal phenomenon, and unlike its equivalents in Christendom never developed into a mark or test of citizenship.

Personnel

Clergy as Priests and Pastors

Only highly trained clergy could produce longer and more technical confessions or teach and preach with ever more detailed catechisms. Each Christian community, and many Jewish and Muslim ones, invested far more from the sixteenth century onwards in educating their clergy and expanding clerical responsibilities and authority to keep the laity clear on what separated them from others. The reformers' drive to purify religion transformed the clergy. The average priest a century earlier could not have met the new standards, and in most cases was not expected to even try. Part of this was due to the changed expectations that came out of the linked revolutions in printing and schooling. But a good part went beyond training and into the question of clerical authority: Reformers of all stripes realized that clergy were on the front lines of a battle for lay hearts and minds. They would have to meet far higher standards for skills, conduct, and behaviour before their communities could trust and follow them. These new standards almost inevitably increased the social distance between clergy and ordinary believers.

A fifteenth-century priest, like the average tailor or carpenter, might not be able to read or write. Literacy was a convenience but not a necessity, and a good memory was a far more valuable tool for anyone who learned an occupation 'on the job' by apprenticing with a master. Some parish priests might get training in a cathedral school, but most apprenticed as young men with older priests. They could administer all the sacraments by memorizing the ritual forms, and perform all their pastoral duties without opening a book or writing a letter. According to the Catholic tradition of *ex opere operans* the priest was a channel for God's grace, and it was ordination by the bishop rather than education by a teacher which gave him the spiritual qualities he needed to do his work in the community. Preaching and teaching required a more intensive education, but those were the work of Franciscan and Dominican friars, other regular clergy, or even lay confraternities. The local priest was not necessarily required or even expected to be able to do either. He had to baptize, marry, and bury his community, hear their confessions regularly, and offer masses. When he put on his robes, lit incense, recited Latin formulas, and raised a host in consecration, he was filling a role that was far larger than himself.

In most parts of Europe, and above all in the rural areas where the majority of people lived, it was local communities themselves that decided which of their young men would apprentice with the priest and take over his ritual duties. They chose with a sharp eye to what was best for the community's overall survival. A strong and healthy boy could do more behind a plough, or baking bread, or butchering pigs, or having many children. The boy who limped, who was physically weaker, or who had little or no inheritance needed a role in the community, too. Assuming that he could learn the formulas and perform the rituals, the community might choose him to become its priest. He moved to the house and properties that the community had put aside for their priests' use over the generations, and often farmed these fields to earn his keep. Community members gave him their tithes, and from this he first took what he needed for his own subsistence, for candles in worship and for shingles on the church roof, and then gave the rest to widows or the sick. He had grown up in his community, and people knew his character and needs, including the physical ones. While he could not marry, he was still a man, and it was far better to look the other way if he lived with a concubine than to hold him to celibacy and then spend a lot of time worrying about his ambitions with the local wives and daughters, let alone the other young men.

What angered many people was less the fact that their priest lived with a woman who was a wife in all but name, than the way the church both forbade the practice but also facilitated it – for a fee. By the early sixteenth century, German bishops were charging their priests annual fines ranging from 1.5 to 2 gulden to keep a concubine, and 'cradle taxes' of an additional 1 guilder to legitimate the priests' babies. This was at a time when, by some estimates, less than 5 percent of priests did *not* keep a concubine. Hypocrisy around clerical sex was a constant theme in religious polemic, leading frequently to strategic exaggeration. A Swiss Franciscan turned Protestant pamphleteer wrote in 1522 condemning Hugo of Landenberg, bishop of

Constance, whose diocese included 2,000 parishes and 15,000 clergy. The pamphleteer estimated that these priests fathered 1,500 infants annually, and that at Bishop Hugo's going rate of 4–5 gulden, this brought in 6,000–7,500 gulden annually: 'There are hardly two pimps in the whole bishopric who take in so much money.' Another former Franciscan turned pamphleteer conveyed these priests' dilemma by writing one's fictitious confession as a bit of Protestant propaganda: 'How shall I preach about chasteness and against promiscuity, adultery, and knavish behaviour, when my own whore goes to church and about the streets and my own bastards sit before my eyes?'

If the fifteenth-century priest took his place beside many others in the *Corpus Christianum*, his sixteenth-century successor was expected to lead the community by theological training and moral example. All religious confessions raised their expectations for clergy. Yet what they expected, and whether their clergy could meet the higher standards, went back to their very different views on Initiation, Presence, and Authority. Apart from education, the differences turn up in some small details of how clergy stood out from or fit in to their local communities.

The earliest Protestant reformers like Martin Luther, Huldrych Zwingli, Thomas Muntzer, and Andreas Karlstadt were all highly educated clerics, most of them former friars and even Observants. Some had witnessed firsthand many 'abuses' among their former brother friars and priests, which needed thorough purifying. Others, like John Calvin, had studied law before moving into theology. Most of the early Radicals were artisans who had no formal theological training at all and no socialization in the clerical profession. Some had little investment in the old order, and others were seriously disaffected by their experience of it; they were ready to completely overhaul it. This was the most purgative generation. Their radical changes to priests' spiritual work and social role set a template that became so common among Protestants that Catholics simply could not imitate it. They rejected celibacy, and some like Karlstadt, Muntzer, and Luther quickly married. When Zurich's new marriage court seized jurisdiction from Bishop Hugo of Constance in 1525, it gave clergy living with concubines two weeks to either marry or separate, on pain of dismissal. Reformers across the Protestant reform also eliminated the clergy's special status – Luther most dramatically by asserting that *all* believers were priests – and made priests and pastors more accountable to lay authorities. They reduced the local priest's ritual role and increased his teaching function.

These changes to what a priest did could have created a crisis in staffing local churches, had it not been for the fact that many localities which reformed their Church Orders also closed their monasteries. They rejected the idea that a whole class of men and women had to stand slightly apart from society and spend their lives praying and performing ritual and charitable services for it. Closing the monasteries provided immediate work for those former friars who were ready to throw in their lot with the new order and whose advanced theological training made them ready to become preachers. Radicals like Karlstadt, Muntzer, and Menno Simons pushed radical purgation in a more egalitarian direction by arguing that it was the community and the Holy Spirit that made the priest rather than theological training. Karlstadt told his theological students to throw aside their books and learn from their parishioners, and early Anabaptists found dreams, visions, prophecies, and piety more compelling signs of a leader's authority than a set of books or a university degree.

Some even believed that the Holy Spirit might inspire women to teach and preach, and in his first edition of *The Institutes of Christian Religion* in 1536 Calvin asked rhetorically, 'Why not?' A few women advocated publicly for the new reform ideas, like the former abbess of a convent of Poor Clares, Marie Dentière, who fled from Tournai to Switzerland, Katherine Zell of Strasbourg, and Argula von Grumbach, a German noblewoman. Yet most reformers were uncomfortable with women taking a public role in religious disputes. Mainline Protestants would soon begin using a few New Testament texts to firmly keep women under male authority. As a sign of how closely they now linked teaching to authority, they held that allowing a woman to preach publicly to a congregation or even teach theology to men in a seminary was against God's divine order and plan. Eliminating women's clerical role and institutional authority by closing the convents and forbidding preaching would prove to be one of Protestantism's broadest and most far-reaching purgations.

Ending celibacy, reducing ritual, closing monasteries and convents, and increasing teaching and preaching by local clergy were forms of purgation and purification rooted directly in Protestant rejection of Catholic beliefs about Initiation, Presence, and Authority. Clergy were not to be ritual actors who by means of ordination gained a permanent special status which enabled them to handle the divine presence in the host. The number and variety of clergy narrowed dramatically. Catholics going about their day could encounter clergy by the dozens: nuns singing, friars preaching, monks farming a plot, parish priests visiting widows, confraternal priests leading processions. Protestants would meet only a handful: their clergy's public and ritual roles were reduced, and female clergy were nowhere to be found. Protestant clergy's ritual functions declined significantly when the sacraments were cut from seven to only two – baptism and communion – and when

Protestantism's radical egalitarianism eliminated their priestly function as intercessors between God and the community. Clerics would still come out of the community and in some sense be even more responsible to it, given that many Church Orders established powerful local, regional, and national lay boards to supervise them. In this system, priests were never permanently ordained in the Catholic sense, but simply employed like any other professional. That employment included a far greater role in educating their community through sermons, catechetical instruction, and personal example. Eliminating celibacy raised the new expectation that male clerics would marry and would become model husbands and fathers. With a reduced ritual function and an increased pastoral role, it made more sense now to call them pastors rather than priests, and so this is what Calvinists and Radicals did.

Clergy as Trained Professionals

Highly trained humanists and friars led the early Reformation and established that education, more than ordination and celibacy, would be what most prepared the new pastors for their role. Luther advocated vernacular day schools supported by government subsidies, but when state funds proved tight, he narrowed this and pushed rulers to focus on funding the Latin schools and seminaries that would train the next generation of pastors. Calvin established an academy to educate clergy, and a system of apprenticing the young graduates in churches in and around Geneva to prepare them for their work as local pastors. He also included teachers together with pastors, elders, and deacons in the consistory, which supervised these young men and indeed the whole church. Church of England priests were expected to go to new Latin public schools and to take some theological training at Oxford or Cambridge, even if they did not take a degree. Protestant cities established Latin schools, and Protestant states erected new universities in Marburg (1527), Leiden (1575), Franeker (1576), and Edinburgh (1583); Cambridge added two colleges, which served as Anglican seminaries, and Oxford graduated the largest number of divinity students in its history from 1610 to 1639. Apart from these universities, an even larger number of colleges, academies, and seminaries emerged across Germany, France, and Switzerland to teach theology. This was all because the ancient Catholic bastions of theological training like Paris, Cologne, or Leuven were now effectively off-limits. Some existing universities turned around when their local governments did, like Basel, Heidelberg, Uppsala, and Wittenberg, where Luther had taught and, as English theatre audiences knew, where the young Hamlet, Prince of Denmark, went to study.

The Protestant emphasis on *sola scriptura* meant that the ideal pastor or priest could read the scriptures in the original Greek and Hebrew, knew the confession and catechism by heart, and studied biblical commentaries and theological treatises to prepare for preaching. He left his community as an adolescent, and his education moved him socially, intellectually, and psychologically far beyond the boys he had grown up with. He was expected to marry a woman from the professional classes or higher (as both Karlstadt and Luther had), and his children would receive an education like his; they would certainly be kept under tight rein. If he was a Calvinist, a Radical, or a conservative Lutheran, he put on a simple black gown – the uniform of professors and of lawyers – before mounting the pulpit to teach from the Word of God. Those Puritans who had returned to England from Geneva fought hard and unsuccessfully to ban other traditional items of clerical clothing or 'vestments', which to their mind smacked of a Catholic view of priestly powers. Over the basic ankle-length black gown or cassock, priests had traditionally added a long and narrow strip of cloth called a stole around the neck, a white tunic called a surplice, a semi-circular cape called a cope, and cloth bands or cords around the wrist (maniple), neck (amice), and waist (cincture). There were many more vestments, often quite elaborately fashioned, and each with its own particular meaning. Some items were only worn when celebrating mass or communion, others only if the cleric filled a particular role like deacon or bishop.

We have to work hard to imagine that the single term 'clergy' united a black-robed upwardly mobile pastor in his Leipzig study in 1580 with someone like a local priest outside Seville in 1480. The latter had 'apprenticed' locally, was still illiterate, worked his fields part time, and may have conceived a series of illegitimate children with a local woman of dubious character who served as his housekeeper and concubine. When the priest of Seville went to his sacristy to put on his priestly vestments and prepare for the mass, he left all that behind. The robes turned him into a different person, and the robes were what his parishioners saw as they entered their church, made their confession, and took communion. This was what the people looked for, and it was one reason why Martin Luther and Elizabeth I both determined that their 'new' clergy would wear the old and familiar robes – these masked the radical changes that were going on in their reforming churches and made it possible for worshippers to still *experience* the old faith in a new church. Both Luther and Elizabeth I accepted that there was a limit to purgation and purification. Both also faced zealots unwilling to compromise on what they took to be God's truth. Priestly robes were such a controversial flash point because they were the most immediate and very public sign of radically different views about who the priest was and what he did. Vestments were a key part of Karlstadt's radical reforms in 1521 Wittenberg, and at the heart of the Puritans' first major challenges to Elizabeth in 1563 and 1566 – a crisis known as the 'vestment controversy'.

As we try to balance the 1480 Catholic priest in Seville and the 1580 Leipzig Lutheran pastor in our heads, we need to remember three things. First, the gap between ideal and reality worked both ways. Not all Protestant pastors met reformers' ideals, and not all Catholic priests exemplified their worst fears. Second, while Protestants were reshaping the expectations for their pastors based around their new views on Initiation, Presence, and Authority, Catholics were similarly re-modelling their clergy on their more traditional theological views. Catholics aimed more to purify, and Protestants to purge the clergy. Third, seemingly small disputes, like what a priest or pastor wore, could generate ferocious debates because they were where abstract intellectual differences became immediate, visible, and public.

The clerical uniform provided one critical example of this, and highlights some paradoxes between Catholic and Protestant views about appearance and reality. Liturgical vestments were never just clothes – they signalled identities, boundaries, and ongoing tensions between what something was and how it appeared, or between a sign and what it signified. In the fierce fights around sign and signified, both Protestants and Catholics rejected certain instances of the tension between appearance and reality in their opponents, while continuing to harbour some version of it themselves. Protestants rejected the Catholic idea of presence in the eucharist, where what looked outwardly like bread and wine was supposedly transformed into the physical body and blood of Christ. Yet reformers like Luther and Elizabeth I were practicing a strategic liturgical 'transubstantiation' of their own when they kept key outward forms (like vestments) unchanged while radically altering the underlying theological substance of what a priest actually was and what spiritual authority he exercised. By the same token, Catholics rejected the Protestant idea of a 'cloak of alien righteousness' in which Christ's freely given grace covered a believer's sin the way a cloak could cover a dirty shirt, and so made the believer *appear* perfect before God even when he or she was still very imperfect in nature. Yet through the doctrine of *ex opere operans*, Catholics equally took comfort that their imperfect or immoral priest was worthy enough to perform the sacraments even when he was personally immoral or impure. When he put on his copes, robes, stoles, and other vestments, he was demonstrating publicly that the power of divine ordination covered over his many ongoing personal imperfections and that he was rendered sufficiently pure to be able to hear confession, offer mass, and be a pure vessel of God's grace.

No group could avoid tension and paradox between signs and what they signified. Change was very slow in coming, and there were always gaps between ideal and reality. In 1599, the Litchfield consistory court summoned Church of England vicar Henry Trickett to answer charges that he did not read the gospels publicly, preach sermons, catechize youths, or celebrate communion by the Anglican rite – and had not done so for at least twenty years. Trickett had never married, but kept up sexual relationships with a series of women, paying off one to keep her quiet and living with another who was known as the 'vicar's whore'. He sired at least one and possibly three bastard children, abandoning one who had been born to a servant girl, and rewarding the man who married the mother of the other two. Everyone considered Trickett to be a Catholic, and he had even been excommunicated five or six times. Yet he had stubbornly refused to defend himself at the bishop's court and had simply never been removed. Whatever it was that finally stirred the Litchfield consistory court to action in 1599, the fact that a priest like Trickett could continue to practice for decades in a parish in the West Midlands reminds us that clerical reforms could move very slowly.

Rogue clergy like Trickett did not stop authorities from trying to perfect the ideal cleric. Trickett's neighbors considered him to be essentially a Catholic in Protestant uniform. Yet Catholic reformers were certainly unwilling to tolerate illiterate, concubine-keeping priests for long, and they worked hard to raise the expectations and norms for all clergy. The bishop of Autun in France complained in 1652 that his secular clergy took a very relaxed view of celibacy, and that it was common for many to have concubines and children; this would continue to be the case in some rural areas of Europe until the nineteenth century. Yet at the same time, a series of reforming bishops in Wurzburg had reduced priestly concubinage from about half of all clergy in the mid sixteenth century to only 4 percent by 1631.

Catholic reformers were not redefining the priest's role by purging it of spiritual powers as Protestants did. Like good Observants, they reinforced traditional rules by tightening up disciplinary procedures, starting as close to the top as they could. There was a lot of talk about reform of the head, meaning the pope and sometimes extending to the curia. Rome did indeed become an incubator and laboratory for the many new religious orders that, as we saw in Chapter 4, put into practice many reform ideas about charity, education, vocation, and mission. Yet the real action was at the level of the bishops, who were pressed to take seriously their duty of overseeing their priests and dioceses. Reformers across Europe held up the model of a good bishop who lived in his diocese, opened a school for his priests, gathered them together often to discuss matters of faith and practice, visited them regularly to check on them and their churches, and established firm disciplinary mechanisms to correct those who went astray. Lutheran and Anglican reforms kept bishops as part of an authoritative and disciplinary hierarchy in their state churches. Catholic reformers for their part thought that too many bishops had neglected their spiritual duties and focused instead on gathering money and power. These lax bishops plotted to win appointment to two or three dioceses and then installed deputies called vicars to carry out the pastoral work that they had no time or energy for. They begrudged any funds spent on schools, and legitimated priests' bastards for a fee. They tolerated the worst abuses and did not do enough to improve illiterate priests or discipline immoral ones.

The picture was not in fact quite so black and white. Many absentee and pluralist bishops promoted schooling and disciplinary reform within their many dioceses. Yet it was the example of a few resident bishops with a clear reform agenda, like Matteo Ghiberti in Verona, that carried the day. The accelerating push for clerical reform came out in a series of fights at the Council of Trent where some delegates, particularly those from France and Germany, wanted everything to be on the table. The theologians argued fiercely over whether priests should be allowed to marry, whether the mass could be in the vernacular, and whether laity could drink communion wine or read the Bible in their own language. All of these changes would have blurred the firm lines between clergy and laity. In the end, the clergy gathered at Trent rejected every one of these proposals, and the Tridentine catechism obscured the fact that there had ever been much debate. Trent did, however, empower and oblige bishops to be the key agents for a new movement of Catholic reform. A bishop could now serve only one diocese, must normally reside in it, and must actively educate and discipline his priests. He must enforce their celibacy and not legitimate their children, set up a seminary where they could become students and teachers of the catechism, visit the churches and confraternal oratories in his diocese to make sure that the liturgical furnishings were in order, and stop old practices like confraternities holding big banquets in their oratories. The bishop could not simply let communities choose their own priests, or let priests apprentice their successors. He needed to control the process by which a man of the community became a man of God, removing him, educating him, and then deciding which parish he would serve.

As we saw in Chapter 2, Catholic bishops also had to police women in religious vocations more closely by enforcing stricter Tridentine regulations on nuns who, though lacking priestly powers or duties, were like the female clergy of Catholicism. One of the last decrees passed at Trent stated this, and

Pius V's *Circa Pastoralis* (1566) reinforced it, turning informal tertiary communities into convents, reducing nuns' personal ongoing contact with the world outside the walls, and imposing tighter spiritual regimens. The obsession with clerical celibacy extended here too, but was complicated because there was more than just a traditional concern with sexual purity. Family marriage strategies forced young women into convents for financial rather than spiritual reasons, as we saw in Chapter 2, and it was because fathers had confidence in the security of convent walls that the numbers of upper-class nuns rose so high. In Florence alone the convent population doubled from 1478 to 1515; by 1552, 12 percent of the female population was in convents. A century later, fully half of all upper-class Florentine girls and 60 percent of Venetian were nuns. In seventeenth-century Lima, 20 percent of all women lived in convents – a minority as nuns, and the rest as servants and students protected by convent walls from colonial society.

Clergy as Public Officials

Catholic bishops and priests were expected to reinforce the boundaries between clergy and laity, and the priest's authority increased together with his education. He organized and supervised new parish confraternities, often bringing in more women as members. Some of these worked to increase devotions around the sacrament of the eucharist and others to teach children the catechism, or carry out charity in the parish. The priest also had to keep the registers of births, marriages, and deaths. As now one of the few reliably literate and accessible professionals, laity called on him to give advice, write letters, and intervene with authorities. Priests and pastors were becoming bureaucrats, and this professionalization increased significantly the local authority of the church. Episcopal reforms moved slowly and erratically, particularly in rural areas, but by the seventeenth century we can see that in most urban parts of Europe bishops had successfully raised clerical standards. Much more tellingly, reforms had raised lay expectations. The women and men of his own parish or congregation could far more effectively discipline a priest than a distant bishop or occasional synod. We see many more cases where laity rejected concubines, reported faults, and gave priests greater respect and deference only if they separated themselves from ordinary lay life by means of their habits, manners, and language.

Protestants and Catholics split radically on their idea of what made a cleric, and what a cleric should do. Yet they agreed that priests and pastors should have more education. They gave clergy more authority to perform a range of new and broader duties around teaching religious identity,

Gens effraenata armis quid quaso laedis inermes / Tastis sacrata Deo audaci spoliare rapina. *Vana superstitio patrum simulachra ferebat / Non furor haec tollat, duce sed ratione geruntur.*

32. Frans Hogenbergh, Iconoclastic rioting (1566). Art Resource NY.

There was a special charisma to the human form, which Catholicism had long emphasized. When Muslim troops seized Christian churches, they might deliberately cut out the heads before plastering over frescoes, as they had in the French crusader church of the Resurrection in Abu Ghosh outside Jerusalem.

For sixteenth-century reformers, iconoclasm was a surgical strike against all forms of Real Presence. Rioters were challenging directly the belief that statues could see, that relics throbbed with a spiritual charisma, and that Christ occupied the monstrance in the form of a consecrated host. Karlstadt dismissed all such veneration as simple idolatry, and most Protestants agreed with his point if not his violent tactics. They found the veneration of images not just a sign of corruption to be cleaned up, but a form of evil to be purged. In many German imperial cities, magistrates who sensed tensions rising quietly removed the images first in order to avoid what they saw as the greater threat of mass rioting and the anarchy of citizens taking things into their own hands. Throughout the 1530s and 1540s, state governments in England, Scandinavia, and across the Holy Roman Empire stripped the altars

33. Iconoclastic damage to a carving of God and the Saints in Utrecht Cathedral. Photo by Ethan Matt Kavaler used by permission.

in a drive that was perhaps less about curbing superstition than about expropriating precious metals and gold. Duke Ulrich of Wurttemberg seized 75 percent of all church lands, and even had his commissioners scrape the gold leaf off altarpieces, while Henry VIII realized well more than 1.3 million pounds when he confiscated monastic lands, buildings, and altar ware. Edward VI moved this state looting from monasteries to parishes, and some English parishioners simply buried the items and then dug them up again a few years later under Queen Mary's Catholic restoration.

If this first form of iconoclastic purgation targeted the statues, altarpieces, and furnishings that filled churches, a second form of purgation wiped their physical structures clean. New Protestant governments had to renovate old Catholic churches. They whitewashed over the frescoed walls and ceilings, and plastered

34. P. J. Saenredam, Interior of St. Bavo Church in Haarlem (1628). Image Courtesy Getty Open Content Program.

over wall carvings; removed rood screens and any remaining statues and altarpieces; got rid of the incense; replaced stained glass with clear; removed side altars lining the nave, and moved the main altar out from the wall so that the priest celebrating communion faced the congregation; constructed larger pulpits if necessary, and highlighted their significance by putting seats or benches around them so that people would not tire through the longer sermons that were the new centre piece of Protestant worship [Fig 34].

Every architectural and sensory trace of the older traditions around Initiation, Presence, and Authority had to be renovated to reflect new understandings: initiation into the community had always taken place at the baptismal font by the entrance to the church or in a separate baptistery; some Protestants now moved this critical site up to the front of the church beside the pulpit and the communion table. They then also moved the baptism ceremony into the regular worship time where the whole congregation could witness it. The purely spiritual presence of the Trinity and the authority of Scripture Alone demanded brighter light so that worshippers could follow along in personal Bibles and then sing religious songs (either drawn from the Old Testament Book of Psalms or newly written for worship) in response. To the extent that they were invoked at all, the senses were directed less to emotional engagement than to a rational comprehension of the truth and a measured and respectful response. Sounding boards over the pulpit projected the preacher's sermon to the back of the church, and since the faith of believers turned rituals into sacraments, he had to speak loudly, in the vernacular, and directly to the people when conducting communion or a baptism.

Different localities and different denominations played a different balancing act in this second form of purgation. Lutherans and Anglicans generally changed less inside the churches than Calvinists and Radicals did. Yet all Protestant authorities closed or repurposed the convents, monasteries, and friaries, which, though usually closed off to the public, could often be the largest buildings occupying the largest stretches of real estate in any town or city. Some became schools, hospitals for the sick or aged, or hostels for travellers. The elector of Saxony gave Luther the Augustinian house where he had lived as a friar, and Luther turned it into a university students' boarding house where he charged rent, presided over the table, and offered sharp comments on current events. Across Protestant Europe, most of these large institutional buildings that had anchored the local *Corpus Christianum* physically and spiritually continued to serve some public religious purpose, though they might now be serving authorities of a distant state government or state church. England's 850 religious houses were expropriated by the crown between 1536 and 1540, and then sold to nobles who either adapted the religious houses into stately homes, or dismantled them entirely and reused the stones. Some of Europe's largest religious houses, like Tintern Abbey and Glastonbury were reduced to ruins or disappeared without a trace, with most of the funds going to pay off royal debts. Shrines and holy places that could not be turned into local churches faced a similar fate. Political and economic considerations drove many of these expropriations and renovations, but even given that, no other form of purgation demonstrates so clearly how Protestants completely rejected the Catholic sense of holy spaces within the *Corpus Christianum*. The practical needs of the Christian community took priority because it was the work of believers in performing worship and conducting charity that made a place spiritual or holy, not some recent miracle or ancient legend.

The third form of purgation followed on the second when early Protestants first started meeting informally or when later Protestants began building new churches. Radicals took seriously Christ's teaching that he was present whenever two or three were gathered, and so might hold their worship services in a simple bare room within a house. Early French Huguenots and Dutch Calvinists moved services entirely out of doors and into open fields in what was sometimes called 'hedge preaching'. It was an immediate and practical step, particularly as many were meeting secretly under threat of persecution, but it also underscored their conviction that worship made a place special rather than the other way around. It is hard to convey just how much this violation of traditional ideas of sacred space and reverence enraged some traditional Catholics. Christ may have been born in a stable, but after death and resurrection, He should not be degraded by being worshipped where cows grazed. Some Catholics thought that they risked Christ's punishing anger if they tolerated worship by heretics in open fields, and one of the signal events sparking the French Wars of Religion came just before Easter 1562 when the duke of Guise slaughtered a group of Huguenots who were worshipping in this way outside of the town of Vassy in Champagne. The duke's purgation triggered a series of similar massacres throughout the Easter season in different parts of France.

French Huguenots did not always worship in fields, but they rigorously rejected Catholic forms and assumptions in the new churches they built, deliberately calling them 'temples' and locating them for convenience alone. In placement, construction, and design these churches advertised that all spaces were equally holy. A place of worship should be built to practical requirements and should not be treated any differently from a house, a workshop, or a stable. When the third- or fourth-generation Anabaptist Mennonites began building their hidden churches in Amsterdam courtyards and homes, they followed the same bare aesthetic. Painters in seventeenth century Holland sometimes showed the interiors of Dutch Calvinist churches as high, whitewashed, and sunlit spaces devoid of furnishings or, for that matter, of people. Catholic painters by contrast seem not to have thought about church interiors as the subject matter for a painting, but continued producing extravagant trompe l'oeil paintings of devout saints and gyrating angels moving through pillars, balconies, and open ceilings straight up to heaven. They were representing the metaphorical space of worship, while Protestants emphasized its physical place.

The whitewashed and sunlit interiors of Calvinist churches were well suited for service as lecture halls for a pastor dressed in a professor's robe preaching catechism sermons. Yet these occupied just one end of the broader Protestant spectrum. In the state churches of Germany and England, there was far more continuity in construction, just as there was in liturgy and vestments. Many Lutheran churches retained the altars, statues, paintings, and even rood screens first installed for Catholic worship. The Church of

England retained its cathedrals, and their deans and chapters retained extensive control over furnishings and liturgies. In many cases, they used that control to maintain traditional practices in regard to vestments, liturgy, and sacraments. This was certainly the case in Westminster Abbey. Although not a cathedral, it enjoyed royal protection, which its clergy used to defend against the purgations to space and sense that Anglican puritans were promoting.

Place, Space, and the Senses

It is tempting but too easy to contrast Protestant place with Catholic space, the first a deliberately plain lecture hall purged of mystery and the second an emotionally and experientially rich sensory world. Few churches changed radically at first because few worshippers could so easily let go of familiar forms and expectations. Protestants did not abandon emotion and mystery entirely, but simply found different ways of working them into worship spaces and services. The pulpit Bible sanctified the worship space with the immediate presence of God as much or more than any relic under the altar or monstrance on the top. Scripture in fact took on the authoritative and imaginative resonance of relics. As they cleared saints' bones in silver and gold reliquaries from their churches, Protestants of most all confessions replaced them with printed Bibles on elaborate brass stands as the physical manifestation of God's power and immediate presence. It had been the relics under Catholic altars that gave those pieces of furniture their spiritual power, allowing the priest to consecrate the host there and sanctifying the entire space of the church. No relic, no altar, no mass. In much the same way, the pulpit now became the real centre of Protestant worship, defining the worship space functionally and imaginatively. No Bible, no pulpit, no worship. The Bible on the pulpit was God's Real Presence in the believers' midst, not as the physical body and blood of Jesus but as the Holy Spirit, the third person of the Trinity, bringing the Word of God through the words of the preacher and into the hearts of the listeners. Protestant communion tables and baptismal fonts were certainly significant as the physical signs of the only two sacraments that Protestants retained. Yet those sacraments had been drained deliberately of any Real Presence, while the pulpit, with the vernacular Bible on it and the preacher preaching from it, spoke to the immediate presence of God the Creator and Judge, to Jesus as the Word or *logos*, and to the Holy Spirit as source of divine interpretation and inspiration. No other part of the Protestant church spoke as strongly to a divine presence within the worship space as the pulpit and pulpit Bible.

Protestant worship also defined and filled space with sound rather than smell. Worship was as much about congregations singing as it was about pastors preaching, not least because it was in song that the laity participated most directly in worship. Zwingli was one of the few who frowned on music and congregational singing, and though he was an accomplished musician, he wanted organs removed from churches. Some English and Scottish reformers followed his lead and dismantled their parish church organs. It may have been the emotional power of the music that made them suspicious. Vernacular hymns and psalms could be deeply emotional laments or sprightly celebrations – Luther famously set religious lyrics to popular tavern tunes and argued that the devil should not have all the best songs, and not for nothing were some of the psalms in Calvin's Psalter known as 'Genevan jigs'. The first Huguenot Psalter appeared in 1533, and soon others were published in Rouen, Caen, Lyon, Geneva, Lausanne, and Strasbourg [Fig 35]. Thomas Tallis (1505–85) composed music for the royal chapel under Henry VIII, Edward VI, Mary I, and Elizabeth I, and managed to tune his style to the very different demands of each. His mass settings for Mary were masterpieces of intricate polyphony, while his anthems and metrical psalms for Edward and Elizabeth offered simple rhythmic harmonizations and clear verse settings of scriptural passages. Singing became for Protestants an aid to memorization and a form of rote prayer, which they could recite anywhere in place of the rosary. Many martyrs were recorded as having gone to their deaths singing psalms or hymns.

In or out of the church building, vernacular song constructed the virtual worship space most meaningful for Protestants, not least because it underscored how their worship took place not just by passively witnessing the priest's action in a sanctuary, but by individual active participation in church, home, street, or field. This built on the rich tradition of lay singing in medieval and Renaissance Catholic confraternities, source of many popular spiritual songs like the Christmas carol. Some Protestant confessions preferred unaccompanied singing, but across the Dutch Republic, Germany, and eventually also in England church organs became the instrument of choice for resonantly expressing the power of God and the varied but deep emotions of believers. From his post in Amsterdam's central Old Church (*Oude Kerk*), organist Jan Sweelinck (1562–1621) profoundly influenced the musicians who spread organ music across Northern Germany and taught the likes of Johan Sebastian Bach (1685–1750). Bach together with Georg Frederic Handel (1685–1759) expanded beyond the organ and congregational singing with more complex cantatas and oratorios in which professional choirs and soloists voiced a narrative recitative of scriptural

35. Psalm 1 and solfege from Huguenot Psalter.
Courtesy of the Thomas Fisher Rare Book Library, University of Toronto.

texts woven through arias, choral works, and purely instrumental passages. Bach himself wrote almost 200 cantatas while serving as a church organist in various courts across the Holy Roman Empire, and Handel's oratorio of *The Messiah* became an enormous success from its first performances at benefit concerts for orphanages in Dublin (1742) and London (1750). Suitable for both concert halls and church sanctuaries, these religious cantatas and oratorios fell in and out of popularity but fed the deep Protestant conviction that a Christian nation's religious orientation should be as evident in its public entertainments as in its formal worship.

Catholic architects shaped churches even more around emotional transport in the period of the baroque, when experiments with the new architectural technology of stucco allowed them more easily (and cheaply) to bend walls, make ceilings seem to disappear, and give extravagant gestures to towering saints and tumbling angels. Yet Catholic reformers also took down

36. Interior of St. Michael's Church, Munich.
Photo by Ethan Matt Kavaler, used by permission.

rood screens and opened spaces in order to promote lay participation, added pews to promote instruction and contemplation, and installed confession boxes to promote repentance. Jesuit architects in Bavaria organized the interior space of St. Michael's church (1583–97) in the heart of Munich, one of the earliest and most influential of their churches in Germany, such that it became the expression in stone, wood, and stucco of Ignatius Loyola's *Spiritual Exercises* [Fig 36]. Jeffrey Chipps Smith has shown, by means of a walk down St. Michael's main aisle, how the span, the massing, the chapels, and decorations can be read as a progressive unfolding of the *Exercises*. By the mid–sixteenth century, Catholics had become despondent at their extraordinary territorial and intellectual losses, and the Jesuits worked tirelessly to reinvigorate the church, not just with their ambitious educational program, but perhaps even more effectively with their patronage of art and architecture, beginning with their own church of il Gesù (1568–84) in Rome.

The Jesuits were the greatest single patrons of art in Germany throughout the period, and what compelled admiration and invigorated their followers was the energy and ambition of Jesuit commissions, and the continuity between the art and the *Exercises*. Both aimed to bring the individual believer to self-awareness, to repentance, and to God. Flemish Catholics who fled towns like Antwerp, Brussels, and Ghent for Cologne absorbed Jesuit aesthetics there, and then became the biggest patrons of Jesuit-style art when they eventually returned to their homes. Protestant iconoclasts had damaged so many medieval altarpieces and statues that there was a great need for replacements, and the returning exiles filled the gap with Jesuit-style religious art. Across Germany, baroque architects in particular managed to find ways of preserving emotional and sensory qualities while introducing the clear glass windows and brilliant sunlight that Renaissance humanists like Pope Pius IV had associated with rational revelation and divine light.

Confessional Monuments and Architectural Catechisms

While both confessions moved progressively towards ever more monumental forms in public churches and religious institutions, the Catholic Church retained a greater attachment to the physical space of worship, and so built more ambitiously and dramatically. This is nowhere more clear than in St. Peter's Basilica in Rome. Like many Catholic churches, it was reconstructed over a very long period (1506–1626). Its consistency and coherence testified to a conviction that this was the earthly centre of a universal church, unifying the separate visions of artists and patrons and demanding an unprecedented scale. The plan and dome of Michelangelo Buonarroti (1475–1564), the facade of Carlo Moderno (1556–1629), and the embracing portico of Gian Lorenzo Bernini (1598–1680) that creates the piazza in front of the church all project a distinctly Catholic conviction of what sacred space must achieve. Its closest competitor for sheer size and impact is St. Paul's in London, constructed by the single architect Christopher Wren in just a quarter of the time (1677–1708), with a dome clearly inspired by St. Peter's and facade bell towers reminiscent of Giulio da Sangallo's early (1513) design [Fig 37a & 37b]. Some English observers in fact found it far too popish a design. Protestant politics were too thoroughly national to allow any single

37(a). A. Joli, St Peter's in Rome. Private Collection. Photo @ Christie's Images/Bridgeman Images.

37(b). R. Barker, St. Paul's in London, Yale Center for British Art, Paul Mellon Collection. USA/Bridgeman Images.

church like St. Paul's to become as iconic for Protestants in other countries as St. Peter's was for Catholics around the globe. More to the point, Protestants generally had enough ambivalence about sacred spaces and enough of a continuing iconoclastic orientation that any physical icon like a towering church would be a paradox and contradiction.

Jewish and Muslim worship spaces were equally shaped by the period's religious and political struggles. The dynamics of internal space and external form that we see unfolding in Catholic and Protestant worship spaces throughout the struggles of the sixteenth and seventeenth centuries were clearly evident in them. The early modern Jewish diaspora created a great demand for new synagogues across Europe, but the ambiguous position of Jewish communities meant that the form of their worship spaces was less often up to them alone. In both Europe and the Ottoman Empire, Jews were prevented by civic law and guild regulations from apprenticing or practicing skilled physical crafts like carpentry and construction, and only after nineteenth-century emancipation do we find Jewish architects and builders becoming active in any numbers. Venetian Jews established five synagogues in the city's ghetto for their separate national communities, but each one was constructed by Christian craftsmen, who inevitably shaped these commissions around their own notions of worship and performance space.

Early synagogues in Erfurt (ca.1100), Avignon (1221), Prague (1270) and Salonika (ca. 1520) had often been discrete and almost hidden places, even though they housed prayer halls, libraries, schools, and administrative spaces. Building restrictions in Christian cities had led to some common innovations like sinking the ground floor well below street level to create a high interior space in a building that was no taller than a house on the outside. That space was made sacred not by physical relics, but by the presence of scripture and the activity of prayer. The French religious historian Jean-Christophe Attias has noted that 'in traditional Judaism, the physical presence of the scripture is at least as important as its content. When Torah is unrolled in service, it is meant to be admired, not apprehended.'

As Jewish diasporic communities established themselves, their confidence took on expanded architectural expression, particularly in areas of somewhat greater toleration like the Polish-Lithuanian Commonwealth and in Dutch Republic. In eastern cities like Kracow (1557–70, 1638–44), L'viv (1582–95, 1632–33), and Vilnius (1633–48), wealthy communities numbering many thousands of Jews employed Italian architects to build masonry synagogues in a baroque style that far outstripped older wooden structures. Over two dozen of these rose in Polish-Lithuanian cities before new political and economic restrictions in the mid seventeenth century forced a new wave of emigration. Amsterdam's Sephardim built three synagogues within fifteen years of winning toleration for public worship in 1603. Yet stiff Calvinist opposition initially forced them to follow local Catholic and Anabaptist examples and fit their 'hidden churches' (*schuilkerken*) into existing buildings leased from Christians. Three congregations then merged to build the first public synagogue in 1636–39, but from the street it looked no different from the neighbouring patrician mansions – a *schuilkerk* in plain view. The fast-growing Ashkenazic community erected a monumental structure in 1670–71 (the *Grote Sjoel* or Great Shul) designed in the style of a great public building by one of Amsterdam's most prominent Christian architects and city planners. Five years later, the Sephardim responded with a yet larger building (the Portuguese Synagogue or *Esnoga*) across the same city square – the largest synagogue in Europe and bigger than many of Amsterdam's churches, though built in a similar classical style. Many Jews and even Protestants looked on the Esnoga as the very image of the temple built by King Solomon in ancient Jerusalem.

Christian architects were building Jewish monuments. Civic ambitions, diasporic realities, and a common imaginary rooted in Old Testament Israel combined to create new forms in these great urban synagogues, which were more public and self-consciously impressive while continuing carefully to reflect local needs and building styles and to fit into an urban fabric. Some of Poland's masonry synagogues were built like fortresses to contribute to civic defense, and both these and the Dutch synagogues added extra rooms, adjoining buildings, and interior courtyards for their communities' schools, charities, and administrative organizations. Their larger scale showed both that Jewish diasporic communities were now more readily accepted into the social and urban fabric of at least a few 'Christian' cities, and also that where there was public acceptance and political protection, they aimed to make a positive public contribution to that fabric by employing the best architects and building on a monumental scale. Amsterdam's Portuguese synagogue reshaped its interior space in ways reminiscent of the hierarchical ordering found in the city's Calvinist churches. There were raised pews allowing the syndics of the governing council (*ma'amad*) to see and be seen, a central seat for the council's lay head, and a slightly lower one for its chief rabbi, and a segregated set of pews for those under discipline.

Political toleration and expanding social and cultural roles were two key factors shaping the scale and profile of synagogues in the early modern diaspora that had been fuelled by the expulsions of the fifteenth and sixteenth centuries. A third related one was Jewish confessionalization. Since Christian and Muslim authorities often preferred to relate to a diasporic community through its religious representatives, specifically religious spaces like the synagogue became more important as centers of Jewish community life. New spiritual movements that developed in the early modern diaspora encouraged more community members, and particularly women, to attend synagogue services regularly. As more women came to pray, synagogues expanded with larger prayer halls ringed by galleries. Jewish confraternities multiplied for charity, education, and socialization, and they too needed space to meet and act. Synagogues in Amsterdam and Hamburg also developed new ceremonies for circumcising and initiating converts, welcoming relatives from Iberia and other Jewish communities, being called to the Torah, and disciplining and publicly humiliating transgressors or receiving their requests for pardon. These new rituals all influenced the shape and use of synagogues across the Sephardic diaspora.

The diasporic town of Savannah in the Dutch colony of Surinam provided a rare instance when Jews could shape urban fabric from the beginning. This was an entirely Jewish community populated by Iberian *conversos* whom the Portuguese had expelled from Brazil in 1654 and whom the Dutch valued for their experience in running sugar cane plantations. The *conversos* saw Savannah as a utopian experiment of sorts, and set their brick synagogue on a hill in the centre of grid town plan whose practical outlines were set by Dutch and Hispanic urbanism but whose imaginary model was intended as a recreation of King Solomon's Temple.

Within early modern Islam, it was the Ottomans who drove major developments in mosque design in the cities they had conquered and that they were repopulating in part through large-scale plantations and relocations of exiles. Their ambitious building campaigns progressed along with their rapidly expanding empire, and were shaped fundamentally by their consciousness of being less the conquerors than the inheritors and preservers of the Byzantine Empire. Occupying Constantinople in 1453 confirmed an architectural hybrid of Muslim and Eastern Orthodox forms, which had started emerging over the previous century. The hybrid merged Islamic minarets and courtyards with Byzantine domes and semi-domes over an open square plan. The new style that Ottomans built in was quite distinct from earlier Arabic, Persian, and Andalusian mosques, and became one of most characteristic and familiar forms of their urbanism. Their mosques were certainly the most highly visible monumental marker of Ottoman domination in cities around the Mediterranean, up into the Balkans and Eastern Europe, and over to Persia. Sultan Murad II gave this new form its most prominent expression when he converted Constantinople's Hagia Sophia, one of the largest and oldest churches in Christendom, into a mosque. But it

38. W. H. Bartlett, Süleymaniye Mosque (1550–58). Private Collection @ Look and Learn/Bridgeman Images.

was the architect Mimar Sinan (1490–1588) who did the most to spread the hybrid form with over 340 buildings across the empire. The most notable was the Süleymaniye (1550–58) commissioned by Süleyman I the Magnificent to crown the highest hill in Constantinople-Istanbul [Fig 38]. He too aimed quite self-consciously to imitate King Solomon, builder of the temple in Jerusalem.

Ottoman expansion into Eastern Europe also provided many opportunities to create Islamic worship spaces out of Orthodox or Catholic churches like Constantinople's Hagia Sophia. Size mattered, and after conquering a town or area, the Ottomans would turn the largest church into a mosque. After seizing Cyprus in 1570, the Aya Sofya Cathedral in Nicosia and Aya Nikola Cathedral in Famagusta were purged of altar, icons, stained glass, and frescoes, and outfitted instead with prayer niches (*mihrabs*) and a pulpit (*minber*). Each also gained a minaret on its gothic facade. Across the island, churches and church properties were converted into endowments (*waqfs* or *vakfs*) providing education, food, water, housing, and worship.

Churches and synagogues were often rectangular and directional, with altar, pulpit, or torah ark and *bimah* giving a linear focus. When converted into mosques, they spoke more to the Ottomans' conquest than to their spiritual values. By contrast, when the Ottomans built new structures, their domes spanned vast open areas for prayer and seemed suspended in space above the rings of windows that flooded the interiors in natural light. The Ottoman mosque was to be as all embracing and inclusive as the empire itself. It was a sacred space, but not because of any relics or icons held within it – these were effectively banned by the Islamic rejection of human images. It was made sacred by the activity that went on in and around it: prayers inside, charity and education in the courtyard, and calls to prayer from the minarets.

Worship space was one of the most public markers of religious identity regardless of confession, and hence one of the most controversial public signs of difference throughout the early modern period. The conquests, divisions, purgations, and migrations of the early modern period triggered an unprecedented wave of adaptations and new constructions, and the builders of each religion and confession were determined to make the worship spaces tell their particular story. Churches, synagogues, and mosques were confessions in wood and stone, and worship spaces were architectural catechisms. As written confessions and catechisms became more detailed and distinctive, the worship spaces followed suit. The colours, smells, sounds, and materials inside these spaces all had particular spiritual meanings for particular traditions and confessions. Rules over who could enter and on what day or time, where they could move, what they could or could not wear or say, and even the language they used – all these marked deeply held views about how a community met God. Every child began his or her socialization into religious tradition by learning what could or could not happen in this space. Not surprisingly, this period's many rioters and conquerors targeted churches, synagogues, and mosques as the object of purifying iconoclastic violence. Magistrates built monumentally to signify power and divine approval. Refugees and diasporic communities hid them away to preserve tacit co-existence, or built grandly to signify arrival and acceptance. The public space of worship was the public face of an entire community. One of the reasons why religious differences became much more clearly fixed and prominent in the seventeenth century was because they were taking monumental architectural form in cities and towns across Europe. These architectural catechisms were more easily read by a broader span of the population than their printed counterparts, and likely spoke more powerfully as forms of religious pride and identification.

Imagination

How might you imagine yourself if you were a Dutch Catholic or French Protestant refugee, a Jew migrating south from Germany after being expelled from Strasbourg, or a Muslim fleeing Spain for North Africa? Were there earlier examples of forced migrants in your tradition that helped make sense of the anxiety? Were there stories you could tell your children to explain to them or to yourself why your God seemed to have abandoned you? With the religious refugee becoming a mass phenomenon in the early modern period, these stories became ever more important to defining and defending identity across all religious groups and confessions. A dynamic made up of anxieties and doubts on one hand, and persecutions, victories, and heroes on the other now lodged at the heart of religious identity. It would shape how religious groups confronted and coexisted with each other until well into the twentieth century.

Leaving home meant leaving the holy spaces that defined you and leaving behind any ancestors buried there. It meant confronting the question of whether you had done anything to deserve God's punishment of exile. Each religious tradition had stories in its scriptures or sacred history that told of obedience and disobedience in terms of divine judgement and the promise of redemption. Each had stories of exile and flight, and stories of those who had been killed before they could escape. Martyrs who had died for a faith were transformed into powerful living symbols of it in books, plays, and paintings. Parents of each tradition drew on these when naming infants in order to remind their children who they were, where they came from, and to what people and God they belonged. We can call this collection of stories, images, myths, traditions, and other creative forms the 'imaginary'. Each refugee community and group of exiles generated its own, which each then used in order to make sense of their experiences and pass on their convictions and preoccupations.

Narratives of Exile and Exiles in the Narrative

The Judeo-Christian Bible was the source for some of the most important stories feeding the refugee imaginary. There were two main themes in the history of the people of Israel as conveyed in the Jewish Bible or Old Testament. The first was the Exodus of the People of Israel from Egypt and their migration to the Promised Land. The second was the destruction of Jerusalem and its temple and the forced deportation of Jews to Babylon for a lengthy period which the biblical accounts rounded off to seventy years.

Archaeological and other textual evidence shows that neither was as black and white as these accounts portrayed. Yet it was in those stark terms that both entered the exile and refugee imaginary as paradigms of God's Liberation and God's Punishment. The burning question for any exile or refugee was this: what is God up to? What have we done?

Punishment and liberation were interwoven in the biblical accounts of the Egyptian Exodus and the Babylonian Captivity. Israel's move to the Promised Land in Palestine was delayed by forty years of wandering due to their disobedience, and the Babylonian Captivity ended in a triumphant return to and rebuilding of Jerusalem and its temple. These themes were common to all religious traditions in one sense or another, each of which expressed suffering and punishment as tests of obedience. Even the Chosen Ones failed, and while God sometimes punished them by forcing them on the road, He always brought them eventually to a Promised Land.

Since the narrative was so critical to many religious communities' self-understanding, it is worth recalling the chief features here. God chose Abraham and made a contract or covenant with him, promising him a rich land and numerous descendents if he was obedient to God's will. God's covenant marked off Abraham and his descendents as God's Chosen People, but it also required Abraham to separate himself from the home, family, and traditions he knew between the Tigris and Euphrates rivers around modern-day Iraq. In order to make a fresh start, Abraham had to move to the land God had promised to him on the eastern shore of the Mediterranean. Muslims, Jews, and Christians took different lessons from his efforts to evade difficulty or to hurry God's timing. Abraham's second son Isaac settled modern-day Palestine and prospered, but the family's wandering was not over. His grandson Joseph had jealous brothers who sold him into slavery in Egypt, but he eventually rose to a position of power that allowed him to save his family during a difficult period of famine and then relocate them to Egypt. After memories of Joseph faded, the Egyptians enslaved Joseph's descendents. Yet God then raised up Moses to liberate them and lead them out of lush Egypt and into a barren desert wilderness before delivering them again to the land promised to Abraham centuries before. Here they developed from a wandering and diasporic tribe into the nation of Israel with a capital in Jerusalem, heroic kings in David and Solomon, and a temple.

According to the historical books of the Judeo-Christian Bible, in the centuries following their arrival in the Promised Land, the people of Israel fell into a rhythm of alternating periods of obedience and disobedience. 'Obedience' meant closely observing the pure law that God had given directly to Moses. 'Disobedience' was any form of religious mixing with other cultures around them. Under weak or evil kings, the Israelites let their distinctive traditions slide and took on animistic practices, resulting inevitably in God punishing them with famine, plague, or military defeat. This set the stage for a good king who revived the old religious laws and practices, and restored Israel's political and military fortunes.

This story of a people's religious disobedience and obedience triggering God's material punishment or blessing planted Observantism at the core of the Judeo-Christian imaginary. Being chosen or elect was as much a burden as a benefit when you served a God who was exclusive, jealous, and powerful. Continuing disobedience split the original twelve tribes into the two antagonistic kingdoms of Judah and Samaria, and centuries later God sent the Babylonians to conquer Jerusalem, exile its people, and force them to retrace Abraham's steps and return east into Babylon. Jews adapted to their Babylonian exile, but their success stirred envy and hatred. Young Jews like Daniel and Esther rose high, but then faced efforts to kill them. Yet God protected those who were faithful to him. Daniel became a prominent and influential servant in the service of his people's captors. When enemies later conspired to eliminate all the Jews in a single judicial slaughter, their plot was diverted at the last minute as Esther, the faithful Jewish queen of the Persian Emperor, exposed their treachery, won the emperor's protection, and secured punishment of the conspirators. The people of Israel would eventually return again to Jerusalem and rebuild a second temple in the Promised Land. But they would again disobey, and God would again punish them in the most total expulsion from the Promised Land when the Romans re-conquered Jerusalem in 70 AD after a rebellion and scattered the Jews west across the entire Mediterranean basin, south to India, and east to China. Jews thought this diaspora was God's judgement on the divisions among the community's religious leaders, the Pharisees and Sadducees, which had divided and weakened the nation.

Disobedience raised the question of who was *truly* God's Chosen People. This was a major preoccupation for all exiles and refugees from the three Abrahamic faiths. Christians thought that the Jewish diaspora was God's final punishment on a people who had rejected and then executed the Messiah, Jesus Christ, whom God had sent to redeem them. This opened the way for Christians to supersede the Jews as God's Chosen. In the eyes of some Christians, both in the early church and in the early modern period, when God's Chosen People had rejected God's Chosen Son, the Jews had effectively broken the covenant that God had made with Abraham. By this ultimate act of disobedience, they damned themselves to eternal wandering without any home at all in this world as their punishment. At the same time, both Jews and Christians believed that the Jews would eventually return to the Promised Land to meet the Messiah and prepare for the Last Judgment at the end of all time. Muslims thought that both the Jewish and Christian narratives were simply the early stages of a story which was fulfilled only with God's ultimate prophet, the Chosen One Mohammed. They certainly had a different understanding of who were really God's Chosen People when they told the story of Abraham and his elder son Ishmael, and of the meaning of Moses' contest with the Egyptian pharaoh, a story to which the Qu'ran returns again and again.

All religious refugees and migrants in the early modern period could draw on this story of the children of Abraham, and apart from differences around who were ultimately God's Chosen People, the three broad faith communities emphasized one part or another of the common narrative according to their own situation. Muslims referred most often to Abraham (or Ibrahim, seen as a model of the perfect Muslim) and Moses (or Musa, the prophet most parallel to Mohammed, leading an exodus from Egypt which was similar to the *hijra* of Mohammed). Both men expressed their faith through pilgrimage, and both were historical examples of the high cost of absolute obedience to God, refusing to abandon the practice of true religion, even if meant leaving homeland, family, position, and wealth. Jews might highlight Moses, Daniel, and Esther. All three had been outsiders who had risen to high positions in potentially hostile political environments, and all three were able to use their positions to save their people. Christians identified with the Children of Israel led from Egypt to the Promised Land and then led again from Babylon back to Jerusalem. They were being tested and tried collectively, and if their hard passage was in some way God's judgment for weak faith or giving in to temptation and following the false prophets of their neighbours, then at least faithfulness and endurance would win them passage to a new Promised Land as a Chosen People.

Jews and Christians wound these biblical characters most thoroughly into their rituals, imagination, and even language. The Jewish festivals of Pesach (or Passover – a term which first appears in English in Tyndale's Bible translation) and Purim marked these liberating events. Passover was the more reflective day, marking Israel's deliverance from Egypt. Since it fell close to Good Friday and Easter, it was also a time when Jews had to guard against violence from Christians. From the early 1490s onwards, a Roman confraternity regularly turned the ruins of the Coliseum into a stage for a Passion play re-creating Christ's trial and crucifixion. They so worked up the crowds that anti-Jewish riots frequently followed, and the pope banned the play in 1539.

Purim was a more celebrative festival marking Esther's success in saving her people. It fell in February and March, often close to Carnival, and Jews celebrated it with the same emphasis on food, drink, costumes, and revelry. Some Iberian *conversos* called her Saint Esther, and observed the festival with a three-day fast. She was for them the model of a Jew who had hidden her faith, risen to prominence, and then used her position to save her people. At Purim, Jews came together to hear how Esther had outwitted Haman, the Persian official who had tried to engineer the slaughter. In the Jewish imaginary, Haman personified evil: thirteenth-century French and German Jewish communities began the custom of booing and hissing when he was named, and in fourteenth-century Avignon, Jews processed with an effigy of him that they later hanged and burnt (a custom which some sources trace to fifth-century Rome). Fifteenth-century Italian Jews continued this tradition of laughing in the face of evil by putting on costumes and masquerades and staging Pesach plays, often of those two other heroic deliverers Joseph or Daniel. It was not all joking. Josel of Rosheim was one of the most prominent 'court Jews' of the sixteenth-century Holy Roman Empire, and in this capacity he had to negotiate the Jews' position with Christian religious reformers. When he wrote about Martin Bucer and Martin Luther, who were arguing publicly that any Jews who refused to convert ought to be eliminated, he reached into the Jewish imaginary and cuttingly called them modern versions of Haman.

If Jews celebrated deliverance from enemies, Christians often focused on the difficult path to a Promised Land. Wouter Jacobsz, prior of the monastery at Steyn where Erasmus had been a monk and ordained a priest, fled with other Catholic refugees to Amsterdam in 1572, where he channelled his anxieties and despair into a long diary that put his community's suffering into a spiritual and distinctly biblical perspective. Jacobsz often compared the besieged Catholics to 'Israel's Children' seeking release. Half a century later, Puritan preachers patterned the migration to America very consciously on the Israelite exodus from Egypt – their sermons described a flight away from a ruler who refused to recognize and obey God's will, and towards a land promised by God as both a refuge and also a 'Light on a Hill'. To counter any ambivalence about abandoning England, Puritan divines waxed eloquent on the spiritual challenge of creating a new Israel in America. This was why those who landed in Massachusetts Bay were so careful about the theocracy they were building. In sermons and pamphlets, they spelled out the threat that any Puritans who relaxed their standards would be following the ancient Israelites' path of disobedience, and so stir up God's punishing wrath. Only clear catechisms, exclusive laws, and citizenship based on strict church discipline could safeguard the Promised Land. This same drive led them to see the North American aboriginals as modern versions of the Canaanites and Philistines, those peoples who had challenged the Israelites for control of the Promised Land and who, in the eyes of the Puritans, were worshippers of false gods who must be purged or converted for God's will to be fulfilled. The Old Testament God had ordered the Canaanites and Philistines eliminated, and at least some settlers believed that this was what God now demanded that they do with those who had not converted to their particular Christian beliefs about truth and civilization. This conviction would be used to legitimize some of the genocidal wars against indigenous groups across the Americas, and the later efforts at cultural purgation in Canada through the forced removal of whole generations of aboriginal children to enclosed residential schools. Run by different churches under government direction, these residential schools imposed regimes of cultural purgation that forced these students to give up their aboriginal language, culture, and family ties and to adopt western learning, languages, and Christian religion. The devastating effects on individuals and peoples have continued over generations.

Preachers and pamphleteers did not usually evoke the biblical narrative of punishment, purgation, and exile to inspire flight as much as to explain or justify it. Many Catholics and Protestants in the upheavals of the mid sixteenth century felt that flight was an unjustified surrender and abandonment of the *Corpus Christianum*. This was certainly the case with Marian exiles of the 1550s and Catholic exiles from the Netherlands in the 1560s and 1570s. In most cases it was only a minority who fled – usually the ones who were more prosperous and literate, and who could draw on biblical imagery and rhetoric as a literary trope. Sixteenth-century refugees most often returned, while this became more difficult and rare in the seventeenth and eighteenth centuries.

The experience of flight radicalized the refugees, who came to see themselves as purer reformers than those who had stayed behind and implicitly collaborated with religiously hostile regimes. Returned exiles frequently rejected compromise and pushed far more radical and purgative agendas, often to the great frustration of those who had stayed behind and who were more interested in co-existence for civil and religious peace. The returned refugees' status and influence meant that they had far greater immediate and long-term influence than their numbers would suggest. Savonarola's followers went underground or into exile after his execution in 1498, and then re-emerged in the 1520s as partisans of a stricter Christian republicanism, which brooked no compromise with the papacy, and responded to a siege in 1528–30 by passing a law proclaiming Christ king of Florence; the fall of that republic ushered in the Medici duchy. The 800 Marian exiles of the 1550s who returned to England under Elizabeth I were determined to introduce Genevan-style hierarchies, vestments, and liturgies, fighting hard throughout her reign and becoming an underground movement that would re-emerge in the seventeenth-century civil wars. Their determined opposition, together with that of exiled Catholics, prevented Elizabeth from realizing the goal of a coherent national church. The Dutch Catholic exiles who fled to Cologne in the 1560s and 1570s returned as partisans of Jesuit spirituality and education, and patrons of a distinctly Jesuit baroque, who eagerly commissioned artists to replace altarpieces destroyed in iconoclastic riots.

Among later refugees, the challenge lay in keeping memory and hope alive. Of 680 Huguenot pastors who fled France after the Revocation of the Edict of Nantes in 1685, 405 went to the Dutch Republic where there was a strong network of French churches and exile communities. The most popular preachers were those who addressed the Revocation and exile directly and emotionally, even though they pulled few punches, and their themes resonated through the sermons of all exile pastors regardless of religious confession. Many ministers described the Revocation as God's punishment of Huguenots for their sins, and His testing of their faith and endurance. In 1688, the Delft consistory ordered its preachers to preach repentance, 'to calm God's ire, which is so strongly inflamed against His Church'. Jacques Abbadie, who led Huguenot congregations in Berlin and London, also spoke of the 'fire of affliction': 'If the faithful suffer persecution, and if they are exposed to all the furies of the world and its rulers, we should not be surprised, because Jesus Christ teaches us that all those who wish to life a pious life will suffer persecution.' Exile always tested a Calvinist's sense of being one of God's Chosen, but to this the Huguenot preachers responded that God only tested and punished those He loved, and that the exiles had in fact demonstrated that they were among the Elect by fleeing. One promised that God 'had still left some grapes, as seeds, and elected residue of his grace', while another promised the refugees that while God had chopped down the 'rotten tree' in France, he would 'by His grace secretly preserve some roots from the remains of this tree, which He will bless, and which will one day sprout from the bosom of the earth.' Preaching manuals advised using emotion, gestures, and theatrical techniques to capture the emotions, and a Dutch diarist indeed noted that the best sermons left listeners 'melting in tears'. This became even more challenging, and perhaps more necessary, as the refugees' children and grandchildren made their own lives in a new land and became more detached from the exile experience. Printed sermons were one answer, but popular culture proved far more effective.

39. The Celestial City & the City of Destruction from John Bunyan's *Pilgrim's Progress* (1684). Courtesy of the Thomas Fisher Rare Book Library, University of Toronto.

Exile accounts worked their way into the collective imagination of many diasporic communities, turning up in songs, stories, plays, and the patriotic language they used to explain their prosperity and vindicate their actions in the world. Stories of exile became stories of pilgrimage, and became common tropes for imaginative and allegorical literature. Perhaps the most famous is John Bunyan's *Pilgrim's Progress* (1678, 1684), written in Bunyan's two periods in prison, which traces the long and winding path of Christian from sin and despair in his hometown City of Destruction through countless adversities to the Celestial City. Part Two follows Christian's wife Christiana as she later follows him with their sons, daughters in law, and a maid [Fig 39]. Like a Puritan version of Dante's Divine Comedy, Bunyan's *Pilgrim's Progress* is at once a commentary on his own time and an allegory of the Christian life that is painted in the most vivid hues. Bunyan was a decidedly less subtle author than Dante, and so the moral lessons lie flat on the surface, signalled by the names of the false and wise guides who help Christian and Christiana in their progress: Mr. Worldly Wiseman, Goodwill, and Faithful can be trusted, while the false friend Pliable, the giants Pope and Pagan, the temptress Wanton, and the judge Lord Hate-Good are best avoided. Very widely translated and never out of print in the centuries since it first appeared, *Pilgrim's Progress* was one of the key texts of English Puritanism and indeed of European evangelicalism. It illustrated Puritanism's conviction that life itself was a long exilic pilgrimage, while underscoring its reputation as dour, obvious, and seriously lacking in imagination.

Saints and Martyrs

Martyrologies and saints' lives were another source of inspiring stories that occupied the migrant and refugee imaginary. Savonarola's followers, Marian exiles, and Dutch Catholics all had their heroes, and they drew on a long Christian tradition to write the narratives that would keep the stories alive. There was a special veneration for those men and women of the early church whose faith had won them terrible tortures, unjust punishments, and finally death at the hands of Roman or Saracen rulers. St. Peter had been crucified upside down, St. Lawrence had been roasted on a grill, St. Bartholomew was skinned alive, St. Lucy had her eyes plucked out, St. Catherine was torn to pieces, Thomas à Becket murdered at the altar. One death was worse than the next in martyrologies, but the souls of those who died for Christ had soared to heaven and been blessed and rewarded by God for their faithfulness, becoming saints who would help believers on earth. In the Catholic imaginary, Heaven teemed with saints and martyrs who all kept a close eye and ear on what was happening on earth. They looked out from icons carrying the signs of their martyrdom – St. Bartholomew held the knife used to flay him and St. Lucy carried her eyes on a plate. Pamphlets, tracts, woodcuts, and treatises brought their stories of martyrdom vibrantly to life and encouraged devotion. One of the leading collections of saints' lives was Jacopo da Voragine's wildly popular *Golden Legend*, a text first penned around 1260, which came out in more editions than the Bible from 1450 to 1500. The *Golden Legend* peopled the imaginative world of medieval Catholicism through print as much as paintings and sculptures did, making the saints and martyrs at the centre of the story accessible, immediate, local, and human avenues to God.

Was martyrdom still possible? It seemed a distant threat, delivered by ancient Romans or Saracens. Yet a group of four Francisan friars were beaten and executed in Jerusalem in 1391 after preaching first on the mosque on Temple Mount, one of Islam's holiest sites, and then at the house of the magistrate where they had been taken for judgment. Their deaths became a European cause célèbre that revived martyrdom as a spiritual goal. John Hus and Jerome of Prague were certainly considered martyrs by the Bohemian Hussites after being executed as heretics at the Council of Constance in

1415–16. A century later, Martin Luther seized on the martyrological possibilities when two of his followers were executed in Brussels in 1523 on the same charge. Luther commemorated them with a hymn, and within five months, printers in seven different cities had produced sixteen editions of a pamphlet praising their sacrifice. These narratives of persecution were powerful tools for promoting cohesion and action in all religious groups. In the yawning chasm that was opening between confessions, one group's heretics were another's martyrs, and there would soon be plenty of both. Luther's hymn writing did not prevent him from endorsing the execution of Thomas Muntzer two years later.

How many martyrs were there? One historian has estimated that approximately 3,000 Protestants and Radicals were executed from 1523 to 1565, a further 1,100 in Flanders and the Netherlands from 1567 to 1574, and perhaps 280 elsewhere in Europe by 1600. Perhaps 300 English Catholics were executed for heresy-treason from 1535 to 1680, and 130 Catholic priests in the Netherlands from 1567 to 1591. We reach a number of approximately 5,000 without taking into account missionaries executed overseas, or Catholic converts executed in China and Japan. At this point definitions begin to break down. Martyrologies did not honour the 3,300 *conversos*, *moriscos*, mystics, and Protestants burned as heretics by the Spanish Inquisition by 1700, or the Roman Inquisition's 1,250, or the Portuguese Inquisition's 221 *conversos*. Were those executed as witches – possibly 50,000 across Europe – victims of a judicial process or martyrs for a faith? Certainly many Protestants, Catholics, Radicals, *conversos*, and *moriscos* burned by their governments as heretics were charged with witchcraft into the bargain, and even John Bunyan was damned by critics as 'a witch, a Jesuit, and a highwayman' – it was hard to know which they thought was worse. Once a culture of purgation took hold, it was difficult to limit its targets.

Even those Protestants who did not smash statues, break stained glass windows, or slice the eyes out of paintings were iconoclasts in the sense of rejecting the belief that saints could, would, or even should intercede with God for believers. For them, modern martyrs filled the gap left by the expulsion of intercessory saints, and martyrologies took the place once filled by works like Voragine's *Golden Legend*. Catechisms taught doctrine, but martyrologies fired the imagination and the emotions. They taught real and invented traditions through the biographies of heroes and victims, and in so doing they taught what allies to favour and what enemies to fear and hate. Common people like Elizabeth Dirks, Janneken Munstdorp, Joan Waste, and Rose Allyn, who we saw in Chapter 3, became models of courage and endurance in the face of appalling injustice. They modelled behavior and attitudes.

The genre of the Protestant martyrology really took off from the 1550s with six volumes coming out in quick succession that voiced the emerging traditions of different Protestant groups: Jean Crespin's *Book of Martyrs* (Geneva: 1554), Ludwig Rabus's *History of the Martyrs* (1554), Matthias Flacius Illyricus's *Catalogue of Witnesses to the Truth* (Basel: 1556), Andreas Cornelis van Haemstede's *History and Death of the Pious Martyrs* (Emden: 1559), John Foxe's first Latin version of the *Acts and Monuments* (Basel: 1559), and the anonymous Anabaptist *Sacrifice of the Lord* (Emden or Amsterdam: 1562). They were wildly popular. Crespin's was published at least thirty-seven times in French, Latin, and German by 1682, and van Haemstede was published twenty-three times by 1671. Most followed Voragine and the Catholic martyrologies in opening with accounts of those early Christians tortured and executed at the hands of the Romans. One key purpose of the Protestant martyrologists was to establish a firm connection linking their budding communities directly to the early church. But they recast the early martyrs as historical models, and not as real presences who took alms, heard prayers, and acted on a believer's behalf. Crespin wrote of the martyrs, 'It is not their bones, nor their hair, nor the limbs of their bodies, nor certain rags or pieces of their clothing, nor fables from Golden Legends that recommend them ... rather it is they themselves, speaking through their writings, consoling and teaching who still remain.'

The martyrologists plagiarized each other extensively. They wrote at length as they went back to the early church and up to executions that may have taken place only a few months or years before. An old line had it that 'the blood of the martyrs was the seed of the church', and these authors were seeding vast fields. John Foxe's *Actes and Monuments*, popularly known as the *Book of Martyrs* would become by far the most famous English martyrology after being translated into English in 1563. Foxe quickly expanded it in three more editions of 1570, 1576, and 1583, which more than doubled the text to 4,000 large folio pages. He used dramatic visualizations – like that of hundreds of Catholics processing through Cambridge with banners and candles to mark a public burning in 1557 of the books and disinterred corpses of two Protestant theologians – to drive home the message that Catholic authorities pursued purgation mercilessly as a solemn religious duty [Fig 40]. Although Foxe died in 1587, editors prepared an abridged version 1589 shortly after England's victory over the Spanish Armada, when its strongly anti-Catholic message was even more politic than before. The first versions had included early Christian martyrs, and the last that Foxe published included Huguenots killed in the 1572 St. Bartholomew's Day massacre in France. It was, after the Bible, the book most commonly found in English households. It has never

40. Burning the Corpses and Books of Protestant Theologians in Cambridge (1557), from Foxe's *Actes and Monuments* (1563). Courtesy of the Thomas Fisher Rare Book Library, University of Toronto.

been out of print (with as many as fifty-five editions and abridgements produced in the nineteenth century alone), which is also to say that this 400-year-old text with its vivid denunciation of Catholicism has never been out of some British households or minds.

Throughout the Thirty Years War and its aftermath, propagandists projected current events through the lens of martyrology and made connections between suffering at home and abroad in order to stir up support. German Calvinists compared themselves to Ulster Protestants who, they claimed, were being persecuted by Irish Catholics. The English Presbyterian Edmund Calamy preached to the House of Commons on 'England's Looking Glasse in 1642' comparing the sufferings of German and English Calvinists, and advocating political and diplomatic support for these co-religionists. His contemporary John La Motte (1577–1655), held an annual celebration of Elizabeth I's coronation where he spoke frequently of 'the great sufferings and bloody persecutions in France and the Low Countries ... as if he had been an eyewitness, yea a sharer in them ... encouraging himself and others to be still mindfull of them in bonds and miseries ... saying, why their case might have been ours, or may yet, who knows?'

Thielemann van Braght's *The Martyr's Mirror* memorializing Anabaptist and Radical martyrs appeared relatively late in 1660, long after the threat of execution had ceased, and even after persecution had tamed considerably. Ironically, van Braght's stirring history was illustrated and published by Calvinist printers whose own ancestors may well have cheered on the executions. Numerous cheap editions of extracts made it more accessible, and the engraved plates took on a life of their own, being produced and sold independently and even sent on tour. Like Foxe's *Book of Martyrs*, it became a highly effective touchstone for group identity into the twentieth century, transferring to new generations of young Mennonites the memory of the fires that had burned their martyrs long after their heat had faded. Martyrologies taught not only whom to admire, but whom to scorn, hate and fear.

Catholic authors realized this as well, and began to publish accounts of the deaths of famous individuals like Thomas More, or of missionaries killed in the field. By 1640, there were at least twenty accounts in English and fifty in other languages of the deaths of English Catholic martyrs. Mission letters, like Marie de l'Incarnation's letters from Quebec to her son in France from 1639 to 1671, or Jesuit letters from Asia were common forms of entertaining and edifying literature that raised hope and horror at the same time. Jesuit fathers in New France wrote of how their baptized allies, the Huron Wendat, were wiped out by Iroquois tribes that had been allied to and armed by Dutch Protestants in a series of battles from the late 1640s. Jesuit authors depicted this long-standing aboriginal dispute as a sharp and genocidal battle of Catholic vs. Protestant tribes, conveniently omitting mention either of the missionary-borne diseases that had triggered the conflict or of the community of Hurons who survived and migrated to an area just outside Quebec City, where the Jesuit's main house in New France was located. Eight Jesuit missionaries also died in the wars, and the order decided at an early stage that they would be considered martyr saints, taking the care to exhume two of the bodies and recover the bones for use as relics. None of the Huron converts were canonized.

Catholics also peopled their imaginary with new saints who were heroes of the Counter-Reformation, some martyred and others not. How did one become a saint? A process which had been rather haphazard and locally driven in the middle ages became ever more precise, disciplined, and centralized from the sixteenth century onwards. Catholic critics wanted more rational investigation to sort through holy fictions comprised of superstition, enthusiasm, and fraud and so establish the truth and accuracy of claims to sanctity. Catholic authorities responded by devising a complex process of gathering and evaluating evidence, staging a trial in which a lawyer acting as the 'devil's advocate' argued against the case, and instituting numerous preliminary steps leading towards the declaration of sanctity. A case like that of St. Bernardine of Siena, canonized within six years of his death in 1444, was remarkable even to contemporaries for its speed. Yet it was one of the last under the old process. From 1523 to 1588, there were none at all. A new Sacred Congregation of Rites and Ceremonies oversaw canonizations and the regulation of saints' cults from 1588, and it approved two saints by 1600, with another twenty-four in the seventeenth and twenty-nine in the eighteenth centuries. Canonization processes under the Sacred Congregation dragged on through decades and even generations, the profile of those canonized changed: there were fewer laypeople and women promoted by enthusiastic followers, and more male clergy, particularly from religious orders that had the money, lawyers, patience, and push to manage the process.

Voragine's medieval *Golden Legend* was inspiring and entertaining, but Protestants and even some Catholics claimed its saints' biographies were more pious fraud than historical fact. Roman authorities published a revised official *Roman Martyrology* in numerous languages from 1584 to reflect rising standards of evidentiary proof and scholarship. Yet the real changes would come in the next century when a series of Flemish Jesuit priests began a yet more exacting scholarly catalogue. Known as the *Lives of the Saints* (*Acta Sanctorum*), the project came to be so closely associated with one of its early authors, Jean Bolland (1596–1665), that the group was known collectively as the Bollandists. Bolland took over some scholarly studies begun by a colleague, and thought that he could finish the project by himself. Yet as its scope and potential dawned on him, he recruited other Jesuits into the work. Their first two Latin volumes appeared in Antwerp in 1643, and by 1681 there were twenty-four volumes. Others picked up the work after the Jesuits were suppressed in 1773, and the Société des Bollandistes published the final instalment in a series now numbering sixty-eight volumes in 1940; it continues to produce scholarly updates and offers a full text database of the Latin series.

Medieval saints like the St. Francis, his close associate St. Clare, their contemporary St. Dominic, or predecessor St. Hildegard of Bingen had battled demonic temptations and modelled heroic self-denial as they spread the faith. Their challenges were largely individual or internal, as they battled against their own appetites and will or against demons that often only they could see. The early modern martyrologies made the struggle to uphold true faith political and public once again, just as it had been when early Christians had faced down the Roman authorities who tortured them, fed them to lions, or executed them for their absolute loyalty to Christ and God. These were the enemies and heroes of the early modern religious imaginary, and these were the stakes. These were the stories that helped communities understand and explain their refugee experience. They did it in terms that held up co-religionists as heroic martyrs like the earliest Christians and that cast contemporary opponents, be they Catholic or Protestant authorities, as no better than some pagan and pathological Roman governor. With the rapid spread of printing, these became the stories shared in homes and churches, told to children, and taught in schools to frame identity around grievance, threat, and heroic rejection of compromise.

Names and Identity

Scripture, saints' lives, and martyrologies established the narrative history of a community and identified the heroes who had shaped or protected it at key points. Just as a family name had always signalled a child's place in the community of ancestors, so naming an infant after one of these scriptural heroes, saints, or martyrs was one of the most powerful ways of signalling religious identity to everyone, including the child. And even adults sometimes reworked their names in order to emphasize a change of profession or direction. This was particularly the case with early modern humanists who often wished to signal their commitment to the classics. Martin Luther's closest colleague for much of his career was Philip Melancthon, who adopted the Greek form of his family name (Schwartzerdt). Johanne Heussgen, later Hausschein, was another of Luther's allies was but is better known by the Greek form of his name ('lamp') as 'Oecolampadius'. At an early point even Luther himself toyed with 'Eleutherius' to add some classical Greek sophistication to his name. The Strasbourg Jewish leader Josel of Rosheim would instead refer sarcastically to Luther in his letters as *lo tahor*, which sounded phonetically like 'Luther' in Hebrew, but translated as 'impure'.

Changing a name to signal initiation, conversion, or a profession was common. It was required in the case with converts, and the names that they chose at baptism said much about their identity. We saw that when al-Hasan al-Wazan converted from Islam to Catholicism in 1520, he very strategically took on the names of his patron Pope Leo X and became Giovanni Leone de Medici. His rough contemporary, the Hungarian convert known as Murad bin Abdullah, took the name of two sultans (Murad I,

1362–89, and Murad II 1421–44; 1446–51) who had conquered Hungarians and combined it with the patronymic 'bin Abdullah' ('son of God's slave') which converts commonly adopted. *Converso* and *morisco* parents in Iberia might come to the Inquisitor's attention if they called their children Abraham, Moses, or David, or Ruth, Esther, Aisha, or Fatima. Neighbours and inquisitors took such names as a sign that the family home, table, and ritual life was still directed to the old ancestral faith rather than to Christianity.

Conversion was meant to purge that tie, and convert parents were to graft their children into the new and purer religious tradition from birth or baptism. As we saw earlier, the Initiation ritual of baptism brought you into a series of connected communities. Catholic naming practices had often merged family and church. Some rulers took names that reflected ancient Germanic or Celtic ancestors ('Adalbert', 'Obert', 'Etheldred') or that expressed fearsome and competitive qualities – the fourteenth-century della Scala rulers of Vicenza and Verona alternated the names Cangrande ('Big Dog') and Mastino ('Mastiff') though the century. Yet from the fourteenth century onwards, the church encouraged parents to use at least a second name drawn from the saints or martyrs. Children were named after their saintly patron, either the saint of their day of birth, or one thought to be more powerful and influential in the heavenly pantheon – one reason why Mary, Magdalen, and Clare were common among Catholic girls and John Baptist (as Giovanni Battista, Jean Baptiste, Juan Battista), Peter, and Francis, were common among boys. Even the della Scala turned to saints' names like Bartolomeo and Antonio.

Protestants marked their own conversion by deliberately bypassing the saints and heading to the Bible. Pastors in Zurich and other cities preached on the issue, and some parents drew voluntarily on Old Testament heroes like David and even Nehemiah. A running dispute in Geneva shows how tensions quickly exploded if parents resisted and clergy attempted to force the issue. Calvin wrote in 1543 against using saints' names for children as a form of veneration, and three years later the Company of Pastors issued a list of suitable and unsuitable names. The latter included the name 'Claude', which was highly popular in Geneva. St. Claudius had been a seventh-century saint who had lived near the city, and was widely considered the patron of Geneva and its citizens. Opposition grew when the city council backed Calvin, quickly becoming less a matter of religion than of locality and control. Prominent local men complained of the influence of 'foreigners,' and they protested to Geneva's City Council when some ministers including Calvin refused to use the names put forward at baptism by parents or godparents.

Seeking some middle ground, the Council in 1553 ordered Calvin and the other pastors to ease up on preaching about the issue and to accept some traditional local names like Gaspard and Melchior – though not Claude. When Calvin's supporters gained control of council in 1555, they restored his list and the names he had deemed unsuitable disappeared from Genevan baptismal records. The list would remain in force well into the seventeenth century.

Later English Puritans would follow John Bunyan and head into metaphor, making personal names out of words like Christian, Faith, Grace, Hope; Catholics followed suit, and 'Charity' became a name found more often in Catholic than Protestant families.

In all religious groups, and for real and secret converts, personal names became more clearly about confessional identity. This was particularly the case through the early modern period, as fixed family names became more common, meaning that there was less pressure to signal family ties through the personal name. Catholic priests and Protestant pastors encouraged parents to use names that evoked either biblical heroes, saints, or martyrs, depending on their confession. Their control over both the baptismal font and the parish register gave them greater authority to over-rule parental resistance, and even to refuse to baptize infants until parents agreed to a name the cleric thought was more confessionally appropriate, a practice that carried on well into the twentieth century.

Confession and Culture

'Confessionalization' is the term historians have used to describe how early modern faith communities shaped their identity and policed the political and religious boundaries that divided them from other states and people. It first emerged in the 1970s to describe boundary-making between Protestant states of the Holy Roman Empire, and historians are divided on whether it applied across other confessions and countries, or whether it even existed at all. Some feel that its rigour and effectiveness have been overstated, and that while strict rules could certainly be found universally across Europe which bound confession to citizenship and obedience, they were seldom enforced to their full rigour.

Others look at confessionalization less as a legal standard or judicial practice than as a cultural process. 'The process of confessionalization was bound up with a general overturning of values: churchlike discipline, the formation of a confessional identity, and the demand for uniformity in dogma and religious practice were combined with a general effort to impose extensive social discipline and to create an obedient community, firm in its belief and faithful to the political regime.' What Yosef Kaplan writes of diasporic Jewish communities could apply equally to Catholics, Protestants, and Muslims. He goes on to describe the paradoxical process in all confessionalization when he notes that the Sephardic diaspora 'regarded Christian Europe as a central point of reference and source of inspiration, a factor for observation and imitation, and at the same time it invested maximal efforts to distinguish itself from Christianity as a religion and belief system.... For those who had left Christianity to rejoin the Jewish people, the dispute with Christianity was an existential need, an integral part of their Jewish socialization process.'

Religious communities had always had to face the Other, but through the early modern period the sheer number, variety, and difference of Others in Europe and around the globe multiplied. Each religious community had to negotiate its own fascination, revulsion, imitation, and aversion to a veritable host of Others that it encountered. The spread of very particular notions of purity, contagion, and purgation from the late medieval period led to expulsions of tens and hundreds of thousands across the continent and turned the religious refugee into a mass phenomenon. In this particular historical context, the early modern Other was not only different, but distinctly dangerous and threatening.

Sometimes the most threatening Other lay within the same broad religious tradition (like Sunni and Shi'a Islam, Lutheran and Calvinist Christianity, Sephardic and Ashkenazic Judaism) and sometimes it lay farther apart (like Catholicism and Hinduism, or Puritanism and Aboriginal beliefs). While they shared questions and concerns, their immediate response was often to emphasize confessional differences and to emphasize the superiority and priority of their own faith or tradition. People of various faiths 'drew upon and perpetuated shared conceptual frameworks that marked the ... age of confessional and imperial polarization in the sixteenth and seventeenth centuries. Catholic-Protestant, Muslim-Christian, and Sunni-Shi'a debates in the age of confessionalization all addressed issues related to spiritual and temporal authority, "correct" rituals, and the authenticity of scriptural traditions employing a shared conceptual vocabulary.' Tijana Krstic's observations about confessionalization in the Mediterranean basin can be extended across European nations and their global empires. 'Within this common conceptual framework, spaces, texts, and political ideas were contested to form communities of difference that nevertheless acknowledged that they were competing for the same moral and religious capital: that is, universal imperial rule and/or the status of the only true religion that guaranteed salvation.'

In many cases the major changes and most vigorous programs based in confessionalization were driven from the top rather than the bottom of society: expulsions, witch hunts, and workhouses were not projects initiated by Europe's urban or rural masses but by its educated elites. They were reforming the social body according to their best lights intellectually and often according to their best personal interests politically and economically. Their efforts amounted to the major cultural shift that we understand as early modernity. This was not a question of elites simply steering their societies in one direction or another, but rather of how creative and influential classes expressed their fears and dreams in ways their cultures found compelling.

Thanks to this, confessionalization as a cultural process of identification and self-fashioning remained important well into the eighteenth century, and took a broad range of forms. While the more violent expulsions did gradually decrease, more mundane and everyday forms of separation, enclosure, prosecution, and purgation carried on as a kind of cultural expectation or reflex prejudice that routinely targeted those who were considered alien. Co-existence certainly became far more common. Yet even though intercommunal social and political relations moderated the longer people lived close together, unpredictable and very violent outbreaks still happened. They recurred often enough to challenge any efforts by authorities to ease restrictions on 'alien' communities even at the very end of the early modern period. London mobs yelling 'No Popery' swept through London in 1780 to protest against efforts in Parliament to eliminate or moderate some of the laws that kept Catholics in a subordinate place in British society. Tuscan mobs burst into the Siena ghetto in June 1799, ransacking it and killing nineteen Jews, only three months after Napoleon's troops had entered the city and emancipated the Jews. We may be able to see the work of agitators behind the violence of occasional outbreaks, but the persistence and wide acceptance of reflex prejudices is something that speaks more to the continuing importance of confessionalization as a broad cultural process rather than to simply a religious or political policy.

Written texts were critical to confessionalization, but, as we have seen communities confessed their faith in far more than just words. Nonverbal forms of confessionalization may have been more influential in shaping cultural attitudes. Worship spaces, architectural forms, liturgical rituals, bloody martyrologies, and imagined histories were more immediate and powerful markers of identity and boundaries. When groups had to negotiate their identity with and against others via the backdrop of violence, exclusion, and purgation, these nonverbal forms became even more vital. People of all faiths identified themselves by their clothing, buildings, customs, and names.

Even before catechism lessons, Sunday Schools of Christian Doctrine, or close study of the Torah or Qu'ran filled in the blanks, children learned a lot about who they were by bedtime stories and popular songs, and by contrasting where they and others worshipped, what they ate and when, or what their priest, pastor, or rabbi wore compared to how other clergy dressed. And while clergy were authoritative transmitters of tradition, their communities also held them to account. While formal texts like catechisms could define the differences more explicitly, the broad-ranging imaginary taught young people more about who they were and who they were not. There were, in the end, likely more carrots than sticks in confessionalization – that is, more food for the imagination than rules for discipline. The visual and spatial forms of religious life set a framework for understanding a community's purity, place, and part in God's plan. As such, they likely shaped the invented traditions, learned behaviours, and legitimizing discourses of early modern confessionalization more than any paper text.

6

RE-IMAGINING THE BODY

ON 28 JUNE 1989. SERBIAN PRESIDENT SLOBODAN MILOSEVIC marked the six-hundredth anniversary of the Battle of Kosovo with a speech calling on Serbs to recover their national pride, sense of mission, and territory. The original battle in 1389 had pitted Serbs against the Ottomans, and killed commanders Prince Lazar Hrebeljanovic and Sultan Murad I together with most of their troops. In the decades that followed, some Serb nobles intermarried with Ottomans, and some resisted, although battles in 1459 and 1540 confirmed Ottoman and Muslim domination of the entire region. By the late twentieth century, Kosovo began looming ever larger in Serb consciousness as the 'Cradle of the Nation', even though ethnic Albanians, most of them Muslim, had come to make up almost 80 percent of the population and had gained significant political autonomy for the province. A million or more Serbs crowded the ancient battlefield in 1989 to hear Milosevic declare: "Today, it is difficult to say what is the historical truth about the Battle of Kosovo and what is legend. Today this is no longer important."

Soon afterward, the Yugoslav Federation descended into the bloody civil war that brought the term 'ethnic cleansing' into headlines around the world. Before the war, Yugoslavia was the most religiously and ethnically diverse nation in Europe, thanks to a mountainous geography, a long history of battles between Ottomans, Croats, Serbs, Bosnians, Hungarians, Venetians, and Holy Romans – some Muslim, some Orthodox, and some Catholic – and the geopolitical fallout of two world wars. After World War II, communist dictator Josip Broz Tito had forcefully turned the faction-ridden state into a multicultural secular federation between Eastern and Western blocs. Tito's death in 1980 and the gradual unraveling of East European communism opened possibilities for many politicians like Milosevic, a one-time opponent of ethno-religious separatism who now found in it the path to power.

41. Stari Most Bridge. NGS Image Collection/The Art Archive at Art Resource NY.

Milosevic spent a couple of years mobilizing Serbs to the defense of a patch of ground and an Orthodox faith that most had long since abandoned. When he spoke of "armed battles" at the Kosovo anniversary, he was evoking both the battle lost in 1389 and also what many took to be an inevitable battle between European Christianity and 'eastern' Islam.

Over the course of the next decade, the partners of the old Yugoslav Federation would fight this battle in valleys and cities across their disputed territories and carve it into a series of separate ethnically and religiously cleansed enclaves. Serb paramilitaries purged Catholic Croats and Muslim Bosnians from areas deemed to be historically Serb, while the Croatian military and Kosovo Liberation Army forced Serb civilians to flee from their emergent nations. Military leaders spoke openly of 'extermination', and mass graves across the former Federation showed this was not just rhetoric. In the historic town of Mostar, the Croatian Defense Council destroyed Serbian Orthodox monasteries and numerous important churches while the Serb-controlled Yugoslav National Army shelled Franciscan monasteries, Catholic churches, a bishop's palace, and numerous mosques. Mostar's most notable monument was the Stari Most bridge built by Süleyman II the Magnificent in 1566 and described by the famous Ottoman traveller Evilya Celebi (1611–82) as being "like a rainbow arch soaring up to the skies" [Fig 41]. It was blown up.

Some Serbian and Croatian nationalists portrayed the civil war of the 1990s as a defense of 'Western values' against Islam. At the other end of the Mediterranean in that same decade, Andalusian separatist groups evoked the glories of the preconquest Muslim state of Granada, and some prominent individuals publicly converted to Islam from the Catholicism imposed by the conquerors of 1492. When an ancient Cordoba mosque, which had been converted into a Catholic church, was restored as a place of Muslim worship, a Saudi official marked the occasion by predicting that the day would come when Muslims would once again rule over Andalusia. In Northern Ireland, members of the Protestant and British Loyalist Orange Order fought to preserve the traditional routes of their annual 12 July marches commemorating the 1690 Battle of the Boyne when William of Orange, the Protestant king, defeated the dethroned James Stuart, the Catholic king. In some towns like Portadown, southwest of Belfast, this provoked serious violence when parade routes passed through areas dominated by Catholics. Riots and violent protests through the later 1990s resulted in five deaths, despite a heavy police and army presence, and the Portadown Orangemen were finally forced to follow a different route in 1998.

Talk of extermination and purgation sounded through the course of the twentieth century, which was history's bloodiest hundred years by far. Ethno-religious Balkan Wars opened and closed the century, bracketing the Armenian genocide, the Ukrainian terror Famine (or *Holodomor*), and the Holocaust, which was the most determined, and nearly successful, effort to erase an entire people from the face of the earth. Those behind these efforts sometimes repeated verbatim late medieval and early modern screeds. After 1933, Nazi anti-Semitic propaganda included reprints of Martin Luther's 1543 tract *Against the Jews and Their Lies,* so that it could look as though the modern German government was simply answering the call this German Protestant reformer had raised centuries before:

> What shall we Christians do with this rejected and condemned people, the Jews? ... First, set fire to their synagogues or schools ... Second ... their houses be raised and destroyed ... Third, their prayer books and Talmudic writings ... be taken from them ... ; Fourth, their rabbis be forbidden to teach on pain of loss of life and limb ... ; Fifth, safe conduct on the highways be abolished completely ... ; Sixth, usury be prohibited to them, and all cash and treasure of silver and gold be taken from them ... Seventh, put young Jews and Jewesses to physical labour to earn their bread in the sweat of their brow ... or toss out these lazy rogues by the seat of their pants.

The Nazis did this and more.

How could a four-hundred-year-old tract have such an impact? Why do centuries-old calls for religious purity and purgation still have such traction in the modern world? Much of modern ethnic-religious violence is driven fundamentally by nationalism, racism, and political and economic competition, and it would be naive to think that religion has been the primary force behind it. But it is equally naive to think that religion plays no significant part in shaping the attitudes, assumptions, and stereotypes that stir people to violence or in justifying the violence they commit against other communities. The violence in 1930s Germany, 1970s Northern Ireland, and 1990s Yugoslavia all went back in some direct and self-conscious way to religious disputes of the late medieval and early modern periods. Each of these modern upheavals has been triggered by opportunistic political leaders. Yet these leaders have all been able to stir up extraordinary inter-communal violence by invoking historical actions and symbols, by using texts first published in the fifteenth and sixteenth centuries, and by using an old language of religious purgation and purification to mobilize societies that had become largely liberal, secular, and tolerant. They have done this with a chilling indifference to what may be truth or invention. As Milosevic said, "Today, it is difficult to say what is the historical truth . . . and what is legend. Today this is no longer important."

Historians have used terms like 'invented traditions', 'imagined communities', or 'legitimizing discourses' to describe how accounts of the past that have been heavily embroidered, exaggerated, or fictionalized can become vital to a particular group or nation's self-image and cohesion. Such histories inevitably play up differences and ignore or suppress early examples of co-operation, co-existence, or collaboration. Modern Scottish nationalists don distinctive kilts to signify their resistance to English domination, unaware perhaps that it was English merchants of the 1820s who drew up the textile pattern books that assigned particular plaids exclusively to particular clans. Spanish authors of the seventeenth century emphasized Spain's historic 'pure' and 'unmixed' Catholicism and deliberately suppressed examples of what one historian has called 'maurophilia', the long-standing integration of Moorish culture into the food, dress, rituals, language, and imaginary of Iberian Christians. Some of the sharpest anti-Semitic woodcuts and tracts circulating in fifteenth-century Germany emerged *after* expulsions; they did not trigger violence so much as justify violence that had already taken place. Narrow threads of fear, suspicion, loss, and victimization woven into the historical narrative can set the dominant pattern. They are the more dangerous for being selective, twisted, and invented. They shape the imagery and language of modern efforts to separate, contain, prosecute, and purge – efforts that are sometimes made by the very groups who were themselves subject to these forms of persecution in earlier centuries.

The obsessions with purity, contagion, and purgation did not originate in the late medieval and early modern world. Yet as we have seen, they took on particularly sharp expression across Europe and the Mediterranean in this period thanks to the conjunction of intellectual, religious, social, and political forces. R. I. Moore noted in *The Formation of a Persecuting Society* that the anxieties generated by heretics, lepers, and Jews from the tenth to thirteenth centuries would have amounted to little had there not been political elites willing to manipulate them. In this book we explore what shape these religious ambitions and anxieties took a few centuries later, how they shaped elites, and how early modern elites then used them to reshape the different societies that existed across Europe and around the Mediterranean through the early modern period. What we still need to consider is how their actions, rooted in a particular place and time, could have an influence extending into the twenty-first century.

Three linked developments of the early modern period were critical: the expanding *scope* of religious community from the local *Corpus Christianum* to the sacred nation, people, or empire; a stronger *direction* of intellectual life towards a recovery of ancient classical models for religious, intellectual, and political life; and the redefined *focus* of religious life around issues of definition, dogma, discipline, and control over self, family, and others.

The expanding *scope* of religious community marked the first critical development. The early modern idea of the 'sacred nation' built directly on the late medieval idea of the *Corpus Christianum* and absorbed that concept rather than replacing it. The move from local to national was the natural corollary of the state church as it evolved in both the Protestant states and city-states of England, the Holy Roman Empire, the Netherlands, Scandinavia, and Switzerland. In Catholic states, the propaganda of sacred dynastic monarchs ruling by Divine Right and with a mission to aggressively (re)Catholicize their nations steadily eroded the practical corporatism of medieval elective monarchies. Each of the leading monarchs of the sixteenth century gained a title which reflected this idea of sacred authority: Francis I was the 'Most Christian King' even after curbing the powers of the pope in France through the Concordat of Bologna and signing treaties with the Ottomans. Henry VIII kept the title 'Defender of the Faith' that Pope Leo X granted, perhaps a little prematurely, and then added 'Supreme Head' of the church after he effectively removed popes altogether from the Church of England. His daughter Elizabeth I adapted this to 'Supreme Governor' in deference to those who believed that scripture did not allow a woman to exercise headship over men. Charles V was crowned 'Holy Roman Emperor' by Pope Clement VII just three years after his troops had sacked Rome and threatened the life of the same pope. It was, in fact, Pope Clement VII who had the dubious distinction of seeing all three of these powerful 'sacred' monarchs assert significant independence in religious matters from Rome. Clement's successors would see the successors of Francis, Henry, Charles, and all other rulers claim for themselves a direct authority over the spiritual life of their subjects as part of their Divine Right to rule.

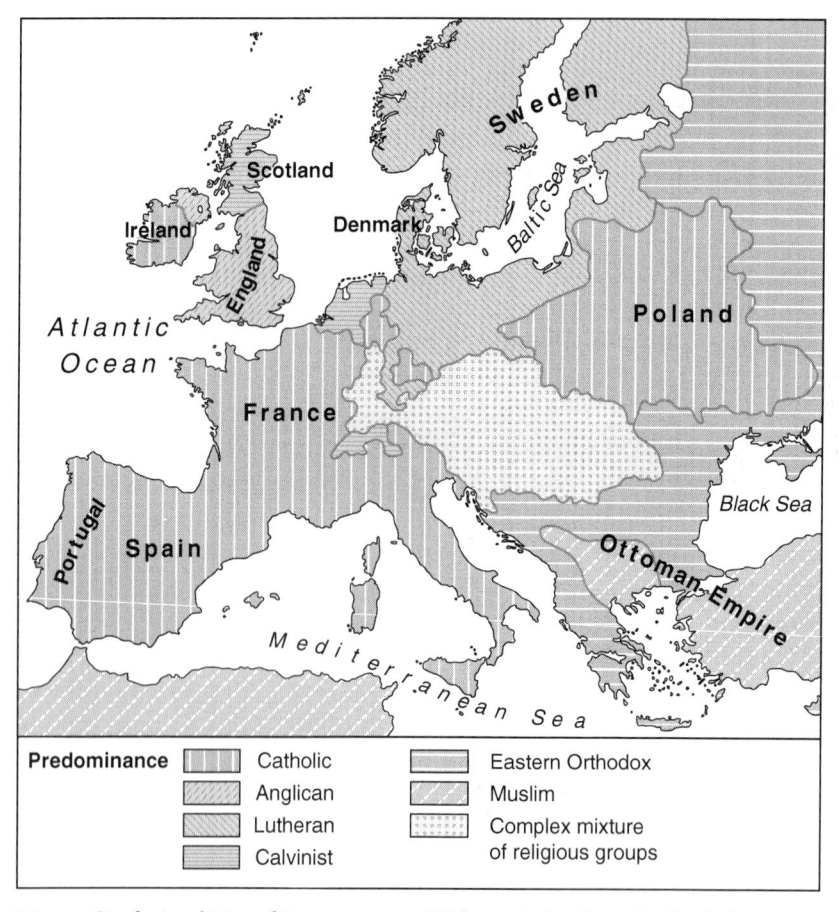

Map 2. Confessional Map of Europe c. 1700. With permission from the *Cambridge History of Christianity*, vol. 7.

There was a long medieval history of disputes between church and state in Catholic Europe, usually around the practicalities of who ultimately controlled appointments to high church offices and their extensive resources in lands and money. These fights were all the more intense because they matched two institutions of roughly equal powers fighting for primacy. The medieval Catholic Church had been a real contender, extending across all of Europe as the only effective continental institution at a time when most states were relatively small and most rulers faced powerful competing forces internally. In early modern Europe, the situation was reversed, particularly after the 1648 Peace of Westphalia ended the continent's civil-religious wars. Monarchs both Catholic and Protestant now effectively controlled the high church offices within their borders. Although they still had to negotiate with local nobles, monarchs were able to use standing armies, more extensive bureaucracies, and national tools for enforcing laws and raising funds in order to do so. The Catholic Church could no longer claim credibly to be equal to these powerful monarchs and their states. Protestant state churches existed only under their direct authority, and any other 'dissenting' or 'free' churches existed only by their permission.

The 1648 Peace of Westphalia brought a pause rather than an end to wars. Over the following decades and centuries, these would be fought more intensely by what we can recognize as modern nation-states. They seized or defended sharper borders, they imposed a restrictive sense of citizenship, and they fought more intensely thanks to relatively strong national institutions (armies, bureaucracies) that not only included but also extended beyond the monarch. Their propaganda turned this monarch into a divinely appointed source of power and unity, even though most of Europe's nations and states continued to be made up of semi-autonomous regions and territories barely held together under dynasties that had to deal and compromise constantly in order to maintain some appearance of power. In this fractious environment, the rhetoric of a sacred nation, a Chosen People, and a holy ruler governing by divine appointment framed a 'consensus absolutism' that was the cheap glue holding everything together. The rhetoric of the sacred nation gave legitimacy and purpose, even if it was all just in the realm of words. The objective division and weakness of these states made it more important to invest meaning in the propaganda around them, particularly in the single institution over which rulers' control was more secure: the church.

It was in order to capture this process of using religious tools to support political power and social discipline that the German historians Wolfgang Reinhard and Heinz Schilling first coined the term 'confessionalization' in the 1970s. They aimed to describe the process whereby confessions, creeds, and catechisms became practical tools for law, order, and public discipline, particularly in the Protestant states of late sixteenth- and seventeenth-century Germany. To enjoy the benefits of the state or participate fully in political and social life, one had to adhere to the confession which the state or monarch had approved. Some historians extended the confessionalization thesis to England, France, and Spain. Other historians have since countered that loopholes, exceptions, and lax enforcement undermined strict confessional rules in most times and places. Local officials looked the other way, wealth and power allowed some individuals to flout the law, and sanity prevailed. Confessionalization was neither automatic nor absolute. That said, the continuing activity of Inquisitions, consistories, and communal bans and excommunications shows that even if confessions had more bark than bite, they did not lack for teeth. More to the point, as we saw in the previous chapter, confessionalism was likely more important as a cultural form and means of socialization than as a form of political discipline. Via space, the senses, the emotions, and the imaginary, it invented those traditions that gave nations an identity and purpose, including a set of threats and enemies to be challenged.

The re-*direction* of intellectual life towards the recovery of 'purer' ancient and classical forms marked the second critical development, particularly to the degree that it fostered a certain exclusive and purgative conservatism. Religious confessions and catechisms did not exist in isolation, but were part of a larger intellectual framework that saw the path to the future lying in a return to the past. The terms 'Re-naissance' and 'Re-formation' both underscore how profoundly reformers believed that classical texts and practices offered superior models around which to build individual character and social life. Some aspects of the Greco-Roman classical past conflicted strongly with the Christian tradition, including the morality of Ovid, the materialism of Lucretius, and the paganism of Olympian gods. Christian elites had long imagined that they were up to the challenge of sifting truth from error so long as the more dangerous texts were kept in Latin and Greek and out of general circulation. As a result, they saw vernacular translations and the printing press as a greater challenge to order and morality than classical Greek and Roman learning itself. 'Humanism' did not yet exist as a philosophy or point of view that rejected religion; 'humanists' were simply those who studied classical disciplines reading classical texts in classical languages. Every major religious figure had a classical education. Every creed and confession was composed and vetted by those with classical educations. Every religious establishment staked its survival on training up new generations of clergy who would receive a classical education.

But what classics? Calvin preferred the Stoics, who emphasized absolute divine power and submission to divinely appointed law and order. Luther preferred Augustine, with his rejection of materialism and emphasis on curbing the will. A century before Luther, Lorenzo Valla added to his notoriety by praising the Epicureans. Valla identified the Epicurean pursuit of pleasure not with hedonism but with a kind of holy love – God is loved for the sake of love, and since God *is* love, this is a way of saying that God is loved for his own sake.

The classical legacy was broad and hardly uniform, and reading or teaching the classics could mean almost anything. Significantly, key thinkers of the fifteenth through seventeenth centuries tended to select some common elements out of classical culture: an emphasis on law and order; an emphasis on personal and social discipline; an emphasis on rationality and order; an emphasis on the supremacy of the state and of the monarch; an emphasis on the primacy of the family and particularly of male authority within it. Individuals like Machiavelli might pick up different streams for different purposes, but they were minority voices and controversial for their views. On the whole, classical humanism, which had celebrated human individuality, emotions, and creativity, gradually became more a conservative than a liberal force. Schools, rather than personal study, became the main vehicles for spreading humanism. As churches and clergy assumed more responsibility for education from the later sixteenth century, they taught a series of texts and sets of values that reinforced orthodoxy and obedience. Their humanism was more technical and instrumental. Few religiously oriented classicists were drawn to the materialism and moral relativism of Lucretius. But few resisted the drive towards discipline, authority, and patriarchal order.

This was the part of the classical legacy that they brought into their theology, their politics, their law, and their social order. Through nearly a thousand years of republic and empire, the ancient Romans had generated many laws regarding women's rights, ranging from strict patriarchal codes to laws that allowed single and married women significant degrees of autonomy. In *their* selective reading of the classics, early modern authorities found patriarchy and discipline most persuasive, and so these became the values that reshaped law codes and redefined women's social role and property rights in far narrower terms. The classical authors they chose to teach and imitate emphasized the authority of men over women, parents over children, literate over illiterate. When it came to political philosophy, some like Machiavelli, Milton, and Montesquieu drew on Roman republican authors like Cicero and Livy, while others like Hobbes and Erastus favored a monarchical absolutism like that practiced by the Roman emperors. Yet all believed that it was important for the state to uphold religion (and vice versa) in the interests of social order.

Machiavelli was perhaps the most cynical in arguing that religion could be the opiate of the masses, but as Marx could see, most thinkers and authorities took the lesson to heart. Although they often diverged on whether the state had the power to compel obedience, they tended to agree that the strongest societies emerged when citizens set aside individual interests for the common good and when secular rulers and governments exercised control over religious institutions. In this way, thinkers across the early modern political spectrum could converge in supporting some concept of a sacred nation or state, even if they divided on the idea of a sacred monarch who transcended differences. As Ethan Shagan has recently shown, English regimes exploited this notion of the monarch seeking a 'middle way' of moderation and civility above the fray as a key to their own legitimacy, even when they worked quite violently to suppress and control opposition.

The redefined *focus* of religious life around issues of definition, discipline, and control that prioritized exclusion over inclusion was the third critical development. John Bossy has noted how certain words changed their meaning over time. *Religio* had meant a profession, vocation, or form of life, and came to mean a creed or body of doctrines. *Caritas* had meant a state of being, and became a set of philanthropic actions. *Communio* had signified the state of union binding members of the *Corpus Christianum* and Christ together; it came to mean the particular sacrament of the eucharist. *Disciplina* had meant the practice of spiritual submission to God, and moved towards signifying judicial actions of punishing or correcting others through formal tribunals of some sort. Verbs were morphing into nouns, and religion was gradually becoming more about dogmas, definitions, and doctrines than about finding modes of living together.

The early medieval church had organized itself around the search for social peace and unity, drawing heavily on the institution of the family and the metaphors of kinship in order to do so. The church used the terminology of kinship (mother and father, sister and brother, parent and child) to reinforce the family of faith. In heaven, God was a father and Christ a son, while Mary gained her high status as the Jesus' mother of Jesus and the earliest saints drew theirs as his siblings and cousins. On earth, the pope was 'father', monks and friars were 'brothers', and nuns were 'sisters'. In their day-to-day lives, individual believers wove a network of symbolic kin relations through god-parenthood, confraternities, and guilds, and preserved the holy fiction that all were equal in the eyes of God. The developing obsession with purity gradually turned this horizontal equality on end as realities of class and hierarchy made social groups in the church more self-consciously vertical and authoritarian. It was an obsession with definition and precision, and it can be traced to the fascination with classical order and discipline, which first emerges in the universities of the twelfth century, but which really expands from the fourteenth.

In Bossy's view, the early medieval church valued resemblances, while the early modern church valued distinctions. Resemblances meant that something new could be acceptable if it was like something known and authoritative, and so this was what believers looked for as they aimed to know what to include in the faith. At least one result of this was that many early communities refashioned their pagan gods as saints, their pagan holidays as Christian feasts, and their pagan shrines as Christian sites. Early modern authorities built their purges and purifications on much sharper distinctions between the holy and the unholy, and in theory – if not always in practice – they rejected compromise and hybridity. Bossy's distinction romanticizes the medieval church somewhat, which could be as dysfunctional a family as any, and his broad generalizations simplify both medieval and Reformation faith and practice. Yet they also help us identify how the deeper intellectual changes of Renaissance humanism and the broad effort to recover the classical past and recast society in the model of classical learning and practice were transforming faith and the church.

Individual discipline was a critical part of that legacy. It took discipline to learn Latin and Greek, and more discipline again to shape one's thoughts and manners around classical writings. Young elite men learned both disciplines in the Latin schools that became the single most important doorway into the social and political elite. Plato, Aristotle, and the Stoics taught discipline directly and even sternly, but even Epicurus taught that the life of pleasure was one lived modestly and within the limits of the world and one's situation so that pain could be avoided. While Stoics may have preached a hard doctrine, even a life of Epicurean pleasure required considerable self-discipline. Baldassare Castiglione's *Book of the Courtier* (1526) was not a particularly original statement of this approach, but it clearly struck a chord: 108 editions appeared from 1528 to 1616, and many Latin and vernacular Books of Manners followed after it. Castiglione drew on Cicero's *Duties of a Gentleman* and *The Oratore* as did the flood of simplified texts that adapted his gentleman's creed to the life of the bourgeoisie, like Giovanni della Casa's *Galateo* (1558), Roger Ascham's *The Schoolmaster* (1570), and Stefano Guazzo's *Art of Civil Conversation* (1579). Civilized manners put civil society on a foundation of self-discipline, sobriety, and gravity above all. The good citizen had to constantly think of being under the eye of an authority, be it father, teacher, priest, king, or God. That judging gaze should shape every action. Until well into the twentieth century, the main Latin schools where elite boys and later also girls were trained were run by religious institutions or according to religious charters and statutes. Clergy served as teachers, and the curriculum emphasized the convergence of the Christian and classical legacies around concerns for order, virtue, and citizenship, with a heavy emphasis on manners, discipline, and self-control. They added a critical religious prod to internalizing these values, which the classical authors had not emphasized. To violate the order was to disobey a Father God who would judge severely, and who had authorized all the other fathers in the house, the church, and the palace to hold individuals to account. The judging gaze of an authoritative father animated the bourgeois morality that shaped Europeans in their waking and sleeping, and cutting out that father's eyes was the iconoclastic act by which Freud began to bring that morality down in the modern era.

Education and socialization helped noble and bourgeois youth develop inner discipline. Lower down the social scale, those thought to be 'naturally weak', like women, children, labourers, the poor, and colonial aboriginals, needed the external discipline of an enclosure, prison, or protective shelter to build up that discipline or compensate for a lack of it. Enclosures shared the ultimate goal of expecting weak, subordinate, and marginalized people to internalize the rules framed by social and religious elites and so live a disciplined life in civil society. The process of 'civilizing' them was a process of weaning them from a naturally animalistic and sinful state marked by appetite and violence, and inculcating them with bourgeois morality. This civilizing code was presented as true religion and the life pleasing to God the Father, regardless of creed or confession. From the eighteenth and nineteenth century, it shaped the curriculum of Sunday Schools and public schools around the globe where vast numbers were educated. In almost all countries, religion continued to be seen as fundamental to education, even if it was now becoming religion of the people, nation, or empire. Specific confessions or more vaguely ecumenical (and more strongly nationalist) creeds appeared in the curriculum as traditions to be learned.

These three critical developments built on each other: the expanding scope of religious community, the direction of intellectual life towards classical models, and the redefined focus of religious life towards dogma and discipline. They take us through the confessionalized culture of the early modern period and into the modern age. They help us understand why Benedict Anderson's typology of the 'Imagined Community' in his analysis of nineteenth- and twentieth-century nationalism resonates with early modernists. In his iconic study, Anderson singled out five factors that drove the development of nationalism under colonialism: the territorialization of religious faiths; emerging models of sacred kingship; the expansion of print capitalism; the spread of vernacular languages linked to national identities; and changing conceptions of time. Anderson argued that these came together to create a religion out of nationalism in the modern era. We can see also see these factors working together as the quasi-sacred nation-state began emerging in the early modern period.

Confessional tribalism as it had developed through the early modern period in fact remained strong through the nineteenth century and into the twentieth, and indeed many of the tools that Anderson's modern nationalists worked with had a clear early modern pedigree. All of Europe's many distinct Christian religious communities experienced revival movements in the decades following the French Revolution, and each very consciously returned to its Reformation history for inspiration. Publishers brought out new editions of the standard martyrologies like Foxe's *Book of Martyrs* and van Bracht's *The Martyr's Mirror* to revive the memories of early martyrs and turn them into highly effective touchstones of group identity for young Anglicans, Mennonites, and Catholics. New statues of past heroes marked the sites of their execution and preserved the memory of conflicts and confessional fires long after their heat had faded. Images of Luther posting the Ninety-Five Theses in Wittenberg started for the first time showing him with a *hammer* in front of the church door. In 1843, evangelical Anglicans raised the Martyrs Memorial at the entrance to Oxford in order to recall the burning of Thomas Cranmer, Nicholas Ridely, and Hugh Latimer by Mary Tudor's Catholic regime. They were keen to stoke up revulsion around Bloody Mary's Catholic tyranny as a means of keeping young university students far from the lures of the quasi-Catholic Oxford Movement led by John Henry Newman who would convert to Roman Catholicism two years later. Monuments to the victims of 'the Killing Time' multiplied across Scotland and the Scottish diaspora to rekindle the memory of the 1680s when English officers had tortured and executed the Calvinists known as Covenanters. Public funds raised the Luther Monument in Worms in 1868 and the Reformation Monument in Geneva in 1909. The former includes four forerunners who suffered persecution or martyrdom (Peter Waldo, John Wycliffe, Jan Hus, Girolamo Savonarola) while the latter is a virtual pantheon of Calvinist religious and political heroes from across Europe.

Many Reformation monuments deliberately merged religious, national, and liberal narratives. They paradoxically recruited early modern religious martyrs to the cause of a modern liberal state, which would formally separate religion and politics, usually by claiming that organized religion – and organized Catholicism above all – was antithetical to liberal democratic values. The Catholic Church's public statements certainly removed any doubt of that. Italian liberal nationalists were claiming Savonarola as a martyr for their cause when they commissioned a statue of him in 1872 and placed it in the Hall of the Five Hundred in Florence's Palazzo Vecchio. This was where the country's Senate had met from 1865 to 1870 when Florence was the new country's capital, and when the national government was at odds with the papacy. A similar statue erected in Ferrara in 1875 bears the inscription, 'Girolamo Savonarola: In Corrupt and Servile Times a Strident Critic of Vices and Tyrants', while Italian Freemasons challenged papal authorities in 1889 by raising a statue of Giordano Bruno on the site of his 1600 execution. In 1915, the five-hundredth anniversary of Jan Hus's execution, Czech nationalists dedicated a monument in Prague's Old Town Square that included a dramatic statue of Hus and twenty-seven crosses marking his executed noble followers. . Decades before this, French authors had lionized the Huguenots as victims of religious intolerance and monarchical tyranny, and their heroism drove the narrative of countless novels, plays, and even operas. Longfellow's *Evangeline* (1847) told the story of young Acadian woman searching for her lost love Gabriel after the British separated them during the deportations of the 1750s. These liberal romanticizations offered black and white plots, highly colourful personalities, and the sharpest stereotypes to advance dramatic action. They moved Reformation debates into popular culture. Individuals and minority groups fought for their freedoms against political and religious authorities of various kinds.

Nationalist martyrologies were catechisms of a different kind, preaching a religion that Hus, Savonarola, Luther, Calvin would not have recognized and likely strongly rejected. They preserved the religious character of nationalism while transferring martyrdom and sacrifice from the religious to the secular sphere. The disputes they described might be distant or even fictional, and always left out inconvenient truths. Longfellow's Evangeline suffers at the hands of the British only, and the poet says nothing of his fellow New Englanders' deep involvement in the deportations. Yet exile, refugee, and martyr heroes were memorialized primarily in order to motivate contemporaries to remain vigilant, active, punitive, and if necessary purgative in the current 'confessional' struggles of nationalism, anti-clericalism, and racial or ethnic purification. In 1914 the language of duty, chivalry, and sacrifice would send hundreds of thousands of men to war 'for God and Country', and after 1918 it would adorn the monuments erected to those who never returned. Religious and chivalric language about 'fallen heroes' and 'evil foes' dressed up and legitimated disputes, and made hatreds somehow holy. The Treaty of Versailles would enshrine national identity and purity as primary values, which had to be defended by political self-determination. It was again about drawing boundaries, and obsessions with national purity and contamination triggered purgative bloodbaths and expulsions both before and after those lines had been drawn by the diplomats gathered in Paris.

The Treaty of Versailles unleashed nationalist purges across Europe, Russia, and the Middle East that wiped out many of the historical diasporic communities first settled by refugees fleeing the religiously purgative campaigns of the fifteenth and sixteenth centuries. Greek nationalists seeking to get the best from the Versailles conference effectively cleansed Salonika of its Muslim and Jewish communities and later expunged even the memory of their presence; it takes a lot of work to find traces of these communities in modern-day Thessaloniki. Stalin's purges followed a tsarist example in clearing Mennonites from rural communities across the Ukraine, which they had first settled in the eighteenth century. Nazi campaigns targeted the large Jewish communities that had developed across Poland and Eastern Europe, and in cities like Amsterdam, Venice, and Salonika; in fact, no Jewish community was too small to escape their notice. Steadily increasing tensions across the Middle East after the creation of the state of Israel in 1948 and the wars of 1956, 1967, and 1972 brought an end to thriving Jewish communities in Baghdad, Algiers, Cairo, and across the former Safavid, Ottoman, and Barbary states. It is telling that we can barely imagine now that such communities ever existed at all. It is one of the tragic ironies of history that so many of the diasporic shelters founded by exiles fleeing the religious purges of the fifteenth and sixteenth century were consumed in the nationalist purges of the twentieth. Purges mark the beginning and the end of a centuries-long period when diasporic communities and exile cultures shaped that part of European culture that was cosmopolitan, polyglot, and multi-cultural.

In order to understand these deeper consequences, we have to recognize a phenomenon like confessionalization as extending far beyond political bureaucracy and social discipline, and even far past the mid seventeenth century when the last of the new confessions were being written. Confessionalization through the senses, emotions, socialization, urbanism, and the imaginary was far more enduring than any particular question-and-answer catechism. It taught children what to suspect, fear, or exclude as much as what to believe. It was the nascent form of nationalism, setting in place the transcendent frameworks, the language, the disciplines, the modes, and the professionals who could benefit from manipulating these. It taught how natural and mundane inter-communal hatreds could be, both at home and abroad. A London audience watching the first performances of Shakespeare's *Othello* (1603) in the Globe theatre would recognize Iago as a Spanish Catholic – for what else could an evil obsessive genius with the name of Spain's patron Saint Iago (i.e., James) possibly be? – pursuing his self-destructive animosity against the converted Moor Othello all the way to the endangered frontier of the polyglot Venetian Empire, where both were mercenaries. Shakespeare did not have to provide a detailed playbill because the many 'Black Legends' of Spanish cruelty circulating in England had already done that work for him. This was a broader 'cultural confessionalism' fed with fears, rivalries, and invented traditions that formed popular xenophobic stereotypes of all foreigners, whether French, Dutch, Spanish, or Italian. This left Shakespeare free to spin a set of characters and settings that resonated with fears of religious and racial miscegenation, insiders and outsiders, purity, contagion, and violent purgation. English audiences would see it all as a commentary on current events when Spain expelled 300,000 Moors and *moriscos* a few years later in 1609.

On the other side of Shakespeare's London, metaphorically speaking, plays brought Dutch traders, Portuguese merchants, French dandies, Italian bankers, and sturdy if sometimes hapless English youths together in an emerging genre called the 'city comedy'. Thomas Dekker (1572–1632), likely the son of Dutch migrants to London, ventriloquized migrant accents and inflated cultural stereotypes in a series of plays that prodded native English xenophobia while showing just how diverse London had become. The lesson in *The Shoemaker's Holiday* (1599) was that the English nobleman would get the girl, but that it would be a close-run against 'foreign' suitors. And the girl he got was the daughter of a wealthy 'Portuguese merchant', hence certainly an Iberian Jewish *converso*. Dekker's comedy filled theatres half a decade before Shakespeare's tragedy did, yet both responded to English audiences' fascination with foreign settings and characters. They demonstrated how blurred lines of religious identity could co-exist with the fear and lure of the confessional other. We could see Shakespeare's tragedy as the sober response to Dekker's comedy, but this reduces them both to dramatic moralizing. What they do show is that discourses of religious and ethnic difference were pungent and present, but above all that they occupied the same stages at roughly the same time.

This book has emphasized the discourses of religious difference: of purity, contagion, exclusion, and purgation. Shakespeare's tragedy about Spaniards destroying each other while serving Venice against the Ottomans picks up some of the main players, locales, and dynamics. We have seen how these bitter realities forced millions from their homes. A relatively small number of these exiles and refugees were forced to move by one government or another at a particular time with particular laws and police actions. Many more decided 'voluntarily' that they could no longer stay in a place which had branded them somehow alien, criminal, and dangerous. Against this, we need to recall the opposite reality of Dekker's comic troupe of migrating expatriates and the eventual marriage of the English aristocrat to the Iberian *converso*. Recent research has emphasized that early modern Europe was in fact full of examples of inter-communal co-existence and co-operation. In this book we have touched on Amsterdam's 'hidden churches' of Anabaptists, Catholics, and Jews; the campaign by the Antwerp migrant Daniel Bomberg to publish the Torah and a host of other Jewish texts in Venice; the Erasmus Foundation's subsidies that brought migrants, exiles, and refugees of different faiths to Basel to live and study; the Transylvanian Diet's decision to allow worship by a wide range of religious groups; and the Edict of Nantes' protection of the Huguenots distinctive worship and culture. We have seen many examples of conversion that force us to question more closely what faith and conversion actually *meant* to early moderns.

Practical religious co-existence could indeed be found across Europe, and nowhere more so than in the Ottoman and Holy Roman Empires. The Ottoman Empire's *millet* system was a model for inter-communal co-existence and a major reason why after the expulsions of 1492 and 1497, the overwhelming majority of Iberian Jews moved there rather than to sites in Christian Europe. The fact that as many as 90 percent of the world's Jews chose to live under Islam says a great deal about early modern Christendom. Yet even within Christendom there were some who refused to limit themselves to a single place, nationality, or identity. Benjamin Kaplan has amply shown that in many multi-confessional towns of the Holy Roman Empire, Christians shared single church buildings – even though Rome forbade the practice and Calvinist ministers described it as bringing together 'God and the devil from hell'. More often, Catholics, Lutherans, and Calvinists kept to different buildings. Civic laws limited the height of their towers or the size of their bells to keep them from intruding too much into each others' physical or sensory space. Protestants in Vienna and other Austrian towns could walk to their own chapels located in nobles' estates out in the countryside, and every Sunday thousands did so in a practice known as '*Auslauf*', or 'walking out'. In 1577, a group of Protestant nobles bought the estate of Hernals just three kilometers from Vienna's city walls, and for almost fifty years it became the main church for the city's Protestants. In some parts of France, Huguenots and Catholics intermarried or stood as godparents for each other's children. The men of the Iberian Jewish Pallache family moved between Morocco, Spain, the Netherlands, and Europe, slipping in and out of various identities with the tacit support of local authorities.

These examples remind us that the discourses of purity and purgation were in dialogue with discourses of integration, conversion, and even hybridity. Communities watched, learned, and bought and sold from each other. Individuals found friends among those whom some of their co-religionists had damned to hell. This practical co-existence of religious communities was not what we would understand as toleration. Modern toleration assumes that faith is an individual and private matter and that the state is a secular institution, which must protect the rights of individuals and communities to their own religious worship. Modern citizens take this for granted, but this was not how early moderns saw the world. They still saw truth as objective, exclusive, and above all *theirs*.

Political necessity and economic self-interest might lead a few rare communities like Amsterdam, Venice, and the multi-confessional towns of the Holy Roman Empire, to practice co-existence. Yet only very few moved from this to the conviction that religion was not a matter of political concern, let alone to any open acceptance of the religious Other. The early Dutch radical David Joris, whom Gary Waite describes as 'the most hated man in sixteenth century Europe', inspired followers called Spiritualists who believed that good and evil were purely interior or subjective qualities. The natural implication was that beliefs were personal and that there should be no use of force in religion. The seventeenth-century Quaker William Penn stated this openly and aimed to practice it in his American colony. Yet even Penn's own children and the colonists in Pennsylvania reverted to passing restrictions on religious freedom (notably against Jews, Catholics, and some other Quakers). It was only much later in the eighteenth century that Penn's ideas about religious pluralism and toleration were taken up by authors like Thomas Paine and Benjamin Franklin. Until then, the best that most religious minorities could hope for was passive co-existence.

Co-existence assumed that communities would *voluntarily* separate themselves and prefer to live with their peers, associates, and co-religionists. Even in the Ottoman Empire, co-existence was often coerced, and was seldom more than purely practical. After the mid-sixteenth century, non-Muslims did not form part of the collective 'we' in Ottoman consciousness, any more than 'aliens' had ever been fully part of the *Corpus Christianum* or sacred Christian nation. It was in the early modern period that these became contradictions in terms. The 'religious clustering' that emerged in Algiers, Granada, Salonika, Amsterdam, New England, and across the early modern world was a psychological distancing reinforced by geographic distancing. Modern toleration and cultural mixing could develop only once secular nationalism had replaced Christian, Jewish, or Muslim dogma as the legitimating doctrine of the modern state, and only once the mass migration of peoples within and beyond Europe and the Mediterranean had broken down psychological and geographic distancing. This might realize the happily inter-marrying polyglot world of Dekker's London, but could it banish entirely the more troubled dynamics of the Spanish who were fighting each other in Shakespeare's Cyprus?

To emphasize purity, contagion, and purgation in the period traditionally known as the Reformation is not to assert that these are the only or even the major characteristics of that religious movement. It is certainly not to say that they are natural or normative characteristics of late medieval and early modern Christianity generally. Nationalism and twentieth-century totalitarianism were far more absolute, extreme, and efficient in their ability to demonize and destroy. To trace exclusionary themes in the broader movements for religious reform is simply to acknowledge that history is created in the exchanges of discourses among groups. Some Europeans were fearful and punitive, while others were not. Some used contemporary religious language to express their ideas, but others rejected that expression. Some saw reformation movements as vehicles for social discipline and exclusion, while others saw them as vehicles for intellectual freedom and responsibility. Some saw religion as promoting centralized monarchy, while others thought it supported a decentralized republic. Some feared heretics, Jews, and witches, while others did not. Some hinted at common humanity. An image of a Moorish mother and child from the Italian edition of Nicholas de Nicolay's *Navigations, Peregrinations and Voyages Made into Turkey* (1577) bears an uncanny resemblance to traditional depictions of the Madonna and Child [Fig 42a & 42b]. It is an anonymous outlier; does it suggest ways in which some aimed to bridge divides or to find forms of expression that brought together what others saw as mutually exclusive? This kind of blending was certainly common enough among some *moriscos* and *conversos*, and among converts in Latin America, Africa, and Asia.

Emphasizing the lived realities of purity, contagion, and purgation simply recognizes that they were ubiquitous across late medieval and early modern society, and that they mattered. Refugees fled, people died, and cultures

42(a). Martin Shongauer, Madonna & Child (c. 1480).
Courtesy National Gallery of Art (Washington).

42(b). Moorish Woman from Tripoli from Nicolay, *Navigations, Peregrinations and Voyages Made into Turkey* (1577). Courtesy of the Thomas Fisher Rare Book Library, University of Toronto.

were reshaped. Examining the expulsions and refugees that multiplied from the later fifteenth century takes seriously the reality that in certain times and places and under the prodding of certain political or intellectual figures, these harsh values could explode with potent force. They still do. They could trigger a cascade of responses that often followed the law of unintended consequences as they rippled across nations. The Iberian expulsions of Jews and Muslims impoverished Spain, but enriched the Netherlands, Italy, and the Ottoman Empire. The intolerance of European Catholic and Protestant authorities was, to a large extent, the making of the Americas both North and South. When Catholic or Protestant refugees fled persecution, at least some, like the Mennonites, found their faith and communities strengthened. Quakers followed the logic of their arguments against compulsion into advocating an end to slavery. Ghettos were meant to isolate and eventually convert Jewish communities, yet often turned out to be effective means of building Jewish solidarity and identity, and so preserving a distinctive Jewish culture. Some consistories and confessors brought erring members back towards communal norms, but many used discipline in a way that pushed these members to other faiths entirely or to a general scepticism about religious ideas and institutions. To emphasize compulsion in early modern religion is certainly not to endorse it, but simply to acknowledge how much it shaped the world from the sixteenth through the twentieth centuries. It also helps us recognize that it is still a powerful reality today.

The Stari Most bridge was blown up in 1993, but by 2004 it was rebuilt, using stones dredged out of the riverbed. Recognizing that we are dealing with discourses means that we must remember both that words can have tremendous power and that at some times they are only words. The memory of persecution is frequently stronger than the memory of co-existence, and violence shapes communal histories and identity more than co-operation. Yet communities contain different voices. Frequently, the push to violent action comes not from broad traditions or masses of people but from those like Adolf Hitler, Slobodan Milosovic, or Osama bin Laden who are willing to exploit the potential to violence found in appeals to purity and contagion. Their most effective triggers are often religious or national or some mix of these. Although they do not speak for all members of their communities, they can incite actions that leave diasporic legacies, which result over time in new and unforeseen mixing. As we have seen, exile and expulsion have always had, as their reverse side, extraordinary cultural creativity.

Dating Europe's Reformation to a German monk's theological preoccupations was a North European conceit. To date it instead to a first act when European Christian culture sought to protect its religious purity by expelling and/or enclosing the Other, thereby triggering harsh violence and extraordinary diasporic movements, gives a more acute view of the roots of some modern global realities. It also allows an expanded conversation among those younger transnational scholars who are coming into the field with different histories, preoccupations, and questions that will help them rewrite its narrative.

SELECT BIBLIOGRAPHY

General Texts

Cameron, E., *The European Reformation*. Oxford: 1991.
  Enchanted Europe: Superstition, Reason, & Religion, 1250–1750. Oxford: 2010.
MacCulloch, D., *Reformation: Europe's House Divided, 1490–1700*. London: 2003.
Walsham, A., *The Reformation of Landscape: Religion, Identity, and Memory in Early Modern Britain and Ireland*. Oxford: 2011.

Research Resources

Bagchi, D., & D. C. Steinmetz (eds.), *The Cambridge Companion to Reformation Theology*. Cambridge: 2004.
Bamji, A., G. H. Janssen, & M. Laven (eds.), *The Ashgate Research Companion to the Counter-Reformation*. Aldershot: 2013.
Bearman, P. J., et al. (eds.), *The Encyclopedia of Islam*. Leiden: 1954–2008.
Comerford, K. M., & H. M. Pabel (eds.), *Early Modern Catholicism*. Toronto: 2001.
Fierro, M. (ed.), *The New Cambridge History of Islam*. Volume 2: *The Western Islamic World, Eleventh to Eighteenth Centuries*. Cambridge: 2010.
Greengrass, M., *The European Reformation c. 1500–1618*. London: 1998.
Ruderman, D. B., *Early Modern Jewry: A New Cultural History*. Princeton: 2010.
Skolnik, F. (ed.), *Encyclopedia Judaica*, 2nd ed. Farmington Hills: 2007.
Whitford, D. (ed.), *Reformation and Early Modern Europe: A Guide to Research*. Kirksville: 2008.

Introduction

Anderson, B., *Imagined Communities: Reflections on the Origin and Spread of Nationalism*, 2nd ed. London: 2006.
Masters, B., *Christians and Jews in the Ottoman Arab World: Roots of Sectarianism*. Cambridge: 2004.
Moore, R. I., *The Formation of a Persecuting Society: Authority and Deviance in Western Europe*. Oxford: 1987.

Nirenburg, D., *Communities of Violence: Persecution of Minorities in the Middle Ages.* Princeton: 1998.

Oberman, H. A., *John Calvin and the Reformation of the Refugees.* Geneva: 2009.

Chapter 1. The Body of Christ: Defined and Threatened

Birdal, M. S., *The Holy Roman Empire and the Ottomans: From Global Imperial Powers to Absolutist States.* New York: 2011.

Black, C. F., & P. Gravestock (eds.), *Early Modern Confraternities in Europe and the Americas: International and Interdisciplinary Perspectives.* Aldershot: 2006.

Casale, G., *The Ottoman Age of Exploration.* Oxford: 2010.

Clark, S., *Thinking with Demons: The Idea of Witchcraft in Early Modern Europe.* Oxford: 1999.

Fuchs, B., *Exotic Nation: Maurophilia and the Construction of Early Modern Spain.* Philadelphia: 2009.

Goffman, D., *The Ottoman Empire and Early Modern Europe.* Cambridge: 2002.

Harper, J. G. (ed.), *The Turk and Islam in the Western Eye, 1450–1750: Visual Imagery before Orientalism.* Aldershot: 2011.

Lynch, K. A. *Individuals, Families, and Communities in Europe, 1200–1800: The Urban Foundations of Western Society.* Cambridge: 2003.

Masters, B., *Christians and Jews in the Ottoman Arab World.* Cambridge: 2001.

Meyerson, M. D., *A Jewish Renaissance in Fifteenth Century Spain.* Princeton: 2004.

Terpstra, N. (ed.), *The Politics of Ritual Kinship: Confraternities and Social Order in Early Modern Italy.* Cambridge: 2000.

Waite, G., *Eradicating the Devil's Minions: Anabaptists and Witches in Reformation Europe, 1535–1600.* Toronto: 2007.

Zika, C., *The Appearance of Witchcraft: Print and Visual Culture in Sixteenth Century Europe.* London: 2007.

Chapter 2. Purifying the Body

Black, C. F., *The Italian Inquisition.* New Haven: 2009.

Bowden, C., L. Lux-Sterritt, & N. Hallett (eds.), *English Convents in Exile, 1600–1800.* 6 vols. London: 2012–2013.

Davis, R. C., & B. Ravid (eds.), *The Jews of Early Modern Venice.* Baltimore: 2001.

Eamon, W., *The Professor of Secrets: Mystery, Medicine, and Alchemy in Renaissance Italy.* Washington, D.C.: 2010.

Ehlers, B., *Between Christians and Moriscos: Juan de Ribera and Religious Reform in Valencia, 1568–1614.* Baltimore: 2006.

Eire, C. M. N., *War against the Idols: Reform of Worship from Erasmus to Calvin.* Cambridge: 1986.

Eletti, M. degli, *The Conversion of a Jew to Christianity.* Trans. D. Chambers, J. Fletcher, & B. Pullan. Toronto: 2001.

Evangelisti, S. *Nuns: A History of Convent Life, 1450–1700.* Oxford: 2007.

Franklin, A. E., R. Margariti, M. Rustow, & U. Simonsohn (eds.), *Jews, Christians, and Muslims in Medieval and Early Modern Times.* Leiden: 2014.

Grieve, P. E., *The Eve of Spain: Myths of Origins in the History of Christian, Muslim, and Jewish Conflict*. Baltimore: 2009.
Harvey, L. P., *Muslims in Spain 1500–1614*. Chicago: 2005.
Janssen, G. H., *The Dutch Revolt and Catholic Exile in Reformation Europe*. Cambridge: 2015.
Kagan, R. L., & A. Dyer, *Inquistorial Inquiries: Brief Lives of Secret Jews and Other Heretics*. Baltimore: 2004.
Kamen, H., *The Disinherited: Exile and the Making of Spanish Culture, 1492–1975*. New York: 2007.
Spanish Inquisition: A Historical Revision. New Haven: 1998.
Kaplan, B., *Divided by Faith: Religious Conflict and the Practice of Toleration in Early Modern Europe*. Cambridge: 2007.
Kaplan, D., *Beyond Expulsion: Jews, Christians, and Reformation Strasbourg*. Stanford: 2011.
Kaplan, D., & M. Teter, 'Out of the (Historiographic) Ghetto: European Jews and Reformation Narratives,' *Sixteenth Century Journal* 40/2 (2009): 365–93.
Melton, J. Van Horn, 'Confessional power and the power of confession: concealing and revealing the faith in Alpine Salzburg, 1730–1734', in H. Scott and B. Simms, *Cultures of Power in Europe during the Long Eighteenth Century* (Cambridge: 2007): 133–57.
Meyerson, M. D., & E. D. English (eds.), *Christians, Muslims, and Jews in Medieval and Early Modern Spain: Interaction and Cultural Exchange*. Notre Dame: 1999.
Moore, Barrington, 'Ethnic & Religious Hostilities in Early Modern Port Cities', *International Journal of Politics, Culture, and Society* 14 (2001): 687–727.
Safley, T. M., *Children of the Laboring Poor: Expectation and Experience among the Orphans of Early Modern Augsburg*. Leiden: 2005.
Stow, K., *Theater of Acculturation: The Roman Ghetto in the Sixteenth Century*. Seattle: 2001.
Walker, C., *Gender and Politics in Early Modern Europe: English Convents in France and the Low Countries*. London: 2003.
Walker, M., *The Salzburg Transaction: Expulsion and Redemption in Eighteenth Century Germany*. Ithaca, NY: 1992.
Walsham, A., *Charitable Hatred: Tolerance and Intolerance in England, 1500–1700*. Manchester: 2006.
Wandel, L. P., *Voracious Idols and Violent Hands: Iconoclasm in Reformation Zurich, Strasbourg, and Basel*. Cambridge: 1994:
Zika, C., *Exorcising our Demons: Magic, Witchcraft and Visual Culture in Early Modern Europe*. Leiden: 2002.

Chapter 3. Dividing the Body: People and Places

Bonney, R., & D. J. B. Trim (eds.), *Persecution and Pluralism: Calvinists and Religious Minorities in Early Modern Europe, 1550–1700*. Bern: 2006.
Coleman, D., *Creating Christian Granada: Society and Religious Culture in an Old World Frontier City (1492–1600)*. Ithaca, N.Y.: 2003.
Crawshaw, Jane L. Stevens, *Plague Hospitals: Public Health for the City in Early Modern Venice*. Aldershot: 2012.
Davis, N. Z., *Trickster Travels: A Sixteenth-Century Muslim between Worlds*. New York: 2006.

Davis, R. C., *Christian Slaves, Muslim Masters: White Slavery in the Mediterranean, the Barbary Coast, and Italy, 1500–1800*. London: 2003.
Dursteler, E., *Venetians in Constantinople: Nation, Identity, and Coexistence in the Early Modern Mediterranean*. Baltimore: 2006.
Fehler, T., G. Kroeker, C. Parker, & J. Ray (eds.), *Religious Diaspora in Early Modern Europe: Strategies of Exile*. London: 2014.
Felici, L., 'The Erasmusstuftung and Europe: The Institution, Organization, and Activity of the Foundation of Erasmus of Rotterdam from 1538–1600', in *History of Universities*, vol. 12 (1993): 25–63.
Garces, M. A., *An Early Modern Dialogue with Islam* [a translation of Antonio de Sosa, *Topography of Algiers* (1612)]. 2011.
García-Arenal, M., & G. Wiegers, *A Man of Three Worlds: Samuel Pallache, a Moroccan Jew in Catholic and Protestant Europe*. Baltimore: 2003.
Gitlitz, M., *Secrecy and Deceit: The Religion of the Crypto-Jews*. Philadelphia-Jerusalem: 1996.
Hsia, R. Po-Chia, & H. Lehmann (eds.), *In and out of the Ghetto*. Cambridge: 2002.
Parker, C. H., *Faith on the Margins: Catholics and Catholicism in the Dutch Golden Age*. Cambridge: 2008.
Rothman, E. N., *Brokering Empire: Trans-Imperial Subjects between Venice and Istanbul*. Ithaca: 2012.

Chapter 4. Mind and Body

de Boer, W., & C. Goettler (eds.), *Religion and the Senses in Early Modern Europe*. Leiden: 2013.
Benedict, P., *Christ's Churches Purely Reformed: A Social History of Calvinism*. New Haven: 2002.
Bynum, C. W., *Christian Materiality: An Essay on Religion in Late Medieval Europe*. New York: 2011.
Fehler, T. G., *Poor Relief and Protestantism: The Evolution of Social Welfare in Sixteenth Century Emden*. Aldershot, 1999.
Gordon, B., *Calvin*. New Haven: 2009.
Harline, Craig, *Conversions: Two Family Stories from the Reformation and Modern America*. New Haven: 2011.
Haskins, S., *Mary Magdalen: Myth and Metaphor*. New York: 1993.
Hsia, R. Po-Chia. (ed.), *The German People and the Reformation*. Ithaca, N.Y.: 1988.
Karant-Nunn, S., *The Reformation of Ritual: An Interpretation of Early Modern Germany*. London: 1997.
McIntosh, M. K., *Poor Relief in England, 1350–1600*. Cambridge: 2012.
More, T., *Utopia*. Trans. G.C. Richards, in *The Complete Works of St. Thomas More*, vol. 4, ed. E. Surtz & J. H. Hexter. New Haven: 1964: 139–41.
Otis, L. L., *Prostitution in Medieval Society: The History of an Urban Institution in Languedoc*. Chicago: 1985.
Rubin, M., *Corpus Christi: The Eucharist in Late Medieval Culture*. Cambridge: 1991.
Sabean, D. W., *Power in the Blood: Popular Culture & Village Discourse in Early Modern Germany*. Cambridge: 1984.
Scribner, R., *Popular Culture and Popular Movements in Reformation Germany*. London: 1987.

Singer, A., *Charity in Islamic Societies*. Cambridge: 2008.
Spierling, K., *Infant Baptism in Reformation Geneva*. Surrey: 2005.
Terpstra, N., *Cultures of Charity: Women, Politics, and the Reform of Poor Relief in Renaissance Italy*. Cambridge, MA: 2013.
Williams, G. H., *The Radical Reformation*, 3rd ed. Kirksville: 2000.

Chapter 5. Re-Forming the Body: The World the Refugees Made

Chambers, D. S., *Popes, Cardinals, and War: The Military Church in Renaissance and Early Modern Europe*. New York: 2006.
Coster, W., & A. Spicer (eds.), *Sacred Space in Early Modern Europe*. Cambridge: 2005.
Finkel, C., *Osman's Dream: The History of the Ottoman Empire*. New York: 2005.
Forster, M. R., *Catholic Revival in the Age of the Baroque: Religious Identity in Southwest Germany, 1550–1750*. Cambridge: 2002.
Freeman, T., *Martyrs and Martyrdom in England, c. 1400–1700*. Woodbridge: 2007.
Gitlitz, M., *Secrecy and Deceit: The Religion of the Crypto-Jews*. Philadelphia-Jerusalem: 1996.
Goodwin, G., *A History of Ottoman Architecture*. Baltimore: 1971.
Graizibord, D. L., *Souls in Dispute: Converso Identities in Iberia and the Jewish Diaspora, 1580–1700*. Philadelphia: 2004.
Gregory, B., *Salvation at Stake: Christian Martyrdom in Early Modern Europe*. Cambridge: 1999.
Kaplan, Y., 'Between Christianity and Judaism in Early Modern Europe : The Confessionalization Process of the Western Sephardi Diaspora', in *Judaism, Christianity, and Islam in the Course of History; Exchange and Conflicts*, ed. H. von Lothar Gall & D. Willoweit. Munich: 2011, 307–41.
The Western Sephardic Diaspora. Tel Aviv: 1994.
King, J. N. (ed.), *Foxe's Book of Martyrs: Select Narratives*. Oxford: 2007.
Krstic, T., *Contested Conversions to Islam: Narratives of Religious Change in the Early Modern Ottoman Empire*. Stanford: 2011.
Marsden, R., 'The Bible in English in the Middle Ages', in S. Boynton (ed.), *The Practice of the Bible in the Middle Ages*. New York: 2011.
Ozment, S. E., *The Reformation in the Cities: The Appeal of Protestantism to Sixteenth Century Germany and Switzerland*. New Haven: 1975.
When Fathers Ruled: Family Life in Reformation Europe. Cambridge: 1983.
Ray, J., *After Expulsion: 1492 and the Making of Sephardic Jewry*. New York: 2013.
Smith, J. C., *Sensuous Worship: Jesuits and the Art of the Early Catholic Reformation in Germany*. Princeton: 2002.
Sponholtz, J., & G. Waite (eds.), *Exile and Religious Identity, 1500–1800*. London: 2014.
Stiefel, B., 'The Architectural Origins of the Great Early Modern Urban Synagogue', *Leo Baeck Institute Year Book* 56 (2011): 105–34.
Terpstra, N., A. Prosperi, & S. Pastore (eds.), *Faith's Boundaries: Laity and Clergy in Early Modern Confraternities*. Turnhout: 2012.
van der Linden, David, *Experiencing Exile: Huguenot Refugees in the Dutch Republic, 1680–1700*. Aldershot, UK: 2015.
Walsham, A., 'Unclasping the Book? Post-Reformation English Catholicism and the Vernacular Bible', *Journal of British Studies* 42/2 (2003): 141–66.

Watt, T., *Cheap Print and Popular Piety, 1550–1640*. Cambridge: 1991.
Wiesner-Hanks, M., *Christianity and Sexuality in the Early Modern World: Regulating Desire, Reforming Practice*. London: 2010.
Yildiz, N., 'The Vakf Institution in Ottoman Cyprus', in M. N. Michael, M. Kappler, & E. Gavriel (eds.), *Ottoman Cyprus: A Collection of Studies on History and Culture*. Weisbaden: 2009: 117–59.

Chapter 6. Re-Imagining the Body

Anderson, B., *Imagined Communities: Reflections on the Origin and Spread of Nationalism*, 2nd ed. London: 2006.
Bossy, J., *Christianity in the West, 1400–1700*. Oxford: 1985.
Grell, O. P., & B. Scribner (eds.), *Tolerance and Intolerance in the European Reformation*. Cambridge: 1996.
Headley, O. P., H. Hillerbrand, & A. J. Papalas (eds.), *Confessionalization in Europe, 1555–1700*. Aldershot, U.K.: 2004.
Rubright, M., *Doppelgänger Dilemmas: Anglo-Dutch Relations in Early Modern Literature and Culture*. Philadelphia: 2014.
Shagan, E., *The Rule of Moderation: Violence, Religion, and the Politics of Restraint in Early Modern England*. Cambridge: 2011
Stacey, P., *Roman Monarchy and the Renaissance Prince*. Cambridge: 2007.

INDEX

Abbadie, Jacques, 295
Abdullah, Murad b., 156, 192, 215, 256, 303
Abi Abdudeyyan, Yusuf b., 192
Abrahamic faiths, 57, 73, 291
Abravanel, Isaac, 134, 135, 136, 156
Abravanel, Judah Leon, 134, 135, 156, 176
Abravanel, Samuel, 135
Acadians, 3, 127, 241, 322
Acre, 40
Acta Sanctorum, 302
Actes and Monuments, 168, 299
ad fontes, 212, 215
Address to the Christian Nobility, 210
Adrian VI, Pope, 65
Against the Jews and their Lies, 311
Albania, 42, 309
Albergati, Niccolò, 252
Albergo dei Poveri, 88
Albigensians. *See* Cathars
Algiers, 6, 44, 154, 157, 177–179, 182, 198, 235, 255, 267, 323, 327
Al-Hasan Ibn Muhammad al-Wazan al-Fasi, 134, 140–142, 156, 303
aljamiado, 109
Allstedt, 170
Allyn, Rose, 148, 149, 156
almshouse, 237, 239
Alpujarras, 108, 109
Alsace, 56
Altoviti, Antonio, 31
Alumbrados, 48
Alva, Duke of, 116, 174
Amish, 101, 125, 170
Amsterdam, 88, 91, 113, 157, 173–177, 179, 182, 198, 216, 226, 228, 232, 234, 235, 237, 255, 267, 277, 279, 285, 293, 323, 325, 326, 327

An Address to the Christian Nobility of the German Nation, 144
Anabaptists, 2, 4, 14, 81, 99, 112, 113, 147, 161, 168–171, 174, 175, 180, 186, 195–197, 203, 232, 260, 285, 301, 325
Anatolia, 157
Ancona, 42, 106, 110
Andalusia, 107, 311
Anderson, Benedict, 12, 320
Anglican, 112
Anglicans, 123
Angola, 5, 96
Antichrist, 81, 247
anti-Trinitarianism, 156
anti-Trinitarians, 180, 199, 215
Antwerp, 23, 26, 60, 100, 167, 175, 231, 282, 302
  Sack of, 116, 173
apocryphal, 214
Apostolic Church, 82
Aquinas, Thomas, 199
Arians, 47
Ariosto, Ludovico, 39
Arius, 47
Armenian genocide, 311
Art of Civil Conversation, 319
Arundel, Thomas, 210
Ascham, Roger, 319
Ashkenazic, 175, 306
Assisi, 106
Athanasian Creed, 248
Attias, Jean-Christophe, 284
Augsburg, 60, 79, 88, 106, 121, 163, 204, 226, 232, 239, 249
Augustine, Saint, 26, 39, 57, 188, 317
Augustinian Order, 67, 80
Aumône Générale, 88

337

Auslauf, 325
Austria, 16, 113, 122, 127, 128, 129, 130, 153, 325
autos da fe, 95, 109
Autun, 33
Avignon, 23, 62, 63, 65, 99, 284, 293
Aya Nikola Cathedral, 287
Aya Sofya Cathedral, 287

Babylonian Captivity, 290
Bach, Johan Sebastian, 279
Badby, John, 50
Baghdad, 7, 42, 268, 323
Bagno Beyliç, 179
bagnos, 179
Bamberg, 103
baptism, 135, 185, 186, 187, 188, 191, 195, 204, 208, 213, 260, 270, 271, 275, 303, 304
  forced, 190–192
  Protestant, 193–195
  radical, 195–197
baptismal registers, 196
baptisteries, 196
Baptists, 124, 181, 197
bar mitzvah, 186
Barbari, Jacopo de', 23, 26
Barbary pirates, 86, 154, 155
Barcelona, 57, 60, 71, 138, 163
Barnabites, 83
Basel, 60, 150, 157, 165–168, 178, 183, 204, 216, 261, 272
  Council of, 64
Bassano, Jacopo, 161
bat mitzvah, 186
Battle of Kosovo, 309
Battle of Mohacs, 43
Battle of the Boyne, 126, 248
Battle of White Mountain, 122
Bavaria, 106, 153
Bayezid II, Sultan, 108, 158
Beaune, 221
Becket, Thomas à, 297
Bedouins, 179
Begijnhof, 237
Belgrade, 6, 43
Benedictine Order, 66, 77
benevolent societies, 163
Berbers, 109, 178, 179
Bern, 204, 208
Bernadone, Francesco di Pietro di. *See* St. Francis of Assisi

Bernardino da Siena, 79, 82, 106
Bernini, Gian Lorenzo, 282
Berti, Michele, 49
bible, 187, 207, 244, 248, 278
  Authorized Version, 209
  Bishop's Bible, 209
  English vernacular, 172
  French vernacular, 172
  Genevan, 209
  Great Bible, 209
  interpretation, 211
  Italian vernacular, 172
  translation of, 209
biblia pauperum, 270
bibliothèque bleu, 247
bimah, 287
bishop, 165, 171, 245, 258, 262, 265, 266
bizzoche, 67
Black Death, 24, 60, 71, 105, 165, 223
Black Sea, 42, 161
Black, Christopher, 99
blasphemy, 72, 99, 100
blood, 54, 58, 138
  blood libels, 59
  of Christ, 200
  of God, 73
Boccaccio, Giovanni, 67
Bodin, Jean, 53
Body, 26
  corruption of, 61
  of Christ, 26, 29, 30, 36, 39, 73, 184
Body of Christ. *See Corpus Christianum*
Bohemia, 16, 50, 121, 122, 123, 207
Bolland, Jean, 302
Bollandists, 302
Bologna, 33, 90, 139, 231, 233, 235, 252
Bolsena, 29
Bomberg, Daniel, 216, 325
Bonaparte, Napoleon, 164, 307
Bonfil, Robert, 268
Bonfires of the Vanities, 79
Boniface VIII, Pope, 49, 85
Book of Common Prayer, 125
Book of Concord, 249, 250, 253
Book of Daniel, 44, 156
Book of Martyrs, 148, See *Acts and Monuments*
Book of the Courtier, 319
Borgo San Sepolcro, 35
Bosnia, 42
Bossy, John, 188, 318, 319
Boston Martyrs, 181

Bracht, Thielemann van, 147, 301
Brandenburg, 121, 123, 173
Braun, Georg, 23
Brazil, 3, 5, 96, 286
Bridewell, 230, 236
Britain, 100, 104, 126
Bruno, Giordano, 154, 322
Brussels, 282, 298
Bucer, Martin, 293
Budapest, 44
Bunyan, John, 296, 298, 305
Buonaroti, Michelangelo, 282
Busbecq, Ogier Ghiselin de, 268
Byzantine Empire, 6, 39, 40, 161, 162, 286

Caesarius of Heisterbach, 23
Cairo, 229, 256, 268, 323
Calamy, Edmund, 300
Calendar of Saints, 59
Calvin, John, 9, 81, 114, 134, 150–152, 156, 167, 171, 172, 173, 193, 259, 261, 304, 317
Calvinism, 121
Calvinist, 112
Calvinists, 2, 205, 261, 276, 277, 300, 325
Campanello, Tommaso, 99
Canada, 294
Canisius, Paul, 253
Capuchins, 79
Cardoso, Isaac, 91
Carlyle, Thomas, 8
Carmelites, 67
Carolina law code, 56
Carolinas, 126
Castellio, Sebastian, 168, 172, 210
Castiglione, Baldassare, 319
Castile, 97, 109, 135, 230
catechism, 233, 244, 247, 248–255, 256, 257, 265, 266, 277, 293, 298, 308
catechumen house, 234
Cathars, 47, 48, 51, 94, 116, 199
cathedral, 138, 170, 190, 257, 269, 270, 271
Catholic Church, 51, 61, 77, 112, 282, 311, 315, 322
  Babylonian Captivity, 62
  Roman, 66
Catholic League, 121
Catholicism, 51, 70
Celebi, Evilya, 310
Cesarini, Giuliano, 65
Cevennes Mountains, 129, 241
charity, 218, 240, 252, 264, 266, 286, 288

Charlemagne, 39
Charles I, King, 125, 126, 153, 180
Charles II, King, 125, 181, 206, 250
  Restoration, 126
Charles University, 50
Charles V, Emperor, 44, 66, 137, 142, 178, 249, 314
Chaucer, Geoffrey, 67
Chrisman, Miriam, 243
Christ. *See* Jesus Christ
Christianity, 73
church, 269
church discipline, 100
Church of England, 124, 125, 181, 204, 205, 249, 261, 278
Circa Pastoralis, 266
circumcision, 185, 186, 191, 194, 195, 198, 199, 286
Cisneros, Ximenes de, 80, 107, 212
city comedy, 324
City on A Hill, 180
civic hospital, 221
civic religion, 4, 30, 31, 32, 37
Clement VI, Pope, 61
Clement VII, Pope, 314
clergy, 48, 49, 51, 53, 61, 64, 68, 85, 106, 124, 143, 144, 177, 190, 191, 200, 201, 257
  regular clergy, 66, 67, 77
  secular clergy, 66
cleric, 266
cloak of alien righteousness, 263
Colet, John, 92
Colettines, 85
College of Cardinals, 65
Cologne, 60, 106, 121, 231, 282
  University of, 53
Common Man's Revolt, 145
Communion, 49, 188, 199, 208, 260
communitas, 36, 37
Community Chest, 225
Commynes, Philippe de, 161
Company of Pastors, 172
Complutense University, 212
Concordat of Bologna, 313
concubinage, 264
condotta, 106
confession, 248–255, 256
Confession, Augsburg, 249
Confession, Dordrecht, 251
Confession, Helvetic, 251
Confession, Schleitheim, 250, 251

Confession, Westminster, 250
Confessionalism, 16, 255–257
Confessionalization, 305–308, 315, 320, 323
confessions, 249
confirmation, 188
confraternities, 17, 24, 30, 31, 33, 34, 35, 49, 200, 226
Connecticut, 181
consistories, 99
consistory, 151
Constance, 208
Constantine, Emperor, 189
Constantinople, 40, 45, 161, 162, 286
  fall of, 41
consubstantiation, 203
convents, 86, 266
Conventuals, 78
conversion, 190, 237, 256, 304
conversos, 45, 53, 91, 95, 97, 107, 110, 134, 138, 146, 151, 159, 164, 172, 173, 190, 198, 218, 235, 255, 286, 293, 298, 304, 327
Cop, Nicholas, 150
Corporation Act, 206, 207
Corpus Christi, 21, 29
Corpus Christianum, 12, 18, 21, 22, 31, 34, 36, 37, 40, 45, 51, 52, 59, 61, 72, 82, 92, 100, 104
  Venice, 161
Corpus Juris Civilis, 92
corsair, 178
Cosimo I, Duke, 31
Cosmografia, 23
Council of Basel, 165
Council of Constance, 50, 63, 64
Council of Florence, 40
Council of Trent, 9, 65, 86, 115, 188, 192, 204, 213, 217, 239, 250, 253, 265
Covenanters, 125
Coverdale, Miles, 114
cradle taxes, 258
Cranach, Lucas, 144
Cranmer, Thomas, 81, 168, 204, 321
Crespin, Jean, 299
Cromwell, Oliver, 124, 126, 181
crusade, 40, 80
Cyprus, 44

dancing, 100
Darnex, Ameyd, 197
Daughters of Charity, 86
death, 68
  personal piety, 70

Declaration of the Rights of Man and of the Citizen', 129
Decree of Toleration, 129
Dekker, Thomas, 324
Delaware, 126
della Casa, Giovanni, 319
della Marca, Giacomo, 106
della Mirandola, Pico, 136
Demon Mania, 53
Demonolatry, 103
Denmark, 123
Dentière, Marie, 260
Description of Africa, 141
devil, 52, 53, 54, 56, 73
devotio moderna, 211
devsirme, 45
Dialogues of Love, 136
Diet of Augsburg, 249
Diet of Worms, 142
Directorium Inquisitorium, 94
Dirks, Elizabeth, 134, 146
Dissenters, 124
Dominican Order, 48, 49, 78, 94, 212, 258
Donatists, 47
Donatus, 47
Donauwurth, 121
Dönme, 159
Douai, 118, 231
dragomans, 160
drunken-ness, 100
Duc de Sully, 117
Durkheim, Emile, 11
Dutch Golden Age, 177
Dutch Observant Province, 78
Dutch Republic, 126, 228, 284

Ebreo, Leone, 136
Ecclesiastical Ordinances, 151
Edict of Nantes, 117, 128, 207, 325
  revocation of, 120, 295
  Edict of Restitution, 123
Edward I, King, 190
Edward VI, King, 236, 274
Efendi, Aziz Mehmed. *See* Zevi, Sabbatai
Egypt, 140
Elizabeth I, Queen, 37, 98, 115, 118, 209, 262, 295
Ellwangen, 103
Emden, 99
enclosure, 84
Engels, Friedrich, 8

INDEX

England, 71, 76, 123, 127, 128, 228, 239
   Civil War, 120, 124, 153, 181, 196
   commonwealth, 124
   plantations, 124
   Protectorate, 124
English Ladies, 153
Enlightenment, 176
Erasmus Foundation, 167, 168, 325
Erasmus, Desiderius, 62, 68, 212
Erastus, Thomas, 155
Erfurt, 60, 284
Esnoga, 285
Esterhazy, 129
Esther, 293
eucharist, 29, 59
Eucharistic, 201
Eugenius IV, Pope, 40, 52, 64, 79, 165
Evangeline, 322
ex opera operantis, 190
ex opere operans, 257
ex opere operato, 190, 193
exorcism, 188
expulsion of the Muslims, 120
Eymeric, Nicholas, 94

Famagusta, 287
familiar, 54
Famine, 71
Fell, Margaret, 125
Feltre, Bernardino da, 106
Feltre, Vittorino da, 92
Ferdinand I, King, 80
Ferdinand II, Emperor, 122, 123, 206
Ferrara, 110
Fez, 141
Ficino, Marsilio, 136
Fioravanti, Ludovico, Doctor, 105
fioretti, 211
five pillars of Islam, 188
Florence, 31, 35, 71, 86, 90, 99, 106, 237
fondaco, 176
Fondaco dei Tedeschi, 163
Fondaco dei Turchi, 163
Forli, 99
Formicarius, 53
Formula of Concord, 249
Fortress of Faith. *See* Salamanca: University of
Forty Hours devotion, 205
Foucault, Michel, 11
foundling homes, 228

Fourth Lateran Council, 29, 78
Fox, George, 125
Foxe, John, 148, 168, 299
France, 71, 76, 104, 123, 127
Francis I, King, 44, 99, 111
Franciscan Order, 49, 68, 78, 85, 258
Franck, Sebastian, 167
Frankfurt, 89, 107
Franklin, Benjamin, 326
Fraticelli, 49
Frederick of Saxony, 142
Frederick V, King, 122
Freedom of the Christian, 210
Freiburg, 60
Friedrich III, Elector, 253
Fugger, Jacob, 233
Fuggerei, 233, 239

Galateo, 319
Galera, 109
Galilei, Galileo, 99
gambling, 100
Gandhi, Mahatma, 9
gemilut hasidim. *See* benevolent societies
Gemilut Hassadim, 222
Genesis, 70
Geneva, 23, 106, 157, 171–173, 178, 183, 204
   grand council, 171
Genoa, 88, 161
George I, King, 127
Gerlach, Stephen, 155, 160
Germany, 71, 76
Ghent, 23, 26, 282
ghetto, 89, 90, 163, 176, 307
Ghiberti, Matteo, 265
Ginzburg, Carlo, 11
Glorious Revolution, 127, 181, 248
Goa, 5, 96, 109
Golden Legend, 149, 297
Gordon Riots, 307
Gospel of Barnabas, 214, 217
Gothic Tyn church, 201
Granada, 40, 108, 230, 327
Gratian, 52
Great Man, 8
Great Migration, 180
Great Shul, 285
Grebel, Conrad, 81, 197
Gregory IX, Pope, 94
Gregory XI, Pope, 63, 210
Gregory XIII, Pope, 234

Grendler, Paul, 252
Grumbach, Argula von, 260
Guazzo, Stefano, 319
Guicciardini, Lodovico, 23
Guide for One's Turning Towards God, 256
Gutenburg Bible, 214
Gutenburg, Johan, 242
Guzmán, Dominic de, 48

Haemstede, Andreas Cornelis van, 299
Hagia Sophia, 286
halakha, 198
halakhic, 218
Halle, 106
Haman, 293
Hamburg, 35, 91
Handel, Georg Frederic, 279
hedge preaching, 277
Hegel, Friedrich, 8
Heidelberg, 154, 261
Heidelberg Catechism, 253
Hell, 73
Henri II, King, 99
Henrietta Maria, Queen, 153
Henry II, King, 228
Henry IV, King, 117
Henry of Navarre, 117
Henry VIII, King, 98, 114, 139, 209, 236, 249, 274
Herp, Hendrik, 80
Herzegovina, 42
Heussgen, Johanne. *See* Oecolampadius, Johanne
hidden churches, 325, *See schuilkerken*
hijra, 292
Hildesheim, 36
Hindus, 109
Hobbes, Thomas, 251
Hoffman, Melchior, 81, 169, 174
Hogenburg, Franz, 23
Holocaust, 311
Holodomor, 311
Holy Roman Empire, 51, 56, 61, 100, 106, 113, 122, 123, 190, 231, 232, 239, 305
Hospital de las Cinco Llagas, 221
House of Conversion, 90
Hrebeljanovic, Lazar, 309
Hufton, Olwen, 236
Hugo of Landenberg, 258
Huguenots, 128, 160, 205, 277, 295, 326
Humash, 216

Hungarian Diets, 129
Hungary, 44, 103, 129
Huron Wendat, 301
Hus, Jan, 50, 63, 122, 321
Hussite, 107
Hussites, 2, 51, 201, 297
Hutten, Ulrich von, 243
Hythloday, Raphael, 219

Iberia, 57, 63, 97, 101, 108, 190
iconoclasm, 116, 166, 231, 272–278
iconoclastic riots, 272, 295
icons, 272
imagined communities, 12, 210, 312
imagined communityies, 12
imams, 269
Imitation of Christ, 34
imitative piety, 34
Imola, 99
incarnation, 199
indulgences, 210
Innocent VIII, Pope, 53
Innocenti, 87, 88
Inquisition, 94, 97, 99, 100, 172, 191, 298
Institutes of the Blessed Virgin Mary, 86, 152
Institutes of the Christian Religio, 150
Institutes of the Christian Religion, 167
invented traditions, 312
Iraq, 44
Ireland, 123, 238
Irish Catholics, 124, 300
Iroquois, 301
Isa, 214
Islam, 39, 51, 73, 187
  Jewish relations, 57
  Shia, 256, 268, 306
  Sunni, 306
Israel, 291
Istanbul, 157
Italy, 71, 106
ivic religion, 33

Jacobsz, Wouter, 293
James I, England, 122
James I, King, 37, 209
James II, King, 125, 126
Jan of Leiden, 169
janissaries, 45
Jerome of Prague, 63
Jesuits, 13, 83, 130, 234, 282, 301
  Schools, 83

Jesus Christ, 70
Jews, 109, 125
John Paleologus VIII, Emperor, 40
Joris, David, 81, 167, 326
Josefov, 89
Josel of Rosheim, 267, 293, 303
Judaism, 51, 57, 73, 187
Julius Excluded from Heaven, 68
Julius II, Pope, 68, 79

Kabiz, Molla, 215
Kaplan, Benjamin, 17
Kaplan, Yosef, 255, 306
Karlstadt, Andreas, 113, 142, 144, 259
Katherine of Aragon, 139
Kempis, Thomas à, 34
King Solomon's Temple, 286
Kingdom of God, 113
Kitzingen, 208
Knox, John, 171
Kosice, 129
Kosovo
    Battle of, 40
Kraców, 89
Kraków, 284
Kramer, Heinrich, 53, 243
Krstic, Tijana, 256, 306

l'Incarnation, Marie de, 301
L'viv, 284
La Motte, John, 300
La Rochelle, 26, 128
ladino, 158
Laski, Jan, 173
Last Judgment, 213
last rites, 188
Lateran Canons, 67
Latimer, Hugh, 321
legitimizing discourses, 14, 74, 312
Leisnig, 225
Leo Africanus. *See* Al-Hasan Ibn Muhammad al-Wazan al-Fasi
Leo X, Pope, 65, 79, 81, 140, 303
Lepanto
    Battle of, 44
Levack, Brian, 103
Leviathan, 251
life expectancy, 70
Light on a Hill, 293
limbo, 189
limpieza de sangre. *See* pure blood laws

Livorno, 110
llyricus, Matthias Flacius, 299
Lollards, 49, 51, 201
London, 71, 232
Longfellow, Henry Wadsworth, 322
Lorraine, 103
Louis II, King (of Hungary and Bohemia), 43
Louis XIII, King, 128
Louis XIV, King, 128
Louis XVI, King, 129
Louisiana, 127
Loyola, Ignatius, 92, 253
Lubeck, 35
Luther Monument in Worms, 321
Luther, Martin, 2, 5, 9, 36, 43, 80, 82, 113, 134, 142–146, 156, 192, 194, 203, 211, 213, 225, 230, 249, 253, 259, 261, 262, 293, 298, 303, 311, 317
Lutheran, 112
Lutherans, 205
Lyon, 31, 35, 139

Ma'amad, 101, 268, 285
Ma'min, 159
Machiavelli, Niccolò, 317, 318
Madonna della Misericordia. *See* Madonna of Mercy
Madonna of Mercy, 22–26
Madrid, 118
Magdalen laundries, 238
Magdalen shelters, 238
Magdalen, Mary St., 146
Maghreb, 140
Mainz, 60
maleficium. *See* Witchcraft
Malleus Maleficarum, 53, 55, 243
Mamluks, 42
Mandeville, John, 142
Manuel I, King, 111
Manutius, Aldus, 161, 211, 216
Marburg, 203
Margaret of Valois, 117
Marian exiles, 209
Marillac, Louise de, 87
marranos, 107
marriage, 188
Marseilles, 57
Marsilius of Padua, 62
Martin V, Pope, 65
Martyr's Mirror, The, 301
Martyrologies, 148, 297

Martyrs, 298
    Female, 146–149
Martyrs Memorial, 321
Marx, Karl, 8
Mary Magdalen, Saint, 237
Mary Queen of Scots, 118
Mary Tudor, Queen, 98, 114, 124, 274
Maryland, 125
Mass
    banning, 204
Massachusetts Bay colony, 125, 157, 180–183
Massachusetts Body of Liberties, 180
Masters, Bruce, 17
Matthys, Jan, 169
maurophilia, 312
Maximillian of Bavaria, Duke, 121
Mecklenburg, 106
Medici, Giovanni de'. *See* Leo X, Pope
Medici, Lorenzo de', 65
Mediterranean, 134, 158, 161, 177
Mehmed, 192
Mehmed II, Sultan, 41, 42
Melancthon, Philip, 227, 303
Memmingen, 208
Mennonites, 101, 125, 175, 196, 197, 277
Merici, Angela, 86
Messianic tradition, 135
Messina, 84, 89
Mexico, 96
Michoacan, Bishop of, 224
mihrabs, 287
Milan, 71, 99, 106, 108
millenarianism, 168, 196
millet, 158, 178, 267
Milosevic, Slobodan, 309
minber, 287
misericordia, 24, *See* Madonna of Mercy
Mission letters, 301
Modern Devotion, 34
modernity, 7
Moderno, Carlo, 282
Mohacs, 129
Mohammed, 39
Mongolfier (brothers), 23
Monte di Paschi, 233
Monte di Pietà, 233
Monte Frumentari, 233
Montenegro, 42
Monteverdi, Claudio, 161
Moore, R. I., 11, 313
Moravia, 106

Moravian Brethren, 170
Moravians, 182
More, Thomas, 137, 219, 224, 301
moriscos, 2, 108, 110, 120, 146, 151, 179, 190, 214, 298, 304, 324, 327
Morocco, 267
mosque, 271, 286
Mostar, 310
Munstdorp, Janneken, 134, 147
Munster, 113, 124, 157, 168–171, 178, 183, 204
Munster, Sebastian, 23
Muntzer, Thomas, 81, 101, 113, 145, 170, 213, 259, 298
Murad I, Sultan, 309
Murad II, Sultan, 157, 286
Muslims, 108, 109, 134, 178
Müteferrika, Ibrahaim, 257

names, 303
Naples, 99
Navarre, 158
Navigation Acts, 181
Navigations, Peregrinations and Voyages made into Turkey, 327
Netherlands, 76, 99, 100, 123
Neuser, Adam, 134, 154–156, 215
New Christians, 111
New Christians', 107
New England, 327
New Hampshire, 126, 181
New Jersey, 126
New Jerusalem, 169, 174, 180
Nicene Creed, 248
Nicholas of Cusa, 65
Nicodemites, 151
Nicolay, Nicholas de, 327
Nicosia, 287
Nider, Johannes, 53
Nikolsburg, 113
Nirenburg, David, 11
Non-Conformists, 124
North Africa, 80
Nuremburg, 31, 60, 100, 106, 204
Nuremburg Chronicle, 64

Oberman, Heiko, 150
Observant Franciscan, 233
Observants, 77
Ochino, Bernardino, 114, 154, 172
Oecolampadius, Johan, 145
Oecolampadius, Johannes, 166

Index

Old Christians, 97
Olivetan, Pierre, 210
On Assistance to the Poor, 225
On Concord and Discord in Humankind, 139
On the Disciplines, 139
On the Harmony of the Spheres, 136
On the Relief of the Poor, 139
Onze lieve Heer op Kelder, 175
Orangemen, 126
Oratorians, 227
Orbatello home, 237
Order of St. John out, 140
ordination, 188, 190
Original Sin, 70
Orlando Furioso, 39, 43
Orthodox, 81
Osman I, Sultan, 40
Othello, 324
Otranto, 42
Ottoman, 157
Ottoman Empire, 42, 44, 123, 129, 156, 157, 159, 164, 176, 178, 179, 215, 268, 269, 287, 323

Padua, 106
Paine, Thomas, 326
Palermo, 89
Palestine, 290
Pamphlets, 246
Paris, 71, 118
Paris Couche, 87
Parma, 106
parnasim, 175
parnassim, 179, 268
Pasha, Rüstem, 268
Passau, 59
Passover, 199, 202, *See* Pesach
pastor, 263, 266
Paul III, Pope, 66, 205
Paul, apostle, 29
Pazmany, Peter, 129
Peace of Augsburg, 232
Peace of Westphalia, 130, 207, 315
Peasants Revolt, 101
Peasants' Revolt, 37, 113, 211, 213, 244
Pelagians, 47
Pelagius, 47
penance, 188
Penn, William, 125, 326
Pennsylvania, 125, 126, 326
Pereyara, Abraham, 101

Periculosa, 85
Perpignan, 237
Peru, 96
Perugia, 24, 72, 106
Pesach, 292
Peter the Venerable, 216
Pfefferkorn, Johannes, 212, 217
Philip II, King, 109, 124, 174
Philip III, King, 109
Philip IV, King, 62
Philippines, 96
Piarists, 227
Piccolomini, Aeneas Silvius, 65
Pilgrim's Progress, 296
pinzochere, 67
Pirckheimer, Caritas, 146
Pirckheimer, Wilibald, 31
Pisa
    Council of, 63
Pius II, Pope, 42, 269
Pius IV, Pope, 250
Pius V, Pope, 213
pogroms, 11, 71, 75
Poland, 16, 101, 113, 127, 128
Pole, Reginald, 114
Polish-Lithuanian Commonwealth, 119, 284
Poor Clares, 85, 152, 260
Poor Laws, 230
poorhouse, 230
Pope Clement VI, Pope, 63
Portinari, Folco, 221
Portuguese Inquisition, 95
Portuguese Synagogue, 111
Prague, 50, 89, 107, 284
Precipitato, 105
Presbyterianism, 205
Presbyterians, 124
priest, 257, 262, 266
printing press, 242
Profession of Faith, 250
Promised Land, 289, 291
Protestant Union, 121
Protestantism, 116, 193, 276
Provence, 158
pure blood laws, 97
Purim, 292
Puritans, 125, 180, 262
pus Christianum, 168

Quakers, 124, 125, 181, 326
Quebec, 128, 301

Quebecois, 128
Quiroga, Vasco de, 224
Qur'an, 207, 308

Rabbis, 102, 175
Rabus, Ludwig, 299
radical, 301
radicalism. *See* radicals
radicals, 113, 118, 135, 180, 195, 203, 205, 232, 259
 Luther dismisses, 145
Rahamim, 222
Rasphouse, 91, 236
Ratio Studiorum, 83
Real Presence, 174, 200, 201, 222
Real Presence of Christ, 29
re-Catholicization, 128
Reconquista, 35, 40, 271
Reformation, 7, 10, 120, 261
 Catholic, 83, 301
 Historiography, 7–11
 Protestant, 81, 242
Reformed Church, 176
Regensburg, 106
Reinhard, Wolfgang, 315
relics, 272, 278
Religious Peace of Augsburg, 115, 121, 152
Remy, Nicholas, 103
Reuchlin, Johannes, 212
Rhine River, 114, 165
Rhode Island, 125, 181
Rhodes, 43, 140
Ribera, Juan de, 109
Richelieu, Cardinal, 128
Ridley, Nicholas, 168, 321
Riedemann, Peter, 203
Roman Inquisition, 96
Roman Martyrology, 302
Rome, 90, 118, 234
rood screen, 270
Rossellino, Bernardo, 269
Rothman, Natalie, 164
Rouen, 118
Ruggiero, Guido, 12
Rule of St. Benedict, 67, 77
Ruoti, Maria Clemente, 146
Russell, J. C., 71

S. Maria Nuova hospital, 221
Sabbateans, 159
Sabbath, 111
sabbats, 54
Sacramentarians, 113, 203
sacraments, 188, 247
Sacred Congregation of Rites and Ceremonies, 302
Sacrifice of the Lord, 299
sadaq, 222
Safavid, 42
Salamanca
 University of, 53
Salonika, 40, 157, 284, 323, 327
salvation, 187
Salzburg, 106
San Gimigniano, 24, 72
sanctuary, 270
Sangallo, Giulio da, 282
Sansovino, Jacopo, 161
Santa Maria della Salute, 72
Sardinia, 96
Sattler, Michael, 250
Savonarola, Girolamo, 35, 36, 62, 68, 78, 294, 321
Savoy, 55, 63, 171
Savoy Hospital, 221
Scandinavia, 100
scapulary, 131
Schilling, Heinz, 315
Schilling, Johann, 79, 204
School Order, 227
Schoolmaster, The, 319
schools, 261
Schools of Christian Doctrine, 226, 252
Schools of Christian Doctrine', 205
Schott, Johann, 243, 247
schuilkerken, 175, 285
Schutzmantelmadonna. *See* Madonna of Mercy
Scotland, 56, 71, 103
scripture mandates, 208
Sefer Torah, 216
Selim I, Sultan, 42, 268
Selim II, Sultan, 155, 160
seminaries, 261
Sensory Worship, 270
Sephardic, 101, 158, 175, 176, 234, 285, 306
Serbia, 42
Servetus, Michael, 154, 172
Servites, 67
seven works of charity, 218
Seville, 89, 95
sexual misdemeanors, 100
Shagan, Ethan, 318

INDEX

shahada, 197
Shakers, 182
Shakespeare, William, 324
Shia, 10
Shoemaker's Holiday, The, 324
Sicily, 96, 108
Siena, 90, 106
Sigismund I, Emperor, 50
Sigismund III, King, 119
Simons, Menno, 81, 134, 147, 260
sin, 187, 193
Sinan, Mimar, 287
Sisters of Charity, 85, 226
Sixtus IV, Pope, 79
Sixtus V, Pope, 65
Smith, Jeffrey Chipps, 281
Socini, Fausto, 154
Socini, Lelio, 154
socinianism, 154
Soed Holim, 222
Sola Scriptura, 143, 208, 210, 227, 244, 262, 270
Song of Roland, 39
Sosa, Antonio de, 178
Sozzino, Lelio, 114
Spain, 123
Spanish Inquisition, 95
Spina, Alfonso da, 53
Spinhouse, 91
Spinoza, Baruch, 137, 176
Spiritual Exercises, 83, 281
spiritualists, 203
Sprenger, Jacob, 53
St George of the Greeks, 162
St. Anne, 146
St. Bartholmew's Day Massacre, 117
St. Bartholomew's Day Massacre, 36, 160, 299
St. Clara convent, 146
St. Francis of Assisi, 48
St. Margaret, 146
St. Michael's church, 281
St. Nicholas of the Greeks, 162
St. Paul, 282
St. Peter's Basilica, 282
St. Simon of Trent, 59
Stari Most bridge, 310, 329
Statenbijbel, 246
Steyn, 293
Stranger Churches, 151, 232
Strasbourg, 60, 114, 150, 167, 169, 204, 272
Stuart, James Francis Edward, 127
Suasso, Antonio Lopes. *See* Suasso, Isaac Israel

Suasso, Isaac Israel, 176
Sudan, 141
Süleyman, Sultan, 43, 44, 178
Süleymaniye, 220
Summis desiderantes, 53
Sunday Schools, 205, 226
Sunni, 10
sürgün, 157
Surinam, 91, 286
Sweden, 71, 123, 228
Sweelinck, Jan, 279
Swiss Confederation, 165, 171
Switzerland, 55, 103
Sylvan, Johann, 155
synagogues, 284
    Amsterdam, 199, 286
Synod of Dort, 246, 253
Synod of Toulouse, 210

Talavera, Hernando de, 108
Tallis, Thomas, 279
Talmud, 198
Temple Mount, 297
Teresa of Avila, 86
Test Act, 206, 207
The Ancient Faith of the One True God... Against the Three-Person Idol and Two-Natured False Deity of the Antichrist., 155
The Babylonian Captivity of the Church, 144
The Bloody Theater or Martyr's Mirror, 147
The Description of the Low Countries, 23
The Freedom of the Christian, 144
The Institutes of Christian Religion, 260
The Killing Time, 125
The Messiah, 280
The Mirror of Perfection, 80
Theatines, 83
Thessaloniki. *See* Salonika
Thirty Years War, 120, 123, 196, 233, 300
Thirty-Nine Articles, 249
Thomist Christians, 109
Timbuktu, 140
tithe, 222
Titian, 161
Tito, Josep Broz, 309
Toledo, 35, 89
Toledot Yeshu, 216, 255
Toleration and Co-Existence, 15–17
Torah, 135, 198, 207, 216, 308, 325
Torquemada, Tomas de, 95
Torquemada, Tomaso de, 97

Toulon, 44, 60
tracts, 247
transubstantiation, 29, 202
Transylvania, 113, 129, 155
Treatise on Islam, 257
Treaty of Versailles, 323
Treaty of Westphalia, 160
Trent, 59
Trickett, Henry, 264
Tridentine catechism, 265
Trier, 103
Trinity, the, 155, 248
Tripoli, 44
Tunis, 44
Tyn church, 206
Tyndale, William, 209

ulema, 269
Ulster, 124
Union of Arras, 115
Unitarianism, 114, 119
University of Alcalá, 138
University of Paris, 150
Uppsala, 261
Urban IV, Pope, 29
Urban VI, Pope, 63
Urban VIII, Pope, 153
Ursulines, 83, 226, *See* Sisters of Charity
Utopia, 139, 219, 224
utraquists, 201
Utrecht, 78

Valencia, 109, 137, 138, 230
Valla, Lorenzo, 212, 317
Valladolid, 35, 118
Vallombrosans, 67
Vecchio, Lazaretto, 92
Venice, 71, 72, 86, 90, 91, 99, 110, 135, 157, 161–165, 215, 234, 323, 326
Vermigli, Peter Martyr, 114, 172
Veronese, Paolo, 161
Vestment controversy, 263
vestments, 262
Vienna, 106, 325
    Expulsion of Jews, 130
Vienne, 33
Vierge de Miséricorde. *See* Madonna of Mercy
Vilnius, 284
Vincent de Paul, 87

violence, 100
Virgin Mary, 22, 32, 68, 146
Virginia, 126
Vives, Juan Luis, 97, 134, 137, 156, 224, 230
Vizzana, Lucrezia Orsina, 146
Voragine, Jacopo da, 297
Vries, Jan de, 71
Vulgate Bible, 213

Waite, Gary, 167, 326
Waldensians, 96, 116
Waldo, Peter, 321
Walloon church, 175
Walsham, Alexandra, 76
waqf, 220, 223, 229, 287
Ward, Mary, 86, 134, 152–154, 156
Wars of Religion, 76, 116, 277
Wartburg Castle, 142
Waste, Joan, 148, 156
Watt, Tessa, 247
Weber, Max, 11
Westminster Abbey, 278
Willaert, Adrian, 161
William III, King, 181, 207
William of Orange, 126
Winthrop, John, 180
witchcraft, 99, 103, 195
witches, 54, 96, 201
witch-hunts, 103–104
Wittenberg, 36, 81, 114, 142, 225, 261
Wurttemburg, 123
Wurttemburg, duke of, 207
Wurzburg, 103
Wycliffe, John, 49, 63, 114, 321

Xavier, Francis, 83
xenodochium, 220

Yiddish, 175
Yugoslav Federation, 309

zakat, 222
Zamora, 35
Zell, Katherine, 260
Zevi, Sabbatai, 159
Zika, Charles, 56
Zurich, 106, 272
Zwingli, Huldrych, 81, 113, 145, 166, 202, 213, 259